MW00861560

3 Shades of Blue

ALSO BY JAMES KAPLAN

Frank:
The Voice

Sinatra:
The Chairman

Irving Berlin:
New York Genius

Penguin Press   New York   2024

3
Shades
of
Blue

Miles Davis

John Coltrane

Bill Evans

and the Lost

Empire of Cool

■ ■ ■

JAMES KAPLAN

PENGUIN PRESS
An imprint of Penguin Random House LLC
penguinrandomhouse.com

Copyright © 2024 by James Kaplan
Penguin Random House supports copyright. Copyright fuels creativity, encourages
diverse voices, promotes free speech, and creates a vibrant culture. Thank you for buying
an authorized edition of this book and for complying with copyright laws by not reproducing,
scanning, or distributing any part of it in any form without permission. You are supporting
writers and allowing Penguin Random House to continue to publish books for every reader.

Page 470 constitutes an extension of this copyright page.

LIBRARY OF CONGRESS CATALOGING-IN-PUBLICATION DATA

Names: Kaplan, James, 1951– author.
Title: 3 shades of blue : Miles Davis, John Coltrane, Bill Evans,
    and the lost empire of cool / James Kaplan.
Other titles: Three shades of blue
Description: New York : Penguin Press, 2024. |
    Includes bibliographical references and index.
Identifiers: LCCN 2023026564 (print) | LCCN 2023026565 (ebook) |
    ISBN 9780525561002 (hardcover) | ISBN 9780525561019 (ebook)
Subjects: LCSH: Davis, Miles. | Coltrane, John, 1926–1967. |
    Evans, Bill, 1929–1980. | Jazz musicians—United States—Biography. |
    Jazz—History and criticism.
Classification: LCC ML395 .K37 2024 (print) | LCC ML395 (ebook) |
    DDC 781.65092/2 [B]—dc23/eng/20230717
LC record available at https://lccn.loc.gov/2023026564
LC ebook record available at https://lccn.loc.gov/2023026565

Printed in the United States of America
1st Printing

Book design by Daniel Lagin

To the memory of Wallace Roney

And to Miles

The only great difficulty with the Jass band is that you never know what it is going to do next, but you can always tell what those who hear it are going to do—they're going to shake a leg.

**April 22, 1917, ad for Orton Bros. record shop
in the (Montana) *Daily Missoulian***

A musician is a scientist and a philosopher.

Lester Young

Man, sometimes it takes you a long time
to sound like yourself.

Miles

Contents

So What?

So, what—

So, what—

is jazz?

Prologue

J azz??

What kind of jazz are we talking about?

A comedian on a late-night talk show did a bit about the awfulness of dating. He said the two worst date ideas he'd ever heard from a woman each consisted of two words: "art walk" and "jazz brunch."

A century ago, jazz was feared and reviled by respectable society because it was Black music. Because it threatened to expose innocent young white people to all that white society imagined and feared about Blackness, sexual abandon being at the top of the list.

Jazz today, when it isn't utterly ignored, is widely disliked for different reasons: because it is old, or anodyne, or hard to understand. Jazz is passé. Jazz is niche. Jazz is the smooth soundtrack to polite brunches in restaurants with potted ferns and bananas Foster and clever young servers. Or it is just loudly squeaking and honking saxophones—noise.

I speak of jazz as an awesome thing. An imperative, an empire. As America's only native art form, one that boiled forth from a gumbo of ethnic musics in late-nineteenth-century New Orleans and coursed up rivers and railroads and blue highways to Oklahoma City and Kansas City and St. Louis and Chicago and New York City, irresistibly, as young men and women, Black then (very quickly) white, became transfixed by its power and seized on it as an unprecedented form of artistic expression.

Geniuses came forth. Waves and waves of them: Buddy Bolden and Scott Joplin and James Reese Europe and King Oliver and Louis Armstrong and Jelly Roll Morton and Bix Beiderbecke and Mamie Smith and Bessie Smith and James P. Johnson and Eubie Blake and Willie "The Lion" Smith and . . .

The three geniuses at this book's heart were born when jazz was already thirty or forty years old; they rose up at the end of World War II, when the big bands of the twenties and thirties and forties were starting to die out, when the idea of jazz as dance music was starting to fade, and something else, jazz as art music, as listening music, was starting to take hold.

With the death of jazz as dance music, the art began to contract. With the movement known as bebop—hard to play and, initially, hard to understand, even for jazz musicians—jazz's already shrinking audience shrank even more severely. (Although when bebop's cofounder, the incomparable alto saxophonist Charlie Parker, released albums on which—quite beautifully, if not audaciously—he played standard ballads accompanied by strings, the audience grew.)

And then, as time and popular culture moved mercilessly forward, bebop came to seem, for jazz's diminished yet passionate audience, foundational, comprehensible, moving, lyrical. And the jazz that followed bebop, known to those who required categories by the under-descriptive, even misleading, label of hard bop, seemed still more comprehensible and lyrical.

Other categories would follow, but I confess that in the genres of bebop and hard bop, jazz created in the quarter century between, roughly, 1942 and 1967, I find almost all of jazz that I want and need. I find magnificent art produced by what bebop's other cocreator, Dizzy Gillespie, called in a slightly different context *superroyalty*—magnificent men (mostly men and mostly Black) of supreme gifts and regal mien, creating masterpiece after masterpiece.

Not antique, not anodyne, not forbiddingly difficult, and viscerally thrilling.

And with all respect to this book's presiding genius Miles Davis, who late in his career proclaimed that he had no interest in returning to the lyrical masterpieces he produced and participated in between ages eighteen and thirty-five (1944 to 1961), saying that to him revisiting that music would be like eating leftover turkey—with all respect to Miles, the thrill of this great and never-fading music is this book's pulse.

Prelude

March 2, 1959—a late-winter Monday in the second-to-last year of the Eisenhower administration. Fair and mild in Manhattan. Among the top stories in *The New York Times* that morning: a fogbound collision between the American Export liner *Constitution* and an oil tanker; the "commuter crisis" caused by ever-rising automobile use in the metropolitan area; tensions between white colonials and Black natives in East Africa. This last article quotes a British banker alleging "the vast unreadiness of the great majority of Africans for self-government."

An older, staider world. On the first page of the second section, a story by the young reporter Gay Talese about "Crazy Couple Clubs"—groups of jaded suburbanites seeking unusual amusements in the city: visits to yoga clubs, night court, Bowery restaurants. And deeper into the section, on what was still called the Theatres page, a review (glowing) by the paper's jazz critic, John S. Wilson, of a Thelonious Monk concert at Town Hall. "He has carried apparent uncertainty to a high and refined art," Wilson wrote. "He makes each performance a fresh and provocative experience."

Buried in the back pages amid the shipping news and weather, a short item about the death by heroin overdose—in the Women's House of Detention, to which she had been remanded after her arrest for drug possession—of one Rosaland Owens, age thirty, of 2492 Eighth Avenue in Harlem. An anonymous, presumably African American woman, a person of no consequence to the readers of *The New York Times*—although four months later in this jazz-momentous year, another African American woman, born Eleanora Fagan but known to the world as Billie Holiday, who suffered from the same disease as Rosaland Owens, would die at age forty-four, handcuffed to her bed in Harlem Hospital.

If the Crazy Couple Club of Manhasset—by the evidence of the photograph in the *Times* piece a prosperous and cheerfully self-satisfied group—had dared to extend their Bowery slumming beyond ethnic restaurants, they might have wandered into the cozy, smoky, messy confines of the Five Spot Café, at 5 Cooper Square, whose owners, two Italian American brothers and ex-GIs named Joe and Iggy Termini, had for the past three years been booking some of the greatest jazz musicians of the day, including Cecil Taylor, Cannonball Adderley, and, most notably, Thelonious Monk, whom the Terminis had helped regain his New York City cabaret card—a conditional ID issued by the police department as a (legally and practically questionable) method of discouraging narcotics use—six years after Monk had lost his card, and with it the right to play in clubs that served alcohol, in a mistaken 1951 drug bust.

Amid the tobacco and reefer fumes and beer reek of that tiny, dark saloon (a glass of gin cost fifty cents; a pitcher of beer, a dollar), the members of the Crazy Couple Club of Manhasset might have found themselves sitting shoulder to shoulder with (though they almost certainly would have failed to recognize) such Five Spot habitués as the painters Willem de Kooning, Joan Mitchell, and Mark Rothko; the writers Jack Kerouac, Allen Ginsberg, and Frank O'Hara; and the young jazz titans Miles Davis, John Coltrane, and Bill Evans.

The Five Spot was closed on Mondays, but on that March Monday Davis, Coltrane, and Evans had other business anyway: in Columbia Records' Thirtieth Street Studio, they were joining the alto saxophonist Cannonball Adderley, bassist Paul Chambers, and drummer Jimmy Cobb to begin making, under Miles's leadership, what would become the best-selling, and arguably most beloved, jazz album of all time, Miles's *Kind of Blue*. March 2 and April 22: three tunes recorded on the first date ("So What," "Freddie Freeloader," and "Blue in Green"), two on the second ("All Blues" and "Flamenco Sketches"). Every complete take but one ("Flamenco Sketches") was a first take, the process similar, as Evans later wrote in the LP's liner notes, to a genre of Japanese visual art in which black watercolor is applied spontaneously to a thin stretched parchment, with no unnatural or interrupted strokes possible, Miles's cherished ideal of spontaneity achieved.

The quiet and enigmatic majesty of the resulting record both epitomizes jazz and transcends the genre. The album's powerful and enduring mystique has made it widely beloved among musicians and music lovers of every category: jazz, rock, classical, rap. This is the story of the three geniuses who joined forces to create one of the great classics in Western music—how they rose up in the world, came together like a chance collision of particles in deep space, produced a brilliant flash of light, and then went on their separate ways to jazz immortality.

1   The blue trumpet

Thirty years later to the month, in March 1989, I found myself riding an elevator, heart knocking, to the fourteenth floor of the Essex House on Central Park South to interview Miles Davis. It was an assignment I'd lucked into through my magazine-editor brother, who knew a *Vanity Fair* editor who'd said he needed a profile of Miles to accompany an excerpt from the trumpet legend's forthcoming memoir, coauthored by Quincy Troupe. The writer, the *Vanity Fair* editor told my brother, should know jazz. My brother, Peter W. Kaplan, told him that I didn't just know jazz; I knew everything there was to know about it.

This was hyperbolic, to put it mildly. I *liked* jazz—liked it a lot, what little I knew of it. My record collection, just beginning to shift from LPs to CDs, was primarily rock and blues, with a bit of classical and a smattering of jazz. I was in the process of educating my ears—still am—but it was and is a long, slow process. I knew Miles Davis was a titan in his field; I knew he'd played with Charlie Parker in the 1940s. That was about it. I owned exactly two Miles albums: 1969's *Filles de Kilimanjaro*, which I'd bought simply because I heard it in a friend's dorm room and it was quietly beautiful, and the dark and menacing 1970 *Bitches Brew*, which I'd bought because, when it was issued, buying it felt vaguely compulsory.

When I complained to my brother that I was very far from knowing all there was to know about jazz, he stopped me. This was *Vanity Fair*, he said, with some italicized heat.

I took his meaning. The magazine, then under the leadership of legend-under-construction Tina Brown, was *the* magazine to write for in those days. And I had a wife and an infant son and a mortgage in Westchester, and a chance to get in the door at *Vanity Fair* would be a plum. One heard they were issuing fat contracts to writers they liked.

I called my brother's editor acquaintance there, and, after surprisingly little discussion of my putative jazz expertise, got the assignment. I promptly went to Tower Records and bought every Miles Davis CD they had, not thinking about when I might have time to actually listen to all of them. Then I phoned Miles's publicist and proudly announced myself as The Writer from *Vanity Fair*.

It was only on that elevator at the Essex House, with the publicist by my side, that the full weight of my fraudulence began to sink in on me. I was nobody! I knew nothing! No Google then, no Wikipedia; no facile way to pose as an instant authority. I'd leafed through the advance copy of Miles's memoir that the publisher had sent me, intimidated by its heft, not to mention its general tone of darkness and anger, not to mention the masses of jazz names I knew little or nothing about. I'd written up a too short and shallow list of questions for him, naïvely hoping that once a flow of conversation was established, further thoughts would occur to me. In my backpack I had my Soviet-style Radio Shack cassette recorder, the size and weight of a dense college textbook (it ran on five C batteries). I also had extra batteries and a half dozen blank cassettes. The backpack was heavy. The publicist had promised me one meeting of one hour, no more. How could I possibly get all I needed in an hour? And what did I need, anyway?

I often think of the line attributed, in various forms, to Mike Tyson: *Everyone has a plan until they get punched in the mouth.* Every interview is a kind of punch in the mouth. You walk in with certain expectations about the person you're about to talk to, and bang, the person is inevitably somebody different from the person you expected, and everything you'd anticipated evaporates. Wise interviewers learn to roll with the punches, to bob and weave and temporize on the spur of the moment. I was anything but wise in those days. In addition, I was thoroughly pre-intimidated by the time we arrived and Miles Davis opened his apartment door, a small but startling presence: dark eyes glittering, naked to the waist, wearing black pajama pants and what looked like an extravagant wig of brown curls.

We settled down to talk. "Now," he said. "What you want to *know?*"

What did I know? Nothing. What did I want to know? Everything.

BUT MILES DAVIS WASN'T ABOUT TO TELL ME EVERYTHING. HE COULDN'T tell me one percent of one percent of everything in our allotted hour—though the one hour turned into almost two, at the end of which I asked timorously if I might have some more time, and Miles rasped, "Come back tomorrow."

Of course I returned the next day, without the publicist this time, and the second session went much like the first, full of Miles's sentence fragments about tangential topics; further discussion about his artwork; stories about matters and people I hadn't the wherewithal to understand; and minimalist, wandering answers to my jazz questions. At the time I had the sinking feeling that I would draw little of substance from him, even over the course of three hours, certainly not enough to make a piece that would satisfy what I imagined were the Olympian standards of *Vanity Fair.*

But the musical standards of *Vanity Fair* in 1989 were far from Olympian. Music was scarcely the point. What the magazine was interested in was celebrity, and style and buzz and dirt, and with Miles and his frequently scabrous memoir, *Vanity Fair* had all of this in abundance. His status as a personage, an icon, had always vied with his stature as a musician. That was the way he wanted it; that was the way he designed it: from the moment he dropped out of Juilliard and joined Charlie Parker's band in 1945, he was an energetic shaper of his own image. He was a visual as well as a sonic phenomenon. He had a lot to work with. He was beautiful and dark, literally and figuratively; he was angry, tempestuous, and always stylish, whether in the Ivy League–bespoke look he favored in the fifties and early sixties or the outer-space outfits of the mid- to late eighties. He was a Black man who lacked any hint of the ingratiation that the white world preferred (or demanded) from its Negro entertainers, and that the entertainers sometimes, doubtless with irony or fury in their hearts, supplied. He wore shades onstage. He didn't announce tunes—he didn't speak at all. He famously turned his back to his audiences, both while playing and laying out.

This was Miles Davis the celebrity. The question of Miles the musician in 1989 was a more complicated matter. From the beginning, his musical life had been a series of restless moltings: of collaborators, of styles, of lovers and friends. From Juilliard to Bird to *The Birth of the Cool* to the Blue Note and Prestige albums to a free fall into the hell of heroin addiction to getting clean and coming back triumphantly in Newport in 1955 to signing with Columbia, the Rolls-Royce of record labels, to the first great quintet (Miles, John Coltrane, Paul Chambers, Red Garland, Philly Joe Jones) to replacing Garland with Bill Evans, to losing Evans, then bringing him back for *Kind of Blue* . . .

After *Kind of Blue* Davis would continue to evolve incessantly, initially with that album's sextet—minus Evans, who'd left to lead a trio of his own, and would maintain that format for the remainder of his career, and then without Coltrane, who became a leader and an artistic trailblazer in his own right. Then, in the early sixties, Miles formed a second great quintet, including saxophonist Wayne Shorter, pianist Herbie Hancock, drummer Tony Williams, and bassist Ron Carter. And then, in the late sixties, he abandoned acoustic jazz altogether, moving to the easy/uneasy blend of jazz and rock that would cause consternation among jazz purists and come to be known as fusion. Then, in 1975, plagued by profuse health problems and addictions, he left music altogether, not to return until 1981.

Audiences and record buyers welcomed his comeback, though jazz's zealous gatekeepers continued to fret about his stylistic excursions and commercial aspirations. Ever since *Bitches Brew*, jazz purists had been decrying what looked like naked commercialism on Miles's part: many knives were sharpened for his every move. His 1985 Columbia album *You're Under Arrest* contained, besides several original compositions, covers of two huge pop hits, Cyndi Lauper and Rob Hyman's "Time After Time" and John Bettis and Steve Porcaro's "Human Nature," from Michael Jackson's megaselling album *Thriller*. *Rolling Stone*'s decidedly mixed review of *You're Under Arrest* spoke of the CD's "instant notoriety" in jazz circles.

It didn't help matters that Miles was inevitably compared with his "anointed heir and label mate, Wynton Marsalis." Marsalis, a mere twenty-three but already world famous when *You're Under Arrest* was released, was the purist-in-chief. A startlingly gifted trumpeter from a brilliant New Orleans jazz family, he first came on the scene in the late 1970s and immediately began making a splash, both with his playing—not only of jazz but also the classical trumpet repertoire—and his outspoken critiques of the contemporary jazz scene, most pointedly of his former idol, Miles Davis.

The young trumpeter was highly opinionated and highly quotable, and from the beginning the music press, sniffing a possible feud, gave Marsalis's venting about Miles—he even critiqued the outlandish outfits Miles had taken to wearing onstage, calling them "dresses"—plenty of column inches. The first time the two met, Miles said, "So here's the police."

Meanwhile, behind the scenes, George Butler, the vice president for jazz A&R (artists and repertoire) of Davis and Marsalis's mutual record label, Columbia, tried vigorously to get Davis to bestow his blessing on the up-and-comer, to little avail.

"George [kept] trying to make friends out of [me and] Wynton Marsalis," Miles told me. "Like, I'd be sketching, right? And the phone would ring. Cicely [Tyson] says, 'It's George.'

"So I said, 'What does he want? Can he tell you?' She said no. So I answer the phone. Say, 'George, what it is?'

"He says, 'Why don't you call Wynton up?'

"I say, 'For what?'

"He says, 'Because it's his birthday. He's in St. Louis.'

"I say, 'Oh, *George*—'"

I laughed.

"See, you laughing," Miles said. "But when that shit comes at you like that, you're like, *What?* And Wynton and I get together and talk about music; he tells me he's tired of playing classical. I said, 'But you're the only one playing it. Of our race. And you play it *good*.'"

This is what Miles *said* he said to Marsalis. But in various public contexts he'd also potshotted right back, often asserting what he'd said after Marsalis recorded his first baroque concerto album in 1982 (and would repeat for posterity in his autobiography): "They got Wynton playing some old dead European music."

And in June of 1986 there had been an incident.

THE EPISODE, AT THE FIRST VANCOUVER JAZZ FESTIVAL, WAS THE MOST exciting thing that had happened in jazz for years, throwing a spotlight on a genre that, in American culture at large, had long since contracted into niche status. The event quickly took on folkloric dimensions. In some accounts, there had even been a threat of physical violence between the frail sixty-year-old Davis and the twenty-four-year-old Marsalis. In Wynton's 2015 retelling, it all started with the goading of the three musicians who played with him at the festival—the drummer Jeff "Tain" Watts, the bassist Robert Hurst, and the pianist Marcus Roberts.

The four were in a car approaching Vancouver, Marsalis recalled, when Roberts, Watts, and Hurst began teasing him about some belittling remarks Miles had made to the press about Wynton and his musical family, New Orleans jazz royalty (his father, Ellis Marsalis Jr., and his three brothers, Branford, Delfeayo, and Jason, were all renowned jazz musicians). How long was Wynton going to stand for this? they asked, jokingly. Was he scared of little old Miles? Davis was going to play that night, they pointed out, and they were off. Why not jump onstage with your horn, barge in on his act?

When Wynton replied, seriously, that he had too much respect for Miles to do that, the others began laughing at him and playfully betting that he was too scared to face off with the great man. Marsalis laughed along with them as they raised the ante. When the bet reached $100 apiece, and Wynton saw that his bandmates were serious, he said he would do it. And so he did.

According to a wire-service report,

> Wynton Marsalis surprised everyone—especially Miles Davis— when he walked onstage with his horn, uninvited and unannounced, as Davis and band were in the midst of a blues number. The upstart Marsalis approached the veteran Davis but Miles

shook his head in a negative fashion. Instead of leaving, Marsalis walked to a microphone and began playing, which resulted in Davis stopping the music. The abashed Marsalis, who has always revered Davis, then walked off. "I don't know why he was up there," Miles said. "We have things that we do and we time everything. If he wants to jam, why doesn't he go out to a club? I wonder what would happen if I did that?"

As Miles recalled the incident in his autobiography, he and his band were playing to a standing-room-only crowd at an outdoor amphitheater. Engrossed in his music, he suddenly sensed a presence in his periphery, and saw the audience reacting strongly—and then Marsalis was standing right next to him and whispering in his ear, "They told me to come up here."

Miles was furious. "Get the fuck off the stage," he said. Marsalis looked shocked. "Man, what the fuck are you doing up here on stage?" Davis said. "Get the fuck off the stage!"

Miles stopped the band, he writes, because Marsalis "wouldn't have fit in. Wynton can't play the kind of shit we were playing."

Marsalis claimed that Davis was playing the organ when he walked onto the bandstand, and that the music was too loud for him to hear anything Miles said. Once the band stopped, Wynton recalled, Miles said a few words to him, but "fuck" wasn't one of them. And even though Davis was physically fragile, Marsalis, remembering that the great trumpeter had once trained as a boxer, watched his hands carefully, certain that any kind of physical altercation would go in his, Wynton's, favor, and wind up making him look like nothing but a bully.

The story, Marsalis said, blew up out of all proportion to what had really happened or what he and his band ever thought it would be. And, he said, he never collected his $300.

One more recollection should be heard: that of the trumpeter Wallace Roney, Miles's friend and only certified protégé, who played at the festival in the drummer Tony Williams's group and was in the audience that night. "Wynton walked onstage—Miles had just taken a solo," Roney told me. "And Wynton went up and said, 'Can I sit in?' And Miles said, 'What?' First of all, his back was to him—Wynton said, 'I would like to sit in, and anytime you want to sit in with my band, you can.' [Miles said] 'No. No. Get off the stage.' And Wynton didn't get off the stage, and Wynton just waited, and he took a solo. You should hear it. You'll hear a big difference between Miles and Wynton, by the way. And then after one chorus of the blues, Miles cuts it off. And the people boo Miles. Miles says, 'Get off my fucking stage, motherfucker.' That's what he said. And Wynton says, back to him, 'Fuck you.' And walks off the stage.

"Now Wynton talks about, he didn't want to do it, and his band [made him do it]—you know, it's bullshit."

The truth may be a combination of all accounts, but let it not be forgotten that ambushing a musician—jumping up on stage in the middle of his set and trying to outplay, or "cut," him—is an ancient and semi-honorable tradition in jazz, one that Miles himself had engaged in as a young man, and certainly one that Wynton Marsalis, the ultimate traditionalist, knew all about.

WALLACE RONEY BROUGHT A UNIQUE POINT OF VIEW TO TALKING AND thinking about Miles Davis. Born in Philadelphia in 1960, he was a musical prodigy who was found to have perfect pitch at age four. When Roney was small, his father, a passionate jazz fan also named Wallace, used to show the little boy off to friends by giving him what were essentially blindfold tests, playing records and asking his son to identify the musicians.

"'Who's that on trumpet, little Wally?'

"And I listened, I'd say, 'Blue Mitchell!'"

"'Who you think is on saxophone there, Wally? Is that John Coltrane?'

"And I listened, and I'd say, 'Well, he's not playing so many notes, and he's got a bluesy thing—gotta be Hank Mobley, it's not Coltrane.'" Roney smiled broadly as he recalled his father's quizzes. "Trane had a *dance* to his playing, I would say," he added.

We were sitting in the cluttered living room of the trumpeter's small house in Clifton, New Jersey, in the spring of 2019. Thirty years to the day, as it happened, after my first meeting with Miles. A gravel-voiced man with a huge belly, Roney drank periodically from a half-gallon bottle of fruit juice that sat on the floor in front of him as we spoke. Perhaps he was diabetic. As we spoke, Wallace Roney had less than a year to live: he would die of Covid-19-related illness in March 2020. He was a brilliant, undersung musician and an incisive analyst of jazz, genial, gentle, and generous, and the only musician of any sort who could ever claim to have been mentored by Miles Davis.

Roney started playing trumpet at six and was awarded a scholarship to Philadelphia's Settlement Music School, studying with the renowned teacher and Philadelphia Orchestra trumpeter Sigmund Hering. At twelve, he became the youngest member of the classical Philadelphia Brass Ensemble. But his real passion was for jazz: "Miles Davis! Coltrane! Herbie Hancock! Art Blakey! Bud Powell! I mean, Monk! I was all in at three years old! I was buying the latest Miles and Lee Morgan records at twelve years old, asking my grandmother for allowance!"

When his parents divorced, he moved with his father to Washington, D.C., where he attended the Duke Ellington High School for the Arts. By the time he graduated, he had met and played for Dizzy Gillespie, Clark Terry, and Woody Shaw. Each trumpeter gave Roney praise and pointers, and he admired all of them, but his unmet idol was Miles Davis.

Roney turned down an invitation to enroll at Juilliard in order to attend Howard University. While he was visiting New York City during the summer after his junior year, he sat in with Philly Joe Jones and then Art Blakey, who invited him to join the Jazz Messengers' tour in Europe. The trumpet chair in the Messengers had previously been occupied by Wynton Marsalis, who had just left to tour with Herbie Hancock.

In the fall of 1983, Columbia Records' George Butler invited Roney to participate in a special event at Radio City Music Hall: "George came up to me and said, 'Listen, we're gonna do a tribute to Miles. And Miles is going to be there; his band's gonna play. But for the first half we're gonna have his alumni play, and I also want to do a thing where seven trumpet players come up and play a fanfare for Miles, then bring Miles up. Would you like to be one of them?'"

Roney shook his head. "Man, I was like, 'Are you kidding?' I would've paid to just go *see* the concert! So we did it"—the other trumpeters were Randy Brecker, Lew Soloff, Jimmy Owens, Art Farmer, Jon Faddis, and Maynard Ferguson—"and everything worked out fine. Then Art Farmer said to me, 'Your man want to meet you.' I said, 'Really?' He said, 'Yeah. I know you want to meet your man. Your man want to meet *you*.'

"We're downstairs in the basement where the Rockettes are—that was our dressing room," Roney said. "And you know, it's a big, long place. And Art starts to walk to the elevator, and I stopped. And my brother [saxophonist Antoine Roney] and [the jazz drummer] Cindy Blackman was with me. And they said, 'What's wrong?' I said, 'Man, what if Miles say something that hurt my feelings?' They said, 'Man, you might not never get this chance again.'

"All this I just told you took place in a matter of twenty seconds. Art didn't even know that I stopped—you know, 'cause Art was older. He's walking to the elevator; I finally jumped on the elevator with Art, I went up—I think Miles's dressing room was on the fifth floor. And that's how I first met Miles Davis. He said, *'I heard you playing that stuff.'*"

Roney was imitating Miles's voice. In the course of interviewing numerous jazz musicians, I've found that virtually everyone who ever met Miles Davis, myself included, loves to imitate that whispery, raspy voice: it brings him back to life a bit, in all his ornery brilliance. And it's fun to say "motherfucker" a lot when you're doing it—after all, the word appears on nearly every page of the Davis-Troupe memoir, often a number of times. Still, some who knew Miles well contend that this—and much else in the book—is more Quincy Troupe than Miles Davis. (Some have also contended that much in the book was lifted wholesale from previous interviews with Davis.) In any case, reducing Miles to "motherfucker" reduces him intolerably.

"He said nice things," Roney continued. "He gave me his phone number and asked me to call him the next day. And the next day—this is beautiful—I woke up like nine in the morning. Shit, I wish I could wake up like that now. And I'm looking at the clock, and I said to myself, 'Should I call him?' I thought, 'I don't want to call too early.' So I'm watching the clock, each hour, thinking—and at twelve o'clock I finally called him up. And he tells me to come over, so I went over."

Roney didn't go to Miles's place at 312 West Seventy-seventh—the fabled five-story brownstone, formerly a Russian Orthodox church, was undergoing renovations. "It was Seventieth Street, West End, penthouse," he told me. "Cicely's place. A doorman. You know. So I go up there, and when they open the door, first thing Miles says to me—*first* thing"—he went back into his Miles imitation—"'I never liked Brown—Clifford Brown. It's not that I was jealous.' First thing! I'm walking in the door!

"'It's not that I was jealous of him,'" Roney-as-Miles said. "'He was a nice enough guy; I just didn't think he played as well as everybody said. Him and Max played fast all the time because Clifford couldn't swing. And Max stopped swinging when he left Bird.'"

Roney grinned in disbelief. "That's the *first* thing he said."

He shook his head. "I didn't say nothing; I ain't arguing—well, why would I? Some people say, 'Well, you should've—' Well, y'all *say* that— I wanted to learn what *he* had to say. So I listened, you know. And from that point on, it was a beautiful—I would say protégé-mentor [relationship]. I would not say friends—I wasn't on his level, to be considered a friend. I would just look at him as my idol."

And—Clifford Brown didn't swing!—all other idols had to be struck down before the mentorship could properly proceed.

AND ACCEPTANCE OF ONE, OF NECESSITY, MEANT REJECTION OF OTHERS. Wynton Marsalis wasn't lacking for important mentors—as a young man he'd come under the affectionate tutelage of the drummers Art Blakey and Elvin Jones, the trumpeter Doc Cheatham, even the great novelist and sometime jazz writer Ralph Ellison—but Miles Davis was in a category all his own, and it couldn't have gone down easily for Marsalis that from the beginning he and his idol failed to hit it off.

"Columbia Records and everybody was pushing Wynton as the next Miles," Roney told me. "And Wynton was talking a lot of *crap* anyway. I don't know if Miles realized that Wynton was talking a lot of crap. But when Miles heard Wynton, he wasn't moved by Wynton's playing. He *really* wasn't moved by it—he felt that Wynton was just a guy that played classical music, that went to Juilliard—but as far as playing *this* music, there was nothing there. His technical facility didn't translate. So Wynton talked shit about Miles because Miles didn't like his playing.

"But what really pissed Wynton off—and I think it pissed Columbia Records off—I think their PR department spent a lot of money promoting Wynton to be the next Miles. When Miles didn't take to Wynton, they tried to write it off as, well, Miles wouldn't take anybody—like a boxer. And then all of a sudden, the person they didn't endorse is the person he did like! I think he heard me play that night in '83, and he liked what he heard! He said he heard something that reminded him of himself, when he first heard Dizzy. And he decided, of all those cats, I like Wally! And then all of a sudden the word's coming out, *Wallace is hanging with Miles.* And I could see Columbia Records saying, 'We invested all that fucking PR money and he went for this one instead!'"

WHEN WALLACE RONEY MET MILES DAVIS IN DAVIS'S RADIO CITY DRESS-ing room, Miles asked him what horn he was playing, and Roney said that he didn't own a horn—he was borrowing one from Giardinelli's, a musical instrument repair shop on West Forty-sixth Street. And when Roney went up to Cicely Tyson's penthouse, one of the first things Miles did, after putting Clifford Brown in his place, was to produce four Martin Committee trumpets and invite Roney to try them out.

The four horns were lacquered in different colors—aquamarine, black and maroon, red, and silver—and the young musician had the giddily rising feeling that his idol was about to give one of them to him. "And I played 'em," Roney told me, "and I saw the horn I wanted."

The horn he wanted was the aquamarine: a dazzlingly beautiful instrument with silver filigree and gold valve keys and tuning slide. The horn Miles gave him was the only slightly less dazzling black and maroon. Its monetary value, given its provenance, would have been in the low five figures; its value to Wallace Roney was incalculable, with a slight, inexpressible disappointment subtracted.

Fast-forward to 1987.

"I was going to Toronto with Tony Williams," Roney remembered, "and as I was getting ready to leave, I got a phone call from Miles: 'Wally—whatcha doin'?' I said I was getting ready to go to my gig. 'Come over.'

"This was the Essex House. The lights is out, you know, it's dark in there—we sittin' on the couch. He not sayin' much. He said, 'What time is your gig?' I had to be at the airport at eight or something like that. He got up and put on his coat and got his keys like he thought the gig was at the Vanguard—I said, no, it's in Toronto.' He said, 'You better get goin'!'

"We laughed, he gave me a hug, then he said, 'Here.' He handed me this little case. And I opened it up, and it was the blue trumpet."

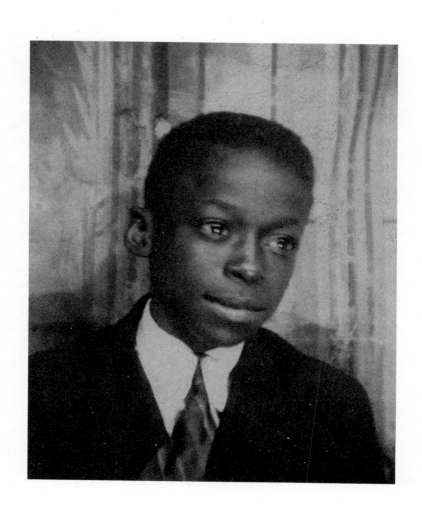

2 Dentist's son

Miles Davis's investiture, unlike Wallace Roney's, began with entitlement. Sometime in the mid- to late 1950s, nobody seems sure exactly when, someone hung the nickname Prince of Darkness on Davis, and while his literal and metaphorical darkness is a subject in itself (and one we will come to), he was a prince from the beginning.

Miles Dewey Davis III came from privilege—or privilege as it was defined (and circumscribed) for African Americans in the early twentieth century: his people, on both sides, were what used to be called (by whites, with amused condescension; by Blacks, with a wide range of attitudes, from envy and contempt to admiration) "Colored aristocracy." Both his parents came from Arkansas. His mother, Cleota, was a violinist, pianist, and music teacher. Miles didn't know much about her side of the family, he said, but the maternal relatives he'd heard about and met "seemed to be middle class and a little uppity in their attitudes."

His father's father, Miles I, was a prosperous Arkansas bookkeeper and landowner; Miles writes that around the turn of the century, jealous whites drove his grandfather off a five-hundred-acre parcel of land he'd bought, but a two-hundred-acre tract near Pine Bluffs, perhaps part of the original parcel, stayed in the family (there was a successful pig farm on the property), and Miles and his older sister and younger brother hunted, fished, and rode horses there as children.

Miles Dewey Davis, Jr., was a dentist with a D.D.S. from Northwestern. As a newlywed he set up a practice in Chicago, but in 1925, around the time Miles Jr. and Cleota's first child, Dorothy, was born, they moved to Alton, Illinois, a Mississippi River town some three hundred miles downstate and just eighteen miles north of St. Louis, Missouri. With a population of just under thirty thousand, Alton was a small city with a big history: in the years leading up to the Civil War it was a hotbed of abolitionism (Illinois was a free state, while Missouri, under the terms of the Compromise of 1820, was the sole Northern slave state; freedom was just across the river). The seventh Lincoln-Douglas debate was held in Alton in 1858, and a coauthor of the Thirteenth Amendment, Senator Lyman Trumbull, was an Alton resident.

Alton also had a sizable and solid African American population, and the arrival of a young Black dentist, a successful practitioner and family man, was news in the community. In an article on a local fundraising event, the *Alton Evening Telegraph* of March 7, 1925, noted: "In the afternoon Madame Evelyn Horton of St. Louis, a well known hair dresser, will speak in regard to the new $6,000 building she expects to erect soon for members of her race. Dr. Miles D. Davis, a dentist of Chicago who is expecting to locate in Alton will also be present to address the meeting."

It was in Alton, on May 26, 1926, that Miles and Cleota welcomed their second child and first son into the world. The following year, perhaps because Dr. Davis wanted to expand his practice, the family moved to East St. Louis, Illinois, a city of seventy-five thousand directly across the river from St. Louis, Missouri. And it was here that Miles Davis III— called Junior by his family, a nickname he hated—grew up, at first in an apartment behind his father's dental office, then in a small house at the corner of Kansas Street and North Seventeenth Avenue.

It was not a happy household. Once the Depression hit, Miles's father had to work harder to support a family that had grown used to living well; he was frequently absent, and when he was present, he and Cleota clashed frequently, sometimes violently. Nor did Miles and his mother—two "strong, independent personalities," by his account—get along well, though he also found much to admire about her:

My mother was a beautiful woman. She had a whole lot of style, with an East Indian, Carmen McRae look, and dark, nut-brown, smooth skin. High cheekbones and Indian-like hair. Big beautiful eyes. Me and my brother Vernon looked like her. She had mink coats, diamonds; she was a very glamorous woman who was into all kinds of hats and things. . . . She always dressed to kill. I got my looks from my mother and also my love of clothes and sense of style. I guess you could say I got whatever artistic talent I have from her also.

For thousands of Black boys growing up in Jim Crow America after World War I and through the Depression, mastering a musical instrument with an eye toward playing professionally was a way of circumventing the dismally scant variety of career choices open to African Americans, a socially (and parentally) sanctioned path out of poverty. Miles Davis, by contrast, could afford to think about Art. He began playing trumpet at age nine; by the time he was twelve he realized music had become the most important thing in his life. Throughout junior high and high school he took lessons from a patient of his father's, a Black jazz trumpeter and music teacher named Elwood Buchanan. Buchanan taught Miles to play with a clear, midrange tone, neither too high nor too low, and without vibrato: he would rap his student's knuckles with a ruler if a wobble crept into a note. (Miles had to be restrained from imitating one of his early trumpet idols, Harry James, whose swaggering solos were built on a lusty vibrato.)

The great trumpeter Clark Terry, also a St. Louis native and six years older than Miles, recalled meeting him then, through his friend Buchanan:

> Buch used to always tell me, "Man, you've got to come over here to school; you've got to hear this little dude. I've got a bad little dude over here." So finally one day, I went over to Lincoln High in East St. Louis and met this little skinny mother. He was so thin that if you had turned him sideways, they would have marked him absent. He was very shy. He couldn't look you in the eye; he would always look down and he spoke very softly. And I heard him play.
>
> Well, he was a bad little dude then; he really could play, even as a kid.

Miles took additional lessons with Buchanan's teacher Joseph Gustat, the principal trumpeter of the St. Louis Symphony Orchestra and a renowned pedagogue whom Bix Beiderbecke himself had once sought out for instruction. (After one look at Bix's unorthodox fingering technique, Gustat decided the young cornetist's talent would blossom more fully if left uncorrected.)

And Miles Davis, renowned as a rebel throughout his career, was an obedient, diligent, curious student. He read everything he could on music theory; he played in the (all-Black) East St. Louis Lincoln High School marching band, and proudly wore its uniform. Clothes were important to him: following his mother's lead, and the movie examples of Fred Astaire and Cary Grant, he took to dressing beautifully in Brooks Brothers suits, high-top pants, and tab-collar shirts so heavily starched, he recalled, that he could barely turn his neck in them.

And he rode horses. In the early forties his father bought a three-hundred-acre farm in rural Millstadt, Illinois, about twenty-five miles south of East St. Louis. The main house was a twelve-room colonial with a white-columned porch in front; there were stables, with horses, and Miles and his sister and brother loved to ride them.

Back at home he formed a jazz combo with a couple of friends, a piano player named Duke Brooks and a hunchback drummer, Nick Haywood; they played social clubs and church suppers in the St. Louis area and made some pocket money. He kept practicing and learning: he taught himself chromatic scales, and won respect from local musicians for the growing depth of his art. At Lincoln High he met his first girlfriend, the portentously named Irene Birth. She was a couple of years older than he, with light skin, a dancer's slim body, and, Miles recalled years later, "pretty little feet." It was Irene who dared Miles to call up a local bandleader named Eddie Randle and ask if he could audition for Randle's Blue Devils, the ten-piece house band at the Rhumboogie Club, above the Elks Club on North Cardinal Avenue and Olive Street in downtown St. Louis.

He got the job, and with it key exposure to the big time. The Blue Devils were a tight, solid band that, over its brief existence, included not just Miles but also Clark Terry and tenor saxophonist Jimmy Forrest. Because the other members of the Blue Devils were grown men with day jobs, Miles, at age seventeen, became Randle's music director, writing arrangements and setting up rehearsals. It was valuable technical experience, and good business experience, too. It prepared him for leadership.

Even as the war raged overseas, the swing era kept swinging (although the loss of musicians to the draft accelerated the cross-fertilization of bands, as the leaders had to hustle continually to fill vacancies). Black and white big bands and territory bands—smaller aggregations usually playing lesser venues—crisscrossed the country by railroad or in their buses: St. Louis, along with Kansas City and Chicago, was a hotbed of musical talent, and an important stop for regal luminaries such as the bandleaders Duke Ellington, Count Basie, and Jimmie Lunceford. A lot of greats and future greats made it their business to go listen to the Blue Devils: Coleman Hawkins, Benny Carter, Roy Eldridge, Kenny Dorham, Fats Navarro, Sonny Stitt. Stitt, who was playing in Tiny Bradshaw's band, asked Miles if he wanted to go on the road with them. Dr. Davis and Cleota vetoed the idea: after all, their son hadn't yet graduated high school.

Then he did, early, in January 1944. It was to be an eventful year for Miles in several ways. His parents separated. Irene gave birth to a daughter, whom Miles, despite his father's heated allegations about Irene's wayward ways, accepted as his; they named her Cheryl. And Billy Eckstine's band came to town, with geniuses on board: Sarah Vaughan. Art Blakey. And Charlie Parker and Dizzy Gillespie.

WILMINGTON, DELAWARE, JUNE 9: THREE DAYS AFTER D-DAY. THEN ON through the South in the dead of summer, mile after mile over two-lane blacktop in the un-air-conditioned band bus, an old Greyhound Silversides. Racks in the back for band jackets. No toilet. Windows wide open; hot breeze gusting in. Washington, D.C. North Carolina, South Carolina, Georgia, Florida, Alabama, Louisiana, Texas, Oklahoma, Missouri. As the band travels, some players are lost to the draft and others replace them. When the drummer Shadow Wilson goes off to the army, his chair is empty; a substitute—always inadequate—has to be recruited in every town. But when Art Blakey is persuaded to leave a gig in Boston and join Eckstine, the band's sound begins to jell. Besides Dizzy and Bird, there are Gene Ammons and Lucky Thompson on tenor sax, Sonny Stitt on alto, Buddy Anderson on trumpet, Tommy Potter on bass. The great Tadd Dameron, helping Dizzy to write the arrangements. Sarah Vaughan, a musical phenomenon with perfect pitch and an infinitely supple voice, is like a great horn herself.

"BILLY ECKSTINE The ROMANTIC SINGING MAESTRO AND HIS ORCHESTRA," the newspaper ad bills them, with a sultry headshot of the leader in half shadow, leaning in romantically, his dark eyes pinning the viewer. And there is romance. Black audiences in clubs and ballrooms and auditoriums, in the thrall of the singer and his hot young orchestra, dance close and slow to the ballads; but then come the fast numbers, and because Dizzy has written these charts, and because these hot young players are impatient with the blues (and, truth be told, ashamed of it, too), there are a lot of them.

"We didn't have it easy; our type of music was more or less a concert style of jazz," Eckstine remembered.

> People would start to dance, and then they'd turn around and lis-
> ten. Sometimes our tempos were almost not danceable either. Diz
> made an arrangement of "Max Is Makin' Wax," which was way up
> there, featuring him and Bird. You couldn't dance to that at all,
> but people would stand there and watch. . . .

"Our breathing and phrasing were different from all the other bands, and, naturally, we sounded very different," Dizzy recalled. "There was no band that sounded like Billy Eckstine's. Our attack was strong, and we were playing bebop, the modern style. No other band like this one existed in the world."

This was both good and bad news. "We never had any problem with the young musicians; they loved it; they loved the band," Billy Eckstine said.

Everywhere we'd go there was a following of young musicians. But the populace, in general, and the powers that be, that booked the bands, and the clubs were used to listening to a certain type of music. They were not thrilled by us coming in; young, wild, crazy young cats playing this style. I remember one place we worked the man wanted to give me some money to go downtown and buy some stock arrangements.

The seeds are being sown both for bebop's bright burst and its demise. The modern style is new and dazzlingly fast and thrilling, but *you can't dance to it*. You can stand and listen to it, but it demands a lot of the listener: ultimately, in many ways, it is musicians' music.

Billy Eckstine understands that something remarkable is happening, and loves it. He loves this band, and they love him back. They call him B., or Mr. B. Dizzy plays tricks while the leader is singing—pointing to him and miming that his teeth are false, or that he is a man who likes to sleep with men. When Eckstine turns around to look, Gillespie is staring heavenward, angelically. Eckstine just smiles.

The band unsettles Dallas and Fort Worth and Tulsa and Oklahoma City . . . and then heads up to St. Louis, where for the first time on the tour they're booked for a two-week residency, in the grandest venue in town, the ominously named Club Plantation.

The Plantation, owned by a minor local mafioso named Tony Scarpelli, is modeled after Chicago's Grand Terrace and the Cotton Club in New York: a plush nightspot where the entertainment is Black and the clientele exclusively white. Because it serves only food, soft drinks, and drink setups—ice and glasses, but no liquor; customers bring their own—local laws allow it to stay open after 1:00 a.m. The Plantation is where Billy Eckstine, afraid of no man, Black or white, strides through the front door to lead the band's first rehearsal and is promptly reminded—by a timid waiter? an imperious manager? Tony Scarpelli himself?—that colored entertainers are to use the rear entrance. And Mr. B.—tall, slim, and cool; immaculately dressed—gives the man *that look* and strides on in anyway.

And this is where Charlie Parker, during a rehearsal break, goes up to each musician sitting with a cold drink and asks, "Did you drink from that glass?"—and on being told *yes*, proceeds to smash each glass on the floor, shouting, "This glass is contaminated!"—ten, twelve, fifteen times.

The management of the Plantation takes his point. Thanks to Eckstine's agents in New York, the residency is quickly switched to the Riviera, a grand establishment farther east on Delmar Boulevard, a place where the skin color of the clientele matches that of the performers. This is the place where, in that summer of '44, one of those young musicians who follow Eckstine's band, the quiet and shy Miles Davis, just turned eighteen, goes with his horn in a case and his friend Bobby Danzig by his side, hoping vaguely to be noticed and—why not dream big?—even asked to sit in alongside Charlie Parker and Dizzy Gillespie in Billy Eckstine's already legendary aggregation.

The band's reputation has preceded it, the word passing along the grapevine up from the South. And though Miles is pre-awed by Parker and Gillespie—two of the only five records he owns are Parker on "Hootie's Blues," with the Jay McShann band, and Gillespie on "Woody 'n' You," with Coleman Hawkins—seeing and hearing them play is a soul-jarring, life-changing experience: "I said, 'What? What is this!?'" he remembered. "It was a motherfucker. Man, that shit was all up in my body. The way that band was playing music—that was *all* I wanted to hear."

And then, as in a dream, he was up there playing it with them.

As Miles recollected, while he and his friend were listening to the band rehearse, a man came running up to him and asked him if he was a trumpet player. He was. Did he have a union card? He did. "So the guy said, 'Come on, we need a trumpet player. Our trumpet got sick.'"

The guy turned out to be Dizzy Gillespie. And the trumpet player who got sick was Buddy Anderson, who as it happened had introduced Charlie Parker and Dizzy Gillespie in Kansas City four years earlier. Diagnosed with tuberculosis when he arrived in St. Louis, Anderson went home to Oklahoma City to recuperate and soon decided to retire, never to play trumpet seriously again. And Miles Davis got to sit in Buddy

Anderson's chair for the Eckstine band's entire two-week stand at the Riviera—though the two weeks were more memorable to the eighteen-year-old than to anybody else. As Eckstine recalled, "Miles, you couldn't even hear him past the reed section."

Quiet and shy, but now firmly resolved: "I decided right then and there," Miles remembered, "that I had to leave St. Louis and live in New York City where all these bad musicians were."

3   It must be heard with the brain and felt with the soul

He arrives in Manhattan in September 1944, agog at the size and speed and bustle of the city of cities (and with the war still on, the town is also filled with soldiers and sailors) yet determined to make his mark in jazz's epicenter. He knows he is destined for greatness. But the part of him that is still a dutiful son has agreed to his father's condition for backing his move to the Big Apple: having passed a trumpet audition, Miles has enrolled at Juilliard, the music school of music schools, a place whose very name sparkles with the high gloss of high art.

Davis will maintain in later years that Juilliard was just "a smokescreen, a stopover, a pretense I used to put me close to being around Bird and Diz"—Parker and Gillespie, by his account, having told him back in St. Louis to look them up if he got to New York. It's the kind of thing people say, breezily, when they have to say something. Were they sincere, or was it just happy talk? How could Bird and Diz have known, given the travel schedule of the Eckstine band, that they would be in New York at the same time as Miles?

In fact, Charlie Parker, "fed up with travel and eager to return to New York," had left Eckstine in August, and Dizzy gave the bandleader his notice a few weeks later. Both were now free agents, and both were back in Manhattan. But Davis would have had no way of knowing this.

No doubt the two geniuses felt for the earnest and quiet young trumpeter; whether they sensed future greatness is another question. Billy Eckstine, for his part, didn't have the luxury of wondering about Miles's potential. With the ruthless practicality bandleading demanded, Eckstine had replaced the trumpeter he couldn't hear over the reeds with one he could, Marion "Boonie" Hazel, for the band's next gig, at Chicago's Regal Theatre. Miles recalled that the rejection dented his self-assurance for a while, but that playing a few gigs around St. Louis helped him to recover his confidence before heading east.

His confidence was extraordinary. The eighteen-year-old spent his first weeks in New York going to classes at Juilliard—then on the far West Side at 122nd Street and Claremont Avenue—and making exploratory trips in Harlem to Minton's and the Savoy Ballroom, and downtown to the clubs on Fifty-second Street, not just looking for Bird and Diz but also checking out the talent. The talent was superlative. But rather than being intimidated, Miles seems to have felt he was finding his peers, many of them barely older than he. At Minton's he reencountered the twenty-one-year-old Florida trumpet wizard Theodore "Fats" Navarro, whom he'd first met and jammed with in St. Louis; he heard, and met, the Detroit vibraphonist Milt Jackson (age twenty-one) and the homegrown tenor saxophonist Eddie "Lockjaw" Davis (no relation), who, at just twenty-three, led the house band.

After the Savoy and Minton's, the smallness and shabbiness of the fabled 52nd Street clubs shocked Miles. The Three Deuces, in particular, had accumulated such renown that he expected it to be "all plush and shit." Instead, the club's tiny bandstand had barely enough room for a piano; the tables for the clientele were practically on top of one another. "East St. Louis and St. Louis had hipper-looking clubs," Davis thought.

It was the same up and down the Street. The clubs, located in the base-ments of the brownstones that lined the block, were former speakeasies, "long, low-ceilinged, narrow, and always looking more crowded than [they were]," little more than holes in the wall. "All the clubs were shaped like shoe boxes, and they had dingy canopies outside," the jazz writer Leonard Feather remembered. "The tables were three inches square and the chairs were hard wood. The drinks were probably watered. They were miserable places. There was nothing to them except the music."

But oh, the music. Fifty-second Street was where audiences—white audiences—went to sit and listen, often not comprehending or approving, to the sea change in jazz. The big bands were dying; the music heard on the Street, the Charlie Parker chronicler Ross Russell wrote, came from "the streamlined band of the future":

> Up front trumpet and saxophone reduced the instrumentation of the big band (seven brass and five reeds) to the lowest common denominator—one brass and one reed. Each horn was a section in itself. The horns played the unison parts. They also exchanged leads, invented counter themes, and, of course, took solos. In the hands of young jazzmen like Charlie Parker and Dizzy Gillespie, everything that the big bands had been able to do was implied by the two horns, and a great deal more besides. The playing was a constant and creative process. There was no band book. No customer at the Deuces ever glimpsed so much as an arrangement or sheet of music paper. The tunes had no names, or numbers. They were simply tunes, heard and carried in the heads of the musicians. The names came later.

The power of these new sounds, heard in close quarters, was startling, overwhelming. "The Parker-Gillespie sets were explosions of musical energy," Russell continued.

> Listeners were rocked back on their heels and numbed by its force. The entire body of American jazz, from Bolden to Basie, was

being subjected to an exhaustive re-examination. Beret at a rakish angle, goatee bobbing, Dizzy would center the horn against his lips and spurt forth festoons of notes. The saxophone would support his escalations, comment on his statements, underline, paraphrase, punctuate, and countervoice. The saxophone solos were still more brilliant. They seemed to begin where the trumpet had stopped. The saxophone was played with an accuracy and at a speed that made the listener's hair stand on end. There had been nothing like this band since the King Oliver Creole Jazz Band, fresh up from New Orleans, with young Louis Armstrong on second cornet, opened at the Lincoln Gardens in Chicago in 1922.

And one feature notably absent from the Fifty-second Street clubs was a dance floor. "We had finally come through to an age of concerts," Dizzy Gillespie said.

It became a listener's groove, instead of just grooving with the dancing. I always liked dancing, but you can have a good time without dancing. Dancing won't make you cry, and crying is a strong emotion. Somebody plays or something, and you say, "Man, I cried. I sat there and cried." Sometimes you can listen to a groove so strong that it'll throw your back outta whack.

The music was changing, faster than even its most ardent fans realized. Swing itself, the marriage of jazz and popular dance music, was growing stale. "Jazz in the Swing Era was so frequently compromised by chuckle-headed bandleaders, most of them white, who diluted, sentimentalized, and undermined the work of dedicated musicians, that a bold new virtuosity was essential," Gary Giddins writes.

Practical conditions on the ground accelerated the revolution. An American Federation of Musicians strike meant no new records from the swing bands for over two years. Out in the territory, the big and medium-sized bands had been hit hard by wartime conditions, primarily fuel rationing and the draft, and the Black bands, usually playing to smaller audiences, were hit hardest of all. After the departures of Parker and Gillespie, Earl Hines lost another half dozen key musicians to conscription; his attention-getting solution, a "draft-proof" all-female string section, was a gimmick that didn't pan out.

And then there was the Federal Cabaret Tax, which, to aid the war effort, was hiked from 5 percent to 30 percent in 1944. The tariff hit music venues hard: the predictable result was a chilling effect on the hiring of big bands. The small groups that pioneered bebop, the quintets, quartets, and trios, were small for economic as well as artistic reasons, and the little clubs on the Street were the perfect setting for the explosion of the new music.

Miles was disappointed with the clubs, but not with the music he heard. On his first visit to the Deuces, he took in a set led by the tenor sax master Don Byas, an elder statesman of the new music at age thirty-two. "I remember listening with awe to him playing all that shit on that little bitty stage," Miles said.

Then someone gave him Dizzy's telephone number. With the impetuousness of youth, Miles simply called up his idol, and the generous-spirited Gillespie told him to come on over to the Harlem apartment where he lived with his wife, Lorraine. Lorraine Gillespie, ordinarily resistant to visiting (read: freeloading) jazz musicians, took at once to the baby-faced teenager. But though the Gillespies were welcoming, Dizzy had no idea where Bird was.

Miles kept looking. One night he was hanging around outside the Three Deuces when the club's manager, Sammy Kaye (not related to the bandleader of the same name), cast a beady eye on this small, very dark-skinned, very young-looking man and asked what he was doing there, telling him that he had to be eighteen to go into the club. Miles said that he was eighteen, and that he was looking for Bird. Kaye then launched into a tirade about what a lowlife drug addict and all-around bad influence Charlie Parker was. Miles, to whom none of this was news, stood impassively, eyes averted, while this white man went on and on. "Where are you from, son?" the man finally asked. Wincing at the appellation, Miles told him: East St. Louis. Sammy Kaye advised him to go back there.

Instead of following Kaye's advice, Davis writes, he walked across the street to the Onyx Club, where the great Coleman Hawkins was heading the bill. Miles was hanging around the entrance to the club, looking for any familiar face, perhaps someone from the Eckstine band, when Hawkins, on a break, stepped outside. The handsome, dapper, pencil-mustached saxophonist, forty that fall, was one of jazz's true luminaries: super royalty. With the brashness of youth, and the persistent though as yet unconfirmed belief that he was somebody, too, Davis went over and introduced himself, informing the great man that he was going to Juilliard, but was really in New York to find and play with Charlie Parker. To Miles's disappointment, Hawkins reacted exactly as Sammy Kaye had, laughing and telling Davis he "was too young to get mixed up with somebody like Bird." Forgetting who he was talking to, Miles got mad. "Well, you know where he is or not?" he demanded.

Hawkins told the upstart to try uptown, maybe Minton's. Then he added: "My best advice to you is just finish your studies at Juilliard and forget Bird."

Of course Miles couldn't forget Bird. Soon afterward he heard through the grapevine that Parker was going to jam at a Harlem club called the Heatwave. With his horn in hand just in case, he went to the club and planted himself at a table, primed and alert, one eye constantly on the door. After waiting in vain for hours, he finally decided to go out for a breath of fresh air. As he stood on the corner, he suddenly heard a voice behind him say, "Hey, Miles! I heard you been looking for me!"

The first thing the fastidious Davis noticed was that Bird was a mess: baggy, wrinkled suit that looked as if he'd slept in it for days; puffy face; red eyes. But to the teenage trumpeter Parker was also the essence of confident cool. And when he walked Miles into the Heatwave with his arm around the young postulant's shoulder, the crowd parting in awe, Miles was *in*.

When Bird put his horn to his lips and began to blow, the "power and beauty just bursting out of him," the transformation from street junkie to genius was complete.

Miles's transformation from unknown music student to rising star began soon afterward, on one of Minton's Monday nights, when Bird and Dizzy beckoned him to come onstage and jam with them. This was the most sought-after opportunity in New York jazz, and it was also the supreme acid test: do or die, sink or swim. Many sank. By his own lights Miles wasn't great that night, but he was good, "playing my ass off in the style I played, which was different from Dizzy's, although I was influenced by his playing at this time." When he was done, the two grand masters smiled.

MEANWHILE, HIS DISENCHANTMENT WITH JUILLIARD, WITH ITS OVERwhelming bias toward European-classical (white) traditions, was growing. "I was learning more from hanging out, so I just got bored with school after a while," he says. "Plus, they were so fucking white-oriented and so racist."

He tells of sitting in a music history class whose teacher, a white woman, said that the reason Black people played the blues was because they were poor and had to pick cotton, which made them sad. At this, Miles relates, he raised his hand, stood up, and told the class that he was from East St. Louis, that his father was a rich dentist, and that he, Miles, played the blues. His father never picked cotton, he said, and he (Miles) didn't wake up this morning sad and start playing the blues. There's more to playing the blues than that, he told the class. The teacher was properly chastened.

As for the boring curriculum, the white Western-European canon, he had found its limits well before coming to Juilliard: "I used to win *awards* in my high school," he told me in 1989. "Then one day I said, 'No, that shit sounds too bad. I can't even feel this.' I said, 'What the fuck am I playing "Flight of the Bumblebee" for?'"

And yet he says in his memoir that he was surprised and disappointed to find, when he first came to New York, that he knew more about music than most of the musicians he met, with the exception of fellow trumpeters Gillespie, Roy Eldridge, and the now forgotten Joe Guy. A lot of Black musicians, he observed, knew nothing about music theory: the pianist Bud Powell was one of the few Miles knew who could both read and write music. Many older players, in his experience, thought that studying theory would cause them to lose the feeling in their playing—would make them sound white. He was incredulous that the likes of Lester Young, Coleman Hawkins, and Charlie Parker refused to go to museums or libraries and study musical scores.

Miles, on the other hand, did just that, frequenting the Juilliard library and taking out scores by Stravinsky, Berg, and Prokofiev.

> I wanted to see what was going on in all of music. Knowledge is freedom and ignorance is slavery, and I just couldn't believe someone could be that close to freedom and not take advantage of it. I have never understood why black people didn't take advantage of all the shit that they can. It's like a ghetto mentality telling people that they aren't supposed to do certain things, that those things are only reserved for white people. When I would tell other musicians about all this, they would just kind of shine me on. You know what I mean? So I just went my own way and stopped telling them about it.

—

OF COURSE, GOING HIS OWN WAY MEANT LEAVING JUILLIARD. ON THE ADvice of a friend, a fellow trumpeter named Freddie Webster, Davis returned to St. Louis to tell his father of his decision not to register for fall classes, news that the elder Davis seems to have taken surprisingly well. By Miles's account, he sprang it on his father while Dr. Davis was in the middle of working on a patient's teeth.

Quincy Troupe is generally so adroit at animating Miles on the pages of the memoir that the persuasion scene between Miles III and Miles II is striking in its unpersuasiveness:

> I said, "Listen, Dad. There is something happening in New York. The music is changing, the styles, and I want to be in it, with Bird and Diz. So I came back to tell you that I'm quitting Juilliard because what they're teaching me is white and I'm not interested in that."
>
> "Okay," he said, "as long as you know what you're doing, everything is okay. Just whatever you do, do it good."
>
> Then he told me something I will never forget: "Miles, you hear that bird outside the window? He's a mockingbird. He don't have a sound of his own. He copies everybody's sound, and you don't want to do that. You want to be your own man, have your own sound. That's what it's really about. So, don't be nobody else but yourself. *You* know what *you* got to do and I trust your judgment. And don't worry, I'll keep sending you money until you get on your feet."

Having delivered his sage advice, Dr. Davis then—by Miles's account—went back to ministering to the patient, who had gotten an earful.

Was there ever a father so wise, nonjudgmental, and bountiful? Who knows how (or if) the scene really went down? The father in Miles's recollection sounds more like the warm and wise dad he wished he'd had than the correct and distant man with whom he shared his name. ("Were you close to your parents?" I asked him in 1989. "Not that much," he said, after a long pause. "You know, my father was a professional man—he had three degrees when he was twenty-four.")

What's certain is that Dr. Davis, in sending his brilliant son to Juilliard, gave Miles an important part of his musical education—even if having something to rebel against was one of the lessons he learned there. "Juilliard didn't have nothing for me," Miles told me in our interview, but that doesn't seem exactly right.

"Miles was very fortunate," the pianist Ahmad Jamal, a friend and artistic inspiration to Davis, said in the early 2000s.

> He was very gifted, very blessed. He was in the right places at the right times, musically. He had the type of parentage that allowed him to go to Juilliard, a place that I wanted to go. That part of my career was aborted, and sometimes I regret that because I think that the young mind should always be buffered. We lose a lot of our greats because they aren't buffered enough. Charlie Parker, Fats Navarro, Tadd Dameron, Billie Holiday. A lot of people we lose, because at eleven years old you shouldn't be in nightclubs. You don't know the difference between yes and no. You're a body of clay, you're absorbing everything, and Miles was fortunate to have exposure in Juilliard and some of the other benefits of his background.

So it was that in the early spring of 1945 Miles returned to the Apple and set about unbuffering himself.

THAT YEAR WAS WHEN HE BEGAN TO SMOKE AND DRINK A LITTLE, HE RE-called. Irene and baby Cheryl having recently (and unexpectedly) arrived at the room he was renting at 147th and Broadway, Miles also spent a lot of time out running with Freddie Webster—across town to the jams in Harlem, downtown to the clubs on the Street and in the Village. But mainly Miles and Freddie ran to hear Dizzy Gillespie, who in his sessions with Bird was redefining jazz trumpet. "Freddie Webster and I used to go down every night to hear Diz," Davis recalled. "If we missed a night, we missed something. We'd go down to Fifty-second Street to hear Diz and get our ears stretched. Stand up at the bar, throw up a quarter, and name the note it came down on. That shit be going so fast; and we'd be testing ourselves."

Freddie Webster was another musical exemplar for Davis: if Gillespie's velocity seemed nearly unattainable, Webster's widely admired style was within reach. "I loved the way he played, that he didn't waste notes and had a big, warm, mellow sound," Miles said. "I used to try to play like him, but without the vibrato." Webster, though almost a decade older than Davis, was his closest friend at this point—the two even wore each other's clothes. His death two years later—in a Chicago hotel room, age twenty-nine, of a heroin overdose—would devastate the younger musician.

Parker had roomed with Miles in the 147th Street place for a while in the fall of 1944; Miles, initially so flattered that he gave Bird a share of the forty-dollar allowance his father was sending every week, quickly came to regret his generosity. Not only did Bird eat all the food in the place, but he was constantly asking Miles for even more money, clearly to buy heroin. One night Davis came home to find Parker sitting on the floor nodding out, having pawned Miles's suitcase. One day Bird hocked his only suit and wore Miles's much smaller suit to a gig, the jacket showing four inches of shirt cuff, the pant cuffs well above the waterline. After Irene and Cheryl arrived, Parker moved to another room in the same building but gave Miles little relief. "He had a kitchenette," Davis said. "But he used to stop by my house and eat up all the fuckin' food. He would go days without eating and when he ate, he ate a lot. I stopped asking him was he hungry."

Miles's feelings about Bird were split right down the middle: "He was a great and genius musician, man, but he was also one of the slimiest and greediest motherfuckers who ever lived in this world," he said.

"Bird was *out*, man," he told me. "He had his own world."

Bird's world was roaming Manhattan, scoring drugs, doing drugs, playing when he felt like it, not playing when he didn't feel like it. He was alone when he wanted to be; when he needed company, an ever-ready, ever-growing cadre of followers and hangers-on were glad to give him company, or pretty much anything else he desired. He accepted it all as his lordly privilege. He was infamous for missing gigs altogether or arriving hours late, walking into a club while all heads turned toward him,

playing as only he could play as he approached the stand. Heroin and alcohol incapacitated merely terrestrial musicians; Bird could be jostled
awake from a drug or whiskey stupor and start playing brilliantly, instantly.

In between all this, he had somehow found the time to read widely; he
could talk with anybody about anything. ("He spoke beautifully, and he
was very kind," the saxophonist Al Cohn told Gary Giddins. "He could
talk to intellectuals about music and art and turn around and talk to street
people as though he were one of them.") He frequently slipped into a pa-
tently phony British accent. Once while he and Dizzy were in the Deep
South (Pine Bluff, Arkansas) with the Hines band, Dizzy was noodling
on the piano in between sets when a white patron dropped a nickel on the
stand and, addressing him with the N-word, ordered him to play "Darktown Strutters' Ball." Dizzy ignored the redneck—and later, when he was
coming out of the men's room, was hit on the head from behind with a
bottle. Charlie Parker sailed to his defense, calling out in full Ronald Col-
man mode, "You took advantage of my friend, you cur!"

They were friends, and geniuses together, even if Gillespie was grounded in all the ways Parker wasn't. Dizzy had a home and a wife and ambition; Bird, a rented room and, largely thanks to his addiction, endlessly wandering ways. ("This is my home, this is my portfolio, this is my Cadillac," Parker once told a friend, showing the track marks on his arm.) Dizzy liked to take a drink and enjoyed marijuana, but never used heroin, at least intentionally. (He once snorted some, thinking it was cocaine, and instantly passed out.) He was in full control of his dizziness: his humor didn't just lighten his world, it gave him a brand—and, notably, a brand that was palatable to white people. This cut two ways. Miles decried it: "I love Dizzy," he says in his memoir, "but I hated that clowning shit he used to do for all them white folks." But Dizzy was zero percent Uncle Tom; like Louis Armstrong, whom many Black musicians accused of Tomming until they learned to know better, he radiated the joy he derived from the music and his brilliance at playing it. His very name was memorable, and—a little tune in itself—fun to say. He was all over the newspapers (the Black and the white newspapers) when Parker, while an object of awe to jazz musicians, was barely known to the outside world. In 1945 *Esquire* gave Gillespie its New Star award for jazz trumpet; the award for alto sax went to Herbie Fields.

In mid-April of that year, Dizzy, ever the practical businessman, secured an eight-week residency at the Three Deuces, and hired Bird, pianist Al Haig, bassist Curley Russell, and drummer Stan Levey to play along with him. (Max Roach, who was on the road with Benny Carter as the stand began, would presently return and replace Levey.) Afternoons, the quintet rehearsed at Minton's, which the manager, the musician Teddy Hill, graciously allowed them to use, and Gillespie and Parker intensified their musical bond, perfecting the ecstatically, blazingly fast unison runs that so often began or ended or just ornamented the new tunes they were playing: "Be-Bop," "Groovin' High," "Salt Peanuts," "Hot House."

The group played to packed houses (at the Deuces, packed meant 125 people) almost every night, many customers drawn by the sheer novelty of the new music; even fellow professionals were sometimes mystified by what they were hearing. "As we walked in, see, these cats snatched up their horns and blew crazy stuff," the veteran drummer Dave Tough remembered. "One would stop all of a sudden and another would start for no reason at all. We never could tell when a solo was supposed to begin or end. Then they all quit at once and walked off the stand. It scared us."

Miles and Freddie Webster were enchanted: they kept coming back for more. The nineteen-year-old Davis, whose reputation was starting to spread, made a strong impression on Stan Levey: "Miles Davis was cocky," he recalled.

> Always dressed in a Brooks Brothers suit with all three buttons buttoned and standing around the Three Deuces when we were there with a matchbook, copying down chord changes. He was walking this hip sort of strut, sort of a bent over shuffle, and he always had his trumpet in his leather case.
>
> One day on a break, we're at the Three Deuces and Miles comes back and he's cocky, you know. He goes up to Dizzy and says, "I can play anything you can play," and Dizzy smiles and says, "Yeah, but an octave lower." Miles was a smart mouth. We were always telling him, "Shut up, Junior, you don't know what you're talking about."

All too soon, all too predictably, Charlie Parker began showing up late, later, or not at all. Dizzy tried to talk to him about it, but Bird's way of talking about it was to deny everything, which only eroded Dizzy's patience and led to an infamous incident: late to the club again one night, Parker came in and immediately locked himself in the bathroom. "After a long while, Gillespie angrily told Roach that Parker was in there with a needle in his arm," Giddins writes. "Gillespie did not realize he was standing next to an open mike. Everyone in the room heard him, including Parker, who felt betrayed."

Affection and mutual respect kept drawing them back together, until the next rift came along. But it wasn't just Yardbird's unreliability that was wearing on Dizzy, who, as Scott DeVeaux writes, "had been struggling to find the center of gravity in his career"; it was the small-club format itself. He wanted to take the new music to more ears, and to show a wider public whose music it was.

A trio of jazz concerts that spring showcased the Gillespie-Parker quintet. The first, on May 16 at Town Hall, on West Forty-third Street, was a mixed success. The quintet came on strong with its power pieces: "Shaw 'Nuff," "A Night in Tunisia," "Groovin' High," "Be-Bop," "Round Midnight," and "Salt Peanuts." But several guest stars advertised to fill out the bill—among them Count Basie, Teddy Wilson, and the bandleader and saxophonist Georgie Auld—failed to show, having been offered an insulting twenty-five dollars to appear.

On June 5 the quintet made a far more successful appearance as part of the All-Star Jazz Concert at Philadelphia's Academy of Music, wowing the capacity crowd, including the teenage John Coltrane and Benny Golson, with its revolutionary sounds.

A second Town Hall concert, on June 22, was recorded in its entirety on state-of-the-art equipment, but for almost sixty years the master discs were thought to have been lost. Then, in 2004, they were discovered, and the high-fidelity recordings show Parker and Gillespie at the apex of their new powers.

At first, actually, it was just Dizzy. As usual, Bird was late, though Gillespie had learned by now to bring along another player as insurance. The jazz disc jockey "Symphony Sid" Torin's introduction makes both facts clear: "I'm almost sure by now that you know the lineup—we're gonna start off with Dizzy Gillespie and his quintet, featuring Charlie Parker—though I don't know whether Charlie has come in yet, so we've got Don Byas workin', standing by."

The group then goes into "Be-Bop," Gillespie and Byas's attempt at a unison intro sounding a little underpowered and tentative, followed by a Dizzy solo that begins a bit haltingly, then grows in power ("Blow, Dizzy!" yells someone in the audience). Byas then solos—quite creditably, though the lower register of his tenor, not blending as well with Dizzy's trumpet as Bird's alto does, makes him sound like the visitor he is. Gillespie then takes a robust second solo, its energy clearly raised by the arrival at long last of Charlie Parker, whose five-chorus solo then makes us understand what all the fuss has been, is, and always will be about. Diz chimes in joyously. Their super-tight unison in the outro is a glorious thing to hear.

Yet even as he blows along with his friend, Dizzy's eyes are on greener pastures. He's tired of waiting for Bird, making excuses for Bird. He's had it with playing to 125 people at a time. There are a lot of people out in America who need to find out who he is. He has immortal longings—or commercial ones, anyway. He wants to lead a big band.

AND THE MATTER IS URGENT, BECAUSE THE WHITE BANDLEADER AND clarinetist Woody Herman and his First Herd are on the radio and out on the road doing sensational business with bebop-flavored numbers, three of them written by Dizzy himself: "Down Under," "Woody 'N' You," and "Things to Come." Herman's trumpeter and arranger Neal Hefti is a proud student of Gillespie's playing and writing, and the band's bassist, Chubby Jackson, also besotted with bop, encourages Herman to hire hot (white) young players who love and understand the idiom. Thus, when Dizzy goes on the road that July with the "Hepsations of 1945"—his orchestra plus the dancing Nicholas Brothers and several other acts—in a sense he is competing with himself.

And there's no competition. The big markets are white, America is rigidly segregated, and Black jazz is ghettoized. Herman, who burst onto the scene in 1939 with the politely bluesy big-band hit "Woodchopper's Ball," is a commercially astute shape-shifter: a genial and charismatic front man who can sing and play Black (blues and bop), white (fast and slow dance numbers), and all stops in between. In the spring of '45, when Louis Jordan's ur-R&B jump blues "Caldonia" ("Caldonia! Caldonia! / What makes your big head so hard?") is number one on the Race Records chart, two big-band versions of the song are also selling: Erskine Hawkins's and

Woody Herman's. Hawkins is Black. His record hits number two on the R&B chart and number twelve on *Billboard*'s pop chart; Herman's hits number two on the pop chart. That summer, Herman and his Herd can be heard coast to coast on CBS radio, while the Dizzy Gillespie Orchestra plays to mostly uncomprehending Black audiences across the South.

"To attract a mass audience to bebop," Dizzy wrote years later, "we had to first establish a feeling for the music among the large Black population of the South by touring the southern states. Things didn't work out the way I'd hoped, and that first big band exists as a blur in my mind. I'd prefer to forget it."

Charlie Parker, meanwhile, had gained in fame through the Three Deuces stand, and now, in Dizzy's absence, his star began to shine more brightly—though because he'd only recorded as a sideman, he was still largely unknown to the general public. In late July he returned to the Deuces for a monthlong stand with the same quintet, with Don Byas subbing for Gillespie—an intriguing combination, of which, unfortunately, no recording exists.

And Miles, initially bereft at Dizzy's departure—"Dizzy's quitting the group shocked everybody in the music world, and upset a lot of musicians who loved to hear them play together"—now stood to gain by it. Club owners on Fifty-second Street were asking Bird who his next trumpet player was going to be. "I remember being with Bird one time in a club when the owner asked that," Davis recalled, "and Bird turned to me and said, 'Here's my trumpet player right here, Miles Davis.'"

He was as good as his word. In early October, Parker began a new residency, this time at Clark Monroe's Spotlite, one of only two Black-owned clubs on the Street, with a sextet consisting of Sir Charles Thompson on piano, Leonard Gaskin on bass, Stan Levey on drums, Dexter Gordon on tenor, and Miles Davis on trumpet.

For all his surface cockiness, the trumpet player was justifiably terrified. "With Bird, Miles is *so* far behind the eight-ball," the saxophonist Dave Liebman told me. "And he knew it. Because with Bird—I mean, he's standing next to the most important voice of the twentieth century. I always say Bird and [Arnold] Schoenberg, as far as people looking at music differently after that. And you're standing next to Charlie Parker—that's a lot to take at twenty-two years old."

Nineteen, actually. Still a minor, albeit married and a father. And Miles's initial terror at "playing with the baddest alto saxophone player in the history of music" wasn't misplaced. He felt at first that since he was stepping in for Dizzy, the fastest and highest-playing trumpeter in the history of jazz, he had to be another Dizzy. And he wasn't. Though Miles understood perfectly what Gillespie was playing, he was simply unable to reproduce it himself. "I just couldn't play it high like Dizzy could because my chops weren't that developed and I didn't *hear* the music up in that high register." He was so nervous, he writes, that he used to ask Bird every night if he could quit. "I would ask, 'What do you need me for?'"

Others were asking the same question. In New York City, the most competitive jazz forum in the world, where cutting contests were rife and even great artists like Roy Eldridge (and yes, like Bird and Diz, too) took sadistic delight in ripping upstarts to shreds on jam nights at Minton's and Monroe's, the word was out on young Mr. Juilliard, and the word wasn't good. "Well, when Charlie started to play the saxophone in Kansas City, when the cats would see him come around, they'd say, 'Oh, no, not this cat again, man!'" Budd Johnson said. "And they did the same thing with Miles Davis on Fifty-second Street. 'If this cat's gonna get on the stand, I'm not gonna play, man.' That's how bad he sounded."

The jazz musician and commentator Loren Schoenberg told me: "Charlie Parker and Dizzy Gillespie have a band together; they're both high-velocity virtuosos. They break up. And Charlie Parker, for whatever reason, hires someone who's in many ways the antithesis of the way he plays. And that's somebody who nobody sees any future in. I knew Howard McGhee, and talked to a lot of the people from those days, and *nobody* could understand why Charlie Parker hired Miles Davis."

I asked Schoenberg what he thought.

"I think it's the same reason that Miles Davis hired John Coltrane [ten years later]," he said. "I think he heard a diamond in the rough, and knew that this guy had something, a potential—which is really hard to hear in the '46 and early '47 Miles. I think that he didn't want another guy who sounded like Dizzy Gillespie. He could've hired Fats Navarro, he could've hired Howard McGhee, he could've hired Red Rodney or Kenny Dorham—people that he hired later. Instead he chose to have a yin for his yang. Somebody who didn't play high and fast."

It's strange to think of the man who would become the Prince of Darkness, the King of Cool, young and raw and scared—even as a furnace of ambition and certitude burned deep within him. But it's hilarious to read Miles's memories of being lectured by Dexter Gordon—who came from an even more privileged background than Davis, was three years older and, at six foot six, almost a foot taller—on his tragic unhipness, and how he might remedy it:

> Dexter used to be super hip and dapper, with those big-shouldered suits everybody was wearing in those days. I was wearing my three-piece Brooks Brothers suits that I thought were super hip, too. You know, that St. Louis style shit. . . .
>
> But Dexter didn't think my dress style was all that hip. So he used to always tell me, "Jim" ("Jim" was an expression a lot of musicians used back then), "you can't hang out with us looking and dressing like that. Why don't you wear some other shit, Jim? You gotta get some vines. You gotta go to F&M's," which was a clothing store on Broadway in midtown. . . .
>
> So I'd say, all hurt and shit, "But Dex, man, these are nice clothes."
>
> "I know you think they hip, Miles, but they ain't. I can't be seen with nobody wearing no square shit like you be wearing. And you playing in Bird's band? The hippest band in the world? Man, you oughta know better."

Then Gordon told Miles, who in his late teens and early twenties had, by his own admission, the face of a pretty girl, that he should grow a mustache or a beard. Miles set him straight:

"How, Dexter? I ain't even got no hair growing nowhere much except on my head and a little bit under my arms and around my dick! My family got a lot of Indian blood, and niggers and Indians don't grow beards and be hairy on their faces. My chest is smooth as a tomato, Dexter."

"Well, Jim [Gordon replied], you gotta do something. You can't be hanging with us looking like you looking, 'cause you'll embarrass me. Why don't you get you some hip vines since you can't grow no hair?"

Miles saved up forty-seven dollars and bought a big-shouldered suit at F&M, and Dexter admitted him to the inner circle of the Truly Hip. To the white-hot center of the new music, though, Miles had already admitted himself.

"4 NIGHT CLUBS PENALIZED," READ THE HEADLINE OF A SMALL ITEM IN the back pages of the November 5, 1945, *New York Times*.

> The cabaret licenses of four night clubs on West Fifty-second Street have been "picked up" by the Police Department after hearings before Cornelius O'Leary, Fourth Deputy Police Commissioner, "to explain why their cabaret licenses should not be revoked for violation of the rules and regulations, in that persons engaged in the traffic of narcotics frequently make a rendezvous of said premises."

Or, in Miles's translation: besides jazz lovers, the clubs of the Street were also attracting

> hustlers and fast-living pimps with plenty of whores, hipsters, and drug dealers . . . both black and white. . . . Them motherfuckers were everywhere doing whatever they wanted to do. Everyone

knew that they had paid off the police, and this was all right as long as most of the hustlers were white. But when the music came downtown from uptown, the black hustlers around that scene came downtown with it. . . . And this didn't set too well with the white cops.

Throughout the war, there had been periodic tension on and around Fifty-second Street between Black musicians and frequently drunk groups of white soldiers and sailors on leave and looking for illicit fun. Dizzy Gillespie told a story about barely escaping a group of angry and inebriated sailors by running down into a subway station. Matters had finally come to a head.

"After the hearings ended Saturday," the *Times* piece continued,

> Commissioner O'Leary reserved decision, but last night the clubs— the Onyx, at 57 West Fifty-second Street; Downbeat, at 66; Spotlight [sic], at 56, and the Three Deuces, at 72—had no entertainment and only a handful of patrons. The license of the Onyx was removed ten days ago, while the others were lifted at 3 A.M. yesterday.

The natural result of the busts was to drive the music back uptown— to Minton's, in the case of Bird's quintet—and for Miles Davis this turned out to be a very good thing for his self-esteem, if not his wallet. The move helped pick his confidence up, he writes: perhaps, he speculates, because the predominantly Black audiences in Harlem were in his corner. Suddenly some of the wild applause following Parker's mind-boggling solos was coming Miles's way, too. He was still struggling with the fast numbers, like "Cherokee" and "A Night in Tunisia," because those tunes fit Dizzy's style like a glove. But he was finding a path.

And all at once, not just playing with Bird, but recording with him, as well.

Savoy Records, a minor label with a specialty in rhythm and blues, was founded by Herman Lubinsky, a Newark record-store owner, in 1942. Lubinsky quickly gained a reputation as "an arrogant bully . . . the quintessential loudmouth, overweight, cigar-smoking record man with little apparent charm" and as "a rather profane cheapskate who had a low opinion of many of the musicians that he recorded." Into Lubinsky's life in 1945 came a "three-hundred-pound-plus, six-foot Jewish promoter born in Harlem . . . raised among the thieves and geniuses of the jazz world, [and] an impassioned fan who mastered the art of networking at an early age." His name was Teddy Reig, and he was one of the characters who haunted Fifty-second Street.

Reig cozied up to the players he admired—one of his chief attractions was an ever-ready supply of marijuana—and made it a point to get close to Herman Lubinsky, convincing him to let Reig produce jazz records for Savoy. And on Monday, November 26, 1945, a historic date by any measure, Teddy Reig did just this, supervising Charlie Parker's first recording session as a leader, for a series of 78 rpm discs to be released under the rubric *Charlie Parker's Reboppers*: a session on which Bird had asked Miles Davis to play, along with, since Bud Powell was unavailable, a Minnesota pianist named Forrest Argonne Thornton (later to become Sadik Hakim), Curley Russell on bass, and Max Roach on drums. The album was intended to introduce Parker to the world, unyoked to Dizzy Gillespie. Dizzy was present as a spectator, yet, somehow inevitably, wound up participating, comping quite respectably on piano on three tracks and playing trumpet on one (and, because he was under contract to a different record label, not officially on the session).

With *Reboppers*, Reig was taking a big step up from being a fixer, drug dealer, and hanger-on. On the session, wrote Dave Gelly of *Jazz Journal*, he "had his work cut out assembling the musicians, paying them cash-in-hand, dealing with the union and turning out four masters per session." On the plus side: "The material consisted entirely of originals, so there would be no publishers to pay."

The November 26 session actually consisted of six recordings: "Billie's

Bounce," "Warming Up a Riff," "Now's the Time," "Thriving on a Riff" (aka "Anthropology"), "Meandering" (built on the chord structure of "Embraceable You"), and "Ko-Ko." Miles played on only three of the numbers, "Billie's Bounce," "Now's the Time," and "Thriving on a Riff." On the first two tunes, both taken at a medium tempo, his solos are tuneful if not quite lyrical: his soulfulness has not yet emerged. This is a competent player, someone in whom Bird saw compatibility and possibilities, but not exactly the greatness that was to be.

The up-tempo "Thriving on a Riff" is different. Davis's muted solo leads it off, at almost Dizzying speed, and it has a jaunty gutsiness that looks ahead to the fully fledged Miles and reminds you of his intense ambition, even in this company and even at nineteen.

His vaunting ambition, though, wasn't enough to make him attempt "Ko-Ko," a blazer built on the chords of "Cherokee." Parker asked him to accompany him on the number, even though, Miles writes,

> Bird *knew* I was having trouble playing "Cherokee" back then. So when he said that that was the tune he wanted me to play, I just said no, I wasn't going to do it. That's why Dizzy's playing trumpet on "Ko-Ko," "Warmin' Up a Riff," and "Meandering" . . . because I wasn't going to get out there and embarrass myself. I didn't really think I was ready to play tunes at the tempo of "Cherokee" and I didn't make no bones about it.

In an interesting bit of psychological self-revelation, Miles says that he was "fast asleep on the goddamn floor" when Dizzy and Bird did their amazing work, in tight unison, then in respective solos, then in unison again, on one of the most legendary recordings in jazz history—out cold, clearly not wanting to hear himself being upstaged, nor to lose face while it was happening.

Miles also noted that the session was punctuated by the arrival of "all these hustlers and dope dealers looking for Bird"—who kept disappearing

into the bathroom, then coming back "all fucked up and shit. But after Bird got high, he just played his ass off."

And there it was, inexorably entwined with the growing fame that this album would accelerate, a coded message to young aspirants, the first two premises of a siren syllogism: *Bird does heroin. Bird plays like a god on heroin.* Young musicians could draw the obvious, but spurious, conclusion. And to the sorrow of so many, many did.

DECEMBER 1945: THE CLOSINGS ON THE STREET HAD PUT ENOUGH OF A damper on business that Miles decided to go home to East St. Louis for Christmas. A few days later, Benny Carter brought his band to the Riviera, and when Miles stopped by to say hello, Carter invited him to join the tour. After St. Louis they were headed to L.A., Carter said, and Miles, with the

ulterior motive of reconnecting with Bird and Diz, who he heard were re-
united and playing at a Hollywood nightclub, Billy Berg's (and with the
further motive of avoiding domestic entrapment whenever possible: Cheryl
was pregnant with their second child), said he'd like to go along.

In Los Angeles, Miles discovered that Gillespie had returned to New
York sans Bird, who'd gone on a bender after the Billy Berg's stand. Davis
sought Parker out, and the two jammed together at the Finale, an after-
hours club in Little Tokyo. Playing with Bird again threw Benny Carter's
music into perspective: though Miles greatly respected the elder bandleader-
musician-arranger, he'd quickly grown bored with the swing-style arrangements the band was playing, and so he quit, despite having no money
and no prospects. He bunked at Lucky Thompson's place, then at Howard McGhee's; at McGhee's urging he took handouts from a glamorous
blonde who was pursuing him.

For his part, Charlie Parker had had enough of costarring with Dizzy
Gillespie; he wanted to shine on his own, to lead his own group, and in
Miles he'd already found someone who wouldn't vie with him for leadership but was an ideal accompanist: a trumpeter playing in the middle register rather than the high, leaving Bird free to showcase his own high-flying
acrobatics. In late February Parker invited Miles to record with him on
his first session for Dial Records, the Bird-centric label recently formed by
Ross Russell. Miles eagerly agreed.

The session was actually the second one Russell had set for Bird, who
had skipped the first for reasons easily guessed. Yet this one really happened, despite a chaotic rehearsal at the Finale on the night of March 27,
with Bird, Miles, and Lucky Thompson in attendance, along with two
(white) musicians, the guitarist Arvin Garrison and pianist Dodo Mar-
marosa. Ross Russell wrote that the evening was marked by "altercations
and a reshuffling of the original personnel. Nor had Charlie written the
promised original compositions."

He must have made the promise to placate Russell; Miles was beginning to form a deeper insight into Parker's compositional process. "Bird

was never organized about telling people what he wanted them to do," he recalled.

> He just got who he thought could play the shit he wanted and left it at that. Nothing was written down, maybe a sketch of a melody. All he wanted to do was play, get paid, and go out and buy himself some heroin.
>
> Bird would play the melody he wanted. The other musicians had to remember what he had played. He was real spontaneous, went on his instinct. He didn't conform to Western ways of musical group interplay by organizing everything. Bird was a great improviser and that's where he thought great music came from and what great musicians were about. His concept was "fuck what's written down."

Charlie Parker had the kind of phonographic memory for music that very few other musicians, no matter how skillful, had. Enclosed in his own Bird-world, he was unable, or at least unwilling, to appreciate this. Musicians were understandably uneasy about stepping out onto that very high tightrope—playing original compositions for posterity with next to no guidance. In time Miles would come to appreciate, and learn from, Bird's non-method method, but at the recording session the next afternoon—March 28, 1946—he found himself scared and a little lost.

"I think everyone played well on this date but me," he recalled.

> This was my second recording date with Bird but I don't know why I didn't play as well as I could have. Maybe I was nervous. It's not that I played terrible. It's just that I could have played better. Ross Russell—a jive motherfucker who I never did get along with because he was nothing but a leech, who didn't never do nothing but suck off Bird like he was a vampire—said something about my playing was flawed. Fuck that jive white boy. He wasn't no musi-

cian, so what did he know what Bird liked! I told Ross Russell he
could kiss my ass.

Miles's account, written over forty years after that momentous Dial
session, doesn't square with Russell's, but even allowing for subjective
memories on both sides, Davis sounds defensive about his nineteen-year-
old self, a teenager who was probably still intimidated to be, as Dave Liebman put it, standing next to the most important voice of the twentieth
century.

And in contrast to the botched rehearsal the night before, and to his
behavior in nearly all contexts, Charlie Parker on this afternoon acted like
a leader, "all business," in Russell's remembering:

> He rolled up his sleeves, unlimbered the saxophone, blazed
> through a few scales, and went to work. The very playing of these
> casual notes seemed to create an atmosphere.
>
> Sturdy and barrel-chested, speaking in a deep, steady voice,
> Charlie began rehearsing his men, first playing the line at the
> tempo he wanted, then drilling the others in their parts. Occa-
> sionally a chord or note was named, but usually it was just played.
> After twenty minutes the band was ready to make the first mas-
> ter. A red warning light alerted the musicians. . . . At a nod from
> Charlie the turntables began rolling.

Russell never called Miles's playing flawed—at least not in his memoir *Bird Lives!*, which was published sixteen years before *Miles*. Rather, he
spoke of "Miles Davis, wooden and dead-panned, not playing much on
his solos but warming the ensemble parts with his broad tone." He continued:

> After each of the takes Charlie would ask to have the master
> played back. Mistakes would be noted and corrected and another

version recorded, until he was satisfied. The mistakes were in all cases *the fault of the sidemen* [italics mine], especially Miles Davis, who was slow to learn new material.

Ross Russell was psychologically acute where Bird was concerned, but what he's overlooking in Miles's case is that the trumpeter was simply young and frightened of being in over his head, a kid putting on an impassive face to save face. It seems unlikely that he was innately slow to learn new material: he was a brilliant musician from the beginning. It's much more likely that he was simply overwhelmed by the occasion.

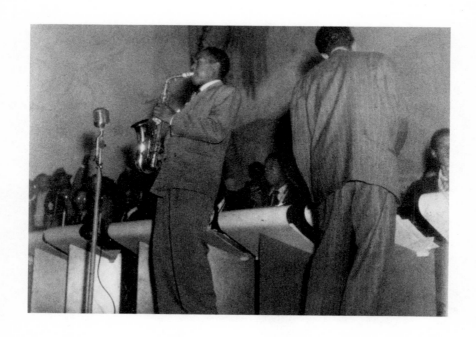

4 Serious

There is a photograph of a young John Coltrane watching Charlie Parker solo. The date is Sunday, December 7, 1947, six years to the day after Pearl Harbor; the place is the Elate Club Ballroom on South Broad Street in Coltrane's hometown, Philadelphia. The occasion is a benefit concert "for little Mary Etta Jordan, who is 6 years old and lost both of her legs in a recent trolley accident." Some three thousand people are in attendance.

Coltrane, who is sitting on the bandstand as a member of the saxophonist Jimmy Heath's orchestra, turned twenty-one that September. At first glance it's hard to see what he's doing or looking at. But zooming in on the image shows that the young saxophonist, laying out while the great man plays, has a lighted cigarette in his hand, and is staring at Bird so intently that it seems as though the cigarette might burn his fingers any second.

Yet if Coltrane is transported by the alto genius's playing, he's showing it in a strange way: the expression on his face is beyond serious—he looks almost resentful.

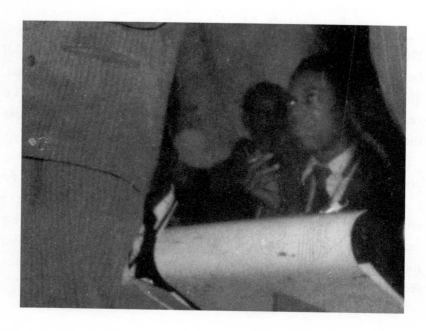

This is not the first time John Coltrane has heard Bird play—that happened two years earlier, on the evening of June 5, 1945, "the unforgettable night," as one writer put it, "[when] bebop invaded Philadelphia." The occasion was an "All-Star Jazz Concert" at Philadelphia's Academy of Music, featuring, as the program put it, "'Dizzy' Gillespie and His Quintet, Starring Charlie Parker." Sitting in the second-to-last row of the balcony, the eighteen-year-old Coltrane and his friend and fellow aspiring saxophonist, sixteen-year-old Benny Golson, were thrilled to see Gillespie, but had never heard of Parker, who at that point had done little commercial recording, and only as a sideman.

The quintet—including, besides Gillespie and Parker, Al Haig on piano, Curley Russell on bass, and Stan Levey on drums—played the Gillespie–Frank Paparelli composition "Blue 'N' Boogie," along with several other tunes in the new style, probably including (if the Gillespie-Parker set list from a concert a couple of weeks later at New York's Town Hall is any indication) Dizzy's "Be-Bop," along with his "A Night in Tunisia," "Groovin' High," and "Salt Peanuts," and Tadd Dameron's "Hot House."

The double-barreled cannon of Gillespie and Parker firing out the new music, with its multiple chord changes at breakneck speed, "hit me right between the eyes," Coltrane later said.

"We almost fell over the balcony," Golson recalled, laughing,

> because this music was so new there was no precedent for it. We were trying to come out of the other kind of music, you know, Jimmie Lunceford and "Flyin' Home" à la Lionel Hampton and "A Train" by Duke Ellington. We heard this [new] music—I mean, our lives were changed. And so, we had to get about the business of finding what it was all about.
>
> After that concert was over, we went backstage, like kids do, and got everybody's autograph. It was an evening concert and Charlie Parker was going over [afterward] for the first show at a place called the Downbeat. And so, John and I were walking up

Broad Street with him, and John was saying, "Can I carry your horn for you, Mr. Parker?" I'm on the other side saying, "What kind of mouthpiece do you use? What kind of reeds do you use? What strength reed do you use? What is the make of your horn?" This crazy kid stuff, and he was telling it all and I thought I was getting the real lowdown.

We got to the club—of course we were too young to go in—and he said, "Kids, keep up the good work," and he went upstairs. We spent the night just standing out front listening to them play from up on the second floor, and walked home talking about it after it was over.

Jimmy Heath, another Philadelphia native, also eighteen, was in attendance that night as well. Many years later, he liked to show his music students, who idolized Coltrane as the seminal figure of jazz saxophone, the photo from the Elate Club concert. "I say, 'Well, if it started with Coltrane, what is he doin' about to burn his hand lookin' at Charlie Parker play, with his mouth open?'"

JOHN COLTRANE MADE HIS FIRST RECORD ON SATURDAY, JULY 13, 1946, AT the Armed Forces Radio studio on Oahu, Hawaii, not far from the base where the nineteen-year-old Coltrane, a seaman first class, was stationed with the U.S. Navy. Coltrane's fellow musicians on the record date—a trumpeter named Dexter Culbertson; a pianist, Norman Poulshock; a bassist, Willie Stader; and a drummer, Joe Theimer—were all white and all fellow sailors, except for the vocalist, a Black army PFC named Benny Thomas. The recording was for private rather than commercial purposes, and the session was a rushed (one hour on the dot) and hushed affair, for like the rest of the U.S. armed forces, the navy was officially segregated. Black and white sailors were not even permitted to fraternize, let alone play music together, and while some racially mixed after-hours jamming was known to take place on the island, John Coltrane had never before met the musicians he recorded with that afternoon. He had come by invitation, having begun to acquire a certain renown as an alto saxophonist in an all-Black navy band called the Melody Masters. Or, as Joe Theimer wrote in a note on the paper sleeve of one of the 78 rpm discs cut on the date, "This session was inspired by John Coletrane [sic], a Bird disciple. . . ."

Bird disciple . . . The phrase rolls easily off the tongue today, but in the mid-1940s it identified Coltrane as a member of an arcane subcult, a branch of the new music that was starting to thrill young players and jazz audiences across the U.S. Bebop was brand-new, and Dizzy Gillespie, charming, photographable, and commercially astute, was its public face— and in the eyes of many, its inventor. "Dizzy was more familiar to record buyers than Duke Ellington or Louis Armstrong," Ross Russell writes. "Dizzy had cashed in while Charlie was in California. Charlie Parker remained a mysterious, prophetic figure, hardly known to the public."

Only those on the inside of the inside understood the transformational power of Bird. John Coltrane had witnessed it at the June 1945 Philadelphia Academy of Music concert, two months before enlisting in the navy.

He had heard it in embryo on the records Parker and Gillespie had made with the leader Clyde Hart and fully fledged on Parker's first Savoy discs. "I went overseas but we still heard Bird's records and I was copying like mad just to see what he was doing," he recalled. The jazz future had arrived, and he wanted in.

The Melody Masters were a tight, competent seventeen-piece band; they played marches for navy ceremonies and swing music—dance music—for social functions, even white social functions. Coltrane might have soloed now and then on these occasions, but like all big bands, the Melody Masters would have been playing from charts—written arrangements. It's more likely that he impressed fellow musicians during some of those after-hours jam sessions, when, with his horn rather than his words (Norman Poulshock remembered him as "a very reserved individual"), he would have preached the gospel of Bird. Word got around: this guy had even *met* Bird.

Coltrane channeled Charlie Parker to the best of his ability on the July 13 session, but it's clear from the recording, which has miraculously survived, that the nineteen-year-old seaman was in the grips of something he didn't fully comprehend—or if he did understand it, like so many budding musicians, like Parker himself during his apprentice years, he heard it in his head but was not yet able to transmit it through his fingers.

Sixty minutes of studio time, seven numbers: a Kai Winding tune, "Sweet Miss"; Yip Harburg and Harold Arlen's "It's Only a Paper Moon"; Mitchell Parish and Cliff Burwell's "Sweet Lorraine"; Charlie Parker's "Ko-Ko" and "Now's the Time"; Tadd Dameron's "Hot House"; and George and Ira Gershwin's "Embraceable You."

Coltrane solos on every song, and the playing ranges from fluid and competent, almost inspired in spots, to, in more spots, halting or painfully discordant. There are riffs that are clearly lifted from Parker, but the teenager's own reservoir of invention is shallow. On "Ko-Ko," for example, he and the trumpeter contrive a new, acceptable-enough, tight-unison intro and outro (very likely because he and Culbertson couldn't figure out how Bird and Diz played what they played on the recording), but while Coltrane's long solo starts with legato verve, he quickly runs out of ideas and starts playing mini-riffs—discrete gulps of notes, many of them flagrantly sour: it's a good thing Jo Jones isn't there to fling a cymbal at him. On three ballads strongly associated with Nat King Cole, the young saxophonist doesn't fare much better.

Astonishingly, Miles Davis heard these records. Equally astonishing is that he seems to have been impressed by them. Three months later, in a letter to a fellow navy musician named Bill Goldstein, Joe Theimer wrote that Dexter Culbertson (who, Coltrane biographer Lewis Porter says, became a protégé of Davis) had played the July 13 discs for Miles, and that Miles "was knocked by Coltrane's playing, isn't that mad!! Trane would flip, if he knew that *the* Miles Davis said that about him, huh! Too much!!"

Porter writes that the letter was dated October 29, 1946—which itself is amazing, in that anyone was already referring to the twenty-year-old Miles, still in the midst of his apprentice years, as *the* Miles Davis. But even if the date is wrong, even if Culbertson was only a bebop hanger-on rather than a protégé, even if Miles was just being polite about Coltrane's playing, a strange sort of connection—as Porter calls it, "the connection that would eventually set Coltrane's career in motion"—had been made.

THOUGH HE DISLIKED THE NAVY (WHOSE RACIST REGULATIONS ALLOWED white sailors to be full-time musicians but demanded that similarly qualified Black sailors perform guard and kitchen duties), John Coltrane seems to have been a diligent sailor. Serious and intelligent, he was promoted from apprentice seaman to V6 (General Service and Specialists) to seaman first class. Upon his discharge in August 1946, he received standard decorations—the Pacific Theater Ribbon, the American Theater Ribbon, a Victory Medal—and marks (on a scale of 1 to 4) of 4.0 for Conduct, 3.6 for Leadership, and 3.6 for Seamanship.

There was a watchful sadness about him, a haunted quality, that began in boyhood and persisted until the end of his short life. Few photographs show him smiling. His childhood, in High Point, North Carolina, was broken in two by loss: for his first twelve years, Coltrane, an only child, lived in the bosom of an intact extended middle-class family in his maternal grandparents' house in Griffin Park, the town's best Black neighborhood. His grandfather, the Reverend W. W. Blair, was the presiding elder of St. Stephen A.M.E. Zion Church; his father, John R. (the younger John was John William), owned a dry-cleaning and tailor shop. It was a musical household, in a serious way. "My family liked church music, so there was no jazz in the house," Coltrane remembered. John R. played violin well; he also had a clarinet and a ukulele, and tinkered a little on both. Coltrane's mother, Alice, had a trained singing voice and played piano. Young John sang in his elementary school chorus and joined the Boy Scouts.

Then, within a few months in the winter of 1938–39, his family suffered a series of deaths—first a beloved aunt, then the Reverend Blair, and then, most devastatingly to John, his father. Suddenly he and his mother were not only bereaved but impoverished. Alice's sister Bettie Lyerly and Bettie's daughter Mary moved in with them, and Alice rented the bedrooms to boarders. Alice, Bettie, Mary, and John slept on cots in the dining room. He had always been quiet, with a subtle streak of mischief, but the rupture of his life turned him even further inward.

He'd been an exemplary student throughout grade school, yet from the moment he entered William Penn High in September 1939, his grades sputtered. Still grieving, he took shelter in music.

African American boys of the early twentieth century were often encouraged—by their parents, by their schools—to take music lessons, as a way to keep out of trouble of all kinds, and as a possible path forward in an America that was not abundant in career opportunities for Black men. Like Charlie Parker and Dizzy Gillespie, and like Miles Davis, John Coltrane began playing an instrument before entering his teens. At twelve he joined a community band led by his scoutmaster, Warren B. Steele, starting out on the alto horn—the valved brass horn that might also have been Charlie Parker's first instrument—then moving to the clarinet.

Steele was a trained musician who knew his way around several instruments and was able to show Coltrane how to hold the clarinet and know if he was playing the right notes. The rest was up to the student—and the boy was a talented and motivated student. From the start, he practiced obsessively. "Even as a child he would sit at the [dining room] table and practice all the time," his cousin Mary remembered. "He practiced *all* the time." He ran scales, over and over. He bought the sheet music to "Blue Orchids," a Hoagy Carmichael song that was a hit for Glenn Miller in the fall of '39. The tune was fairly complex, with a wide range and several chromatic passages; Coltrane learned it note for note.

The success of Steele's community band inspired the principal of William Penn to start a school band, which Coltrane joined as a charter member. The band's director and teacher was Grayce W. Yokely, a pianist who had studied with the Black composer Nathaniel Dett. In 1991 Yokely reminisced to a newspaper reporter about the young Coltrane: "He was interested in wanting to learn, and he always showed great potential for music. He showed great interest in wanting to get everything just right. He was a very rhythmic fellow, and he paid attention."

Rhythm was suddenly important to him. Growing up in a cloistered household, he hadn't heard much jazz. All at once, his hormones were starting to kick in, and his ears were wide open. "My interest in jazz was started in high school," he recalled.

> It started through the regular dance we had—from the beginning it was a matter of just dancing to jazz. I liked bands like [R&B saxophonist] Louis Jordan's. I enjoyed Louis' music and out of that I started to listen more to the horns. I didn't hear much Duke [Ellington] during that time. We didn't get much of that type of music. It was mostly what you call rock and roll.

Around the fall of 1940, inspired by Jordan and by Lester Young (even though Young played tenor), Coltrane switched from clarinet to the alto sax, and seems to have become even more focused. "John played his horn all the time," a bandmate named Floyd B. Phifer recalled. "I just played mine during practice [rehearsal], because I was interested in other things. He played his horn in all his spare time, so therefore he was advanced. He had the rhythm, he knew how to make the tone mellow—his horn wasn't squeaking."

"He kept that saxophone with him all the time," a friend named Rosetta Haywood remembered, "and you could hear him all the time [after school], from any other part of the building, back in the music room practicing by himself. I think it was jazz. He just loved that horn."

Without telling anyone, he had decided to make music his life. "I wanted to progress quickly," Coltrane told the French critic François Postif in 1961. "This was something new for me, and I threw myself into it body and soul."

Sometime during his senior year, his mother moved to Philadelphia to try to find better employment than what High Point offered. Around the same time, his aunt Bettie and cousin Mary moved north, too. Back in North Carolina, John sat moodily at the dining room table, practicing his horn and writing lonely postcards to Alice and Mary. On Friday nights he partied with his friends, having found a new consolation besides music: whiskey and wine.

AFTER GRADUATING, HE MOVED TO PHILADELPHIA TO JOIN HIS MOTHER, who'd gotten a job as a live-in maid with a white family. Alice returned on weekends to the apartment she was sharing with Bettie and Mary; now John joined them. He quickly found work, first at a sugar-refining plant in town, then at the Campbell Soup factory across the river in Camden. He practiced his saxophone before leaving for work every morning and after he returned each afternoon. When the neighbors complained, the minister of Bettie and Mary's church gave John a key to the building and told him he could play there anytime.

And he began to study music seriously, attending the Ornstein School of Music, where he took saxophone lessons and theory classes from a reed player named Mike Guerra, and quickly found that without having known anything about it, he had moved to a city that was a hotbed of jazz.

Rashied Ali. Kenny Barron. Clifford Brown. Ray Bryant. Joe Chambers. Buddy DeFranco. Sonny Fortune. Jimmy Garrison. Benny Golson. Jimmy, Albert, and Tootie Heath. Philly Joe Jones. Jymie Merritt. Hank Mobley. Lee Morgan. Odean Pope. Red Rodney. Archie Shepp. Jimmy Smith. Bobby Timmons. McCoy Tyner. Wilbur Ware. Reggie Workman. In later years, Pat Martino. Michael and Randy Brecker, Kevin Eubanks, and Christian McBride. All were born in, or grew up in, the City of Brotherly Love.

The history of jazz in Philadelphia was already well advanced when young Coltrane arrived. As early as 1917, white Philadelphians could—daringly, for the time—go to dance halls that featured Black jazz bands. (They could also go, less daringly, to B. F. Keith's vaudeville theater and be entertained by acts such as Ralph Dunbar's Old Time Darkies, "A Quartette from the South.") By the early thirties, with the Great Migration well underway, the city's growing Black population had places of their own to dance to jazz, and the local scene was vibrant enough to support a Colored Musicians Union, whose secretary, the bandleader Frankie Fairfax, hired the teenage John Birks Gillespie for the trumpet section of his band. By the time of Coltrane's arrival, as the pianist Ray Bryant recalled to Lewis Porter, "there were many social clubs in the Black community that sponsored cabaret parties and dances at such places as the Elate Ballroom, Elks Lodge, Bombay Gardens, and the O. V. Catto Lodge."

The city also teemed with bars and clubs where jazz could be heard. Near Coltrane's Twelfth Street apartment was an after-hours joint, the Woodbine Club, where the regal likes of Lester Young, Coleman Hawkins, and Duke Ellington now and then dropped by to listen and jam after playing gigs elsewhere in town. And the kids who were coming up, too young to go to clubs, found their own outlets. "We had so many jam sessions all over Philly, at everybody's house," Benny Golson remembered.

"We never looked at John as a genius, he was John," his cousin Mary said. "We all just lived in those two rooms, and he would just sit there all the time and practice and smoke cigarettes. He would sit at my vanity and look at himself in the mirror playing his horn."

Was *this* vanity, or a way of practicing his fingering, or both? Or, perhaps, something else altogether—a way of trying to see himself as a real musician, to take in this new self, as he struggled through the process of getting what was in his head into his horn?

Coltrane appears to have started playing professionally around the time he first met Benny Golson: early 1945. His artistic ideal then was the exquisitely lyrical, creamy tone of Duke Ellington's lead alto player Johnny Hodges—a ballad player.

He joined the musicians' union and, for a time, was part of a trio. "I played with a pianist and a guitarist," he told Postif. "It was a kind of cocktail music, but it kept me alive!"

And then, to keep from being drafted, he joined the navy.

Upon mustering out in August 1946, Coltrane—not yet twenty—returned to Philadelphia and went all in on becoming a working jazz musician. By night, he put together a living by freelancing around town with small groups, sometimes playing with Ray Bryant. By day he attended the Granoff Studios music school, his tuition paid by the GI Bill, studying theory and classical music with the jazz guitarist Dennis Sandole, who became a mentor to the serious young aspirant. Coltrane also studied his instrument with a saxophonist named Matthew Rastelli. Rastelli noted that at first his pupil could barely read music. This changed rapidly.

That fall and winter, Coltrane toured with the Indianapolis-based, R&B-oriented Joe Webb band, which featured the blues shouter Big Maybelle: it was his first travel gig, and felt like a professional turning point. Shortly after returning, he went out on the road again, as lead alto in the seventeen-piece dance band of the Kansas City trumpeter King Kolax (William Little), who had briefly employed Charlie Parker before the war. Coltrane would later compare working for Webb and Kolax to playing in baseball's minor leagues: "A good place to learn, anyway."

On February 19, 1947, while the band was playing Los Angeles, he attended a Charlie Parker recording session for Dial at the C. P. MacGregor Studio; later, either at the studio or at Lester Young's apartment, he jammed with Bird, at Parker's invitation. All at once, he was way out of the minor leagues.

From May of that year until the end of 1948, Coltrane once more freelanced around Philly, often now in the recently formed, and highly expert, band of his fellow altoist Jimmy Heath. Suddenly, strikingly, as Heath recalled years later, "Trane was [now] a great reader . . . an excellent musician in every sense of the word."

Almost everyone associated with John Coltrane took note of his voracious appetite for learning about music in general and his instrument in particular. Late at night, so as not to disturb anyone, he would go over key fingering for hours on end, not playing a note. Like Charlie Parker, he made a point of learning to play in every key; also like Parker, and like Miles, he listened broadly and deeply, not just to jazz but also to the modern Europeans: "Trane and I," Jimmy Heath recalled,

> used to go to the Philadelphia Library together and listen to Western classical music—they had the earphones, you know. We would play Stravinsky and people like that and listen to all this music that we could. We listened to the *Firebird Suite* and *The Rite of Spring* because we heard that Parker was carrying around miniature scores of Stravinsky. We were in tune with whatever was happening with Bird and Diz. We knew that that was what we were supposed to do!

What Coltrane was also supposed to do was make a living. To that end, he signed on for a tour with Eddie "Cleanhead" Vinson (so named because he shaved his skull after a botched conk job) and his new band. After his last tour, Vinson had simply fired his old musicians and hired a new sextet, all of whom had one thing in common: "Aside from the leader," the *Detroit Tribune*, an African American newspaper, reported in

January 1949, "there is not a single member of the sensational new combo, put together by Mr. Cleanhead, who is more than twenty-four years of age."

Besides Vinson, an elderly thirty-one, the new aggregation consisted of Coltrane on tenor, Johnny Coles on trumpet, James Young on baritone sax, William "Red" Garland on piano, James Rhodes on bass, and Charlie Rice at the drums. "Many veteran musicians questioned the wisdom of the new plan," the *Tribune* piece continued, "but Vinson argued that 'If you're going to play modern music, the kind youth appreciates and understands, then there is none better able to produce it than the generation that creates it.'"

Coltrane's switch to tenor was a matter of necessity: there was only room for one alto in the band, and Eddie Vinson, the leader, was it. Trane's audition was a trial by fire—during the last night of Vinson's old band's stand at Emerson's Tavern in Philadelphia, "they played a song that had this tenor solo in it, so Eddie told John, 'Pick up the tenor, play the tenor solo,'" Benny Golson remembered. "John was a little hesitant about it, and Eddie insisted, 'Pick up the horn!' He picked it up and he sounded like Dexter Gordon, of all people."

Coltrane had come far in the sixteen months since the Oahu session. But all his thousands of hours of practice and study had been on the alto. To pick up the larger horn and at once sound like an established young master of the new music—Gordon, though just three and a half years older than Coltrane, had been recording under his own name since 1945—was an impressive feat. And Mr. Cleanhead was impressed.

"Luckily for Coltrane," Lewis Porter writes, "Vinson (1917–88) was a sophisticated musician who appreciated bebop. He was also a popular performer and recording artist who could promise lots of work."

But those two sides to the bandleader's musical personality were essentially in conflict with one another. Lots of work meant a series of one-nighters in southern ballrooms and tobacco warehouses, before Black audiences and white audiences, and, sometimes, rowdy audiences. This was a far cry from the *Firebird Suite*. For all his understanding of the new music, Vinson made his money as an entertainer—a rocking sax player and blues shouter who played dance tunes. As both Billy Eckstine and Dizzy Gillespie discovered when they led bands, bebop numbers could be sneaked in here and there, but a wise leader had to pick his spots: if customers (who would often stand outside a venue listening before deciding to buy a ticket) couldn't dance to it, they kept their wallets in their pockets.

Unlike some young musicians, Coltrane, who, after all, had been weaned on R&B, had no problem with the blues. But as Cleanhead Vinson recalled, he was slow to gain confidence on the new instrument:

> "Yeah, little ol' Coltrane used to be in my band," Vinson remembers with a paternal smile. "He never wanted to play. I used to have to play all night long. I'd ask him, 'Man, why don't you play?' He'd say, 'I just want to hear you play.'"

The remark was at once evasive and deeply felt. "When I bought a tenor to go with Eddie Vinson's band, a wider area of listening opened up for me," Coltrane recalled.

> On alto, Bird had been my whole influence, but on tenor I found there was no one man whose ideas were so dominant as Charlie's were on alto. Therefore, I drew from all the men I heard during this period. I have listened to about all the good tenor men, beginning with Lester, and believe me, I've picked up something from them all, including several who have never recorded.

Yet in another context, he admitted that despite his own immortal longings, Bird's titanic example stood in his path. "I wanted to find my own way but I wasn't ready," he said. "I had to learn to play straight. There was so much to learn yet. I wasn't trying—not reaching out for too much. Charlie Parker had me strung up. He was way ahead of me and I had trouble just keeping up with him."

5 Move

While John Coltrane was busy hiding his considerable light under a considerable bushel, Miles Davis had been much occupied with becoming Miles Davis. Just four months older than Coltrane, Miles at twenty-one was bubbling with ambition, presumption, energy. Entitlement. He was a prince and a genius; he knew it.

He'd stayed on the Coast for a few months after recording with Bird (who had been arrested in July after either purposely or inadvertently setting his hotel bed ablaze, and remanded to the Camarillo State Mental Hospital), rehearsing with the formidably brilliant and irritable bassist and composer Charles Mingus, and then, having become considerably more audible and accomplished than he'd been two years earlier, accepting Billy Eckstine's invitation to rejoin his band. This aggregation, some twenty pieces strong—including Sonny Stitt, Gene Ammons, and Cecil Payne on saxophones; Erroll Garner's brother Linton on piano; Tommy Potter on bass; Art Blakey on drums; and Miles, Hobart Dotson, Leonard Hawkins, and the versatile King Kolax on trumpets—played around

California, then worked its way east to New York. It was a great band filled with great players playing great music, but by late 1946 the writing was on the wall for the big bands: even Duke Ellington could only get booked for one-nighters.

In January Eckstine denied rumors that he was breaking up the band; in February, as they swung east through Ohio and Pennsylvania, he admitted to the press that he might be about to downsize. But then Mr. B. finally threw in the towel. "People still talk today about that legendary Billy Eckstine band," he said years later. "Man! The legendary Billy Eckstine was about to starve with that motherfucker, so I decided to break it up."

Back in Manhattan and at liberty, Miles wrote arrangements for Sarah Vaughan and Budd Johnson; he made a record with the honking tenor player and bandleader Illinois Jacquet. When Bird got back to town in early April, reenergized after leaving Camarillo, and re-addicted, too—"They can get it out of your blood, but they can't get it out of your mind," he said—Miles was waiting for him.

PATIENT NEGOTIATIONS BY ROSS RUSSELL AND CHARLIE PARKER'S NEW York girlfriend Chan Richardson had landed Bird (whom the booking agencies wouldn't touch) a lucrative four-week contract at the Three Deuces, with a quintet. The original plan was to include Howard McGhee (trumpet), Erroll Garner (piano), and Wardell Gray (tenor sax), but commitments shifted, and by July, Bird still hadn't been able to put a quintet together. That month, though, while now and then sitting in with Coleman Hawkins's quintet at the Deuces—Hawkins, Miles Davis, pianist Hank Jones, bassist Curley Russell, and Max Roach—Parker recruited Miles and Roach. Tommy Potter and the pianist Duke Jordan soon signed on, too, and an opening at the Deuces was set for August 7.

"All of Charlie's sidemen could have worked for higher wages elsewhere," Ross Russell wrote, "but the inducement of being with Bird outweighed any other considerations." Quite unusually for him, Bird called a rehearsal a week ahead of the opening—and then, as was all too usual, neglected to show up. Davis rehearsed the band for the whole week.

The Street was freshly resurgent after the war, and on opening night the Deuces was packed. "We ain't seen Bird in a week, but we'd been rehearsing our asses off," Miles recalled.

> So here this nigger comes in smiling and shit, asking is everybody ready to play, in that fake British accent of his. When it's time for the band to hit, he asks, "What are we playing?" I tell him. He nods, counts off the beat and plays every motherfucking tune in the exact key we had rehearsed it in. He played like a motherfucker. Didn't miss one beat, one note, didn't play out of key all night. It was something. We were fucking amazed. And every time he'd look at us looking at him all shocked and shit, he'd just smile that "Did you ever doubt this?" kind of smile.

Bird in flow was a wonder to behold—and for the musicians who tried to keep up with him, a terror. Miles again: "Everything he played—when he was on and *really* playing—was terrifying, and I was there every night! And so we couldn't just keep saying, 'What? Did you hear *that*!' all night long. Because then we couldn't play nothing."

The Deuces stand ran from early August to September 24, and the quintet returned for another week in late October. They came back in January and March of 1948, then played the Onyx, across the street, in early July. As history congealed around these evenings, the quintet came to be known as the Golden Era Bebop Five. Miles, as well as the blind avant-garde pianist Lennie Tristano and the guitarist Tal Farlow, both of whom opened for the group at the Deuces, all testified to the jazz chronicler Phil Schaap that Parker was *really playing* throughout 1947 and 1948, that these Three Deuces and Onyx gigs represent the peak of his genius. Yet this is history, or History, talking: this is how legend is born. More instructive, and infinitely more entertaining, is to listen to the recordings made by the obsessive Parker chronicler Dean Benedetti at the Three Deuces on the night of March 31, and at the Onyx on July 6, 7, 10, and 11, 1948.

Benedetti, a decent tenor saxophonist himself, first heard Bird on record in 1945, and like so many others, realized he had to rethink everything he thought he knew about jazz. In order to study Parker's solos, he needed to transcribe them, and the only hope of breaking down all that velocity into notes on staff paper was to record Bird. He started at the Hi-De-Ho Club in Los Angeles in late February 1947 (where Parker, just out of Camarillo, was playing as a sideman in a Howard McGhee–led quintet), on a Sears portable disc cutter that produced acetate 78 rpm records. In order to try and understand how Parker did what he did, Benedetti only recorded his solos, leaving out the boring (to him) parts where other musicians played. But on some of the Deuces and Onyx tracks enough of Miles is audible—particularly the March 31 recording of "All the Things You Are"—that his easy ability to dovetail with, and shine alongside, Parker's overpowering brilliance is apparent. The spontaneous freedom and lightness and energy of these evenings is electric.

The quintet made its first commercial recordings in 1947. In October, Ross Russell, having moved Dial east to follow its raison d'être, produced Bird's first New York record for the label:

> The first session was made October 25 at WOR Studios, Forty-eighth and Broadway. Benefiting from experience in California, I reserved the studio from eight p.m. on and instructed the musicians [Miles and the rest of the Deuces quintet] to be on hand at seven. Again Charlie crossed me up. When I arrived at six-thirty he was already there. He was uptight and said he needed fifty dollars. He had instructed his [dealer] to meet him at WOR. This made the current rumors official. "So you're back on," I said as I handed him the money. He said nothing and went into the men's room to prepare his fix. Twenty minutes later he was all smoothed out, in a "mad, blowing mood," as the Dial studio log shows.

Had heroin not been available to Parker, he would have had to ingest a substantial amount of alcohol to take the edge off, which would have led to a very different, undoubtedly much worse, kind of recording session. Instead, by Russell's account, the four-hour date was a marvel of efficiency and creativity, requiring just fifteen takes for six sides: "Dexterity" ("rhythmic and Lestorian, reminiscent of his Kansas City roots"), "Bongobop" ("intriguing Afro-Cuban overlays"), "Dewey Square," "The Hymn" ("a tour de force, metronome 310, after the manner of his famous 'Koko'"), and finally, two ballads, "Bird of Paradise" (closely based on "All the Things You Are") and the non-retitled "Embraceable You."

Non-retitled, but stunningly remelodicized by Bird, in one of jazz's greatest improvisations, a staggering feat of on-the-spot composition—Bach and Mozart, too, were improvisers—and a sad reminder that the vast majority of Parker's genius solos occurred at clubs and jams in the wee hours of the night, floating out to the ether, gorgeous, glittering, and unrecorded.

Bird was the main event, and, confirming the evidence of the Benedetti recordings, Miles was his able costar. Everything that Charlie Parker had detected at the start in the baby-faced trumpeter, when nobody else could understand what he heard in him, was now coming to fruition. Davis's muted, silken, midregister solo is nearly the inventive equal of his idol's, and a foretaste of Miles's mature style: meditative and lyrical, at once understated and richly sexual. To hear his "Flight of the Bumblebee"–fast playing on "The Hymn" is to understand that he could now compete at velocity with Dizzy and Fats Navarro, but to hear his ballad playing is to realize that he was in a class of his own.

The Dial session was actually the third record Miles made with Bird in 1947: the previous two, on May 8 and August 14, were for Savoy—and on the August date the precocious Davis was in charge. "Playing with Bird and being seen and heard every night on 52nd Street helped lead to my first record date as a leader," he writes. And he was the leader in every sense: he wrote and arranged all four tunes on the ten-inch LP, titled *Miles Davis All Stars*: "Milestone" (sometimes called "Milestones"—and

sometimes credited to the pianist John Lewis—but not to be confused with Miles's great modal 1958 composition), "Little Willie Leaps," "Half Nelson," and "Sippin' at Bells" (Bell's was Miles's favorite Harlem bar). The all-stars of the title were Miles, Charlie Parker on tenor sax, Lewis, Nelson Boyd on bass, and Max Roach at the drums.

Yes, Bird on tenor, not alto. So strong was the young leader's artistic confidence that he had the great Charlie Parker, his idol, change horns to better contrast with his trumpet and add sonic spice to the album's palette. "Miles's musical gift," the pianist and bandleader Jon Batiste told me, "is understanding the essence of what something is, and being able to execute that on his horn. And his conceptual gift is being able to understand how that will be viewed in the future, and also how to assemble the right people to create this essence."

Another gifted musician and arranger was in Manhattan at the same time and made it his business to meet Miles Davis—though, like the rest of the world, he first came to Miles through Charlie Parker. The Canada-born Gil Evans (no relation to Bill) had been writing charts for Claude Thornhill's big band since the late thirties, but a decade later Evans and Thornhill's professional relationship was coming to a crisis point.

The trademark Thornhill sound was mood-inducing: rich and low (in both range and volume), vibrato-free, and anchored by two instruments rarely if ever found in big bands, French horn and tuba. But the sweet music was starting to smell faintly musty to Evans. Like so many others, he'd become smitten with Charlie Parker and bebop, and much as Dizzy Gillespie and Billy Eckstine had done with their bands, he began bringing the new sounds to Claude Thornhill's romantic-ballad orchestra.

The mid- to late 1940s were an inflection point for jazz. As the big bands faded and the new music captured the imaginations of jazz fans, the art of written arrangement was receding and—with Charlie Parker's godlike solos serving as a beacon—the art of improvisation had grown dominant.

Charlie Parker's ears were part of his phenomenal musical gift: he adored Bach, Beethoven, Chopin, and Debussy, and modernists such as Bartók, Stravinsky, Shostakovich, and Schoenberg; he incorporated snippets of their works into his solos, especially when he knew there was someone in an audience who would get the reference. He dreamed of studying composition with Nadia Boulanger in Paris; late in his career, full of regret at never having learned music theory, having grown bored with blues and popular-song forms, he begged the ultramodernist composer Edgard Varèse to take him on as a student. "Take me as you would a baby and teach me music," Parker said. "I only write in one voice. I want to have structure. I want to write orchestral scores."

Instead, Bird was ruled throughout his short life by chaos, hopelessly leashed to his appetites and addictions and doomed to remain one voice, intuitive and brilliant though it might have been, worshipped but set apart, isolated by his genius. Miles Davis, whose ears were no less great than Charlie Parker's, was a different matter. His artistic ambitions—and limitations—led him on a lifelong quest for collaboration and broader musical meaning, and Gil Evans joined him at the start of his voyage.

In 1947, Evans hired the stellar twenty-year-old alto saxophonist Lee Konitz, an intrepid explorer of the new music, for the Thornhill band. When I met with him in late 2018, Konitz was a very old man with a fading memory, but when I asked about Gil Evans's storied midtown apartment, he smiled. "I remember there was a lot of pot smoking," he said.

Like many other musicians, Black and white, like John Lewis and Gerry Mulligan and, soon, Miles Davis, Konitz spent a lot of time in the basement flat, next to a barbershop and behind the Asia Laundry, at 14 West Fifty-fifth Street. Through the force of his quiet, generous personality, along with an infinite musical curiosity, Evans turned his long, low-ceilinged apartment into a kind of Bateau-Lavoir for postwar American jazz, a combination crash pad/clubhouse for young musicians on the rise, conveniently located "within stumbling distance of 52nd Street," and open to all comers: the door was never locked, whether Evans was home or not. It was a cozy, messy place, with exposed pipes that ran across the walls, an upright piano, a pot of stew or soup usually bubbling on the hot plate, a fat black housecat named Becky, and, now and then, a snoring Charlie Parker passed out on the single bed. A fragrant cloud of reefer usually hung in the air, mingling with the cooking smells.

It was a warm place, Konitz recalled, both literally and emotionally, its general air of scruffy congeniality and total acceptance a direct reflection of the personality of its leaseholder and presiding spirit. The tall, lean, hawk-nosed Evans was a kind of den father to the young musicians who frequented his place: in his mid-thirties, he was a decade or so older than most of them. Rather than being paternalistic, though, he was a free spirit with an air of Zen holy man about him. Miles remembered him coming to listen to Bird's quintet at the Three Deuces:

> He'd come in with a whole bag of "horseradishes"—that's what we used to call radishes—that he'd be eating with salt. Here was this tall, thin, white guy from Canada who was hipper than hip. I mean, I didn't know *any* white people like him. . . . Here was Gil on fast 52nd Street with all these super hip black musicians wearing peg legs and zoot suits, and here he was dressed in a cap. Man, he was something else.

Something about Evans's Canadian-ness also let him skirt the initial wall of suspicion many Black artists put up with white people. Great players frequented Gil's apartment as much for the heady musical atmosphere as for the hospitality. "I was always interested in other musicians," Evans told the jazz critic Nat Hentoff. "I was hungry for musical companionship, because I hadn't had much of it before. Like bull sessions in music theory."

"When you went to Gil's place," the trumpeter and composer Johnny Carisi recalled, "he was playing the latest recordings of twentieth-century composition—Stravinsky, Ravel, Bartók, and so on. . . . To have a place where there was a group of guys listening to contemporary classical, that was special. Gil really had a lot of influence on all of us at the apartment because he was really stretching out musically in those years, and we started utilizing what we learned from him."

Stretching out musically meant looking beyond bebop, though that didn't happen all at once. Sometime in the fall of 1947, probably at the Three Deuces, Gil Evans told Charlie Parker that he really liked Bird's tune "Donna Lee," recorded on the quintet's first Savoy session in May. Bird told Evans that Savoy had erred in crediting him for the song; in reality, it was Miles's composition—the first Miles Davis tune ever to be recorded.

The error was understandable: with its rapid-fire, upbeat-but-not-sweet, switchback melody, its fast-moving unison sax-and-trumpet intro and outro, "Donna Lee" was bebop incarnate; it *sounded* like a Charlie Parker song—which was why Evans was drawn to it. Now, though, he and Miles were meeting for the first time and conversing, cordially but a little cagily. Davis recalled:

> He was asking for a release on my tune "Donna Lee." He wanted to make an arrangement. . . . I told him he could have it and asked him to teach me some chords and let me study some of the scores he was doing for Claude Thornhill. He really flipped me on the arrangement of [Sir Charles Thompson's song] "Robbins Nest" he did for Claude.

"After talking for a while and testing each other out, we found out that I liked the way Gil wrote music and he liked the way I played," Miles said in his memoir. "We heard sound in the same way."

THE STAGE WAS SET FOR MUSICAL CHANGE. GIL EVANS ARRANGED "DONNA Lee" and several other bebop numbers—"Anthropology," "Sorta Kinda," "Yardbird Suite"—for the Thornhill orchestra, which played them at shows and recorded them. To listen to them today is to hear an offbeat, musically rich way of reframing bebop, but paying dance customers didn't like the numbers, and Miles, for all that he and Evans heard sound the same way, wasn't fond of what Thornhill had done with Gil's arrangement of "Donna Lee": "It was too slow and mannered for my taste. . . . I could hear the possibilities in Gil's arranging and writing on other things, so what they did on 'Donna Lee' bothered me less, but it did bother me."

All of it bothered Claude Thornhill. He was musically astute enough to respect and even like Evans's charts, but bandleaders must be business-people as much as they're artists, and the sight of paying customers shaking their heads and walking off the dance floor whenever the new tunes were played was enough for Thornhill. Eventually he would knock on Evans's door at three in the morning and tell him he didn't want to play bebop anymore.

Meanwhile, though Miles had gained greatly in fame and confidence by playing with Charlie Parker—he'd just won the 1947 *Esquire* New Star award, and had tied Dizzy for first place in the critics' *DownBeat* poll—he was finding himself increasingly out of tune with his idol. Bird's helplessly self-centered life made him more undependable than ever, and, with his renown growing, more high-handed. Sometimes he would simply refuse to pay his musicians. Almost as bad, Davis felt, was the way Parker hammed it up, performing a kind of minstrelsy for the Street's white audiences. Once he introduced a song as "Suck You Mama's Pussy." "It was embarrassing," Miles recalled. "I didn't come to New York to work with no clown."

All the while, he was spending more and more time in the warm and stimulating atmosphere of Gil Evans's place, talking and thinking about new sounds. "By spring 1948," Evans's biographer Stephanie Stein Crease writes,

> Davis was an active participant in the running dialogue taking place among Gil, Mulligan, Johnny Carisi, John Lewis, and [avant-garde composer] George Russell on the subject of what they called their "dream band."
>
> Months earlier, Gil had already sketched out some pieces for an eleven-piece band. The motive . . . was to use the lush sonority of the Thornhill sound—still so unusual in a jazz context—in a smaller setting, allowing more flexibility for writer, improviser, and ensemble.

As originally conceived by Evans and Mulligan, the dream band would be just that: "a rehearsal band, something for the group members to write for and fool around with." But Miles, with masterly ambitions, had something more real in mind. As he tells it, Gil and Gerry came up with the idea and the instrumentation, but "the theory, the musical interpretation and what the band would play, was my idea. I hired the rehearsal halls, called the rehearsals, and got things done."

Mulligan confirmed this. "The musical direction ultimately fell into place when Miles became interested because Miles was our choice to play lead anyway," he said. "And it's kind of fascinating that we loved the way Miles played, even though at the time he was *not* widely respected as a trumpet player."

The rap on Miles, before Miles became Miles—before the world understood what Gil Evans and Gerry Mulligan already knew—was that he was deficient in technique: specifically, that he couldn't play fast. But for one thing, this came from a bebop perspective, at a moment when bebop was beginning to cool off and other styles were starting to emerge. For another, very soon it simply wasn't true. ("Listen to him with Dizzy [and

Fats Navarro, on the 1949 recording] *Metronome All-Stars*," Wallace Roney told me. "He's outplaying Fat Girl!") And for another, Miles was charting a new way forward: a way of leading by playing with exquisite lyricism, at medium volume and in the middle of the trumpet's range.

And as an artistic pioneer, he had no desire to be closeted: a dream band was a pretty idea, but in Miles's mind, a band wasn't a band unless it played in public and recorded. Gerry Mulligan again: "Miles made the move to materialize it and had all the relationships with people that he wanted in it that I never would have thought of—Max Roach, for one, Max was perfect in that band."

And Miles would be in charge. Starting with the August 1947 Savoy session on which he knew Bird should play tenor, and continuing through 1948 and 1949, Miles was starting to think as a leader rather than a sideman. A significant part of his artistic gift, then and for the rest of his career, was knowing what great painters or movie directors or orchestra conductors knew: what—whether colors or actors or sounds—to put where. The colors and textures of the Thornhill orchestra were lovely, but eighteen pieces were twice as many as Davis felt necessary for this new band; even eleven were more than enough. Miles wanted the band to sound like a choir, a quartet of human voices: soprano, alto, baritone, and bass. He could create all the rich sonorities he wanted with nine discrete instruments: trumpet, trombone, French horn, alto sax, baritone sax, tuba, piano, bass, and drums.

After Bird had pulled one too many stunts at the Deuces—the last straw, Miles said, was humiliating Sammy Kaye by calmly eating crackers and sardines in the dressing room while Kaye begged him to go out and play as he was supposed to—the Parker quintet began gigging at a new club on Broadway between Forty-seventh and Forty-eighth, a cellar joint called the Royal Roost (it had begun its existence as a fried-chicken restaurant; the WMCA jazz DJ Symphony Sid Torin persuaded the owner, Ralph Watkins, that bringing in bebop bands would be good for business). Bird's decamping was one of the final coffin nails for Fifty-second Street. After a little burst of vitality at the end of the forties, mainly fueled by the Parker quintet's sets at the Deuces and the Onyx, the Street was beginning to go down for good—the jazz clubs were turning into strip joints. And Miles, for his part, was branching out, playing as a sideman and leader with other groups, further exploring his new lyrical voice.

In September 1948, at Miles's urging, the promoter Monte Kay booked the nonet that Gil Evans and Gerry Mulligan and Miles had conceived, for a stand at the Royal Roost. Davis writes that the band was scheduled for two weeks, from late August into early September, billed second to Count Basie's orchestra. The reality seems to have been more complicated: it seems both Miles's nonet and Basie's orchestra played the Royal Roost that month, but so did Charlie Parker's quintet (with Bird, Miles, Tadd Dameron on piano, Curley Russell on bass, and Max Roach on drums), Tadd Dameron's sextet (Dameron, Fats Navarro, Allen Eager on tenor sax, Milt Jackson on vibes, Curley Russell, and Kenny Clarke on drums), and a Miles Davis–led quintet (Miles, Lee Konitz, John Lewis on piano, Al McKibbon at the bass, and Roach).

Nine pieces may have been the minimum necessary to create the new sound, but nine pieces were four too many for the club's owner. "When we opened up at the Roost," Miles recalled,

> I had the club put up a sign outside that said, "Miles Davis's Nonet; Arrangements by Gerry Mulligan, Gil Evans, and John Lewis." I had to fight like hell with Ralph Watkins, the owner of the Roost, to get him to do this. He didn't want to do the shit in the first place, because he felt it was too much for him to be paying nine motherfuckers when he could have paid five.

Introducing the nonet for the first time ever, live on a WMCA hookup very late one September night, bebop's sonorous, tireless champion Symphony Sid tried as best he could to soften the shock of the new:

> And right now, ladies and gentlemen, we bring you something new in modern music, we bring you Impressions in Modern Music

with the great Miles Davis and his wonderful new organization, featuring Max Roach on drums, John Lewis on piano, Al McKibbon on bass, Lee Konitz on alto, Gerry Mulligan on baritone—you all remember Gerry from the Disk Jockey Jump that he did with, ah, Gene Krupa and the band—Bill Barber on tuba—that's right, Bill Barber on tuba—Junior Collins on French horn, and Mike Zwerin on trombone. Ladies and gentlemen, let's give them a big hand for something new in modern jazz. Ladies and gentlemen, the Miles Davis organization, as they do for you a John Lewis arrangement—their first tune, a thing called "Move" . . .

And then there it was. "Move," written by the drummer-composer Denzil Best as a bebop number, but rearranged by Lewis into something else . . . a propulsive, melodic thing, beginning like a bebop tune with a theme statement played in fast unison by Miles and Konitz, and then salting in solos along the way . . . but. The resemblance to bop ended there. The tempo was quick but not blistering. The thing clearly had been *written*—written freely, so that it felt like improvisation, but written, nonetheless. The arrangement had a driving, masculine sweetness: the horns played chorded commentary throughout, and there were unison passages that hinted at fugue. To a listener today, "Move" sounds like modern big-band music—but this is because modern big-band music evolved from what was being presented at the Royal Roost for the first time, to unprepared ears.

The general reaction seems to have been admiring puzzlement, but puzzlement nonetheless. The applause, as heard on radio air checks of the sets, was polite. A September 23 review, after gushing about Basie's band, didn't even get the size of Miles's nonet right:

Holding down bandstand at the Basie band's absence is Miles Davis and his Quintet featuring all that's new in the way of modern music. The Davis Quintet produces music not akin to the Basie offerings in any respect thus making for a variety of musical entertainment. His outfit is unique in that he has tuba and a French horn playing along with the regular Be-Bop boys. The music at times tends to be a bit haunting by virtue of this innovation.

Basie himself, after listening for a few nights, was almost as nonplussed: "Those slow things sounded strange and good," he said. "I didn't know what they were doing, but I listened, and I liked it."

"Move" was slower than bebop, but couldn't exactly be called slow. On the other hand, the nonet's version of the Glenn Miller ballad "Moon Dreams," played at the Roost on the night of September 18, was—though filled with rich harmonies among the horns, embodying Miles's ideal of a choirlike sound—trancelike, if not dirgelike: it's hard to guess what the club's bop-loving audience could have thought of it. Still, not a cough or a clinking glass can be heard on the air check of the WMCA radio broadcast. And the modernist composer and arranger Pete Rugolo, then working as a producer for Capitol, was impressed enough that he asked Miles at the end of the evening if he could record the nonet once the current AFM strike (which had begun in January 1948) ended.

Meanwhile, Miles's discontent with Bird was building toward a crisis. In mid-December, owed several weeks' salary by Parker, Davis accosted him as he was sitting at a table in the Royal Roost, enjoying a king-size order of fried chicken and "drinking and higher than a motherfucker off some heroin." Miles asked Bird for his back pay; Bird went on eating and drinking as though Miles weren't there. Miles grabbed him by the collar and threatened to kill him if he didn't pay him. Bird gave him half of what he owed him.

Just before Christmas, once more at the Roost, Miles demanded the rest of his money. Once again, Bird put him off. Then, during the show, as Parker was clowning around, shooting a cap gun at Al Haig, blowing up a balloon and letting the air out into the microphone, Miles walked off the bandstand. Roach soon followed suit. Davis would return briefly, even recording with Bird several more times—most notably with the

Metronome All-Stars in January 1949—but he would never be in Charlie Parker's orbit again. From here on, others would orbit Miles.

THE STRIKE ENDED; CAPITOL PRODUCED THREE SESSIONS WITH THE nonet, on January 21 and April 22, 1949, and March 9, 1950. The personnel shifted somewhat from session to session, but Miles, Mulligan, Konitz, and Bill Barber the tuba player were constants, with Gil Evans and John Lewis writing the arrangements. The first release came soon after the January session, with the four upbeat tunes recorded that day doubled on two 78 rpm singles, one containing Gerry Mulligan's "Jeru" on the A-side and George Wallington's "Godchild" on the flip, and the other with Bud Powell's boplike composition "Budo" (aka "Hallucinations") paired with Best's "Move."

The purple Capitol label on each disc credited "Miles Davis and His Orchestra," and listed complete personnel; the records were categorized as "Bop Instrumental." And—despite the fact that every note on every number had been written on staff paper and read by the nine musicians—it was as bop instrumentals that the world understood, or, really, misunderstood them. Hence the capsule review in the record column of the March 13, 1949, *Amarillo Sunday News-Globe*:

> "Budo" is one of Capitol's first steps in the trek down the bebop trail, a frantic uptempo original performed by Miles Davis and band. A bevy of top bop instrumentalists turn in a series of interesting and exciting solos to spark the inventive arrangement. Flip is "Move," another fast-moving instrumental, a strictly bop affair, with the Davis trumpet highlighting a brilliant performance.

It appeared that the word "bebop" had officially lost its meaning, having come to signify any weird new sounds in jazz, or any unexpected quality of the musicians who played those sounds. ("There is a strange vein of

Mohammedan conversions, baggy clothes, and beat-up trumpets," as another paper put it.)

And then there was the record columnist for the African American newspaper *Cleveland Call and Post*, who wrote: "Vooph! It's great to see someone get Miles on wax." Davis at twenty-two had become a name to conjure with—then and forever after, the single word "Miles" told many people all they seemed to need to know about jazz.

But even his ascension did nothing to move merchandise if the product wasn't fully appreciated. Over time, the nonet's recordings from the Royal Roost sets and the Capitol sessions would acquire legendary status as *The Birth of the Cool*, the start of the next new jazz trend to follow bebop, the apple seeds Gerry Mulligan would take back to his native California to help spawn West Coast Jazz. But in the late forties and early fifties the new sounds were just Impressions in Modern Music, a bland, eat-your-vegetables catchall, and the records didn't sell.

STILL, MILES WAS A NAME TO CONJURE WITH, AND IN THE SPRING OF 1949 he and Tadd Dameron got an invitation to the new Festival International de Jazz in Paris, a celebration of postwar cultural rebirth. It would be Davis's first trip overseas. The festival's directors had invited a dozen or so American musicians representing different epochs in jazz history, including such elder statesmen as the New Orleans clarinetist Sidney Bechet (born in 1897), boogie-woogie pianist Pete Johnson (born 1904), and trumpeter Oran "Hot Lips" Page (born 1908), as well as Bird and his latest fivesome—Kenny Dorham on trumpet replacing Miles, plus Haig, Potter, and Roach—all of whom were in their twenties except the old man of the group, the thirty-year-old Potter.

In his memoir, Miles claimed that his quintet with Dameron—with James Moody on tenor sax, an expatriate American bassist named Barney Spieler at the bass, and Kenny Clarke on drums—was the hit of the festival, "along with Sidney Bechet." Ross Russell, leaving Miles out of the account entirely, said that Bird's set was "warmly received by the avant garde claque," but the bebop quintet's sound was "almost private, too intimate for the huge music hall." By contrast, the great Bechet, whose rousing, raspy, blues-based playing harkened back to the origins of jazz, "had the crowds dancing in the aisles."

Who knows? On the evidence of recordings from the festival, the Dameron-Davis five played with great boppish energy, Miles blowing in unusually Gillespie-esque, fast and high form, and received enthusiastic applause. The jazz writer Dan Morgenstern holds that playing as a leader opposite Bird and Kenny Dorham "represented both liberation and challenge to Miles, and he rose to the occasion."

But even if European ears were still largely attuned to prewar sounds, Europe itself was a revelation to Miles. He had lived for twenty-three years with the foot of American racism on his back; all at once, without expecting it, he was liberated. "I had never felt that way in my life," he said. "It was the freedom of being in France and being treated like a human being, like someone important." He was free, he was in the full flower of his young manhood, in the most beautiful city in the world, in spring. And quite naturally, he fell in love.

Juliette Gréco had already lived a lifetime at twenty-two: as a member of the Resistance during the war, a bohemian cabaret singer and actress, a muse to the postwar existentialists, a close friend to Jean-Paul Sartre, a lover of Albert Camus. Petite and dark-haired, with dramatic Mediterranean features, she instantly drew Miles's gaze when she attended one of his rehearsals. He crooked a beckoning index finger; she came. "When I finally got to talk to her," he remembered, "she told me that she didn't like men but that she liked me. After that we were together all the time."

It was a brief but electrifying affair, lasting just for the early-May week that Miles was in Paris (though he and Gréco would rekindle their romance when he returned in 1957), yet its effect on him was as powerful as that of the city itself. She introduced him to Picasso and Sartre. (Bird had his own memorable encounter with the existentialist: "I'm very glad to have met you, Mr. Sartre," he said; "I like your playing very much.") They walked along the Seine, holding hands and staring into each other's eyes, communicating just by touch and sight: that neither spoke the other's language only raised the heat.

And the fact that Miles was a married father of two was a side issue. "I cared a lot for Irene, but I had never felt like this before in my life," he said. Yet when the festival ended, though Kenny Clarke decided to stay in Paris, Miles knew he had to return to the blighted breast of the place he knew best. "Man, I was so depressed coming back to this country on the airplane that I couldn't say nothing all the way back," he recalled.

> I didn't know that shit was going to hit me like that. I was so depressed when I got back that before I knew it, I had a heroin habit that took me four years to kick and I found myself for the first time out of control and sinking faster than a motherfucker toward death.

6   Walking the bar

Eddie "Cleanhead" Vinson's tour broke up sometime in the spring or summer of 1949, possibly due to the leader's drinking problems, and Coltrane returned to Philadelphia. But in September he landed a dream job when Dizzy Gillespie hired him and, soon afterward, his pal Jimmy Heath, to play alto in Diz's big band, alongside the likes of Count Basie alumnus Paul Gonsalves (tenor sax), the great young bebop trombonist J. J. Johnson, the bassist Al McKibbon, and the drummer Specs Wright. It was "a beautiful band," Gillespie remembered, wistfully; "technically . . . the best I ever had."

Technically speaking, the band was a smoothly running machine. This was a delight to Coltrane's ears, but also a frustration. Back on alto—and lead alto, to boot—he indeed had to play straight, almost always reading arrangements and rarely soloing. And the organization's technical strength was also its weakness: dance gigs were where the money was, and as Gillespie's plainspoken wife, Lorraine, put it, "A dance band, you are not!"

"Dancers," Dizzy wrote, "had to hear those four solid beats and could care less about the more esoteric aspects, the beautiful advanced harmonies and rhythms we played and our virtuosity, as long as they could dance." But the harmonies and rhythms and virtuosity were so arresting that instead of dancing, they listened. "They'd just stand around the bandstand and gawk, so the dance-hall operators stopped sending for us."

Gillespie was also bucking a powerful cultural trend. As the big bands died out, singers, who could make money with minimal accompaniment, were coming to the fore, as was R&B, the progenitor of rock 'n' roll. Like Billy Eckstine, Dizzy quickly found that between salaries and transportation, his twenty-man orchestra was costing more than it was bringing in. "It's either me or the band," Lorraine told him. In June 1950, with a sigh, he pulled the plug on his dream.

And, always energetic and practical, got going again almost immediately, with a much smaller group, which once more featured Coltrane—but this time on tenor. At the end of August, Gillespie went on the road with a septet that also included the other future greats Jimmy Heath on alto, Milt Jackson on vibraphone, and Jimmy's big brother Percy Heath on bass, as well as Specs Wright on drums and one Fred Strong on congas. As always, Dizzy was good newspaper copy (Dorothy Kilgallen mentioned him often in her syndicated gossip column): with his soul patch and big grin and fizzy shave-and-a-haircut name, he was a star, a fun national character, while somewhere back east, Bird still labored in relative obscurity.

Under the smiles, though, was trouble, and Coltrane was at the center of it. He and Jimmy Heath had both been using heroin for a couple of years—snorting it, though Lewis Porter maintains that Coltrane may have started injecting it back in Philadelphia. (Charlie Parker had told Heath, "When you put it in your nose, you're still a gentleman; when you put it in your arm, you're a bum, exposed to all the world.")

Musicians mostly snorted it—unbeknownst to Gillespie, six of the players in his big band had been doing so—and those who put it in their nose rather than in their arm were better able to stop when they wanted. But while the septet played Dayton, Ohio, that fall, Coltrane and Heath, sick and nervous from the diluted heroin they'd had to purchase in the hinterlands, got relief when "Specs Wright brought in a girl named Dee Dee . . . who came in with a set of 'works' (needles and supplies), and she helped them all with shooting up, mainlining. That way they all got high instantly."

It was the beginning of a hellish seven-year addiction for Jimmy Heath. Coltrane's relationship with self-soothing substances was more complicated. He gobbled sweets, which led to problems with his weight and his teeth. He treated his frequent dental woes with heavy drinking. He also drank when he couldn't get heroin or was trying to stop. In October 1950, while he was in Los Angeles with the Gillespie group, he passed out in his hotel room after shooting up; Heath found him and revived him.

The incident put enough of a scare into Coltrane that he switched to alcohol—but when he passed out again at a later stop on the tour, this time when he was supposed to be onstage, Dizzy, who had just fired Jimmy Heath and Specs Wright after catching them with a hypodermic, threatened to drop Coltrane as well. Coltrane begged Gillespie to give him another chance, and the leader relented.

Dizzy Gillespie's stern hard-drug policy was a matter not of moral superiority but commercial practicality. Along with being a great musician, he was a bandleader and a businessman, justifiably proud of his product, great jazz, and wanting to present it consistently to audiences. Cheerful and generous by nature, he loved the brilliant musicians he hired and was endlessly generous about imparting his formidable musical knowledge to them: all he really wanted was to lift everyone in the band to the same high technical level. He largely succeeded. But he never succeeded in stopping all his players from using drugs.

Since jazz's beginnings, substance abuse among its musicians had been a nearly unavoidable occupational hazard. From 1900 to 1940, booze was the drug of choice among musicians, with marijuana running a close second. Then heroin came into vogue, with Charlie Parker as its prime exponent.

Bird, of course, was the ideal. His genius was so otherworldly, and his heroin use so blatantly extreme, that it was hard for young players prone to magical thinking (and all artists are prone to magical thinking) not to draw a connection between the two—and, having drawn the connection, hard not to see heroin as the royal road to jazz mastery. "I heard Charlie Parker and that was it," Red Rodney said.

> When you're very young and immature and you have a hero like Charlie Parker was to me, an idol who proves himself every time, who proves greatness and genius. . . . When I listened to that genius night after night, being young and immature and not an educated person, I must have thought, "If I crossed over that line, with drugs, could I play like that?"

Communion, and conformity, were as powerful as magical thinking: "You want a sense of belonging," Rodney said. "You want to be like the others. . . . Heroin was our badge. It was the thing that gave us membership in a unique club, and for this membership we gave up everything else in the world. Every ambition. Every desire. Everything. It ruined most people."

And it ruined Bird, but it took a while. In the meantime, his genius, combined with a powerful physical constitution and the occasional ability to play his best while high, led to the myth that he was *always* at his best on heroin. An awestruck Hampton Hawes wrote of watching Parker "line up and take down eleven shots of whiskey, pop a handful of bennies, then tie up [and shoot up], smoking a joint at the same time. He sweated like a horse for five minutes, got up, put on his suit and a half hour later was on the stand playing strong and beautiful."

This, in its own dark way, was like John Henry or Paul Bunyan: a classic American folktale, with Bird as the superhuman hero. On the other hand, Hawes also remembered driving Parker to a club gig "and he'd be too high to get out of the car. Howard McGhee would ask me where Bird was. I'd say, Sittin' in the car. No point in trying to pull him out, he wouldn't have been able to play anyway." After he'd sat there awhile,

Parker would get himself together and perform his time-honored coup de théâtre, walking into the club and blowing as only he could as he wove through the tables up to the stand.

But what of all the many times he simply never showed up?

Only Bird was Bird. As for all the others, every player had different needs and vulnerabilities, but the traps and pitfalls of the musician's life were remarkably consistent. "When you are working regularly, playing and rehearsing, [heroin] just doesn't come up," said Dexter Gordon, who fought hard against his addiction and kicked it more than once, sometimes for a couple of years at a time. "But when things are slow, you get bored and idle and depressed and the pushers start coming round—before you know you are back on it again. Boy, those pushers really made a believer out of me."

The pressures were everywhere. "I started using around 1945 when just about all the big names were," Gordon told an interviewer years later. Bird. Sonny Stitt. Bud Powell. Fats Navarro. Gene Ammons. Billie Holiday. And white musicians, like Stan Getz, Gerry Mulligan, Red Rodney, Chet Baker. In his memoir, Miles speaks of the younger musicians who became heavy users in the mid- to late 1940s, starting with Gordon and also including Tadd Dameron, Art Blakey, J. J. Johnson, Sonny Rollins, Jackie McLean. And himself.

When I asked Sonny Rollins why he thought drugs were so pervasive in jazz in the 1940s and '50s, he said, "Well, I think there were several things. For one, drugs were being introduced by criminal syndicates into communities. Also, jazz musicians were always looked down upon and marginalized in society."

Especially Black musicians. But, Rollins continued, both the substance and presentation of bebop represented a sea change from what had gone before: "To me," he said, "bebop was not just a different music, but I think [it represented] a break from when jazz players had to be entertainers. And especially bebop as exemplified by Charlie Parker, who used to stand up straight—he didn't dance around and all that stuff. He played all this great music. And it sort of was a harbinger of things to come in the social world. All races of people appreciated what a great music bebop was. And with Charlie Parker especially—I think there was a sort of racial thing where it was trying to straighten up American society."

A funny way to put it, but the meaning was clear. In the old scheme of things, it was perfectly natural for a redneck club patron to slap a nickel down and command Dizzy Gillespie to play "Darktown Strutters' Ball." These were the rules of minstrelsy. In the new era, those who'd been treated as minstrels felt ever freer to see themselves as aristocrats, with their own coded language and customs. Drug use, in Sonny Rollins's view, was one of the customs.

"I think the musicians sort of found something to have of their own, away from things that were happening in society," he told me. Heroin, he said, was "something that we had. It was our thing. So it was our fight against discrimination, our way of fighting against American culture."

It's an extraordinary statement, and a way of thinking that, no matter how wholehearted and seemingly justified, would have increasingly tragic consequences, as heroin took over the lives of many young musicians, then took their lives, period. What Rollins told me about his own heroin addiction—which began when he was a just-out-of-high-school musical sensation and continued until 1955, when at age twenty-five he committed himself for experimental methadone treatment at the Federal Medical Center in Lexington, Kentucky—rang similarly to Miles's story, and their lives and careers intersected often in the early 1950s.

Charlie Parker's iron constitution allowed him at times to play gorgeously while high. But Parker wasn't just a physical phenomenon, Ross Russell contends; he was also a kind of nihilist: "That Charlie was never able to make a meaningful break with his addiction was a matter of lifestyle, and despair. In spite of his successes and growing prestige Charlie saw no future for the music he played, or for his race in America. To live once, and to the limits—that was his game plan."

As for Coltrane, as greatly as he admired Charlie Parker, and as mountainously difficult as he found trying to catch up to Parker musically, he never confessed (on the record, anyway) to any magical imaginings that heroin could make him play like Bird. His own use of the drug seemed to come from a different place: one of loss and deep sadness, demons that had afflicted him since early adolescence, long before he ever heard of Charlie Parker. In all the hundreds of pages of interviews in *Coltrane on Coltrane*, Coltrane himself makes no reference to his drug use—although apparently he did speak candidly in 1960 to the Swedish journalist Björn Fremer about his addictions to alcohol and narcotics, and his "deep regret that he'd wasted so many years of his life because of them"—but then asked Fremer to remove that part of the interview from the article. Coltrane only touched on the subject when speaking with Gene Lees in 1961 about an unnamed player then working for him: "It's just so hard for any-one," Coltrane said, "and it's even harder for a musician, because there's so little to look forward to. It's such an uncertain business."

This when he was one of the most celebrated, beloved, and successful jazz musicians in the world.

IN EARLY 1951 DIZZY GILLESPIE AND HIS SMALL GROUP, NOW A SEXTET (Gillespie on trumpet, Coltrane on tenor, Milt Jackson on vibes, Billy Taylor on piano, Percy Heath on bass, and Art Blakey on drums), were back in New York, playing an extended stand at Birdland. Dizzy loved—pined for—the greater spectrum of musical and emotional colors he could produce with a big band, but he could also create amazing depth and power with six pieces. Some of the Birdland shows were broadcast on the radio, some were recorded, and Coltrane's solos can be heard on them. To listen to them is to realize how very far he had progressed since the Oahu disc: one bluesy solo, on "A Night in Tunisia," speaks of all his thousands of hours practicing and his sometimes enjoyable, always educational, stints with R&B bands. It is magnificent: fluid, inventive, soulful, hot.

Yet for the next four years, John Coltrane labored in a kind of self-imposed anonymity, for reasons both clear and murky. In 1961 he told the French jazz journalist François Postif, "See, I stayed in obscurity for a long time, because I was happy to play what was expected of me, without trying to add anything. I saw so many guys get fired from bands because they tried new things that I was somewhat disgusted to try anything else!"

Perhaps Coltrane was revolted by the unoriginality of the bands he played with after Gillespie, but what he really seems to have been disgusted by was himself. This period was the nadir of his heroin addiction. Billy Taylor remembered that during breaks at Birdland, when the rest of the sextet sat at a table together or went out for coffee, Coltrane was nowhere to be found. "[His] habit got in the way, so I didn't hang out with him as much as I might have had he not had other things to do. He was a very soft spoken and nice guy. It was frustrating for me because he was one of the first people that I met that I said, 'Gee, I wish there was something I could say or something I could do to convince him not to do this.'"

But addicts are compelled by an overpowering physical need, as well as the knowledge of the hell that accompanies going without. And early loss is a trauma that has lasting effects on the body as well as the mind, and John Coltrane, with his persistent quiet sadness, the haunted air that's so striking in photographs, seemed to be in the grips of physical and emotional forces he was nearly powerless to resist.

AFTER THE BIRDLAND STAND WAS OVER, HE RETURNED TO PHILADEL-phia and a life of study and freelancing. He continued taking theory lessons with Dennis Sandole; he met with other musicians, including the advanced and eccentric pianist Hasaan Ibn Ali (who would also influence McCoy Tyner), to exchange ideas. He played with Jimmy Heath again, in a group called the Dizzy Gillespie Alumni; he sometimes sat in with Miles Davis when Miles was playing the Club 421 on Wyalusing Avenue in West Philly.

Then it was back out on the road. In January 1952, Coltrane and Specs Wright joined Gay Crosse and His Good Humor Six, a minor, Louis Jordan–influenced R&B band based in Cleveland. Two months later, they took a big step up, signing on with the bandleader and tenor saxophonist Earl Bostic. With his propulsive, growling sound, Bostic wasn't just a nationally known leader, he was a great player, fully capable of going head-to-head with Charlie Parker in jam-session cutting contests. Bostic, Coltrane later remembered, "showed me a lot of things on my horn. He has fabulous technical facilities on his instrument and knows many a trick." Two skills Bostic almost certainly demonstrated to Coltrane were playing bravura passages in the altissimo range and the mystical art of circular breathing—simultaneously inhaling through the nose and pushing air held in the cheeks through one's instrument.

Coltrane recorded with Bostic but never soloed. "All this time musically I was progressing very little in the way I wanted," he told Fremer in 1960. "I was learning just by being in this great company. But I had not reached the point when I could take active steps by myself."

Which meant that for the time being, he was stuck in show business. Earl Bostic could duel with Bird, but he hadn't become a nationally known leader and recording artist by playing bebop. Pulse-stirring R&B-style dance music was his bread and butter: sometimes his musicians, John Coltrane included, had to sing backup vocals. There were nights when Coltrane, playing Philadelphia clubs with pickup bands, had to "walk the bar": literally to solo, as brassily as possible, while treading among the cocktails and beer bottles. Benny Golson, Porter writes, "once entered the Point Bar when Coltrane was on the bar, and Coltrane was so embarrassed that he said, 'Oh, no!' and walked right out of the club."

After Bostic came further R&B stints: with Daisy Mae and the Hep Cats, whom Coltrane would describe to Bill Evans as "the kind of band you'd find in Las Vegas lounges ten years later," and with another forgotten figure of the early 1950s, Bull Moose Jackson, a tenor player/vocalist whose subspecialty was jump-blues tunes with raunchy lyrics.

Then Coltrane landed another dream job, joining the small group of one of his idols, the great altoist Johnny Hodges, aka Rabbit. Between 1951 and 1955, Hodges took a four-year hiatus from Duke Ellington's orchestra to lead his own band; Coltrane, on tenor, signed on in early 1954. The personnel varied from seven men to twelve. John Coltrane played on two recording dates with the group that summer, though he didn't solo.

However, on a startlingly clear private recording of the band in concert during the period, he can be heard soloing extensively in three numbers: the Al Sears blues "Castle Rock," Duke Ellington's "In a Mellotone," and Dorothy Fields and Jimmy McHugh's ballad "Don't Blame Me." His playing is beautiful and fully fledged Coltrane: growling and blowing with all the verve his R&B training has inculcated in him; navigating fluidly and soulfully through the medium-tempo "Mellotone" and the slower "Don't Blame Me," interjecting little Parkeresque excursions into unexpected harmonic territory, riffs that speak of greatness forming.

"We played honest music in this band," Coltrane said, years later, of his months with Hodges. "It was my education to the older generation." At twenty-eight, an age when many other jazz musicians were established veterans, John Coltrane still considered himself a student, still unwilling— or afraid—to take active steps by himself.

HIS ADDICTION WAS BOTH A SYMPTOM AND A CAUSE OF HIS INABILITY TO move forward. Unlike the heedless, defiantly sociopathic, endlessly self-involved Charlie Parker, who lied and cheated and stole constantly to feed the monkey on his back and only occasionally regretted it, "Trane knew he was sick, and he knew he had the habit, but he controlled himself very beautifully," said the pianist James Forman, who'd begun playing by Coltrane's side at the Elate Club in 1947. "He didn't try to rip anybody off. He told me one time he was going to stop. He said, 'Man, I spent eighty dollars today. I gotta cut this out!' That was a lot of money back then."

Bird, the heroin paragon, was a swashbuckling narcissist; Coltrane, soft-spoken and eternally modest, had strong ties to family and friends. In 1952, his drug outlays notwithstanding, he took a GI loan of $5,416, putting 10 percent down to buy a house in Philadelphia's Strawberry Mansion neighborhood as a home base and as a home for his mother, his Aunt Bettie, his cousin Mary, and an old school friend, James Kinzer.

But his habit still had a grip on him. After one too many goofs by Coltrane—whether it was not showing up on the bandstand at the appointed hour, or nodding out in front of an audience—Johnny Hodges let him go, in Los Angeles in the summer of 1954. (It's said that the young multi-instrumentalist Eric Dolphy, whom Coltrane had met while playing in L.A., had to lend him the money to return home.) That September, Coltrane was back in Philadelphia and freelancing again.

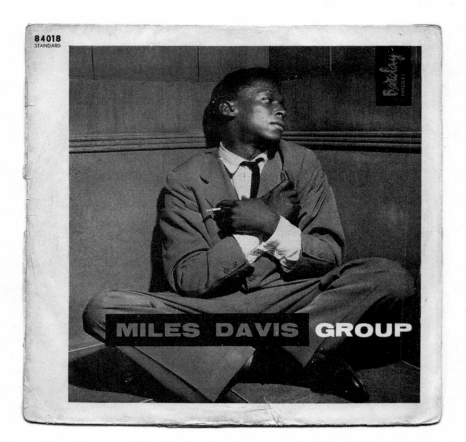

7 Junkie time

Miles's return from France was a rude comedown—from rapturous love and Paris in the spring, from adulation and even basic respect. In Paris he had learned that all white people weren't the same, that some were capable of standing face-to-face with him and speaking with him simply as human to human. In the New York of 1949 he was not only an ocean away from Juliette Gréco, he was once again a second-class citizen: in the eyes of white America, just another Negro. To add to the indignity, work was hard to come by: "White musicians who were copying my *Birth of the Cool* thing were getting the jobs."

"Those were listless years," the veteran jazz observer Dan Morgenstern wrote of Davis's late 1940s and early '50s. In the summer of 1949 Miles was masquerading as a family man, living with Irene and their two small children in an apartment on a quiet street in St. Albans, Queens, and quietly going crazy—bored, lovesick, and broke.

Small wonder, then, that Harlem exerted a powerful pull. On an installment plan, Miles had bought a used blue 1948 Dodge convertible so he could commute easily to the place that knew him best—and where he knew he could score drugs. Harlem saw and respected him, even loved him a little, but the love was conditional. He was *Miles Davis*, he was on the cutting edge of coolness, but coolness, for all its roots in rebellion, had its own set of rules. Communion and conformity.

Heroin was our badge . . .

"I just know that when you got high at that time, you were further into the clique," said the pianist Walter Davis, Jr. "It was in to be doing that. [When somebody was playing well] the conversation went like this: you would always hear somebody say, 'Who the hell is that?' Guy say, 'Well, that's such and so,' and the next question would be, 'Does he get high?' You say, 'Yeah, he gets high as a motherfucker.'"

Miles started by just snorting heroin and cocaine now and then— chipping, in street parlance—but soon the now and the then got closer together. One day, he recalled, he was standing on a corner in Queens feeling miserable—chills, a runny nose, possible fever—when an acquaintance, a hustler called Matinee, walked up and asked what was happening. Miles told him he'd been snorting drugs, but on that day he hadn't gone to Manhattan to score. Matinee gave him a withering look and told him he had a habit.

"What do you mean, a habit?" Miles asked.

"Your nose is running, you got chills, you weak. You got a motherfucking habit, nigger."

Matinee bought him some heroin nearby; Miles snorted it and felt better at once. But the next time he saw the hustler, Matinee told him, "Miles, don't waste that little money on getting some to snort, because you still gonna be sick. Go on and shoot it, then you'll feel much better."

That, Miles said, was the start of "a four-year horror show."

Bix Beiderbecke, 1903–1931
Bunny Berigan, 1908–1942
Lester Young, 1909–1959

Billie Holiday, 1915–1959
Freddie Webster, 1916–1947

He began shooting heroin in the late summer or early fall of 1949, when, exactly as in Dexter Gordon's formula, things were slow and Miles was idle, bored, and depressed. For up to six blessed hours after injecting the drug, he could feel that all was right in the world, and that the problems of underemployment and poverty and responsibility to his two small children and their mother had drifted off like a smoke ring and vanished. Then he would nod off into sweet oblivion—and, when he came to, feel a craving in the marrow of his bones to return to the blessed state: to score more heroin, no matter what it took or how much it cost.

It was never as good as it was the first time, though the fantasy that it could be, combined with the deepening physical effects of addiction, kept him on the run, always looking for more. Heroin was fast becoming Miles's boss—his impossibly demanding boss.

"When we first came to New York everyone was so bright and eager," Irene recalled. "Then suddenly everyone was nodding." Miles was spending so little time at home, and had so little interest in her sexually, that at first she suspected he was having an affair. Then she found blood on his shirtsleeve and put two and two together. Gregory Davis, just three or four at the time, remembered his mother hiding Miles's shoes so he wouldn't be able to go out to score.

In early 1950 he left Queens and moved himself and his young family into the Hotel America on West Forty-seventh Street, one of the few Manhattan hotels south of Harlem designated by *The Negro Travelers' Green Book* as hospitable to African Americans, within easy walking distance of Birdland, Bop City, and other Broadway clubs—and closer to sources of drugs. The America was home to a number of jazz musicians, including his old St. Louis friend Clark Terry, and Miles promptly consigned Irene and the kids to the care of another hotel resident, the up-and-coming young singer Betty Carter, who idolized him. Meanwhile he hung out with Sonny Rollins and his Sugar Hill Harlem crowd, basically a kaffeeklatsch of heroin users who also happened to be great musicians: the teenage altoist Jackie McLean, the pianist Walter Bishop, Jr., the drummers Blakey, Roach, and Art Taylor. Doing drugs with other addicts relieved loneliness; it also made it easier to score. Miles continued to work, even as his addiction dragged him steadily downward.

In February he led a sextet at Birdland, with J. J. Johnson, the twenty-three-year-old tenor player Stan Getz, Tadd Dameron, the bassist Gene Ramey, and Roach. With varying personnel, Miles would return to the club, the one place that consistently welcomed him, until early July. In March, after a long gap, he recorded with the *Birth of the Cool* nonet for the third and last time, laying down four tunes arranged by himself, Gerry Mulligan, and Gil Evans: again, Capitol released them on ten-inch 78s; again, reviews were excellent and sales were thin.

At Birdland in May he led another sextet, then sat in with Charlie Parker's band, playing alongside a dying Fats Navarro. Miles's beloved Fat Girl, the only trumpeter in the universe who could make high and fast sound lyrical, reduced to skin and bones and racked by coughing, would succumb in early July, at twenty-six, to the combined effects of heroin addiction and tuberculosis.

By that summer, Miles recalled, heroin had changed him from "a nice, quiet, honest, caring person into someone who was the complete opposite," a man who desperately wanted to stop injecting heroin but couldn't. "I'd do anything not to be sick, which meant getting and shooting heroin all the time, all day and all night." Which meant somehow coming up with the money to pay for it. Pawning his trumpet bought him some time, but just a little. Fitfully employed (when he had a gig, he would rent a trumpet from Art Farmer, at ten dollars a night), behind on his hotel rent and car payments, he began pimping to support his habit. But, John Szwed writes, this was pimping "not in the sense that white people use the term . . . as someone in The Life, a man who runs women on the streets for profit. He was a pimp only in that he took gifts from women who lived by selling sex, as well as from those who didn't."

There was nothing sexy about this. Heroin had neutralized Miles's libido. Women gave him money because he was young and cute and vulnerable, and—this might have been the main thing—because he listened to them. He had, he said, become "a professional junkie."

One day Clark Terry came upon Miles sitting on the curb, his eyes red and his nose running. Terry bought him breakfast and told him he was about to go on the road with Count Basie, and that Miles could stay in his room until he felt well enough to leave—all he had to do was lock the door behind him. Miles returned the favor by stealing and pawning Terry's clothes and one of his trumpets. Somehow Terry found it in himself to forgive him.

Feeling that leaving New York for a while might help him, Miles put Irene and the children in the Dodge convertible—Sonny Rollins had nicknamed it the Blue Demon—and drove his little family to East St. Louis. Soon after he parked the car in front of his father's house, the finance company repossessed it.

In his memoir, Miles and his coauthor finesse a number of subjects, including Irene's third pregnancy. Miles and Troupe write as though Miles learned she was expectant after they arrived in Illinois, but some sources say Miles IV was born in August, and at least two date his birth to November 11, 1949. If the child was born in August 1950, Irene's condition would have been apparent for months—and if the baby had arrived in the previous November, that would've made quite a carload for the Blue Demon. In any case, Miles says he knew the child wasn't his: he hadn't been having sex with Irene. In addition, "a friend" notified him that he'd seen Irene and another man leaving a hotel together. It's unclear, then, why Miles named the boy, or allowed him to be named, after himself. But then, not much about Miles's life was clear in those days.

The trip home marked the end of his common-law union: "At the end we didn't have no argument or nothing like that, it was just over," Miles said, sidestepping the inconvenient question of what to do about six-year-old Cheryl and four-year-old Gregory, not to mention Miles IV. He returned to New York alone, then joined Billy Eckstine once again, this time as part of a sextet accompanying Eckstine on a city-to-city bus tour that would culminate in Los Angeles. Miles didn't have much taste for backing Eckstine's romantic ballads, but musicians he respected, including Art Blakey, Dexter Gordon, and Budd Johnson, were in the band, and he had few if any other offers.

After the L.A. show, Miles, Blakey, and Gordon were driving to the Burbank airport to fly to the next gig in San Francisco when Blakey decided to stop and buy some drugs from a dealer he knew. When they got to the airport, a police car pulled them over. It was an era when police departments around the country, following the lead of Harry Anslinger, the crusading and notoriously racist commissioner of the Federal Bureau of Narcotics, paid particular attention to jazz musicians, who were often drug users and often Black. Since both possession and use of drugs were illegal, even needle tracks on an addict's arm could be used as evidence. In this instance the L.A. cops, who'd followed Davis, Blakey, and Gordon from the dealer's house, found heroin capsules in Blakey's pocket and observed track marks on Miles's arm. The musicians were immediately arrested. When the cops demanded their names, Davis and Gordon complied, but Blakey insisted on giving his new Muslim appellation, Abdullah Ibn Buhaina. "Cut that shit out and give me your fucking American name, your right name!" the cop taking everything down yelled.

This was one big problem in a nutshell: the reason Black musicians adopted Islam, and Muslim names, was to leave behind any vestiges of slavery and white dominance. And Blakey/Buhaina had a particular issue with white cops: while touring the South with the Fletcher Henderson Orchestra in the late thirties, he had been beaten so badly by an Albany, Georgia, policeman (allegedly for violating the city's segregated busing laws, but as Blakey later said, "I was arrested for being black, for being a nigger; that's what I was charged with") that he had to have a steel plate put in his head. And so he refused to relent to the L.A. cops, and he and Davis were remanded to the county jail.

It was Miles's first incarceration, and he was horrified. "He was very soft," said Hadley Caliman, a saxophonist who happened to be in the cell

Blakey and Davis were put into. "He cried a little bit. He didn't like the fact that he was incarcerated with these thugs."

As usual in those days, Miles sought his father's help, placing his one phone call to Dr. Davis, who tapped his network of distinguished African Americans, reaching out to a dental-school classmate, who in turn contacted a young Black Los Angeles lawyer named Leo Branton. Branton was just then making his bones by fearlessly bringing malfeasance cases against the notoriously racist L.A. police; he would go on to a long career of representing high-profile Black defendants. He got Miles released on bail—then shocked him by telling him that in exchange for lighter treatment, Blakey had told the police that Miles, not he, was the drug user. In fact, Miles had, of necessity while traveling with Eckstine, been going lightly enough on heroin that he believed he might be in the process of kicking—but the police had no way of knowing how old or new the track marks on his arms might be.

Miles's account says nothing about how Dexter Gordon fared in this instance, but Maxine Gordon writes that at twenty-seven, the saxophonist was a veteran of Los Angeles's punitive criminal law system for users: he was first arrested for "transporting drugs" in 1946, at age twenty-three, and spent his first time behind bars in 1948. Davis says he stayed with Gordon for a while after they were released, and that because Dexter had good access to heroin, Miles began shooting up again.

He was acquitted at his November trial, but in the court of public opinion he'd already been convicted. For a musician to be outed as a user of drugs—any drugs—was a major scandal in the days before drug use in jazz was a sad cliché, and Miles's name, already one to conjure with in jazz circles, was tarnished. On November 18, the *Jackson Advocate*, a Black Mississippi newspaper, reported, slightly inaccurately but damagingly enough: "Word comes from out on the coast that ace drummer man Art Blakely [sic] and trumpeteer Miles Davis, both of New York, have been arrested for carrying some weeds in their possession." But the day before, a much bigger hammer had come down: *DownBeat*—which had published its first feature on Miles in January, a long and highly sympathetic profile that rated him "a mild, modest, quiet young man of 23, [with] a lot of respect for his elders"—ran a scathing editorial on the narcotics problem in the music business, citing Miles and Blakey's Los Angeles arrest as a case in point. The almost instant result for both men was an evaporation of employment opportunities—although strikingly, the Hi-Note in Chicago, where Miles had backed Anita O'Day the previous Christmas, hired him again to accompany Billie Holiday, whose own drug arrests had been public knowledge for years, over the 1950–51 holidays. The two-week engagement drew capacity audiences: for some clubgoers, the aura of the forbidden around the two stars would have added spice to the great music.

And Miles was in clover, or some version of it. "He was in a marvelous hotel then," the pianist Gil Coggins recalled.

> I think it cost $28 a week, and *then* . . . that was a pretty nice hotel! And that time he was messing around with everybody. His old man was sending him $75. . . . Shit was cheap, you could get a capsule for a dollar. . . . It was pure, you know, potent.

And while club owners on both coasts were giving him a wide berth, the head of one New York record label wanted badly to work with him.

Tadd Dameron, 1917–1965
Charlie Parker, 1920–1955
Joe Guy, 1920–1962
Wardell Gray, 1921–1955
Fats Navarro, 1923–1950

BOB WEINSTOCK WAS A NEW YORK JEW OF A TYPE THAT BARELY EXISTS anymore: big, tough, and fat, rough around the edges, and, as the expression once went, straight from the shoulder. A *shtarker* with a sensitive soul. He was first smitten by jazz at age eight, when his father took him to a record store sale and bought an armful of 78s at nine cents apiece, discs by

Duke Ellington, Benny Goodman, Count Basie, Louis Armstrong. He listened raptly, again and again. By fifteen Bob had started a mail-order business, selling jazz discs out of his family's Upper West Side apartment; he was successful enough that by age eighteen, in 1947, he was able to open a store on West Forty-seventh Street, the Jazz Record Corner.

Jazz was always playing in the store; musicians working in the neighborhood were intrigued. "On the way to work at the Royal Roost they'd hear the music and come look where it was coming from," Weinstock recalled.

What they found was a treasure house of jazz discs. Bob Weinstock prided himself, as he later said, on carrying "everything from Bunk to Monk"—everything, that is, from the early New Orleans trumpeter Bunk Johnson to Thelonious Monk. Yet while Weinstock sold bebop records by the thousands—particularly Charlie Parker on Dial and Savoy—at first he had no taste for the new music.

Then a series of jazz enthusiasts changed his life. Alfred Lion, the German émigré who'd cofounded Blue Note Records in 1939, had long done well with recordings of traditional jazz artists like clarinetists Sidney Bechet and George Lewis, records that Bob Weinstock sold in quantity. Weinstock and Lion grew friendly. Blue Note had begun recording Monk in 1947, and though the revolutionary pianist didn't sell well at first, Lion believed in him: so much so that he brought Bob Weinstock a Monk disc and urged him to listen. "When someone like Alfred Lion, who I respected for recording the old jazz, got into Monk, it really opened my eyes," Weinstock recalled.

His education continued when the drummer Kenny Clarke, a regular customer at the store, took him to the Royal Roost and introduced him to Monk, Tadd Dameron, Fats Navarro, Dexter Gordon, Wardell Gray, Bud Powell, Max Roach, and other masters of the new music. Weinstock became such a passionate convert to bebop that Clarke recommended he start a record label of his own.

In the fall of 1947 Ross Russell, who'd also become a friend through the big business he and Weinstock did together, moved Dial Records from Hollywood to New York. Weinstock attended a couple of Charlie

Parker Quintet recording sessions in Manhattan and met Bird—and Miles, clearly a star in the making—for the first time. Weinstock invited the young trumpeter for a drink; Miles said he'd rather have an ice cream cone. Weinstock was charmed.

The record seller began to see the logic in Kenny Clarke's suggestion. The major record labels had no interest in bebop: sales numbers simply weren't big enough. But as Dial and Savoy had shown, a small outfit, with far lower overhead, could do well in what had become a lively niche market.

In January 1949 Bob Weinstock inaugurated his new label—called, sensibly if not memorably, New Jazz—by producing a Lee Konitz–Lennie Tristano session and issuing it as a ten-inch LP, *Subconscious-Lee*. "It was a smash hit in jazz circles," Weinstock said. "All the critics gave it five stars. Stores all over the United States would call up and order it. I was swamped with orders." In short order, Weinstock changed the name of his label to Prestige.

It's unclear why Bob Weinstock didn't sign Miles at once. It could be that through 1948 Davis was too definitively Bird's sideman for the new producer to consider recording him as a leader. And then the next two years began Miles's lost period. But sometime in late 1950, Bob Weinstock conceived a determination to record Miles Davis—who at this moment was persona non grata in the jazz world and off the radar screen. As Miles tells the story, in the early winter of 1950 Weinstock called every Davis in the St. Louis and East St. Louis phone books until he reached Miles's father, who told him Miles was at the Hi-Note in Chicago. "I said, 'Please, if you should hear from Miles, ask him to call me in New York,'" Weinstock recalled.

Once Davis returned to the Apple, Weinstock offered him a one-year contract with Prestige, beginning immediately—January 1951—for $750 (the equivalent of some $8,800 today): not much money, Miles wrote, but enough "to lead a group of my own choosing, lay down some music that I wanted to record, and put a little money in my own pocket"—and also in the pockets of his drug suppliers. Weinstock, Miles said, "knew I was a junkie, but . . . was willing to take a chance that I would eventually come around."

Bob Weinstock liked Davis's nonet recordings but preferred the Miles of the Dial sessions with Bird. As he later put it, with a blatant lack of musical and political correctness:

> Miles, at that time, although he still dug the cool music of Mulligan and Evans, some of the primitiveness in him started to come out. I say primitiveness, because to me the music of the bop masters is primitive music, like the original New Orleans music of King Oliver and Louis. He sort of drifted back into that element, and he liked Sonny Rollins, as crude as Sonny was at that time, and John Lewis. On his first date, you can hear a very different Miles Davis than on the Capitols.

If different terms are substituted for the incendiary word "primitive," what Weinstock was trying to say becomes clearer—well, a little clearer, anyway. The early New Orleans jazz of King Oliver and Louis Armstrong contained strong African and Afro-Caribbean influences, both harmonically and rhythmically, and more of a straight line than Armstrong perhaps would have liked to admit can be drawn between that music and the bebop of Bird and Diz, with its flatted fifths, plunging velocity, and rhythmic strangeness. "The cool music of Mulligan and Evans"—which had at least as much to do with Miles's artistic vision as with Gerry's and Gil's—was, in its essence, *arranged*, giving it a far different energy than the urgent, head arrangement–cum–improvisation of bebop. It must be said: to certain ears, at certain times, the nonet recordings sounded anodyne.

"Musically speaking, the cool period always reminded me of white people's music," Dizzy said, with his always thrilling capacity for not holding back.

> There was no guts in that music, not much rhythm either. They never sweated on the stand, Lee Konitz, Lennie Tristano, and those guys. This music, jazz, is guts. You're supposed to sweat in your balls in this music. I guess the idea was not to get "savage"

with it, biting, like we were. But that's jazz to me. Jazz to me is dynamic, a blockbuster.

But then he let Miles off the hook:

Miles wasn't cool like that anyway. Miles is from that part of St. Louis where "blues" comes from. Just part of his music is played like that, cool. They copped that part—the cool—but let the rest, the blues, go, or they missed it.

Interesting, then, to see what Weinstock got from his new artist the first time out. In his memoir, Miles recalls January 17, 1951, as "cold and mushy . . . a day when snow can't seem to decide if it wants to be snow; a fucked-up, raw day." This is dramatic; the day's actual weather, according to *The New York Times*, was fair and milder. Maybe Miles was remembering his inner state. He actually played three sessions on the seventeenth: not just his first one for Prestige, but earlier in the day, a date with Charlie Parker for Bird's new label, Mercury, and last, a single number, Miles's composition "I Know," also for Prestige, featuring Sonny Rollins (over the mysterious reluctance of Bob Weinstock to see the twenty-year-old Rollins as the prodigy he was).

Miles says that Bird was in ebullient spirits that day, and the evidence is there: Parker played beautifully on four numbers: his compositions "Au Privave," "She Rote," and "K.C. Blues," plus the Gene de Paul–Don Raye standard "Star Eyes." Davis felt that everyone (Bird and himself, Walter Bishop, Jr., on piano, Teddy Kotick on bass, and Max Roach on drums) acquitted themselves well on the Parker session. And Miles did play well in pieces and patches—but there are also sections, such as his solo on "Star Eyes," where he sounds halting, almost lost. As he says himself, the trumpet is a physically demanding instrument: its masters have to work at it like top-flight athletes. And he admits that his lack of work, combined with the distraction of addiction, was affecting his embouchure.

He carried his uncertainty to his sextet session (Bennie Green on trombone, Rollins on tenor, John Lewis on piano, Percy Heath on bass, and Roy Haynes at the drums). In the ripening of his career and the re-blooming of his confidence after kicking drugs, Miles would come to have his own way with standards, altering notes and emphases for expressive purposes and to make a song new; here, though, the music is just having its way with him: at several junctures he seems simply bewildered, especially on two takes of Rodgers and Hart's "Blue Room," where at one point he's so unhorsed that Lewis has to play him back into the song. ("Davis is rather unfamiliar with the tune," *DownBeat*'s reviewer would write in April, rating the side 4 out of 10.) He sounds, dishearteningly, like the junkie he is.

On the Rollins session, Miles didn't play trumpet at all: instead, since Lewis had to leave, he sat in on the piano, block-chord comping nicely behind Sonny's spectacularly mature solo.* Afterward the musicians teased Miles that his piano playing had been better than his horn playing that day.

Weinstock would stick with him anyway.

Elmo Hope, 1923–1967
Wilbur Ware, 1923–1979
Dinah Washington, 1924–1963
Bud Powell, 1924–1966
Sonny Berman, 1925–1947

Miles recalled that after the record date, as he and Sonny Rollins headed uptown to buy heroin, he thought, "If only I could kick this habit, then things might be all right." But, he continues, he was a long way from kicking, and he knew it.

---

*See Art Matthews's explanation of block chords at artmatthewsonlinepianolessons.com /ac-22-block-chords-what-are-they-how-to-use-them. See also Miles's beautiful recording of Harry Warren's "You're My Everything," on which Davis whistles Red Garland's slightly corny intro to a halt and commands him to use block chords instead: youtube.com/watch ?v=ekbWB6kBW2I.

The drug-shaming drumbeat continued. In February *Ebony* printed a feature titled "Is Dope Killing Our Musicians? Famed Orchestra Leader Sees Use of Narcotics as Dire Menace to Future of Band Business." The piece, under Cab Calloway's byline, read in part:

> There are many alarmists among us who say that dope is slowly killing our musicians and that the jazz business is doomed to destroy itself in a poisonous cloud of marijuana smoke to the sinister accompaniment of heroin hypodermic needle "pops." I am not an alarmist. I know that the drug menace in music is very real, and that unless immediate steps are taken it will lead to the deterioration of a splendid art. I do not think, however, that the advance of the dope habit is irresistible. It can be checked.

The feature was illustrated with photos of prominent musicians who'd been associated with drugs: Bird, Blakey, Dexter Gordon, Billie Holiday, Howard McGhee, Gene Krupa, and Miles. With seeming sympathy, Calloway wrote:

> One young trumpeter, recently picked up on the West Coast for possession of heroin, happens to be one of the most brilliant minds in contemporary jazz. He has contributed mightily to the growth of the modern jazz movement and is widely admired for his talent. Music needs this man, the country needs to hear his music, we all need the joy and beauty his playing can bring into our lives.

Nobody reading the piece would have had any question about whom Calloway was referring to.

There were many common threads among jazz musicians addicted to heroin; each also danced his or her own dance with the drug. Charlie Parker was locked in a lifelong embrace with it, about which he was now and then sorrowing, sometimes ashamed, but often defiant. Sonny Rollins, as we've seen, also felt this defiance. "Using drugs was, in a strange way, a negation of the money ethic," he said. "Guys were saying, 'I don't care about this, I don't care how I dress or how I look, all I care about is music.'" Dexter Gordon said, "We were the revolutionaries. We did what was new and hip with no forethought of consequences. Heroin just became part of the scene."

And at first, the mortal perils of the drug notwithstanding, many musicians enjoyed it unapologetically—and not just heroin itself but everything about it: talking about it in a special, coded language; obtaining it; administering it. Speaking from sorrowful knowledge decades later, Gordon recalled that he "loved shooting up . . . part of the charm, the romance, is sticking a needle in your arm."

Rollins felt similarly:

> When I was in New York and using drugs and playing my horn
> and beginning to get recognized as a young, up and coming player,
> I was really in a happy situation. . . . I recall telling somebody that
> I would never stop using drugs because it felt good and it put me
> in the place I wanted to be, mentally and physically. I remember
> really being an advocate of drugs at one time.

Art Blakey told an interviewer that he started using heroin "because I liked it. There isn't any other reason. It makes you feel good. . . . Nobody ever found out about it, because I had a lot of money. Money can cover up almost everything."

We've seen that Miles gravitated to the drug out of depression and boredom, looking for escape. Then the tightly wound genius discovered an added benefit. "The first time I used heroin, I just nodded out and didn't know what was happening," he remembered. "Man, that was a weird feeling. But I felt so relaxed."

Inevitably, heroin found its way into the making of the music itself. "Alcohol throws your talent out; your technique gets sloppy," Jimmy Heath said.

Marijuana makes you get plenty of ideas, but then your mind moves too fast. You move off one idea to another. Heroin was a concentration drug. . . . If you can concentrate better, you can work on things very meticulously. Coltrane used to get high and practice all day. When I would go to see him, he would have nothing on but a pair of pants. Sometimes it was so hot in his house that he would be drenched in sweat, and he would practice endlessly.

"It made you feel like playing," Randy Brecker told me. "There's a phrase, 'junkie time,'" he said. "You kind of end up playing behind the beat—it's just a little lag—and it's a great way to play."

In a couple of years, after Capitol Records and Nelson Riddle resuscitated his recording career, Frank Sinatra would come to the same conclusion independent of drugs (but strongly influenced by the singing of Billie Holiday and the playing of Lester Young): if he placed his vocals just a bit behind the beat, listeners would unconsciously feel a continual cycle of tension and resolution, something akin to sexual pleasure. And he would sound cool and masterful in the bargain.

Miles was cool in the jazz sense, but in almost every respect he was anything but masterful. He had let his appearance go: he'd stopped processing his hair, the five dollars per treatment being money for which he had another, more urgent use. His clothes were often less than clean; his suits were wrinkled. It was a terrible cycle: the worse he looked, the worse he felt about himself; the worse he felt about himself, the less inclined he was to do anything about it. Added to this was the fact that he was all but unemployable on a steady basis—Oscar Goodstein, Birdland's manager, was the only club operator who would hire him more than once. Like all jazz musicians since the beginning of jazz, he played dances when he had to—and now he had to. "Miles used to do these dance jobs in the Audubon [Ballroom] . . . way up on Broadway," John Coltrane remembered. "And I think on one of the jobs he had Sonny Rollins, and Bud [Powell], and Art Blakey, forgot the bassman, and myself." One hell of a dance band. It was a Sunday afternoon, March 11, 1951. In all that year Miles was able to work just six or seven weeks.

High or junk sick, he blew around the city like a tumbleweed. He lived for a while at Stan Levey's place on Long Island, then he didn't. He bounced from hotel to hotel—the America again; the University on Twentieth Street. He ran around town with the nineteen-year-old Jackie McLean. Miles was six years older than McLean, vastly more experienced, with a name in the music business and, to some extent, in the world at large. But hanging with Jackie brought out Davis's inner teenager: when they weren't shooting dope together, the pair took in Forty-second Street movies, watched the boxers at Stillman's gym, and—most fun when they were high—rode the subway convulsing with laughter at the corny shoes and clothing of their fellow passengers.

Meanwhile, his music career was barely alive. Late that summer *DownBeat* reviewed two more releases from Miles's January Prestige session, "Down" and "Whispering." The reviewer called them

> two very bad sides from Miles. . . . Sonny Rollins, Benny Green, John Lewis, Percy Heath, and Roy Haynes give aid. But no one seems at all interested in playing, and a completely lifeless and uninspired performance results. Release of items like this can do neither the artist nor the label much good.

Yet somewhere inside the disheveled junkie an ember of pride glowed fiercely. Miles was determined to do better on his upcoming second Prestige session in October—all the more so since Weinstock had told him that on this date the label would be using a new technology, microgroove, and that Miles would be one of the first jazz musicians recorded with it. By contrast with the old 78 rpm discs, which could only contain one three-minute song per side, each side of the new ten-inch 33⅓ rpm discs could hold up to fifteen minutes of music. With the new format, players would be able to show their stuff as they'd only been able to do in live performance.

He practiced, using whatever concentrative powers heroin allowed him. He assembled a band—Rollins, Blakey, Tommy Potter, Walter Bishop, and Jackie McLean—and rehearsed it through a song list: a pair of originals by George Shearing ("Conception") and McLean ("Dig"), as well as three of his own ("Out of the Blue," "Denial," and "Bluing"), and two standards ("My Old Flame" and "It's Only a Paper Moon").

The session, on October 5 at Apex Studios, in Steinway Hall on West Fifty-seventh Street, was a highly fraught occasion, and not just for Miles. Jackie McLean, who had never recorded before, was a nervous wreck—and to make matters worse, his idol Charlie Parker had stopped by to observe from the engineer's booth. (Charles Mingus also showed up and played uncredited on "Conception.") But once Bird had reassured McLean that he sounded fine, the young altoist settled down and fulfilled Miles's faith in him.

As did everyone else on the date. Once again, Sonny Rollins, just eight months older than McLean, played with amazingly mature, free-swinging virtuosity. And Miles redeemed himself—or at least believed he had. The sextet recorded two LPs worth of music that day: the first, *Miles Davis: The New Sounds*, Davis's first album as a leader, was released a couple of months later, containing two tunes per eleven-minute-plus side: "Conception" and "Dig" on side 1, and the two ballads "My Old Flame" and "It's Only a Paper Moon" on the flip.

The session inspired both supporters and detractors in quantity. Miles felt he'd recorded his best work in a long time on the date. (He was especially proud of his melodic ballad-playing on "My Old Flame.") It's true that the session has strong links to the recent past: "Conception" is very similar to "Deception," a nonet recording of the previous year; and the sheer velocity of "Denial" is nothing if not bebop-ish. Yet in the unashamed lyricism of "Dig" and "Out of the Blue," something altogether new can be heard.

But the reviews were less than positive. When Prestige released the seven-and-a-half-minute "Dig" as a two-sided 78, *DownBeat* gave it just two stars, opining oddly that "Miles, altoist Jack [sic] McLean, tenor

Sonny Rollins are not helped a bit by the rude, unswinging drumming of Art Blakey." And when the label released its second Miles LP, *Miles Davis: Blue Period*, containing "Bluing" and "Out of the Blue" from the October date (the former, logging in at almost ten minutes, occupying the entire A-side), along with the unfortunate "Blue Room" from the January session, the jazz journal said:

> *Blue Period* is the title of this LP, and it was certainly that for us, as we thought back to Miles' great Capitol sides and reflected how sadly that great promise, that exceptional talent, has been betrayed. . . .

But where *DownBeat*'s reviewer, compelled to stick to the sad narrative of Miles's lost promise, heard lethargy and sloppiness, modern ears can hear compositional beauty, liberated by the new long-play format. This is Miles stretching out, rising toward a new kind of greatness. One pictures Bob Weinstock listening raptly in the engineer's booth (along with the session's official producer, the twenty-two-year-old jazz journalist Ira Gitler), then suddenly realizing almost ten minutes into the entrancing groove that it has to end: you can imagine Weinstock, behind the glass, twirling his hand in a wrap-it-up gesture, Miles signaling his musicians to bring it to a close—and Blakey, not wanting the bliss to stop, puckishly ka-chinging his ride cymbal right through, and on past, the final notes. At which point, Miles speaks, right on the record, telling Blakey, "Hard for [us] to *end* this, man—you know that, right?"

As startling as the unusual ending is the sound of Miles's youthful voice, before the trademark rasp set in.

One wonders why Weinstock left the talk on the record. As a producer, he would develop a reputation for avoiding session rehearsals and extra takes—a money-saving policy for sure, but he claimed it was to maintain artistic freshness. In keeping this imperfect "Bluing" on permanent record, Weinstock was able to preserve the beauty of the piece and have a poke at the critics at the same time. Change was happening no matter who objected: *New Sounds* was more than a catchy title. Bebop was cooling, and Miles, hobbled as he was, was inventing what would come next.

Art Pepper, 1925–1982
Ernie Henry, 1926–1957
John Coltrane, 1926–1967
Hampton Hawes, 1928–1977
Bill Evans, 1929–1980

Mostly, though, he was suffering: "in a deep fog, high all the time and pimping women for money to support my habit." Thinking he might be able to sweat his way out of his addiction, he asked a trainer at Gleason's Gym, a former prizefighter named Bobby McQuillar, if he would work with him. The streetwise McQuillar saw at once that Miles was high even as he made the request. Disgustedly, the trainer told him to go back home to Illinois and get clean. Once again, Miles called his long-suffering father.

As Miles tells it, he was playing a gig one night at Le Downbeat on West Fifty-fourth Street when he suddenly saw Dr. Davis standing in the middle of the audience like a ghost or a figure in a dream, wearing a raincoat and staring at him balefully. Father and son caught a train back to East St. Louis that night, Miles feeling "like a little boy again going with his daddy." He swore up and down to his father that this time he was going to give up dope for good.

He went to the farm in Millstadt: he rode horses and breathed fresh air. But he quickly grew bored—he always did—and, as withdrawal sickness began to overtake him, boredom turned to misery. Easily enough, he found a connection in St. Louis and began shooting up again, paying for the drugs with small sums borrowed from his father, to whom he swore he'd stopped using. He hooked up with Jimmy Forrest, the great, bluesy tenor saxist and a fellow addict: they played gigs together at a city club called the Barrelhouse, and scored and shot up together, too. Miles found a new friend and source of ready cash, a "young, fine, rich white girl whose parents owned a shoe company." But his ever-hungry habit demanded even more money, so he went to his father again.

And this time, having been tipped off by Miles's sister, Dorothy, that he was using again, Dr. Davis turned him down. Miles proceeded to have a screaming tantrum right in the dental office, cursing his father out as he never had before. Calmly, Dr. Davis made a phone call, and two large men materialized and dragged Miles off to a jail in Belleville, Illinois.

He stayed there a week, furious and miserably sick. When he got out, his father explained to Miles that he was in desperate need of help, and that he, Dr. Davis, was going to take him to the federal facility for drug addiction in Lexington, Kentucky. Exhausted, Miles agreed to go. Dr. Davis and his second wife drove him, making the six-hour road trip in the dentist's new Cadillac.

But when they arrived, Miles balked at volunteering himself for incarceration. He hated any kind of jail, and even though Lexington was an extraordinarily humane and innovative facility, Miles was too sick and mistrustful to give himself over to it. At this point he hadn't used in two weeks—maybe he'd kicked, he reasoned. Dr. Davis was skeptical and worried, but his hands were tied: his son was no longer a minor. And so they went their separate ways, the dentist and his wife back to Illinois and Miles returning to New York to pick up where he'd left off.

Chet Baker, 1929–1988
Hank Mobley, 1930–1986
Dick Twardzik, 1931–1955
Sonny Clark, 1931–1963
Wynton Kelly, 1931–1971

"Miles in the past year has seen his career slip away from him while his imitators have been progressing," Leonard Feather wrote in the London *Melody Maker* in February 1952. When Miles remembered this period, he broadened the focus: "A lot of white critics kept talking about all these white jazz musicians, imitators of *us*" [italics mine]—the likes of Stan Getz, Dave Brubeck, Kai Winding, Lee Konitz, Lennie Tristano, and Gerry Mulligan—"like they was gods or something. And some of them white guys were junkies like we were, but wasn't nobody writing about that like they was writing about us."

But he saved his special rancor for one white trumpeter (and fellow addict):

> What bothered me more than anything was that all the critics were starting to talk about Chet Baker in Gerry Mulligan's band like he was the second coming of Jesus Christ. . . . Now, I knew that among all the younger players, Clifford [Brown] was head and shoulders above the rest, at least in my opinion he was. But Chet Baker? Man, I just couldn't see it. The critics were beginning to treat me like I was one of the old guys, you know, like I was just a memory—and a bad memory at that—and I was only twenty-six years old in 1952. And sometimes I was even thinking of myself as a has-been.

Gary McFarland, 1933–1971
Paul Chambers, 1935–1969
Bobby Timmons, 1935–1974
Woody Shaw, 1944–1989

8   Take off

Shit took me three years to break it," Miles told me, spritz-
ing his luxuriant curls with an atomizer. We were in his
suite in the Essex House, in the early spring of 1989.

"How'd you do it?" I asked.

"I went out to my father's and shut the door and that was it."

Well, but—there were those three years.

HEROIN DIDN'T INCAPACITATE MILES DAVIS IN 1952 AND '53—ALTHOUGH,
as Peter Losin notes, "his addiction made him unreliable, and his contract
with Prestige had not been renewed. He had no working band."

He bounced north from Lexington in April. That week's *DownBeat*
carried a strange little item: "Miles Davis back in town (25 lbs heavier)
and working Birdland as a single." It's hard to imagine twenty-five extra
pounds on Miles's small frame, but maybe those country breakfasts in
Millstadt had plumped him up. The pickup gigs at Birdland were with a

female leader, the Philadelphia pianist Beryl Booker. And it isn't quite true that he had no working band in all of 1952: the engagements with Booker were successful enough that Oscar Goodstein offered Miles a week at Birdland at the beginning of May. For seven nights of that year he had a sextet: Jackie McLean on alto, Don Elliott on vibes, Gil Coggins on piano, Connie Henry on bass, and Connie Kay on drums.

Miles carried forward two of those players, McLean and Coggins, to his first Blue Note session, on May 9. The record date pointed up the paradoxes of his life. It allowed him to work with great musicians—he'd also hired J. J. Johnson, Oscar Pettiford, and Kenny Clarke—and Miles mostly played beautifully: on "Dear Old Stockholm," a Swedish folk melody jazzified by Stan Getz, on Dizzy's composition "Woody 'n' You," and on Jerome Kern's powerfully melancholy ballad "Yesterdays." He was continuing to make lyrical and poignant new inroads into post-bop jazz—yet this was his only record date in 1952.

That spring Sid Torin, who'd relocated to Boston, put together a tour he called "The Symphony Sid All Stars," and Miles, without much of anything else happening, signed on. The tour was a mixed bag, a slightly motley and, behind the scenes, somewhat disharmonious affair. On the one hand, it was a couple of months' steady work for the musicians involved. On the other, Sid, who through his jazz broadcasts from Birdland and elsewhere had become something of a celebrity across much of the Northeast and Midwest, was very much in charge. Because, after a few personnel shifts, all the musicians were Black, there was the uncomfortable (to the musicians, not to white audiences) sense of the white ringmaster bossing the help around.

Like other Black musicians, Miles had mixed feelings about Torin. Sid was, in the style of those radio days, a smooth and sonorous DJ—a slick and phony character on the face of it, but also, as Miles has pointed out, a man who was passionately promoting this life-changing music and bringing it into people's homes. Loving bebop and identifying with those who played it, he'd perfected a line of hipster patter to introduce the band

and announce each tune (and he also walked the walk: a marijuana bust in New York may have been part of the reason he left town).

As would be the case with many rock disc jockeys five or six years thence, Symphony Sid felt himself somehow *part of the music*. But on this tour especially, what he really was was the Man. Receipts were rich: "Sid is convinced of the salability, let alone the durability of modern jazz, when properly booked and presented," read a dispatch from the tour's first stop, Boston. "And his grosses prove it."

His grosses. In his memoir Miles goes on at aggrieved length about how much money Torin was pocketing as both booking agent and announcer ("and, he thought, star"), and how little he was paying the musicians. Tension built as the tour traveled from Boston to New Haven, Toronto, and Atlantic City; Youngstown and Cleveland; the Apollo and Le Downbeat in New York. Tensions also built within the band: in Ohio, where heroin was scarce, Miles and Jimmy Heath were often absent while trying to score or getting high. Sometimes the rest of the band had to start without them. Clarke, Jackson, and Percy Heath made their unhappiness known, often and loudly, to Miles.

And as the tour was ending in New York, J. J. Johnson spoke up to Torin about money the emcee owed him—fifty dollars, not much today but a lot then. Torin fluffed him off. A few days later the syndicated gossip columnist Dorothy Kilgallen let the whole country know what happened next: "Disc jockey Symphony Sid took the bop treatment the hard way the other night—right on the jaw. The solid sender was trombonist Jay-jay Johnson." Miles's account was more graphic: "J. J. just up and knocked Sid's false teeth out of his mouth; they went skipping and sliding across the floor."

Furious, Torin brought in some gangster cronies to put a hurt on Johnson, but when Miles and the other players stood beside the trombonist, Sid calmed down and paid up. Then the tour was over, and Miles was back to scrambling. Between the end of the tour in early August and the end of the year, he played in public exactly once, at a midnight jam session at the Howard Theatre in Washington. In *DownBeat*'s year-end poll, he came in second on his instrument to the Canadian trumpeter Maynard Ferguson, a member of Stan Kenton's all-white band.

HIS ADDICTION HAD ONLY GOTTEN WORSE, BUT FOR WHATEVER REASONS—perhaps because the worst publicity had receded—1953 was a busier year for Miles. There were club dates at Le Downbeat in New York and the Tijuana in Baltimore, and Bob Weinstock had come around and offered him a new, nonexclusive contract—at around the same time as Blue Note's Alfred Lion asked him to record. That year Miles led four recording dates (which was four times as many as the year before): three for Prestige and one for Blue Note. Peter Losin calls the sessions "desultory," meaning, I suppose, that lacking a working band, Miles wasn't building a repertory or artistic consistency; yet despite everything—and there was a lot of everything—his confidence in his playing was growing.

The year got off to an inauspicious start with the chaotic Prestige session of January 30. Playing for Miles on the date were Sonny Rollins, Walter Bishop, Percy Heath, Philly Joe Jones (recording with Davis for the first time), and Charlie Parker, who supplied the chaos, having recently switched from heroin to gin after his trumpet player, Red Rodney, had been arrested and imprisoned for heroin possession. Parker, under contract to Mercury, billed himself as "Charlie Chan" on the date, and once again played tenor instead of alto. Ira Gitler, who produced, recalled that while familiarizing himself with his new horn, Bird drank a full fifth of gin and promptly fell asleep.

Miles's recollection was that Parker so infuriated him with his unprofessionalism—not to mention acting as though he, not Miles, was leading the session, and chiding him in his fake British accent—that Miles began playing badly, and then, when Gitler called him on it, started to pack up his trumpet and leave. At which point Bird snapped out of his stupor and said, "Ah, come on, Miles, let's play some music." And so, Miles remembered, "we played some real good stuff after that."

He kept playing good stuff, even as the other kind of stuff continued to consume his life. Of the April Blue Note session, Miles mainly recalled that he and Jimmy Heath began feeling junk sick and contrived to leave the studio to score by telling Alfred Lion an elementary-school-level tale: that Heath needed to buy some reeds, and Miles had to help him carry them. As Davis points out, a box of reeds isn't any bigger than a bar of soap. In any case, Lion let them go, Miles not knowing whether Lion believed him or was just going along with the ruse to get some music recorded. "So we were higher than a motherfucker when we made that record," Miles and Troupe write.

And it's a beautiful record. On "Tempus Fugit," a dark but fast-paced number by Bud Powell, Davis's high-velocity staccato runs are pinpoint accurate. And two ballads from the session, "Enigma" and "I Waited for You," are achingly lovely; Miles's unmuted tone is rich and full. A newspaper-column review of the Blue Note album, *Man with a Horn*, tossed him a bland bone: "Not his best by any means, but it's still Miles, and he swings." I think it was better than that. I think it was a time when people simply didn't know what to make of Miles Davis, as he rose toward the light from dark depths.

IN EARLY 1953 MILES RETURNED TO HIS FATHER'S FARM TO TRY TO KICK his habit again—and failed again. In May he filled in at Birdland for Dizzy, who was in Toronto playing the legendary Massey Hall concert with Bird, Bud Powell, Charles Mingus, and Max Roach. Davis found himself accompanying a comic bebop vocalist named Joe Carroll, who tickled Dizzy's funny bone but only reminded Miles of "that clowning shit [Gillespie] used to do for all them white folks." Yet Miles needed the work, and his habit needed the money. A couple of nights later he was standing on the sidewalk between shows, high, dirty and disheveled, when Roach walked up, told him he was "looking good," and put a couple of new hundred-dollar bills in his jacket pocket.

As high as he was, Miles felt acutely ashamed. Fastidious by nature, exquisitely attuned to every article of clothing he wore, he was suddenly aware of how far he had fallen. And here was Roach, a close friend, looking clean and sharp and together, trying to help him out but also signaling pity for him, and, whether consciously or not, showing superiority as well. Instead of taking the money to a dealer, Miles took a bus back to Illinois.

Once again Dr. Davis welcomed the prodigal home, and once again the cycle kicked in: hope and warmth quickly congealed into boredom. Miles had friends in Illinois, but he was more aware than ever how much he had changed and they hadn't. Soon he was shooting up again—then, late in the summer, Max Roach called.

Roach was driving cross-country, he said, to take the drummer Shelly Manne's place in Howard Rumsey's Lighthouse All-Stars. The Lighthouse was a Polynesian-style bar in Hermosa Beach, on the Pacific in Los Angeles's South Bay section, where Rumsey, a bassist with an entrepreneurial bent, had started a band in 1949. In short order the Sunday concerts there, with a rotating cast of musicians, became a hub of the growing West Coast jazz scene. Rumsey was white, but from the start he welcomed Black musicians from Central Avenue clubs—and points beyond—to the All-Stars. Roach, who was traveling with Charles Mingus, asked Miles if they could stop and see him in East St. Louis; Miles invited them to stay with him in Millstadt.

He would have still been smarting from Roach's noblesse oblige in front of Birdland—and to underline his prosperity, the drummer pulled up at the farm in his shiny new Oldsmobile—but here, in his father's affluence, was a way for Miles to regain face. Everything about Dr. Davis's rural homestead amazed Roach and Mingus: its grand size, its plentiful livestock, its resident cook and maid. Miles had always carried himself with a certain air; now the drummer and bassist understood better where it came from. The three musicians stayed up all night talking jazz, and when Roach and Mingus left the next day, Miles went with them. He spent the whole drive west listening to the voluble bassist hold forth about the evils of white people, animal rights, or anything else that crossed his mind, now and then breaking the monotony by getting into heated arguments with him.

Davis spent a couple of months on the Coast, sitting in occasionally with the All-Stars—and, for the first time, meeting his nemesis, the square-jawed, baby-faced, endlessly photogenic overnight sensation Chet Baker. It wasn't just the critics who'd been talking about Baker: when Charlie Parker traveled to Los Angeles the previous spring, he'd selected Baker over numerous auditioning trumpeters to accompany him on a two-week stand at the Tiffany Club.

In person, Chet proved surprisingly agreeable, especially when it became clear that Miles was his idol. The young trumpeter (twenty-three years old to Miles's twenty-seven) expressed proper embarrassment about having come in ahead of Dizzy Gillespie in the *DownBeat* poll—from which both Miles and Clifford Brown had been left out altogether. "I didn't hold it against him personally, although I was mad at the people who picked him," Miles said. "Chet was a nice enough guy, cool and a good player. But both him and me knew that he had copied a lot of shit from me."

True enough. Yet this damning with faintish praise can actually be seen as a high tribute, the edgy giant guarding his flanks, in much the same manner that Miles would diminish Clifford Brown to Wallace Roney a quarter century later. Baker had an amazing ear and musical memory: he *could* play. And he was similar to Davis in many ways—both were slim and handsome and wore clothes beautifully; both were junkies. Both were fond of dogs and powerful cars, and both were supremely attractive to women. Baker could also do something that Miles could not: he was an affecting, even haunting ballad singer, with a light, boyish voice that— much like the tone of Miles Davis's trumpet—conveyed ardor and distance at the same time.

WHILE IN L.A., MILES ALSO MET FRANCES TAYLOR, A STRIKINGLY BEAUTIful young dancer in Katherine Dunham's troupe who six years later would become his first wife. There was electricity between them at first sight, but Taylor was also much in demand: she was seeing both "a rich white guy" and Sammy Davis, Jr., who had just put her in a TV pilot he was working on. Then Miles left town.

His memoir describes a fistfight with a racist bartender at the Lighthouse as the inciting incident that led to his kicking heroin for good—but the reality seems to have been more nuanced. Three days after Labor Day, Miles arrived at San Francisco's Downbeat with his mouthpiece in the wallet pocket of his suit jacket, but without a horn—not hard to guess why. He was there to fill in for Gerry Mulligan, who was in jail on narcotics charges. Joining the pianist Kenny Drew's trio (Art Farmer's twin brother Addison on bass, George Walker on drums), Davis stayed on for four weeks, then went to Chicago, where he played the Nob Hill club for another month. Then something, we'll never know what, sent him back home one more time.

Miles's accounts of a climactic withdrawal from heroin in Millstadt come across variously as overwritten, highly romanticized, or as incoherent as the fever dream it surely was. Locked in a second-floor bedroom in the guesthouse at Millstadt for a week or more, he writhed, sweated, hallucinated. His description of the episode to me in 1989, fragmentary and seeming to run backward and sideways in time, conveyed its chaos and terror but left me with one lasting question:

JK: How'd you do it?

MD: I went out to my father's and, uh . . . shut the door and that was it.

JK: Mhm.

MD: Just . . . I smell like chicken soup. . . . I started to jump out the window but it . . . it was too far down.

JK: Mhm.

MD: I said, I'd knock myself out, but I might break a leg. And I could hear his footsteps—he ran a colonial house on like about 265 acres.

JK: Mhm.

MD: And I went up—there's like a . . . master bedroom over here, after you come up the stairs. And the same thing on this side. Two rooms. So I just shut the door.

JK: Mhm.

MD: You know. And the maid would ask me, [calling] *Junior, you want breakfast?* I said, *Fuck you!* [*Blech!*] *Breakfast?* I drink some orange juice, that shit come right up. But it was . . . [*coughing/retching sound*].

That was all. And I wondered for years: chicken soup?

Then, decades later, I found a *Rolling Stone* interview with Miles that had been published in 1969. The syntax was suspiciously perfect, but this story of the ordeal jibed with the oblique, almost abstract tale he'd told me—and cleared up the mystery of the chicken soup:

> I laid down and stared at the ceiling and cursed everybody I didn't like, I was kicking it the hard way. It was like having a bad case of flu only worse. I lay in a cold sweat, my nose and eyes ran. I threw up everything I tried to eat. My pores opened up and I smelled like chicken soup. Then it was over.

The romanticized account in his memoir once more features a moving speech by a wise, big-hearted Dr. Davis: "Miles, if it was a woman that was torturing you, then I could tell you to get another woman or leave that one alone. But this drug thing, I can't do nothing for you, son, but give you my love and support. The rest of it you got to do for yourself."

And the book has another stirring scene when the ordeal is done:

> Then one day it was over, just like that. . . . I felt better, good and
> pure. I walked outside into the clean, sweet air over to my father's
> house and when he saw me he had this big smile on his face and
> we just hugged each other and cried. He knew that I had beat it.

The problem was, he hadn't.

WORRIED ABOUT RETURNING DIRECTLY TO THE BIG APPLE'S TEMPTA-
tions, Miles decided to give himself a buffer by spending some time in
Detroit, where the drugs were scarcer and weaker—Philly Joe Jones famously remarked that for all Motor City heroin was worth, you might as
well have saved your money and bought a Hershey bar—and where, in the
winter of 1953–54, there was a dynamic jazz scene, including such starry
local musicians as Donald Byrd, Betty Carter, Tommy Flanagan, Curtis
Fuller, Barry Harris, Elvin Jones, Thad Jones, and Yusef Lateef. He went
to work at the Blue Bird Inn, a small club northwest of downtown, sitting
in with the house band, led by the saxophonist Billy Mitchell and including Elvin on drums, Flanagan or Harris on piano, and assorted bassists.
The Blue Bird was Black owned and operated, and for the most part,
Black patronized. The manager was a local numbers runner named Clarence Eddins, and rumor had it that Miles was so down and out that he
was working for drugs.

Carl Hill, the club's doorman, recalled:

> When Miles first came to the Blue Bird . . . he was strung out and
> living in Sunnie Wilson's hotel on Grand River and the Boule-
> vard. . . . It was in the winter and Miles walked from the hotel to
> the Blue Bird, and the joint was packed; everybody was waiting for
> Miles Davis. So when he came in he had on this grimy white shirt

and a navy blue sweater and Clarence told him to go home and put on a tie. . . . So Miles went outside and took a shoelace out of his shoe and tied it up under his shirt and said: "How do you like this, boss?" and went on the bandstand and played.

"Miles' existence in Detroit was especially chaotic even within a life that was never particularly orderly," John Szwed writes. "Sleeping late in the day in a darkened room, eating virtually nothing, drinking cognac, he spent much of the time waiting, usually for his daily care package from his man Freddie Frue—'Frue with the Do.'"

"It was hard to kick my habit," Miles writes, "because of guys like him and because I was weak."

There's a famous Miles story from this period: Max Roach and Clifford Brown were in Detroit, playing, depending on who was telling the tale, either Baker's Keyboard Lounge (still in business today) or the Crystal Bar & Grill. Roach, Brown, and the rest of the quintet—Bud Powell's younger brother Richie on piano, Harold Land on tenor, George Morrow at the bass—had just played a blazing set, torn the house down, when the door opened and Miles walked in out of the pouring rain, coat collar turned up. According to the painter and journalist Richard "Prophet" Jennings,

He went over to Clifford Brown and asked for Clifford's trumpet. He reached in his inside coat pocket, took out his mouthpiece, put it in Clifford's trumpet. . . . Now, the stage was still on fire. It was still burning. . . . Miles got up on that stand with the support of the piano to hold his ass up. He put that motherfucking trumpet to his mouth and that motherfucker played "My Funny Valentine." Clifford Brown stood up there and looked at him and just shook his head. . . . That little black motherfucker, behind all that fire, he made people cry. . . . When he got through playing and took his mouthpiece out, he put it back in his coat, gave Brownie his trumpet, and split. That's what he did. I saw this. I was *there*!

———

SOMEHOW, SOMEWHERE BETWEEN DETROIT AND MANHATTAN, TO WHICH he returned in late February of 1954, Miles kicked heroin for good. If there were any *Snake Pit*–like scenes of withdrawal horror or sweet breezes of rapturous redemption, they're lost to history. Dr. Davis and his farm were not involved. Miles claims to have been positively influenced by Detroit musicians, so many of them clean, so many looking up to him; he also cites the inspiring example of "one of the few idols I ever had," the stylish, charismatic, and thoroughly professional middleweight champion Sugar Ray Robinson: "Sugar Ray was the hero-image that I carried in my mind. It was him that made me think that I was strong enough to deal with New York City again. And it was his example that pulled me through some real tough days."

Sick as he'd been in Detroit, he'd managed to play a lot: his chops were solid. Feeling "strong, both musically and physically . . . ready for anything," he moved into the Arlington Hotel, on Twenty-fifth Street near Fifth Avenue, and called Bob Weinstock and Alfred Lion. He was off drugs, he told them, and he wanted to make records again. They were happy to hear it.

New York seemed different to Miles—over the five months he'd been absent, somehow the scene had clicked over into something new. He claimed in his memoir that Bird was in eclipse: "all fucked up—fat, tired, playing badly when he bothered to show up for anything." But in fact Parker was on the West Coast at the beginning of that year, on tour with Stan Kenton, in something called the Jazz Festival of Modern American Music. In March, shortly after the tour ended, Bird's three-year-old daughter Pree, who'd been born with cystic fibrosis, died in New York. Shattered, Parker came back east and went into a slow downward spiral.

In the meantime, everyone seemed to be talking about cool jazz: about George Shearing and Lennie Tristano and Chet Baker, and about John Lewis's ultra-cool Modern Jazz Quartet, which had recently finished its first stand at the club named after Bird. The (ironically enough) horn-free

MJQ was changing the paradigm: no solos, no showmanship, just four ultra-serious young Black men in dark suits and dark ties (Lewis on piano, Milt Jackson on vibes, Percy Heath on bass, Connie Kay at the drums), playing jazz originals and American Songbook standards in a style infused with European classical counterpoint—quietly swinging, never dangerous, and at such low volume that the four often had to play even more softly to embarrass audiences into listening.

Miles wanted to return to quartet format himself, picking up where he'd left off on his last Prestige session the previous May. And from the moment he checked in at the Arlington, he had a pianist in mind—a fellow hotel resident, Horace Silver, a twenty-five-year-old of Cape Verdean ancestry. Silver, who'd been recording as a leader and as a sideman since 1952, had an upright piano in his room, and Miles began to spend time with him, listening and demonstrating ideas of his own.

Silver's first album, Blue Note's *New Faces New Sounds (Introducing the Horace Silver Trio)*, had presented an astonishingly self-possessed young pianist who seemed to have leaped fully formed from the respective brows of Thelonious Monk and Monk's great protégé Bud Powell. Powell, sometimes called the Charlie Parker of the piano, could, like Bird, improvise brilliantly at high speed: the literary critic Harold Bloom put Powell's 1951 recording of his (Powell's) percussive and urgent "Un Poco Loco" on his short list of the American Sublime in the twentieth century. And on his first album, just a year after that, Horace Silver recorded a hard-driving tune of his own, "Safari," that came close to rivaling "Un Poco Loco." Silver could also play beautifully on ballads; he could even sound like Monk; but his greatest enthusiasm seemed to lie in producing a propulsive, minor-toned funk all his own, a sound on top of which Miles eagerly wanted to play.

Davis's Blue Note recording session of March 6, 1954, was his first record date for almost ten months and his first time working in the Hackensack, New Jersey, home studio of the soon to be legendary optometrist turned recording engineer Rudy Van Gelder. John Lewis had been the pianist on the May 1953 quartet recording; now that Horace Silver was on the piano bench (Percy Heath was back on bass; Art Blakey replaced Max Roach), Miles went in a different direction altogether.

The first tune recorded on the date was Miles's composition "Take Off." The tune was based on the chords of the 1950 nonet number "Deception," which Miles's sextet replayed the following year, in head-arrangement form, as "Conception." On the nonet version, Miles is listed as the composer, whereas "Conception" is credited to George Shearing. To nonprofessional ears, "Take Off" sounds less like a tune than a beguiling exercise related to the spiky harmonic experiments of George Russell and Gil Evans: music for musicians. In Miles's good hands, the song has rhythmic drive, verve, and cheerful charm, but—again to nonprofessional ears—it presents a puzzle. It isn't just noise; it is clearly up to something as a song, but what? At several junctures, for a few breathless seconds, the rhythm section seems to stand in place: as Silver and Heath play a repeated three-note figure—*bong bong bong, bong bong bong*—Miles blows along on top, *fast* but with entrancing gentleness, following "Deception"/"Conception"'s chord progression—which follows no harmonic scheme familiar to amateur ears. Again, this is not a tune like "All the Things You Are" or "Blue Moon"; rather, it is its own thing, the further assertion of something new, something taking off into uncharted territory. "If no one had understood it before," Szwed writes,

> it was becoming clear that Davis was rebuilding the jazz trumpet tradition from a different set of principles from those that guided the hot players of the past. There was a softness to his attack on "Take-off" and a considered approach to note choice new to trumpet playing, one that found him landing on unexpected notes again and again, all of it at a high speed of execution.

Those *bong bong bong* interludes are known in jazz as *pedal point*: a repeated note, typically in the bass, during which at least one dissonant harmony is sounded in the other parts. Szwed calls them "moments of harmonic and rhythmic suspension, the trumpet soloing over a repeated single chord—a device somewhere between an old-time break, an interlude, and what would soon be called modality in jazz. Jazz had from its beginnings hinted at what might happen if the melody broke loose from harmony."

Free from heroin (though not from drugs: liquid cocaine, which Miles claimed wasn't addictive, helped propel him and his musicians through long record dates and late-night gigs), Davis went on a blistering recording run in 1954, leading five sessions for Prestige between March and December, the first (and the first under his new contract) just nine days after the Blue Note date, and with the same players, Silver, Heath, and Blakey, at the Beltone Studio in Midtown. Miles led the quartet exuberantly through the first two numbers—"Four," an upbeat Eddie Vinson composition that Davis would continue to play live for the next decade (and claim as his own), and Burton Lane and Yip Harburg's standard-to-be "Old Devil Moon"—but when the third, a slow blues, bogged down for some reason, Jules Colomby, a young wannabe trumpet player and part-time Prestige employee in the studio, suggested turning out the lights, with the result that "the grooviest blues you ever heard came out of there. It was like making music by the light of a cigarette." But what really made it groovy was Miles's superbly assured and tasty playing, "his command of phrasing and tone," Losin writes, "in striking contrast to the Prestige dates of the last couple years." The power of this deep blues—eventually titled "Blue Haze"—came not just from his musicianship but from his new strength: the power to draw from his Blue Period, rather than be trapped in it.

And strength built on strength. Miles was back at Van Gelder's in early April, this time with a quintet—Silver and Heath still on piano and bass, but now with Kenny Clarke on drums and a brilliant young Charlie Parker imitator named Dave Schildkraut on alto sax. There was nothing arbitrary about these personnel changes. Miles was feeling his potency as a painter with sound: he'd determined that the palette of this session would be of a certain softness. He himself would play every tune with a cup mute, and Clarke, whose touch with brushes Davis loved, would use them throughout, even on the upbeat numbers. And Schildkraut wasn't just stunt casting: he really did sound a lot like Bird, only with a softer, sweeter sound.

The quintet laid down four tunes: Miles's "Solar" (which he would often play live later, but only recorded this once) plus three standards, Gene de Paul and Don Raye's weeper "You Don't Know What Love Is," Walter Donaldson and Gus Kahn's "Love Me or Leave Me," and de Paul and Raye's (and Patricia Johnston's) great "I'll Remember April."

The immortal seven-minute-fifty-second recording of "April" begins with a clever, perky, Chinese-sounding figure played by Miles and Schildkraut, and then it takes flight. Losin: "Davis's two-chorus solo is chock full of ideas. Silver's two choruses are, too—'hard bop' is here already.* Schildkraut's two choruses are Bird-like gems, but without Parker's occasional harshness of tone. Silver takes another chorus, borrowing some phrases from Bud Powell. Heath takes the bridge, and Davis has another chorus on the way out." The number closes with a bookend repeat of that same Chinese-sounding figure.

And on this afternoon in Hackensack it *is* April, the springtime of Miles's resurrection.

HE WAS ON FIRE. SWITCHING OUT SCHILDKRAUT FOR LUCKY THOMPSON, a tenorist with a big, warm tone who could play everything from swing to R&B to bebop, Miles took the quintet to Birdland for the latter half of April, doing good business and earning strong reviews. In the meantime, he sat with Horace Silver at Silver's upright in the Arlington and worked out sounds for the next Prestige date, which he wanted to be as forceful as the last one had been velvety. On the twenty-ninth he returned to Van

---

*Mysteriously, at 3:26 of the song, the pianist slips in a seeming quote of Lerner and Loewe's "With a Little Bit of Luck"—two years before *My Fair Lady*.

Gelder's with Thompson, Silver, Heath, Clarke—and, to add an exclamation point, the always dynamic J. J. Johnson on trombone. The only thing he didn't have with him, according to Jules Colomby, who was once again present, was his trumpet.

It's unclear why Miles hadn't brought his horn along. Had he pawned it for the umpteenth time? In any case, Weinstock, who'd already paid a substantial sum to set up the session, "turned white" at the news, Colomby recalled.

> So I said to Miles, "I've got a trumpet in the trunk of my car. It's an old Buescher I've had since I was 13." Miles said, "Bring it in." I walked to the car knowing the horn was full of leaks, and I thought, "How in the world is he going to play it?" Miles warmed up by just going over the valves with his fingers, to see if they were loose.

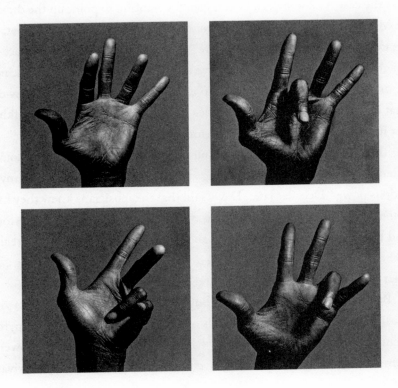

A note on Miles's fingers: they were extraordinary. In 1986 Irving Penn took a series of black-and-white photographs of his hands, for Miles's album *Tutu*.

Colomby's account continues:

> Then he counted off the tempo to "Walkin'" without saying a word. It was just a blues, and everyone knew the tune. Miles played and I couldn't believe how beautiful he could make that trumpet sound. Forget about take two, it was one of the best records he'd ever made. The band just went right into "Blue 'n' Boogie," an uptempo blues that Dizzy wrote.

Losin says the recording order was the opposite: that "Blue 'n' Boogie," a breathlessly fast, eight-minute-plus blues combining bebop-ish fire and spontaneity with Silverian funk, came first, and "Walkin'" second. If this was the case, Colomby can be forgiven for wanting to point up the drama of Miles recording a historic number on a crummy borrowed trumpet.

Unlike "Blue 'n' Boogie," "Walkin'" proceeded at an ambulatory pace—for thirteen minutes and twenty-five seconds, room enough for all kinds of drama. Lucky Thompson was so enthused, Percy Heath told Szwed, that he wouldn't stop playing: "Miles came up behind him, but he didn't get it. Weinstock showed him the stopwatch, but he kept on playing."

Though Davis would play the number live for many years to come, often at a far faster tempo, this song at this cadence had a great and mysterious power. Decades later, Davis said that the musicians knew they had something good once the recording was over—that even Bob Weinstock and Rudy Van Gelder were excited about it. But, he said, "we didn't really feel the impact of that album until it was released later on that year. . . . That album turned my whole life and career around."

Bebop at its best had been thrilling: in its *newness*, its velocity, its virtuosity, and, especially in the hands of Charles Parker Jr., its sheer pyrotechnic inventiveness. But bebop had limited communicative powers: there weren't many bebop tunes you could hum or whistle. It was a private language, for adepts to play and enthusiasts to feel in on. Now it, along with Bird, was fading; "Walkin'" was something new under the sun.

IN THE MIDDLE OF MAY CHET BAKER CAME EAST WITH A QUARTET AND played Birdland for two weeks opposite Miles and his quintet. The billing wasn't advertised as a battle, East Coast vs. West, soul vs. cool, but it might as well have been. Though Baker had stirred national interest through his good looks and deadpan playing and singing, the Birdland stand was an unequal contest. "Chet Baker's New York debut was successful in terms of the crowds he attracted to Birdland," *DownBeat*'s reviewer wrote. "Musically, his unit might have sounded more impressive if it hadn't been for the strikingly contrasting presence on the same bill of a Miles Davis band that made the Bakermen sound rather frail and, I'm afraid, a little dull."

ONLY A HALF-YEAR CLEAN, MILES HAD A REPUTATION TO LIVE DOWN: that of, as one writer put it, "a gig-skipping, note-fluffing junkie." Reviewers of the early fifties consistently—if vaguely—faulted his "articulation and intonation," and to some extent Davis agreed with them: his addiction did his chops no favors. In the vicious cycle of ignominy and unemployment, both his embouchure and his confidence suffered. Yet as gigs and his confidence returned, and with them his physical mastery of his horn, his "wrong" notes, his often wayward ways with known melodies, lingered. He was making a virtue of former vices, preserving the uncertainty and vulnerability of his down days, solidifying a style.

AT THE END OF JUNE, ANOTHER PRESTIGE SESSION AT VAN GELDER'S. THIS time Sonny Rollins joined Miles, Silver, Heath, and Clarke, contributing three originals to the date: "Airegin," "Oleo," and "Doxy." Miles added the fourth, the Gershwins' "But Not for Me," as a tribute to a lyrical young pianist he'd begun to admire, Pittsburgh's Ahmad Jamal, in whose repertoire the tune was a staple (and probably as a dig at Chet Baker, in whose repertoire the tune, both played and sung, was also a staple).

Listen to *Miles Davis with Sonny Rollins* and you'll hear some astonishing music: from the opening notes of "Airegin," which has become a jazz standard, the idea that outside this recording studio is an America of rounded cars, blue highways, and Eisenhower seems absurd—these sounds are fresh and timeless. As is the sound of Miles's muted horn on the next number, the bright and breezy "Oleo." That instantly identifiable, Harmon-muted tone that seems so definitive of Miles Davis is being recorded here for the first time.

He'd often used a mute before, but always, in the past, the straight or cup version that trumpeters had been employing since time immemorial—in a pinch, a small salad bowl or derby hat would do just as well. The Harmon (or wah-wah) mute had a hole in the center, in which a metal stem could be pushed or pulled, causing a variation in tone. Miles took out the stem altogether, and suddenly he had the sound he wanted: as before, midrange- and vibrato-free, but now with a new quality, one that was at once intimate and distant. It was a sound as singular and instantly identifiable as his speaking voice, an instant trademark. The trumpeter Jon Faddis, whose ability to play high and fast caused many to speak of him as a legitimate successor to Dizzy Gillespie, made an important point: "Before Miles, most people thought of the trumpet as a very extroverted instrument," he said.

> Miles was more introverted in his approach. He used a Harmon mute—it wasn't really popular before he started to use it—and it's a very beautiful sound. . . . Before Miles came on the scene in the 1940s, we had players who were more technically proficient, but he really didn't have the technique at that time to play like a Dizzy Gillespie, so he wanted to go in a different direction. He developed in a way that suited his cool persona. When you listen to Miles, it feels like you get to know the person. You hear in the music: "This is who I am. Check it out."

This is who he was: "His star was on the rise and he had an absolutely charming balance of the cocky and the elfish in his humor," said Jean Bach, a midwestern society girl and jazz lover who gravitated to New York in the early fifties and became a radio personality and, ultimately, the filmmaker of one of the great jazz documentaries, *A Great Day in Harlem*.

> The things he would say. Oh, he was just such an *imp*. He wasn't funny; he was witty. But his wit could put you on the floor, I tell you. There was always an unusual angle to what he said and what he saw. He was sort of a handsome leprechaun. Small, beautifully built, and full of mischief. Things were panning out for him and he intended to enjoy himself. But there was always this kind of sadness about him. It was there and very penetrating. You knew he had been hurt by something or was sunk in some kind of deep melancholy. Miles could withdraw into his sadness and it could seem as if he wouldn't be able to come out of it. His unhappiness could trap him and hold him down. It really could. Depression was one of his struggles.

In a world where whiteness was valued, the mahogany hue of his skin caused him particular sadness. "The Miles I knew was sensitive and ailing, bruised by the hurts this life metes out," Cicely Tyson wrote. "With trembling lips, he told me of the years during his childhood in East St. Louis when he'd been called Blackie by his friends and even some of his family, gazed down upon as a nobody, rendered invisible by his dark hue."

Miles was nothing if not an emotional personality—and yet as he emerged from his bleak period, seeming cool became increasingly important to him, and to his growing fan base. More and more, he appeared to embody a concept that was gaining a powerful niche position in popular culture, even though nobody quite seemed to agree on, or even really understand, what exactly *cool* was. Some say that it was Lester Young, a great coiner of jazz argot, who introduced the word as a term of approbation sometime in the 1930s. But what did cool mean in 1954?

The nonet recordings that would come to be called *The Birth of the Cool* weren't called that originally, and when Capitol issued a compilation LP of eight of them in mid 1954, as Miles was making those landmark albums for Prestige, it wasn't called that, either: rather, it was titled *Miles Davis— Classics in Jazz*. It wasn't until 1957 that Capitol reissued the compilation, with three more tracks added, as *The Birth of the Cool*. What, exactly, had been birthed? From jazz's beginnings, improvisation had been celebrated; not everyone loved the arranged coolness of the nonet recordings. Many of jazz's high priests looked askance at the cool jazz Gerry Mulligan helped create on the West Coast. And the new new music Miles was instrumental in creating in 1954, jazz imbued with fire and funk and spontaneity, was anything but cool, except in the approving sense of the word.

And yet Miles cultivated coolness, in the emotionally distant sense of the word. Clean of heroin and getting stronger (physically, musically, emotionally) all the time, he no longer had to worry about the club owners who once wouldn't hire him or the critics who carped about his articulation and intonation. Fuck them! "I had a lot of anger in me about things that had happened to me in the last four years; I didn't trust hardly anyone," he said in his memoir.

> When we would go to places to play, I was just cold to the motherfuckers; pay me and I'll play. I wasn't about to kiss anybody's ass and do that grinning shit for nobody. I even stopped announcing tunes around this time, because I felt that it wasn't the name of the tune that was important, but the music we played. If they knew what the tune was, why did I have to announce it? I stopped talking to the audience because they weren't coming to hear me speak but to hear the music I was playing.
>
> A lot of people thought I was aloof, and I was. But most of all, I didn't know who to trust.

9   Left-handed pianist

In 1951 the twenty-two-year-old tenor player Benny Golson, his stellar career as a jazz saxophonist and composer mostly ahead of him, joined a small dance band led by the clarinetist/altoist Herbie Fields. "When I joined the group," Golson remembered,

I met an unknown piano player who looked and played like a country hick. He bore no resemblance whatsoever to any talented jazz pianist I had ever known. He looked like a college student majoring, perhaps, in archeology or advanced botany. Although it pains me to admit this, he was a classic nerd. His name was Bill Evans. He later became *the* Bill Evans. When we first met, however, he was far from being the path-breaking, transformational piano shaman whom everyone came to respect and adore. His playing was corny and stiff, with spastic movements augmenting his cornpone squareness. This version of Bill Evans sat rigidly straight, bouncing up and down when he became engaged in the

music. His sound was reminiscent of Milt Buckner, a longtime pianist and organ player with Hamp [Lionel Hampton], though he
lacked Milt's residual drive and swing. This early incarnation of
Bill Evans had an absurd way of patting his feet. Notice I said *feet*.
While he played, he would lock his feet together and roll or wobble their knotted unity back and forth from beat-to-beat—heels
then toes, over and over, again and again, creating a kind of
rocking-chair gait with both feet clamped together like a vise. I
have never understood how he did that. I assure you, he had a performance persona so estranged from any jazz posture or attitude
or, for that matter, from any musical self-presentation that I encountered before or since that I truly cannot fathom how the great
musician he became could have originated from that.

About four years later, having long since moved on from Herbie Fields,
Golson reencountered Evans:

Unbelievably, the Bill Evans I had briefly encountered years earlier had disappeared. Someone with the same name took his place,
an utterly different Bill Evans. What I heard across those ear-
opening moments left me breathless. This former "cornball" played
some of the most beautiful chords and voicings I had ever heard.
That night he touched my heart again and again: amazing tonal
complexity, unearthly lyric beauty. I listened flabbergasted. How
could this be? Not only were Bill's chord choices enchanting; his
pace and time sense were otherworldly. He knew when and how
to suggest dark and light shades, holding overt dynamic contrast
in reserve. He had a knack for jumping ahead to compress or elaborate his melodic narrative. His playing kept me riveted and off
guard. I did not know what to expect at any moment. I was overwhelmed with admiration. This was musical genius.

What had happened?

Golson was gobsmacked enough to put that very question to Evans, who answered with almost Monk-like ellipsis: "Sometimes we have to make changes."

Benny Golson's first take on Bill Evans was almost completely physical and behavioral rather than musical: he simply can't get over the pianist's nerdy presentation, his un-jazziness, his—dare we say it?—extreme whiteness. As for the playing itself, it's "corny and stiff," with no further explanation of what exactly this might mean. Does it have to do with time, rhythm, or lack thereof—some fatal inability to swing? This would seem odd given that by all accounts, Herbie Fields's smallish band—seven to nine players, depending on the gig—played something more akin to R&B than to jazz. "I have often been condemned for not playing strongly," Evans recalled years later. "But when I was with this band I would come off the stand with split fingernails and sore arms." Fields's one hit record, a 1947 cover of the twenties dance number "Dardanella," had a driving boogie-woogie beat. Why would he have hired a piano player who couldn't swing?

In 1947 Bill Evans was still four years away from joining Herbie Fields. After graduating high school in Plainfield, New Jersey, that year, he entered Southeastern Louisiana College, in Hammond, forty-five miles northwest of New Orleans, on a music scholarship.

If anything, what the young Evans seems to have been is a gifted musical chameleon. He'd studied (and loved) classical piano from a tender age: "From the age of six to thirteen," he later said, "I acquired the ability to sight-read and to play classical music . . . performing Mozart, Beethoven, or Schubert intelligently, musically."

And yet, he added: "I couldn't play 'My Country 'Tis of Thee' without the notes."

As one whose musical life had been changed in his teens by hearing Stravinsky's *Petrushka* and Darius Milhaud's *Suite provençale*, but also by listening to the swing music of Harry James and Tommy Dorsey on the radio, Evans was baffled at first by the concept of improvisation. Then, playing for his Plainfield high school rehearsal band, he had an epiphany:

"One night we were playing 'Tuxedo Junction,' and for some reason I got inspired and put in a little blues thing," he recalled. "'Tuxedo Junction' is in B♭, and I put in a little D♭, D, F thing, bing! in the right hand. It was such a thrill. It sounded right and good, and it wasn't written, and I had done it. The idea of doing something in music that somebody hadn't thought of opened a whole new world to me."

That world was jazz. Soon he recorded a homemade disc of himself playing "the fastest boogie-woogie in Central Jersey." His sight-reading skills also allowed him to earn money by playing dance music at weddings and other events. During summer vacations from college he went home to New Jersey and, in a trio with a couple of friends, did gigs at seashore resorts. He also sat in from time to time with a group of older musicians, "more of a jazz band than the high-school band," Evans remembered.

> On some of the jobs, the people expected to hear jazz, so I just dived in and tried it. I have recordings from the very beginning that show I was very clear in what I was doing. . . .
>
> I was buying all the records . . . anybody from Coleman Hawkins to Bud Powell and Dexter Gordon. That was when I first heard Bud, on those Dexter Gordon sides on Savoy. I heard Earl Hines very early and, of course, the King Cole Trio. Nat, I thought, was one of the greatest, and I still do. I think he is probably the most underrated jazz pianist in the history of jazz.
>
> I'd play hooky from school and hear all the bands at the Paramount in New York or the Adams in Newark. Or we'd try to sneak in the clubs on 52nd St. with phony draft cards, just to hear some jazz. I got a lot of experience with insight that way.

Yet for all his growing rapture with the Great American Art Form, Evans dived even more deeply into the study of European classical piano at Southeastern Louisiana. "[His] studies in the classical repertoire, two weekly lessons of an hour and a half each," wrote his biographer, the concert pianist Peter Pettinger, took in sonatas by Mozart and Beethoven and works by Schumann, Rachmaninoff, Debussy, Ravel, Gershwin (the Piano Concerto in F), Villa-Lobos, Khachaturian, Milhaud, and others. The constructional knowledge of music that Evans later brought to jazz was firmly rooted in this European tradition, as was his thoroughly trained and exquisitely refined touch at the keyboard. In later years, when interviewers observed that certain aspects of technique—his pedaling, for instance—were unusually polished for a jazz musician, Evans was invariably baffled, for the whole process had been quite unconscious for as long as he could remember.

Drafted at the height of the Korean War, Evans was fortunate to spend his tour of duty in the Special Services entertainment branch, playing flute and piccolo in the Fifth Army band at Fort Sheridan, Illinois, in the Chicago suburbs. While there, he helped run a jazz show on the camp radio station and, on leave, frequented Chicago jazz clubs. He would stay up all night playing piano and smoking Mexican reefer and return to base not having slept a wink. Soon the combination of marijuana and sleeplessness hurt his playing, both when he was high and when he wasn't, and undercut his musical confidence: "I was very happy and secure until I went into the army," he said. "Then I started to feel there was something I should know that I didn't. . . . I was attacked by some guys for what I believed, and by musicians who claimed I should play like this pianist or that. Pretty soon . . . I began to think that everything I did was wrong."

After mustering out in January 1954, he recalled, "I went home to my parents and took a year off. I set up a little studio, acquired a grand piano and devoted a year to work on my playing. It did not come easy. . . . I don't consider myself as talented as many people. But in some ways that was an advantage. Because I didn't have a great facility immediately, I had to be more analytical. I had to build my music very consciously, from the bottom up."

If there is one hallmark quality to Bill Evans, it is his sheer *consciousness*, not just of music but of everything around him: he was an incessantly

analytical human being. And though he felt guilty about leaving European classical behind, and though his teachers had told him he had the
technical and artistic wherewithal to be a concert pianist, his heart pointed
him in a different direction.

"It's obvious now that jazz is the most central and important thing in
my life," he said a decade after his apprentice years. "But I never knew
that. You know, I went to college and got a teacher's degree, because I
thought I might teach, but when the moment came, bang, I went out into
jazz. It was like—it was so much a part of my inner life, and I didn't realize it. It's like you ask a kid, 'What do you want to be when you grow up?'
Well, I would've said anything. Because I didn't really know, and I don't
think most children do. But I just became so involved with jazz that that
was the natural road—it pulled me here and pulled me there, and finally
it revealed itself as the most important thing in my life."

LATE IN HIS SHORT LIFE, EVANS WOULD INSIST TO HIS YOUNG GIRLFRIEND
Laurie Verchomin (she was twenty-two at the time of his death, at fifty-
one, in 1980) that his boyhood had been a blissful one. I spoke with Verchomin in the fall of 2018, and it was touching and occasionally funny to
hear the highly evolved perspective, by turns loving, respectful, and gently
mocking, that this almost sixty-year-old woman brought to revisiting her
youthful relationship with this complex, contradictory, needy, but tough-
minded genius. She imitated Evans: "'I don't know why I'm such a junkie,
strung-out, blah blah blah, because I had a perfect childhood.'" She
laughed. "He just didn't have the awareness of whatever was going on
there. I think he felt very protected by his mother. His relationship with
his mother was really close."

His relationship with his father was not. Harry Senior, Pettinger
writes, was "gentle and easygoing in character—when sober, that is, for by
all accounts he was a heavy drinker." His forebears were Welsh, and
Wales's tradition of vocal music seemed to have run strong in him: "He
loved singing and barbershop harmony," a nephew remembered, "and he

and his buddies would get together with a bottle and start singing and drinking. . . . Harry was always a playboy, and pleasure was more important to him than his family, which he frequently neglected. After his alcoholic abuses he would cry and say how sorry he was, but two days later it would be the same old story all over again."

Evans's mother, born Mary Soroka, was of Ukrainian ancestry; her parents emigrated to northeast Pennsylvania in the 1890s. Her father was killed in a coal-mining accident in 1904, and the family was left destitute: Mary and a sister were raised in an orphanage run by Russian Orthodox priests. She met and married Harry Evans when she was thirty—old in those days—and gave birth to their two sons in 1927 and 1929. She soon discovered that her husband was anything but dependable.

"The marriage was stormy," Harry Jr.'s widow, Pat, writes, "brought on by [Harry Senior's] heavy drinking, gambling, and abuse." He worked in the printing business, but his heart wasn't in it. "Harry Senior slept his life away, never learned to drive and primped for hours before he left the house. . . . There was a period when [Mary] sold corsets door to door to keep bread on the table."

And yet, as Pat recalls, it was a complicated household. Various relatives—Mary's mother, an aunt from Harry Senior's side, a couple of cousins—lived with the Evanses from time to time, and the house was "saturated with music." Mary had a beautiful alto voice: "Birthdays were more than singing 'Happy Birthday.' They were family choirs." The boys took piano lessons and played in bands as they grew up. And they were inseparably close, "One thinking for the other, laughing, protecting, risking for the other. They shared an old black Pontiac, ties, cuff links, and girls."

As they grew up, the muscular and assertive Harry Jr. protected his "bespectacled, introspective . . . smart and weak" younger brother. But as Bill's musical skills widened and deepened, Harry began to drift. At seventeen he lost interest in school and enlisted in the navy. A year after Bill was accepted to Southeastern Louisiana on a scholarship, Harry followed him and enrolled, too. And majored in music, too.

Pat Evans, who met her husband-to-be there, writes that the brothers "roomed together in a house they shared with other music majors . . . frequented Kelly's bar to shoot dice and dined in style at the Casa de Fresa Hotel. They played in the College Orchestra, the Marching Band at football games and the College Jazz Band." Yet Bill "immersed himself in the music, living in the music building, practicing in his every spare moment, not as an onus, but as a joyful way of discovery. . . . Students began to sit in the hall outside the door of his practice room, just to hear him play."

10 Now's the time

orking on Fifty-second Street in the fall of 1945, newly hired by Bird but not truly believing that he deserved the job (and all too aware that many others shared his disbelief), Miles would now and then leave the Spotlite during a break and dash over to the Downbeat to catch Coleman Hawkins and Hawkins's singular piano player, Thelonious Monk. "He used to come in with his horn," Al McKibbon remembered, "and he'd sit up on the bandstand and he'd listen to us play, watch what Monk was doing. And sometimes Monk would hit something strange . . . and [Miles would] figure it out on his horn, but he'd never play. He would just sit and listen and laugh to himself."

In his side of the story, Miles gave himself a more active role:

I used to ask Monk, every fucking night, to play "'Round About Midnight" [*sic*]. I'd say, "How'd I play it?," because he wrote it, right? And he'd say, "You didn't play it right." Next night. "Did I play it any better?" "A little bit better, but that ain't the way it goes." And one night I asked him [and he said], "Yeah, you can play it." . . . I [finally] got the sound. . . . It took me a long time to be able to play that song."

Davis said, "Monk taught me more than anyone on the street when I was down there. [He's] the one who really showed me everything." A man of few words, Monk, as his biographer Robin D. G. Kelley writes, "taught by demonstration rather than explanation. He would say very little, and when he did explain something he [might] say it once. . . . You had to pay strict attention and see everything he was doing if you wanted to learn." Or, as Miles put it, "If you're serious you could learn from him, but if you're bullshitting you wouldn't see nothing."

Nine years later, much had changed. Approaching middle age, Monk had continued to develop as a composer—much to the delight of those who played his songs or lifted phrases (or entire tunes) from him—but had failed to catch on commercially. He was still playing what sounded like wrong notes, and his idiosyncratic tempos could baffle even sophisticated musicians. His personal and musical oddities endeared him to fans of the avant-garde, but also kept him a fringe figure: an outsider artist. The critical establishment (Leonard Feather was a particular antagonist) frequently put him down in withering terms, calling his playing primitive, simplistic, childlike. "Two left hands," some said. Meanwhile, Miles, still only twenty-eight, was rising toward superstardom.

Monk had had a hard time earning a living in the best of times, but in 1951, after a false heroin bust (he was sitting with Bud Powell in Powell's car when cops appeared; the drugs they found belonged to Powell, but Monk refused to betray his friend in court), he had lost his cabaret card, and with it the right to perform at New York City clubs that served alcohol—meaning all New York City clubs. Enforcement was looser in the outer boroughs, however, and in late 1953 Monk managed to secure a steady gig at Tony's Club Grandean, a Black-owned Brooklyn dive bar at the corner of Grand Avenue and Dean Street.

One weekend in late March of 1954, Kelley writes,

> Monk shared the bandstand with Miles Davis, [composer and tenor saxophonist] Gigi Gryce, Charles Mingus, and Max Roach.... Earlier in the week, Davis and Roach met at Thelonious's apartment to go over the music. Monk's nephew, Theolonious ("Peanut"), who just happened to come in from playing basketball, witnessed Miles, Monk, and Max crammed into the tiny front room with the upright piano. The session turned sour when Miles made disparaging remarks about Monk's playing. Monk just glared at first, but Miles would not relent and soon the dispute escalated into a shouting match. "Max didn't say nothing," recalled Theolonious, who was fourteen at the time. "Uncle Bubba [Monk] stood up and towered over Miles and they were about to go to blows.... And Monk said, "This is my band, my music." Miles said, "But you're not playing it right, Monk." Miles looked up at Monk and I thought he was going to hit him with the trumpet. Then Monk finally said, "I think you better leave. This is my mother's house and I don't want no violence in here."

By all accounts, the fractious rehearsal had no ill effect on the gig itself, though Monk managed to exact a measure of revenge on Miles: while the trumpeter soloed, the prankish pianist "left the piano, snuck up behind Miles . . . reached into [Miles's] shirt pocket for a pack of cigarettes, and dug into his jacket pocket for matches. After he lit up, he put everything back into Davis's pockets." Miles never missed a note. But Monk had made sport of him in public, and he would remember.

In December, Bob Weinstock put together an all-star group, meant to showcase Miles, for a Christmas Eve recording session at Van Gelder's. Monk was the pianist on the date, along with three-quarters of the Modern Jazz Quartet: Milt Jackson, Percy Heath, and Kenny Clarke. Prestige would bill the quintet as the Modern Jazz Giants. Each of the three stars had brought a tune: Miles, a presciently modal composition called "Swing Spring"; Jackson, his signature standard "Bags' Groove"; and Monk, a number he'd written with Denzil Best, the Caribbean-flavored "Bemsha Swing."

It was a legendary date in more than one way, and riven with tension, with most of the unhappiness emanating from Monk. For starters, he didn't want to be there: more than any of the jazz colossi, he was a family man, and he would have far preferred to spend this holiday eve with his wife, Nellie, and their soon-to-be five-year-old son, T. S. (Toot), and their year-old daughter, Barbara (Boo Boo). Equally galling for the pianist was the fact that he was on the session as a sideman, working for scale. He was under contract to Prestige, but his albums as a leader had failed to sell: Weinstock was calling the shots, Miles was leading the session, and Monk needed the money. "So when Monk arrived at Van Gelder's studio around two in the afternoon," Kelley writes, "he was already a bit agitated."

Then Miles instructed Monk when he should play and when he shouldn't. "I just told him to lay out, not play behind me, except on 'Bemsha Swing,'" Davis said. "Monk never did know how to play behind a horn player. (The only horn players he ever had that sounded good playing with him were John Coltrane, Sonny Rollins, and Charlie Rouse.)" But the trumpet, Davis argued—and especially his trumpet—was a different matter: "A trumpet player needs the rhythm section to be hot even if he is playing a ballad. You got to have that kicking thing, and most of the time that wasn't Monk's bag."

On the first tune recorded that afternoon, "Bags' Groove," Monk does just as ordered, laying out entirely during Miles's long initial solo, then coming in behind Jackson (another rhythm instrument, after all), inserting his uniquely Monkian chords in his inimitably unpredictable rhythms. Monk's own solo, coming right after the vibraphonist's, is a thing of strange, sideways beauty, beginning with a bugle-call sequence of right-hand Cs and Fs "followed [Losin writes] by an F# (at 6:59) that critic André Hodeir described as 'one of the purest moments of beauty in the history of jazz.'" When Miles returns for another chorus, Monk obediently drops out again.

By the evidence of the recording, Monk has taken Miles's directive easily, turned the lemons of his subsidiary role into ambrosia. In the studio and in the moment, however, things got strange. When Miles started his long solo at the beginning of "Bags' Groove," Monk walked over and stood right next to him. As was his custom when recording, Miles played while sitting in a chair, pointing the bell of his horn at the floor; the bearlike Monk towered over him, his poker face betraying nothing, and stayed there for the whole solo. "Why did you do that?" Miles asked Monk once the take was over. "I don't have to sit down to lay out," Monk said.

Monk seemed to settle down during the next two numbers, "Bemsha Swing" (during which, appropriately enough, since it is his song, he accompanies Davis—quite effectively—the whole way) and the modal "Swing Spring," though Ira Gitler remembered that the pianist ruined one take by asking, "Where's the bathroom?"

But then, as the quintet began to play the final song, "The Man I Love," the session's only standard, the tension that had been building popped. No sooner has Milt Jackson begun to hit the romantic opening chords than Monk blurts, "When should I come in, man?" Jackson stops, there's a collective groan, and someone says, "Man, the cat's cuttin' hisself." Monk complains, "I don't know when to come *in*, man. Can't I start, too? Everybody—"

Miles breaks in. "Hey, Rudy, put this on the record," he says. "*All* of it."

What was going on in the moment? Was Miles angry? Was he being provocative? Or was he just trying to make a joke, let some tension out of the room? Rumors sprang up over the years that there was a physical confrontation between Monk and Davis during the session, but everyone involved denied it, including the principals. When Ira Gitler (who'd left Van Gelder's before the date was done) asked Monk about it in an interview a couple of years later, the pianist chuckled. "Miles'd got killed if he hit me," he said.

Miles agreed. "Monk was like a little baby," he said.

> He had a lot of love in him and I *know* Monk loved me, and I loved
> him, too. He wouldn't ever fight me even if I stomped down hard
> on his feet for a week, because he just wasn't that kind of person.
> Monk was a gentle person, gentle and beautiful, but he was strong
> as an ox. And if I had ever said something about punching Monk
> out in front of his face—and I never did—then somebody should
> have just come and got me and taken me to the madhouse, because
> Monk could have just picked my little ass up and thrown me
> through a wall.

And Monk would later assert that being asked to lay out was no big
deal: "When Miles asked me to lay out during his solo on that record," he
told another interviewer, "I never thought nothing of it—Roy Eldridge
had his piano lay out years ago."

In the end, whatever sparks of tension may have flown during the session, a great quintet with Miles very much in charge (and feeling stronger
than he had for years) prevailed. "Later that night, at Minton's," Gitler recalled, "I saw Kenny Clarke, who answered my 'How did it go?' with
'Miles sure is a beautiful cat,' which was his way of saying that despite the
obstacles, Miles had seen it through and produced something extraordinary and lasting."

And for all the tales of bad blood between them, Monk recalled that
when the session was over he invited Miles to come back to his place to
spend Christmas Eve with his family, and Miles had stayed into the early
hours of the morning, when Monk had had a hard time getting rid of the
lonely leader.

MILES WENT INTO 1955 "FEELING REAL GOOD." HE'D KICKED HIS HABIT, HE
was playing better than he'd ever played, and people were starting to buy
his albums again. Then he got arrested.

It was early March, and Irene, now living in Brooklyn with ten-year-old Cheryl and eight-year-old Gregory, had gotten tired of chasing Davis for child-support money and hired a lawyer, one Maxwell T. Cohen, the man who handled Billie Holiday's tangled affairs—and who would later mount a successful challenge to New York City's corrupt cabaret-card system. Cohen was a legal bulldog, more aggressive than Irene had bargained for: Miles was arrested and taken to Rikers Island. "I didn't know they were going to [do that]," Irene later said. "I just thought he had the money and would pay me. When I heard that he was in jail, I cried and cried." Miles was upset, too. Bob Weinstock went to visit him at Rikers; as he was leaving, Miles screamed, "Get me out of here!"

Davis's next visitor, a lawyer named Harold Lovett, was just the man he wanted to see. A familiar face on the jazz scene (he represented Max Roach), well dressed, exuberant, and Black, he would later become a good friend of Davis's. But before they could even discuss his case, Lovett had calamitous news for him: Bird was dead.

Charlie Parker had died early in the evening of Saturday, March 12, in the Fifth Avenue hotel suite of the Baroness Pannonica de Koenigswarter, where he'd stopped to rest before driving to a gig at a Boston club, George Wein's Storyville. De Koenigswarter, called Nica by her friends and the Jazz Baroness by the gossip columns, was a rebellious and eccentric scion of the world's wealthiest family, the Rothschilds; she was also a passionate lover of jazz and a close friend and patron to many musicians, but especially to Thelonious Monk and Bird. Fortyish, angular, and handsome, witty and sardonic, she drove a Rolls-Royce that she called "the silver pigeon." Her elegantly appointed apartment in the Stanhope Hotel, across the street from the Metropolitan Museum of Art, was a salon for musicians, who might stop in at any hour for food, drink, and conversation as jazz played on the hi-fi and the suite's many cats roamed and nestled.

Bird's health and mental state had been precarious since the death of his daughter; he was feeling especially depressed and unwell when he dropped by Nica's place on Wednesday the ninth. The previous Saturday night, a comeback engagement at Birdland—Parker leading a quintet

with Kenny Dorham, Bud Powell, Charles Mingus, and Art Blakey—
had fallen apart before a note could be played when Powell, in the grips
of schizophrenia, had a mental breakdown and walked off the bandstand.
The evening ended with Parker standing at the microphone, calling over
and over in an anguished voice, "Bud Powell! Bud Powell! *Bud Powell!*" as
the customers filed out of the club. (Taking another mike, Mingus added
his own counterpoint: "Ladies and gentlemen, please don't associate me
with any of this. This is not jazz. These are sick people.")

Midweek, traveling to Boston for a solo gig with a pickup rhythm section was the last thing Parker felt like doing. His stomach hurt and he was
having difficulty breathing when he walked into Nica's place; he went to
the bathroom and vomited blood. The baroness called her personal physi-
cian, who arrived promptly, told Parker he was a very sick man, and recommended he be hospitalized immediately. Parker, who hated hospitals,
refused.

The doctor returned several times between Wednesday and Saturday,
recommending hospitalization each time, Bird refusing each time. Early
Saturday evening, Parker was sitting in an armchair in Nica's living
room, watching *The Tommy Dorsey Show* on TV, laughing at a comic jug-
gling act, when he began to choke and collapsed. Nica grabbed his wrist
and felt a faint pulse, but by the time the doctor arrived, Charlie Parker
was gone.

The police and the medical examiner followed quickly. Detectives
questioned the baroness; forms had to be filled out. Nica's doctor attributed Parker's death to stomach ulcers and pneumonia, with contributing
factors of advanced cirrhosis and a possible heart attack. He estimated the
decedent's age as between fifty and sixty.

The baroness tried to contain the news until Parker's girlfriend Chan
Richardson could be located, but the story leaked "due to the chance remark a morgue attendant made to a newspaperman," Ross Russell wrote.
The story hit the papers on Tuesday the fifteenth; the tabloids gave it
headlines, juicily insinuating something between the baroness and the

Black jazzman; the *Times* put it on page 17, in two quarter columns sand-wiched between a piece about radioactive fallout from atom-bomb tests in Nevada reaching New Jersey and an ad for Allegheny Airlines:

CHARLIE PARKER, JAZZ MASTER, DIES

A Be-Bop Founder and Top Saxophonist Is Stricken in Suite of Baroness

Charlie Parker, one of the founders of progressive jazz, or be-bop, died here last Saturday night.

The news of the death of the noted musician, known as "The Yardbird," spread quickly last night through Tin Pan Alley, where he was affectionately referred to as "The Bird." A virtuoso of the alto saxophone, Mr. Parker was ranked with Duke Ellington, Count Basie and other outstanding Negro musicians. . . .

The piece concluded by noting, "The police said Mr. Parker was about 53 years old."

Charlie Parker was thirty-four.

BIRD'S DEATH "FUCKED EVERYONE UP," MILES SAID, BUT IT ALSO TURNED a page. Some musicians began making serious efforts at kicking heroin—Sonny Rollins would sign himself into Lexington in September—and even amid the widespread grieving for Parker ("Bird Lives!" graffiti began appearing around New York soon after March 12; I remember seeing the faded inscriptions when I first went to college there in 1969), there was a sense that bebop was grievously wounded, if not over, and new things had begun to happen in jazz. And Miles's album releases on Prestige were gradually making it clear—albeit to the limited audience of enthusiasts who bought independently distributed jazz records—that he was at the arrow tip of the change.

In the meantime, though, his finances were nil and his reputation among critics and club owners still checkered. After Weinstock and Lovett sprang him from Rikers with an advance on a gig at Philadelphia's Blue Note, Miles took a new quintet there in April: Sonny Rollins, Red Garland, a dazzling young bassist named Paul Chambers, and Philly Joe Jones. Chambers, barely out of his teens, could already play unexpected harmonies and meters; he could also bow his instrument beautifully. And there were several things about Garland that Davis liked: he was a former welterweight boxer who'd once fought an exhibition match with Sugar Ray Robinson, and he was a hip, expressive pianist with a light touch, able to channel Miles's new lyrical inspiration Ahmad Jamal. In a Prestige session that June, Davis recorded with Garland for the first time, in a quartet featuring Oscar Pettiford and Jones; two of the tunes on the album, "Will You Still Be Mine" and "A Gal in Calico," were Jamal standbys. Davis's playing, with an open trumpet on the first and Harmon mute on the second, is exuberant and assured: liberated.

IN HIS MEMOIR, MILES SAYS THAT THE NEWPORT JAZZ FESTIVAL AT which he played in July 1955 was the first Newport Festival. In actuality, the first had taken place the previous July, at a time when Davis, though free from heroin and starting to make those wondrous—though only gradually released—albums for Prestige and Blue Note, was still thought of among jazz fans, critics, and club owners as a fallen star. In point of fact, Miles hadn't been invited.

Newport began as a collaboration between a jazz-loving socialite couple, Elaine and Louis Lorillard, and the Boston club owner George Wein: the Lorillards provided the cash and Wein booked the artists. The first-year roster put an emphasis on the traditional, with players ranging from Eddie Condon to Gene Krupa to Stan Kenton, and a scattering of new Young Turks like Gerry Mulligan, Lee Konitz, and Lennie Tristano.

Black artists were well represented—Dizzy Gillespie, Milt Jackson, and Oscar Peterson were present, as were Billie Holiday, Ella Fitzgerald, and Erroll Garner—but little would have challenged the ears of the predominantly white audience, which, given Newport's plutocratic population, naturally included some of the Lorillards' fellow swells.

The '55 festival was similarly grounded in tradition. Louis Armstrong, Count Basie, and Duke Ellington all brought bands, as did Woody Herman—and Stan Rubin and His Tigertown Five, playing Dixieland. But jazz's new sounds had more of a presence in the event's second season: Konitz was back, and the Clifford Brown–Max Roach Quintet made their first appearance, as did Chet Baker and the West Coast pianist Dave Brubeck. Thelonious Monk was also there, and, as an eleventh-hour addition, so was Miles Davis.

In his account, Miles finesses his last-minuteness, but he was not listed on the program for the festival's third and final evening of Sunday, July 17. The Modern Jazz Quartet began the proceedings, followed by a small group led by Count Basie reuniting with Lester Young. While stage changes were made for the Brubeck quartet, then at the height of its popularity—Dave Brubeck had appeared on the cover of *Time* the year before—there was to be a twenty-minute jam session, with Zoot Sims, Gerry Mulligan, Thelonious Monk, and the MJQ's bassist and drummer, Percy Heath and Connie Kay. "But at the last second," Szwed writes, "the festival's director, George Wein, added Miles Davis to the group. Wein thought Miles was something special, 'a melodic bebopper, a bebop Bobby Hackett,' a player who could reach a larger audience than most other musicians."

Miles and George Wein had history. One early stop on the 1952 Symphony Sid tour had been in New Haven, at a Storyville club Wein had recently opened. When the sextet arrived, Sid cautioned Wein not to give Miles any money. "Miles, who was deep into drugs at this time, probably owed Sid some money from their last gig," Wein wrote in his memoir.

Later that same night, Miles approached me.

"George," he said, "give me ten dollars."

"Sid told me not to give you any money, Miles. I can't do it."

"George," he said, as if he hadn't heard me, "give me five dollars."

"Come on, Miles, I can't do it. The man said not to give you any bread."

"George, give me a dollar."

"Miles—"

"Give me fifty cents, George. Give me a quarter. George, give me a penny."

That was my first conversation with Miles Davis.

Three years later, Wein was in New York, planning the second Newport Festival, when he walked into Basin Street East, a midtown nightspot, and saw Miles sitting alone at a table in the corner. "We didn't have much of a relationship," Wein recalled.

But when I walked into the club, he called me over and asked a question.

"Are you having a jazz festival up at Newport this year?"

"Yeah, Miles," I replied.

He looked me in the face and rasped: "You can't have a jazz festival without me."

"Miles," I said, "do you want to come to Newport?"

"You can't have a jazz festival without me," he repeated.

"If you want to be there, I'll call Jack," I said. Jack Whittemore was Miles's agent.

"You can't have a jazz festival without me," he said again. Miles had a way of getting his point across.

Wein might not have liked Miles, but liking wasn't the point: he knew that he had to fit him onto the bill, even though Davis still didn't have a working group. But the post-bebop and pre-hard-bop economics of jazz were such, Wein wrote, "that it was difficult for *anyone* to keep a band. Players took whatever work they could get."

He added Miles to the jam session, though the programs had already been printed without his name.

While Miles's memoir is often candid about his vulnerabilities, he says nothing about his emotional state as he prepared for what would be, arguably, the biggest concert of his life. In the weeks after Newport he would downplay the significance of his appearance that Sunday night, making it out to have been just another gig. It was not.

After the Basie group finished its set, Duke Ellington, the master of ceremonies that evening, stepped to the microphone. "Thank you very much, ladies and gentlemen, for Count Basie, Jimmy Rushing, and all of the other Kansas City kids," he announced, in clarion tones.

> Uh, I have another listing here of a group that's coming up. It looks like these gentlemen live in the realm that, ah, Buck Rogers is trying to reach. Ah, we start with a couple of gentlemen you've heard before, Percy Heath, bass, and Connie Kay, drums, of the Modern Jazz Quartet. And then we go on down to *Miles Davis*, trumpet! Miles Davis!

The mention of Miles drew surprised and enthusiastic applause—he wasn't on the program!—and Duke's showmanlike repetition of the name acknowledged the crowd's response. Maybe Ellington, too, was surprised. Seven years earlier, he had tried to hire Miles for his band, liking the way the young trumpeter played, liking too the way he dressed and handled himself. Though greatly flattered—Ellington was a particular idol of his—Miles had declined with thanks, telling the great man that he was in the midst of the *Birth of the Cool* sessions. What he didn't say was that having already served his big-band time with Billy Eckstine, he never again wanted "to put myself in a musical box, playing the same music, night after night after night."

Duke Ellington would have been well aware of Miles's fall from grace. Yet if the truth be told, Ellington wasn't doing so well himself at this strange moment in jazz: for almost a decade he and his great band had been limping along—they'd even played skating rinks. In 1955 the great Duke Ellington didn't have a recording contract.

And so his reference to Buck Rogers—the spaceman hero of a sci-fi comic strip set in the twenty-fifth century—was humorous but pointed. As grand as he was, as brilliant as he was, as singular as he was, might Duke Ellington have worried that the world now saw him as old hat?

He finished his introduction:

> Zoot Sims, tenor . . . And my very dear friend, ah, the cool one, Gerry Mulligan . . . And the . . . high priest of bop, the inimitable Thelonious Monk. . . .

Miles wanted this audience to know that he was back. He knew that his unheralded presence was a surprise, even a shock, and he wanted to maximize his impact, to demonstrate vividly to every professional or amateur critic in the audience that the Miles Davis they thought they knew, the addict and outcast, was a thing of the past. When he walked out onto the stage, crisp and clean in a white seersucker jacket and black bow tie, and strode to the microphone, his presence and his bearing said the same thing he'd told George Wein: *You can't have a jazz festival without me.* Leaving nothing to chance with the festival's fluky sound system, he placed the bell of his horn squarely over the microphone and began to blow.

The sextet played three numbers, two by Monk—the jaunty "Hackensack" (named in honor of Rudy Van Gelder's studio) and "'Round Midnight"—and the bebop anthem "Now's the Time," in honor of its composer, Charlie Parker. There is a whole Talmud of opinions on those momentous twenty-odd minutes of music: since we have an audiotape of the proceedings but no video record, commentators are forced to microanalyze audience reactions and reverse engineer them into a gauge of Miles's performance.

From the opening notes of "Hackensack," his playing was as crisp as his seersucker, as authoritative as his dark-eyed stare, and in the soft passages of Monk's great ballad, as devastatingly lyrical as only Miles could be. (And Monk and Miles, for all their problems with each other, complemented each other throughout like hand and glove.)

Davis's memoir says that he played "'Round Midnight" with a mute—he didn't—and places it as the climactic number (it was the second of the three), after which he "got a long standing ovation." (Doesn't quite sound that way.) "Everybody was looking at me like I was a king or something," he says; "people were running up to me offering me record deals."

Maybe people were; maybe he was exaggerating. One fact is incontrovertible: even if people, plural, weren't running up to Davis with record deals, one very important person was.

George Avakian, the head of Columbia Records' popular-music division, was in the audience that night with his brother Aram, a film editor and photographer. Before Miles had finished his beautiful solo on "'Round Midnight," Aram turned to his brother and said, "Sign him—now! After tonight everybody will know he's back." By the time the band began "Now's the Time," George was headed backstage. When Miles walked into the dressing room and saw the record executive, he gave him a big grin. They too had history.

An ardent jazz lover since his early teens, George Avakian had gone to work for Columbia Records in 1940, while still an undergraduate at Yale, creating a groundbreaking reissue series, Hot Jazz Classics, that brought the important early work of Louis Armstrong, Bix Beiderbecke, Fletcher Henderson, Bessie Smith, and Billie Holiday to a wide public. After serving in the army during World War II, Avakian returned to Columbia and was put in charge of popular albums, then in transition to the label's revolutionary 33⅓ rpm long-playing technology. And he had a revolutionary idea of his own: jazz shouldn't be ghettoized in its own department; rather, it should be positioned as part of popular music.

Columbia was a major label in the late forties and early fifties, but its jazz catalog still mainly consisted of reissues—Louis Armstrong's 1920s Hot Fives and Sevens and Benny Goodman's Carnegie Hall concerts of 1937 and 1938 were solid sellers—and polite nostalgia (*Ralph Sutton Plays Music of "Fats" Waller*). Miles Davis wanted to change that. He and George

Avakian had first gotten to know each other in the late forties, and Miles had begun pestering the young record executive immediately. "Every time I saw him, he'd ask me to sign him," Avakian recalled. "I lived near him, and he'd come by to hang out. He'd tell me that he'd been asking me to sign him 'for years': at first it was two years, then it was four years, then six years."

There were problems. The first was Miles's big problem between 1949 and 1954. Ross Russell, Bob Weinstock, and Alfred Lion could countenance their recording artists' drug use up to a point, but Russell, Weinstock, and Lion ran their respective labels, and Dial, Prestige, and Blue Note were small independent companies. Avakian was part of a corporate structure in a subsidiary of CBS, and responsible for his bottom line. Missed or botched record dates cost money. "I didn't want any part of junkies," Avakian recalled. "I'd been around them enough to know that they're nothing but trouble. It was terrible to see it in Miles. Around 1952 he was hardly working and would come sit in at Birdland on Mondays when they had an open-door policy. He looked slovenly and his playing had deteriorated. It was a sad thing."

The second problem flowed from the first: Davis had no working band. A working band meant identity, continuity, and commercial solidity: an excellent ad hoc group might be assembled for a recording session, but if the players were no longer together to publicize the record when it was issued, sales could suffer.

George Avakian had long been intrigued by Miles: "Of all the young musicians who came out of the immediate post-war jazz period," he would later write, "Miles Davis is perhaps the most lyrical and most instantly communicating." Yet Avakian felt that Davis's musical reputation didn't do justice to his greatest strength: "Those who had heard of Miles at all then mostly thought of him as a bebop player," Avakian told *The Wall Street Journal* on the fiftieth anniversary of that Newport Jazz Festival. And from the beginning, George Avakian had had little interest in bebop: "I knew [it] would never connect on a large scale," he said. "It was ingenious music but far too complicated for the average ear and too hard for the mass market to follow the melodies.

"But I saw Miles in a different way. I saw him as the best trumpet ballad player since Louis Armstrong. It could be jazz ballads like "'Round Midnight,' but I thought it could have a broad appeal on the basis of being very pretty music—easy to listen to on one level—yet of a very high quality for jazz fans." With his keen commercial instincts, an absolute survival skill in the cutthroat world of the big-label recording industry, Avakian also recognized something else: even beyond his music, there was a magic to Miles himself—in his darkly beautiful (and often dangerous) looks, his finely calibrated sense of style; in the Proustian sorcery of the sound of his name. "In certain contexts," Avakian wrote, "he has proved to be an artist of enormous appeal to people who know nothing about jazz."

Much as the farsighted Capitol record executive Alan Livingston had met intense company resistance when he signed a down-and-out Frank Sinatra two years earlier, Avakian encountered little enthusiasm for Davis at his label. "Within Columbia there was absolutely no interest in Miles," he recalled. "He wasn't a factor in the business we were doing, which was getting to be huge. Fortunately, there was no need for me to ask anyone's permission to sign him."

There was just one pesky detail: Davis was already under contract to Prestige. But here the trumpeter himself came up with a brilliant workaround: "Miles suggested that I tell Bob Weinstock that if he'd allow Miles to record with Columbia while he was still under contract with them, and hold the masters until the contract ran out, then Prestige could benefit from the publicity that Columbia would generate when his first records for them were released. It was a wild idea, but just might work."

Two days later, over lunch at the storied Times Square restaurant Lindy's, Avakian signed Miles to a two-year contract, with a two-thousand-dollar advance against a royalty of 4 percent—just one point less than Doris Day, a major Columbia star, was earning. "It was," Ben Ratliff writes, "a lot of money for jazz." Davis's contract with Prestige would run out at the end of 1956. As part of the agreement, Avakian asked Miles to form a working band that would still be together when his first Columbia album was released, about a year and a half thence.

———

DAVIS LIKED THE QUINTET HE'D TAKEN TO PHILADELPHIA IN APRIL. BUT Sonny Rollins, then in the thick of his own serious heroin problems, was making noises about leaving New York to try and kick. So Miles needed a saxophone.

As fate would have it, a brilliant new saxophonist had materialized in Manhattan that summer, seemingly out of nowhere, bursting on the scene in an incident that, while the still-stunned jazz world was still trying to process the death of Charlie Parker, became the stuff of myth. Julian Adderley, twenty-six—he'd been nicknamed Cannonball as a boy, in tribute to both his voracious appetite ("Cannibal" had naturally morphed into "Cannonball") and his rotund silhouette—came to New York from his native Florida, where he was a high school band director, to take a graduate music course at NYU, with an eye toward earning his master's and getting a college teaching position. His younger brother Nat, a cornetist who'd recently been cut from the Lionel Hampton band for missing a gig, had come along with him. One Sunday night in June 1955, Nat's friend and former Hampton bandmate, the trombonist Buster Cooper, took the brothers to the city's hottest new jazz club, Café Bohemia, on Barrow Street in Greenwich Village, where the house band was led by Oscar Pettiford. Both Adderleys brought along their instruments, in the same spirit that had driven the youthful Miles to take his trumpet to the clubs he visited when he was a student at Juilliard: you never knew when you might get to sit in.

As it happened, Pettiford's saxophonist, Jerome Richardson, didn't show up that night, so Pettiford was down one man—but then he spotted the tenor player Charlie Rouse at a table down in front. Rouse, however, had come without his horn. The problem seemed easily fixable when the bassist saw the husky young man sitting with a saxophone case at his feet. Pettiford sent Rouse to borrow the horn of "the dude over there."

What Oscar Pettiford didn't know was that Charlie Rouse had once played a gig with Cannonball Adderley at a club in Florida and knew how good he was. Rouse therefore decided to have a little fun with Pettiford. He doesn't like lending his horn to anyone, he told the bassist. But he'd be happy to sit in.

As the story goes, Pettiford was so annoyed by this that he decided to teach the kid a lesson. As soon as Cannonball took the stand with his King Super 20 "Silversonic" alto, the bassist counted off "I'll Remember April" at a double-fast tempo. And then, after the first chorus, pointed at the plump young upstart: *Your solo.* Half hoping that the fat kid would freeze, or squeak out a few bars of embarrassing incompetence. And of course the unknown proceeded to blow such a gorgeous cadenza that the audience gaped, and then shouted with the sheer joy of it. Soon afterward, Pettiford summoned brother Nat to the stand, where he displayed his professional, if less pyrotechnic, chops.

That did it for NYU.

Record companies were soon falling over themselves to try and sign Cannonball; the one he chose, EmArcy, a division of Mercury, began a marketing strategy that Adderley disliked intensely. "Jazz circles are touting an ex-schoolteacher, Julian 'Cannonball' Adderley, as the logical successor to the late Charlie Parker," Dorothy Kilgallen wrote in her syndicated column that September. The jazz circles Kilgallen was writing about chiefly consisted of EmArcy's advertising department. Those who had ears to hear realized that although Cannon played alto with amazingly fluid technique, the resemblance to Parker ended there. Julian Adderley was his own thing: a prodigious blues improviser with a "gorgeous swooping tone and plump vibrato," and a strong rhythmic pulse.

Miles quickly made it his business to get down to the Bohemia and sit in with Pettiford and the Adderleys, and in short order he'd found his new saxophone. To his exquisitely attuned ears, Cannonball sounded nothing like Charlie Parker, but there was this congruence: just as Parker had hired Miles Davis, with his spare, vibratoless, midregister sound, to contrast with his own cascading, note-saturated flights, Miles could counterpose Adderley's cheerful musical garrulity with his own lyrical economy.

Adderley was literally garrulous, as well. Miles loved talking with Cannon about all kinds of things, because the saxophonist knew all kinds of things. The Adderleys' parents were both college graduates and school-teachers, and the household where the brothers grew up was filled with books. Both Julian and Nat were readers, thinkers. Like Charlie Parker, Cannon had been taken under the wing of a talented high school bandleader, and like Bill Evans and John Coltrane, he had served in the armed forces and played in a military band, the Thirty-sixth U.S. Army's. Miles's one complaint about him was that since he was smart and articulate and deeply grounded musically, he could be a know-it-all on the subject that Miles knew even better: "Cannonball thought he knew everything back then, so when I would talk to him about some of the silly chords he was playing—I told him he ought to change the way he approached them—he just kind of fluffed me off."

Adderley would soon admit the error of his ways, Miles says; but then, sought-after though he was, Cannon let his super-developed sense of responsibility trump the uncertainties of the jazz life, and returned to Florida to complete his teaching contract, which ran until December.

Miles still needed a saxophone.

The young (just turning twenty-four) tenor player John Gilmore was a trailblazing musician, who'd found his musical calling in the transcendental stylings of the pianist, bandleader, and pioneer Afrofuturist Sun Ra. Ra, born Herman Blount in Alabama, disavowed his terrestrial origins, claiming to be an alien from Saturn sent to Earth to preach peace through music. He called his band the Arkestra. Gilmore, who felt that Sun Ra's explorations in harmony were revolutionary, "had been pushing the [tenor saxophone] to new limits," according to John Szwed, a biographer of Sun Ra as well as of Miles Davis.

In early September Gilmore joined Miles, Garland, Chambers, and Jones for a week at the Blue Note in Philadelphia. But while Davis had great respect for the saxophonist's abilities ("a hell of a player"), his sound didn't fit into the palette that Miles, the master painter, had in mind for his band. "And then," he writes, "Philly Joe brought up John Coltrane."

11   Why he picked me, I don't know

After Johnny Hodges fired him, John Coltrane was back in Philadelphia and spottily employed—so spottily that he was without a job for New Year's Eve of 1954. And so, out of pity, and in gratitude for some musical pointers Coltrane had given him, a trumpeter friend named Ted Curson took him along to a gig in Vineland, New Jersey. Curson, who went on to have a solid jazz career, remembered the evening decades later. "He played 'Nancy with the Laughing Face,' I'll never forget that," he said. "I never heard anything so great, so intense, with so much feeling."

Along with all his other musical strengths, Coltrane had a beautiful way with ballads. But his work problems had nothing to do with musical skill. He was a heroin addict, with the same set of handicaps that had crippled Miles Davis's career from 1949 to 1954: unreliability and general dishevelment made steady work next to impossible. Leading a working band was out of the question. So he picked up whatever gigs he could, when he could. One now-and-then job in 1955 was as part of an ad hoc trio called the Hi-Tones, with the great jazz organist Shirley Scott and the youngest Heath brother, Albert ("Tootie"), on drums. All three were dead-serious, technically sophisticated players. "We were too musical for certain rooms," Coltrane recalled.

"Coltrane was phenomenal even then," Scott said. "We played in and around Philadelphia on and off for at least a year. . . . We played bebop (including 'Half Nelson' and 'Groovin' High'), straight-ahead music. . . . We did rehearse a lot, and we had a lot of arrangements, most of them John's."

Then came the call from Philly Joe Jones.

Philly Joe—Joseph Rudolph Jones had taken on the nickname to differentiate himself from the great swing drummer Jo Jones—went way back with Coltrane: the two had started gigging around town with Percy Heath soon after Coltrane's discharge from the navy. Three years older than the saxophonist, Jones was as different from the quiet, serious, monomaniacal Trane as different could be: he was a brilliant, highly articulate extrovert, a skilled tap dancer and mimic. He was also a serious heroin addict. "Philly Joe Jones was the Babe *Ruth* of junkies," one longtime observer of jazz told me. "I mean, he was *the* junkie. He was *the* cat."

Jones and Miles also went back: for a while during Davis's dark years, the two had barnstormed around the Midwest together, Philly Joe going ahead of Miles to pick up local sidemen in each city. The results were consistently disappointing. Still, it had fed them for a while—fed the monkey on their backs, too.

Miles never made a secret of the fact that Philly Joe was his favorite drummer. "He *knew* everything I was going to do, everything I was going to play," Davis said; "he anticipated me, felt what I was thinking." Jones had a special rim shot that he liked to hit immediately after a Miles solo: it became known around jazz as a Philly lick. Soon, other musicians began asking their drummers for it, too. "I left a lot of space in the music for Philly to fill up," Miles said. "Philly Joe was the kind of drummer that I knew my music had to have. (Even after he left I would listen for a little of Philly Joe in all the drummers I had later.)"

Miles had tapped Jones to contact Coltrane much as he'd deputized the drummer to find sidemen back in the day, only in this case the need was more urgent: Jack Whittemore had set up a tour for the Miles Davis Quintet—Baltimore, Detroit, then back to New York at Birdland and Café Bohemia—but with Sonny Rollins and now John Gilmore out of the picture, the quintet was a quartet.

Coltrane was working at Spider Kelly's in Philadelphia with the organist Jimmy Smith when Philly Joe called and asked if he could come rehearse with the band. Recognizing that this could be his shot at the big time, Trane asked Smith for a few days off and went to New York, where things did not go well.

John Coltrane would ultimately become a jazz deity, by virtue of his supreme technical skills, his ceaseless exploration of the far bounds of the music, and the intense spirituality that informed his life and art. But in 1955 he was an awkward outsider, as far as possible from any kind of distinction in his field. (Even his heroin addiction—desperate, furtive, ashamed—didn't fit into the cool model of jazz culture.) In auditioning for Miles he was virtually coming out from hiding, having spent the past decade freelancing around jazz's seamy outskirts as he searched musically; yet even as his playing improved, he gained little faith in his own abilities. His ceaseless questing for musical and spiritual enlightenment filled him with questions about everything, especially music. And in reencountering a newly ascendant Miles Davis, he was coming up against the ultimate non-answerer.

"Miles is sort of a strange guy," he would tell François Postif in 1961. "He doesn't talk a lot, and he rarely discusses music. You always have the impression that he's in a bad mood, and that he's not interested in or affected by what other people are doing. It's very hard, in a situation like that, to know exactly what you should do. . . ."

Two good things quickly became apparent in those September tryouts: that Coltrane's abilities as a player had advanced considerably since that long-ago gig at the Audubon Ballroom, and that he knew Miles's repertoire. What was less good, Davis recalled many years later, was that

"Trane like to ask all these motherfucking questions . . . about what he should or shouldn't play. Man, fuck that shit; to me he was a professional musician and I have always wanted whoever played with me to find their own place in the music. So my silence and evil looks probably turned him off."

It was an odd business, this angry aloofness of Miles: on the one hand it seems to have been kind of worked up, put on like a vestment of fame and entitlement; on the other hand, at first he and Coltrane seem to have genuinely rubbed each other the wrong way. After a couple of days of rehearsing, the saxophonist told Davis he had to go back to Philadelphia, and left.

If he had secretly wanted Miles to cut out the unpleasant behavior and hire him, Coltrane couldn't have come up with a better strategy than walking away. The first date on the tour, at Baltimore's Club Las Vegas, was rapidly approaching, and Davis still had a hole in the lineup. Coltrane could play, and he knew all the tunes: "We practically had to beg him to join the band," Miles recalled. Coltrane joined.

Another important joining happened around the same time. In Philadelphia a year earlier, at a Saturday jam session at the home of the bassist Steve Davis and his wife, the jazz singer Khadijah Davis, Coltrane had met Khadijah's friend Naima (born Juanita) Austin, and a relationship between the two began. Serious and shy, solemnly dedicated to his art, John Coltrane had never been a sexual adventurer like Miles Davis and Philly Joe Jones and so many other musicians: his adventures, seemingly, were all within his art. And Austin, the single mother of a four-year-old girl and a devout—and abstemious—Muslim, matched his seriousness. He hoped she could help him in his quest to become a better man.

On September 27 Coltrane joined Miles's band at the Club Las Vegas, and Naima soon followed him to Baltimore. On October 3, the day after the quintet's weeklong engagement ended, the two were married, with Davis, Garland, Chambers, and Jones all standing as best men. Just like that, the chemistry between Trane and Miles had shifted: "As a group, on and off stage, we hit it off together," Davis said.

ON OCTOBER 26, IN COLUMBIA'S EAST FIFTY-SECOND STREET STUDIOS, Miles made his recording debut for the label, with George Avakian supervising. Though Avakian's grand plan for marketing Davis was to sell him as a ballad player, this first session consisted entirely of up-tempo numbers with a bebop flair. (There would be two subsequent sessions for Miles's first Columbia album—it wouldn't be issued for a year and a half—with several ballads recorded, including the one that would give the LP, 'Round About Midnight, its title.)

Transcripts of this first date show that as a producer George Avakian was respectful but thorough and assertive, stopping takes short several times when the sound struck him as not exactly right, asking Davis and Coltrane to move closer to the microphone or farther away or, in Coltrane's case, to try to play more confidently: "Miles? Miles, excuse me," Avakian says, stopping take 6 of "Budo" forty-nine seconds in:

> Could we, could we take it once again from the top? There are a
> couple little clams there, and John, again we've got a little spit
> sound, that's probably 'cause you're blowin' soft, you know? If you
> go back, you'll, ah, you'll enable you to blow a little stronger. . . .

Blow a little stronger. Coltrane's solo on the final take of "Budo" (originally a Bud Powell tune called "Hallucinations," then appropriated by Miles as "Budo" for the nonet album, with himself listed as cowriter) is fluid but strangely diffident—as though, cowed by his sudden elevation, he's hesitant to really let go.

Just after Coltrane joined the quintet in Baltimore, Miles had asked George Avakian to come down and listen to him—essentially to sign off on this odd, recessive saxophone player. Avakian heard what Miles had heard. "I remember well that Coltrane just knocked me out with the last set," he said in 2005. "That was the thing I needed to push me over the line."

But Avakian was in the minority. To the jazz world, Loren Schoenberg told me, Miles's hiring Coltrane "was as odd a move as when Bird hired [Miles]—nobody in 1955 could understand why the hell he hired John Coltrane. A junkie and an alcoholic. With a bad rep. Already been fired from Johnny Hodges's band, been fired from Dizzy's band; very, very strange choice."

"I was around when the group started," Bill Evans would later recall. "[And] most people wondered why Miles had Coltrane in the group. He was more or less withdrawn, plus sort of off to the side of the bandstand, sort of half—not fumbling exactly, but just sort of searching."

He played with his eyes closed, introspective rather than performative. Coltrane, Miles said, wouldn't have noticed if a beautiful woman was standing stark naked in front of him.

"Coltrane was like a guy that wasn't really of this world," Sonny Rollins told me. "He was always on another level, to me. He was so involved with music. I shouldn't say just music. Music in an otherworldly, spiritual sense. I hate the word 'spiritual' because it's so overused. But that's the only thing I can think of. Coltrane was a spiritual person with his music. But not just his music—music was his thing that he was doing, but he was doing it in a spiritual way. He was just a spiritual being."

And he was *old*, in jazz terms: twenty-nine, a rather advanced age for a musician who was still arguably a journeyman. Coltrane's first and toughest critic was Coltrane. "When I first joined Miles in 1955 I had a lot to learn," he told an English jazz journalist in 1961.

> I felt I was lacking in general musicianship. I had all kinds of technical problems—for example, I didn't have the right mouthpiece—and I hadn't the necessary harmonic understanding. I am quite ashamed of those early records I made with Miles. Why he picked me, I don't know. Maybe he saw something in my playing that he hoped would grow. I had this desire, which I think we all have, to be as original as I could, and as honest as I could be. But there were so many musical conclusions I hadn't arrived at, that I felt inadequate. All this was naturally frustrating in those days, and it came through in the music.

One way of working through his underconfidence—in performance, not on recording sessions—was to use his solos as explorations, blowing for chorus after chorus as he tried to figure out how to play what he really wanted to say. The method wasn't always popular with his fellow players—or with the bandleader. "Miles would say to him, 'Can't you play 27 choruses instead of 28?'" the drummer Jimmy Cobb recalled. When Coltrane explained that he couldn't figure out how to stop, Miles dryly offered, "You might try taking the horn out of your mouth." But this was just Miles being Miles: in those early days he seemed to understand, Cobb said, "that [Coltrane] was working on something."

In hiring John Coltrane, Miles knew exactly what he was doing. "In Coltrane's dense, vertical style, gritty sound, and emotional ferocity, Miles had found the perfect foil for his own sound and style," Dan Morgenstern writes. "It was a bit like the contrast between himself and Parker—only this time, it was the trumpeter who played lead."

And this time, the leader was a minimalist rather than a maximalist. As for Coltrane, like Charlie Parker, he played a lot of notes. Only unlike Parker, whose improvisations traveled through the chord structure of a blues, standard, or bebop original, searching for harmonies that related to the melody, Coltrane ran all conceivable harmonies of a tune as an end in itself, searching for notes no one had ever thought of using before.

Miles recalled that as the quintet set out on tour, it coalesced with magical quickness: "Faster than I could have imagined, the music that we were playing together was just unbelievable. It was so bad that it used to send chills through me at night, and it did the same thing to the audiences, too."

In fact the process was more gradual, and not always ecstatic. Audiences who'd heard many recordings of Miles playing with Sonny Rollins, the free-swinging young genius, were disappointed at Rollins's unexplained absence; instead, here was this unknown quantity whose tentative explorations on the stand came across as underwhelming, if not tedious. The new tenor had to rely on Miles's patience and implicit pleasure in his playing—there certainly wouldn't have been any pep talks—and his own incessant practicing, which allowed him to make incremental improvements. His growing musical and personal closeness to Red Garland, Paul Chambers, and Philly Joe—who were quickly coming to be known around jazz as the Rhythm Section—was key.

Coltrane's progress was as careful as the man himself, but there was an important breakthrough when the quintet played Jazz City in Los Angeles in January 1956. One night Stan Getz, slightly younger than Trane but already a major star, came up to sit in with the band, and Coltrane was so intimidated that he tried to leave the stand: Miles had to order him to stay. As it happened, Getz was rusty that night—his own drug problems may have had something to do with it—and he couldn't quite mesh with the rhythm section, which by this time fit Coltrane effortlessly. Getz blew a shaky solo, Coltrane soloed smoothly, and though no one had called a cutting contest, Coltrane clearly won the encounter, impressing the audience, and maybe even himself.

Miles's quintet hit the Coast hard. "The sound of New York—funky hard bop with a sophisticated lyrical edge—impinged on cool territory where Gerry Mulligan and Chet Baker had debuted their pianoless quartet a few years before," Ashley Kahn writes. "Nobody knew what to expect," the jazz composer and arranger Sy Johnson told Lewis Porter. "It literally blew everybody out of the water. It destroyed West Coast jazz overnight."

The quintet was busy from the start. In the fall and early winter of 1955 their tour took them to Baltimore, Detroit, New York, Boston, Cleveland, Washington, D.C., and Philadelphia; after L.A. in early '56 they proceeded to San Francisco, Chicago, Quebec City, Boston, and back to New York. Meanwhile, Miles's odd arrangement with Weinstock and Avakian kept him recording for Prestige, now with Coltrane, Garland, Chambers, and Jones, even as he continued to prepare his first Columbia LP.

Miles owed Prestige five albums before he could leave for Columbia. One, recorded in November of '55, was released the following April as *Miles*. Soon after that—two weeks before Davis's thirtieth birthday—the quintet did the first of two marathon dates for Prestige that year: in May at Van Gelder's studio, they recorded thirteen numbers; returning at the end of October, they laid down a dozen more. Over the next five years, Prestige slowly doled out the material in four LPs: *Cookin' with the Miles Davis Quintet*, *Relaxin' with the Miles Davis Quintet*, *Workin' with the Miles Davis Quintet*, and—delaying the release of the last album until mid-1961—*Steamin' with the Miles Davis Quintet*.

The albums were masterpieces, as fresh and vigorous as their apostrophized titles. Due to the very modest terms of Miles's contract with Prestige, the musicians were paying for their own studio time: accordingly, the band laid down each number in a single take unless blatant errors were made. As a result, every disc had the feeling of live performance. (And to add to the freshness, in the style that had become customary on Prestige, a certain amount of studio chatter is included.) This was very different from Avakian's methodical production approach—but then, of course, he had a lot more money to work with.

Yet neither the Prestige albums nor *'Round About Midnight* suffers by mutual comparison. The Prestige LPs are lighter on their feet; the Columbia has better production values: the music is great all around. In each case the rhythm section is perfection. In each case you can hear Miles at the height of his powers and Coltrane ascending toward his. The difference between the saxophonist's rather tentative outing on "Budo," recorded in October of 1955, and his gorgeous, assured, swinging solo on "'Round Midnight," less than a year later—his first great solo—is staggering.

The third Columbia session was called for the morning of September 10, 1956: a fair, cool day with a hint of autumn in the air. Leonard Bernstein, another Columbia artist, was present in the Thirtieth Street Studio that day, to supervise the quintet's recording of one of the numbers on the agenda, the old jazz chestnut "Sweet Sue, Just You." Among his many other endeavors, Bernstein had achieved great currency as a TV lecturer on music; for his regular segment on the popular show *Omnibus* he planned to demonstrate jazz's evolution through clips of various bands playing "Sweet Sue." He would also release a companion record album, to be called *What Is Jazz*.

As recordings of the between-takes chatter show, Bernstein was every inch the maestro in the studio that day, but of course Miles was a maestro, too; we can hear that the conductor and Miles accorded each other a certain amount of deference. Bernstein's deference stopped there, however. At one point during a rehearsal of the song, Red Garland asks, "Hey, how many choruses on this?" and Miles says, "One each." Bernstein then elaborates: "One for Miles and one for, um—" "Coltrane," Miles quickly interjects.

As hard as it is to imagine John Coltrane as an outsider, a virtual unknown, this is just what he was when he joined Miles and for the next two years, as he refined his art on and off the bandstand and—slowly—began to impress a jazz world that initially had difficulty figuring out what to make of the strange beauty of his playing.

"I don't think we would have known Coltrane's potential or [had] the great contributions that he's made, except for Miles and Miles's belief in his potential," Bill Evans said, years later. "But Miles really knew, somehow, the depth and the development that Coltrane had coming, and just gave him all the room, just gave him all the room, man."

BACK IN LOUISIANA, EVANS HAD EMERGED FROM HIS YEAR OF DOUBT AND study with strengthened confidence and determination. He later said, "I can remember coming to New York to make or break in jazz and saying to myself, *Now, how should I attack this practical problem of becoming a jazz musician, as making a living and so on?* And ultimately, I came to the conclusion that all I must do is take care of the music, even if I do it in a closet. And if I *really* do that, somebody's going to come and open the door of the closet and say, *Hey, we're looking for you.*"

His new home wasn't quite a closet, but it was close. In July 1955 Evans moved into a Bird-less Big Apple, tapping his savings to rent a tiny studio apartment on West Eighty-third Street, which his Knabe grand piano filled almost entirely. On the music stand were pieces by Chopin, Ravel, and Scriabin, as well as Bach's *The Well-Tempered Clavier*. When he practiced he loved to play classical then modulate into improvised jazz, the tempo turning to idiosyncratic rhythm, the harmonies close cousins to those in the European music.

He gave himself five years to make it in jazz. In the first year he paid the rent mostly by playing dance music: "the Friendship Club in Brooklyn three nights a week, and the Roseland Ballroom on Wednesday afternoons. He chased a bewildering variety of 'Tuxedo gigs': society balls, Jewish weddings, intermission spots, and, most depressing of all, the over-forty dances. He rode down to Rockaway on the subway and played in some bar or other till five in the morning for a pittance."

He also enrolled in the Mannes College of Music, then on the Upper East Side, for courses in composition: he satisfied his intellectual hunger by studying twelve-tone technique and writing songs set to the poetry of William Blake. Blake was very important to him. Years later Evans would tell an interviewer:

> He's almost like a folk poet, but he reaches heights of art because of his simplicity. The simple things, the essences, are the great things, but our way of expressing them can be incredibly complex. It's the same thing with technique in music. You try to express a simple emotion—love, excitement, sadness—and often your technique gets in the way. It becomes an end in itself when it should really be only the funnel through which your feelings and ideas are communicated. The great artist always gets right to the heart of the matter. His technique is so natural it's invisible or unhearable. I've always had good facility, and that worries me. I hope it doesn't get in the way.

Intellectual though he may have been, his visceral love of jazz led him to the clubs: Basin Street, the Hickory House, the Embers, Birdland. Evans began to sit in with established players, everyone he accompanied hearing at once that he was a pianist of superlative abilities who sounded a bit like Bud Powell, a bit like Ahmad Jamal, but mostly like nobody else. "His apprenticeship at Southeastern," Pettinger writes, "had stimulated his ear for tone color, the potency of harmony, as well as for mood and emotion, in a way that only the European classical repertoire could."

Nineteen fifty-five and 'fifty-six brought more and more sideman work. He toured in quartets with Tony Scott, an ambitious, classically trained clarinetist he knew from the Chicago jazz clubs he frequented while he was in the army. And in August of '55, soon after moving to the city, Evans accompanied a now forgotten singer named Lucy Reed on her album *The Singing Reed*. He'd first seen Reed perform at those same Chicago jazz clubs: she was a superbly tuneful and tasteful vocalist, imparting a dry and knowing quality to the often lesser-known American Songbook pieces she chose to perform; and Evans, with his quiet, exquisitely voiced chords, was a perfect accompanist for her.

One hot morning that August, Reed phoned a friend of hers, the jazz composer and arranger George Russell, and told him she'd like to visit with a friend named Bill. Russell, who lived with his wife, Juanita, in a small room in an east twenties residential hotel called the Beechwood, suggested they all beat the heat by taking a ride on the Staten Island Ferry.

Russell had no idea who this Bill was, and his first impression wasn't promising: "plain-looking fella, very quiet, very withdrawn." This is going to be like pulling teeth all day, he thought. "Eventually," Pettinger writes,

> they returned to the Russells' place at the Beechwood Hotel, where the stove, bed, ironing board, and piano were crammed together into one room. George was paying his dues working behind a lunch counter while working on his theoretical magnum opus [the *Lydian Chromatic Concept of Tonal Organization*]. As it happened, some of his arrangements had already come Bill's way for a concert with Lucy. The ironing board was moved onto the bed so that Evans could play, while Russell, expecting the worst, hovered at the door ready to make an excuse. Instead, "It was one of those magic moments in your life when you expect a horror story," he now recalls, "and the doors of heaven open up—I knew then and there he wasn't going to get away."

Born in 1923 to a white father and a Black mother, George Russell was a nonesuch, a brilliant musical theorist destined to change jazz, yet fated to remain all but unknown himself. His *Lydian Chromatic Concept* had actually been published in 1953, while Russell was working as a salesclerk at Macy's, and his music had been known to jazz musicians since at least 1947, when Dizzy Gillespie, seeking to meld the music he and Charlie Parker had cocreated with Cuban jazz, recorded Russell's two-part Afro-Cuban composition "Cubana Be/Cubana Bop." In 1950 Artie Shaw recorded another Russell tune, "Similau."

These two numbers didn't sound like conventional jazz tunes because, unlike popular songs or bebop numbers, they were based on greatly simplified chord structures—just one or two chords rather than a progression of several—and on unusual *modes*.

Modes are scales—scales with distinctive sounds and emotional colors. There are dozens of modal variations in world music. (And much of world music is played on string and wind instruments, which, unlike a piano, allow many gradations in tone between one note and the next.) Different modes can make a piece of music sound Spanish or Middle Eastern, Chinese or Indian. In Western music, most popular and classical pieces are based on the Ionian mode (the major scale, e.g. C D E F G A B C on a piano, with half-steps between E and F and B and C) and the Aeolian (the natural minor scale, which can be heard in the white keys from A to A). The blues are usually in Dorian (from C: C D E♭ F G A B♭ C) or Mixolydian (from C: C D E F G A B♭ C).

Popular songs are built on chord progressions, sometimes simple, as in Irving Berlin's "Always," and sometimes complex, as in Jerome Kern's "All the Things You Are" or Billy Strayhorn's "Lush Life." Bebop tunes were often contrafacts of popular standards—meaning they were built on the same chord structures as American Songbook standbys like "How High the Moon" (Charlie Parker's "Ornithology"), "What Is This Thing Called Love" (Tadd Dameron's "Hot House"), or "I Got Rhythm" (too many to name). And bebop was so notorious for cycling through chord changes at such breakneck speed that—as early as the late forties but especially after the death of Charlie Parker—jazz began to react by looking for new directions. Influenced in part by modern European-classical composers like Debussy and Bartók, jazz musicians began to move beyond traditional major/minor tonality, toward new modes and simplified chord structures.

George Russell was an important explorer of these directions. Jazz players heard something completely fresh in his music: "George composes things which sound improvised," Bill Evans later said. "You have to be deeply involved in jazz and understand all the elements to do that." The things that Russell composed had dauntingly odd names, and sounded— still sound—formidably strange to untutored ears.

In late 1956, RCA tapped George Russell to compose and lead an album in a new series of recordings the label called Jazz Workshop. The result was *The George Russell Smalltet*, including Hal McKusick on alto and flute, Art Farmer on trumpet, Barry Galbraith on guitar, Milt Hinton on bass, Paul Motian on drums, and Bill Evans on piano. In the months after the Staten Island ferry ride, Evans and Russell had become good friends; with teasing affection, Russell and his wife nicknamed the pianist "the minister."

All the compositions on *Smalltet* were by Russell, and they were as singular as their appellations: "Ye Hypocrite, Ye Beelzebub," "Livingstone I Presume," and "Knights of the Steamtable," among others.

If this is indeed a jazz record, then what's being talked about is a very broad definition of jazz—but then, the form had been cross-pollinating with modern European classical almost from its beginning in the 1910s, and had been broadening since the demise of swing around the end of World War II. And on the evidence of listening to the *Smalltet*, George Russell's language, which even to some of its players sounded strange at first, was one in which Bill Evans felt thoroughly comfortable.

No track on the album gives stronger evidence of this than "Concerto for Billy the Kid"—no relation whatever to Aaron Copland's 1938 vernacular ballet score on the same subject. For all its dissonances and unexpected syncopations, its almost complete lack of any passage one might hum or whistle, this is a strangely exciting piece, with a driving energy all its own: busy, energetic, cooking. It could be the theme music for an outer-space western. And around two and a half minutes in—2:28, to be exact—a remarkable thing happens: the other instruments drop out, and Evans begins a darting, swooping, dazzlingly fast solo, shooting sprays and bou-quets of rapid-fire single-note leaps and pirouettes *with his right hand only*, punctuated by occasional stop-time *chunk*s on bass, drums, or guitar.

Russell designed the piece, and particularly the solo, "to supply a frame to match the vigor and vitality in the playing of Bill Evans," he said.

A player Evans saw a lot of during that period was an old friend, the Mississippi-born guitarist Mundell Lowe. The two had met at Southeast-ern Louisiana and had gigged together there, and then again after Bill moved to New York City. On one of these recent engagements, a 1956 trio date with Lowe, Evans, and the bassist Herman "Trigger" Alpert, Alpert turned on his Ampex reel-to-reel tape recorder and memorialized the oc-casion. He had a specific aim in mind: both he and Lowe felt it was time for Evans to make his first record as a leader, and both knew that the pi-anist's generally low level of confidence and high level of self-criticism would prevent him from seeking to do so—or even recording a demo—on his own.

Mundell Lowe had put out a couple of quartet and quintet LPs with a scrappy new independent label called Riverside. Cofounded by a pair of old college friends named Bill Grauer and Orrin Keepnews, Riverside had begun in the early fifties with reissues of albums by early jazz artists like Jelly Roll Morton and Ma Rainey. Then, in 1954, Grauer and Keepnews signed their first contemporary jazz musician, the young pianist Randy Weston. (In their shoestring operation, Grauer handled the business end and Keepnews, who'd long dreamed of being a record producer, simply started doing it and found he was good at it.) In 1955, in an artistic coup, Riverside picked up Thelonious Monk, whose previous label, Prestige, had had little commercial success with LPs of the pianist playing his own compositions. Riverside paid Prestige $108.27 to buy out Monk's contract—then had him put out two albums of standards to gain broader acceptance.

A mental exercise: Imagine a world in which there is a wide jazz-listening public. Now further imagine that to that public, Thelonious Monk is a pianist with a comical name and hard-to-understand compositions, and Bill Evans is a pianist with a generic name who is all but unknown. This was the real world of America in 1956.

To press their case for Evans, Lowe and Alpert called Grauer and Keepnews and played Alpert's tape recording over the phone. The young record executives were impressed enough to go listen to Evans playing live, which impressed them even more. And so, in a reversal of usual procedure, in which an artist was a supplicant, the artist's manager or agent pleading the artist's case to a label by presenting a demo, Grauer and Keepnews wooed Bill Evans, going to some lengths to persuade him to record with as little protective mediation as possible: in a trio setting, and under his own name.

Evans's contract with Riverside was bare bones, but the label extended him one major accommodation, allowing him two recording sessions to make his first album, rather than the single session a new artist would customarily receive. The result was *New Jazz Conceptions*, an LP whose earnestly generic title belied its fresh contents.

On September 18 and 27, 1956, at Reeves Sound Studios on East Forty-fourth Street, with fellow Tony Scott alumni Teddy Kotick on bass and Paul Motian on drums, Evans laid down the album's eleven tracks, which included five standards—Cole Porter's "I Love You"; "I Got It Bad (And That Ain't Good)," by Duke Ellington and Paul Francis Webster; "Easy Living," by Leo Robin and Ralph Rainger; Kurt Weill and Ogden Nash's "Speak Low"; and Rodgers and Hart's "My Romance"—along with two jazz pieces by others, George Shearing's well-traveled "Conception" and Tadd Dameron's "Our Delight," and four original compositions by Bill Evans: "Five," "Displacement," "Waltz for Debby," and the blues "No Cover, No Minimum."

To a certain extent, Evans and Orrin Keepnews were playing it safe. The album was a bouquet of different styles, each of its tracks played with impressive technique and great youthful brio. There was something for everyone. The pianist harmonized the five standards beautifully enough to make them sound new. He played the more challenging material—his Monk-ish "Five," the literally offbeat "Displacement," Shearing's bebop-period (lots of chords) "Conception"—with infectious energy, spurred on by Motian's propulsive drumming. And the three solo pieces—"I Got It Bad," "My Romance," and "Waltz for Debby," all of them under two minutes long—were gorgeous miniatures, each a jewel box of lyricism. The meltingly lovely "Debby," which Evans had composed two years earlier for Harry and Pat Evans's toddler daughter, was destined to become a classic, and, as Pettinger writes, "classical in another sense . . . comparable to a piano vignette of, say, Robert Schumann's."

Released in February 1957, *New Jazz Conceptions* would sell eight hundred copies.

SOMETIME IN THE SUMMER OF 1956 CAME WHAT EVANS ALWAYS THOUGHT of as his big break, a solo gig opposite the Modern Jazz Quartet at the storied Village Vanguard, on Seventh Avenue South. "Nobody knew me, of course," Evans recalled,

> and you could hear a pin drop during their sets, and despite the fact that Milt Jackson gave me a really fine introduction every time, this intimidated the audience into about five and a half seconds of silence, and from then on it was thunderous din. But I just kept playing. . . . Now one gratifying thing: one night I looked up, opened my eyes while I was playing, and Miles's head was at the end of the piano listening.

JOHN COLTRANE LOVED THE RHYTHM SECTION IN MILES DAVIS'S QUINTET— loved the three players musically and personally. But his friendship with Red Garland, Paul Chambers, and Philly Joe Jones, gratifying as it was, contained an element that would lead to the dissolution of the band.

Miles's quintet was great, but, as Eric Nisenson writes, "the group almost immediately got the appellation 'the D and D' band—'Drunk and Dope.'"

"Red often came late to gigs," Szwed writes.

> Chambers was frequently drunk, even passing out while he ate. And Joe and John were usually high. Stories of Davis' problems with this band were legion. Miles may have been the only member of the band free of heroin at the time, and he spent much of his time on the road keeping watch over them, trailing after them, keeping them away from the cops, getting them fed, or sobering them up. Miles sometimes wrote out checks to Philly Joe with sardonic notes on them saying that they were for dope. Unbeknown to the band, he even kept a stash of heroin in case of an emergency with one of them.

Miles had turned thirty in May; suddenly he was the adult in the room. And of course, not so suddenly: rebuilding his reputation had taken months of herculean effort, and he was determined to hold on to it. He was in the big leagues now, signed to a major label, making real money. The last thing he needed was more ignominy.

Coltrane, the other frontman in the quintet and therefore the most conspicuous player along with Miles, was becoming the particular focus of his disapproval. Now that New York had become Trane's home base, he had access to the strongest heroin in the country; when he wasn't drugging he was drinking, and both were affecting his performance. He kept trying to quit but couldn't. Although he had married Naima with the intention of pulling himself together, he hadn't had enough of a home life over the past year to profit by her influence. In June she and her daughter, Syeeda, moved to New York to be close to John, who was playing often at Café Bohemia; but then he spent much of June and July on tour in the Midwest. It was a haunted summer: on June 26, Clifford Brown and Bud Powell's brother Richie were killed in a car wreck, upending the jazz world and sending Max Roach, who'd founded a dynamic and successful group with Brown, into a tailspin. Brown was just twenty-five. (In a horrible irony, the sweet-tempered trumpeter, who seemed beloved by everybody, was one of the few major jazz artists who neither drank nor did drugs.)

Miles and the band were back at the Bohemia for all of September, and Ira Gitler was there often. "A lot of times you wouldn't see Coltrane between sets," he remembered. "He would be in the basement practicing, and he was drinking a mixture of wine and beer. I guess he was trying to kick heroin. He just wasn't too communicative."

At Storyville in Boston immediately afterward, "Coltrane was in particularly bad shape, nodding off on the bandstand, showing up late most nights, or not at all, his clothes sometimes filthy and foul." When this continued upon the band's return to Café Bohemia in mid-October, Miles fired Coltrane, or he quit; Sonny Rollins, back on the scene after kicking heroin, replaced him. Some sources say that Coltrane then returned, played alongside Rollins for a couple of nights—then left again after more arguments with Davis and went home to Philadelphia. But then he was back at the end of the month for the band's ultimate marathon session for Prestige.

On October 31 Miles suspended the quintet and went to Europe to tour with the so-called Birdland All-Stars: Lester Young, the Modern Jazz Quartet, and Bud Powell—who, though he was on the bill for concerts in France, the Netherlands, Belgium, Germany, and Sweden, was in such an advanced state of schizophrenia that he could barely play. A French rhythm section accompanied Davis and Young; Miles had a romance with the sister of his piano player and friend René Urtréger. He also reconnected with Juliette Gréco on the trip, and, despite the good time he was having musically and personally, told an English jazz writer that much as he would like to stay longer in Europe, he couldn't extend the tour after its allotted one month: "I've got to get back home. . . . I've got four guys depending on me back there. I've got the best rhythm section in the world right now. Philly Joe Jones is just great and you know that Coltrane is the best since Bird."

Actually, the English jazz writer, Alun Morgan, knew nothing of the sort. Though all the recordings for *Cookin'*, *Relaxin'*, *Workin'*, and *Steamin'* were in the can, as were the three sessions for *'Round About Midnight*, it would be months, or in the case of the latter three Prestige titles, years, before the albums were released. The only Coltrane Morgan could have heard would have been on *The New Miles Davis Quintet*, the LP that *DownBeat*'s reviewer had docked a star for the saxophonist's "general lack of individuality." Alun Morgan politely changed the subject and moved on to other matters.

UPON HIS RETURN FROM FRANCE, MILES WAS AS GOOD AS HIS WORD: HE reassembled the quintet and embarked on a five-month tour: Washington, D.C., Chicago, L.A., San Francisco, Pittsburgh, Chicago again, Baltimore, and finally, back to the Café Bohemia in April 1957. But the drinking and drugging continued, and sometime in the middle of the trip, Davis's patience began to fray—especially with Coltrane and Philly Joe, who were often "showing up late, sometimes not at all. Here was Trane up on the bandstand sometimes nodding out, high off heroin."

While they were playing Preview's Modern Jazz Room in Chicago, his frustration emerged in a strange way: during a break, Miles announced to a couple of journalists that he was quitting jazz. "I've had it," he said. "This is no sudden decision. I've been thinking about it for a long time and after I close here I'm calling it quits." He said he'd been offered a teaching position at Howard University and a job as music director at a record company. He had all the money he needed, he said; he was fed up with the business. He was tired of jazz. He didn't even like the word anymore.

Miles loved Coltrane. Though they were too unalike to hang out the way he and Philly Joe did, Davis understood the saxophonist's basic decency, his soulfulness. He'd explained to him over and over that record producers had been coming to their gigs, wanting to give the saxophonist a contract, but when they saw him nodding out on the stand, they lost interest. "He seemed to understand what I was talking about, but he kept right on shooting heroin and drinking like a fish."

According to Jackie McLean, who was playing (with Art Blakey) opposite Miles's band when the quintet returned to the Café Bohemia, Coltrane had finally decided to go cold turkey, "but he came to work every night being sick. Of course he was drinking quite a bit and trying to fight it off. . . . He was in miserable shape in the same clothes, same shirt, all creased up and dirty, same tie. . . ."

This was doubly offensive to Miles, not only reminding him sharply of his own bad time but clashing severely with the clean, commercial image he was now trying to project. More than commercial. Columbia was trying to make him a star—one night George Avakian came to the Bohemia with a publicist for the label, who "immediately declared that with his Italian suits, Cole Porter tunes, and seductive use of the mute, she could get [Davis] into *Newsweek* or *Time*." And Miles was fine with this. The club's name notwithstanding, he had no bohemian misgivings about fame or wealth—bring them on.

And here was his saxophone player, "playing in clothes that looked like he had slept in them for days . . . standing up there when he wasn't nodding—picking his nose and sometimes eating it."

Things came to a head when the Bohemia gig ended. On April 28, Miles fired both Coltrane and Philly Joe, Jones having not only hindered the band with his own bad behavior but, Miles felt, been a bad influence on Trane. Sonny Rollins and Art Taylor would replace them.

Miles says in his memoir that he didn't just fire Coltrane. He was so fed up with the saxophonist, he writes, that "I slapped him upside his head and punched him in the stomach in the dressing room." The book claims that Thelonious Monk, who'd stopped by to say hello, witnessed the assault, upbraided Miles, and told Coltrane that he didn't have to put up with it. "You can come play with me anytime," Monk is said to have said—and as we'll see, there is good reason to believe that he actually said it.

12 I began to accept the position in which I had been placed

Thelonious Monk wasn't one to do anything casually, let alone drop nonchalantly by a club dressing room to shoot the breeze with a fellow musician. Though his actions were sometimes mysterious to those around him, even his intimates, he was guided by deep feelings, and as an early fan of the Davis quintet's shows at the Café Bohemia—despite his fraught history with Miles—he'd recognized John Coltrane at once as a brilliant musician and a kind of fellow sufferer.

Monk wasn't an addict, strictly speaking—reefer and alcohol, the latter sometimes used to excess, were his occasional drugs of choice—but he'd seen too many colleagues and friends brought down by heroin, and, his biographer Robin Kelley writes, he "developed a soft spot for the quiet and self-deprecating saxophonist. A fellow homeboy born and raised in High Point, North Carolina, 'Trane in turn had long admired Monk's music ever since he recorded "Round Midnight' with Dizzy Gillespie back in 1949." And, of course, he had recently recorded it again with Miles.

Kelley postulates that Monk and Coltrane became close when Monk played a two-week gig at Philadelphia's Blue Note in November 1956, while Miles was in Europe and Coltrane had returned home for the month. Paul Chambers, also at liberty, was part of Monk's quartet: "So it is conceivable that 'Trane either came out to the Blue Note to hear the band or Chambers accompanied Monk to Coltrane's house on Thirty-third Street. Whatever the case, the timing of Monk's Philadelphia gig allowed the two men to get to know each other a little better outside of New York. Here, in the City of Brotherly Love, the seeds of a longstanding friendship were sown."

Five months later, Coltrane was out of a job. But while Miles had banished him in no uncertain terms, he'd also told him, well remembering his own experience, that he would take him back if he kicked heroin. Accordingly, Porter writes, the saxophonist "took this opportunity to get his career and his personal life together. He had begun rehearsing informally with Thelonious Monk."

Nica de Koenigswarter, the Jazz Baroness, having been evicted by the Stanhope after the unholy frenzy surrounding Charlie Parker's death, had relocated to another hotel, the Bolivar on Central Park West, where a constant parade of jazz musicians, Monk prominent among them, streamed through, jamming on and around her Steinway at all hours. This, too, ended badly. "People complained about the noise, not realizing that they were hearing this fantastic music they would never hear again in their lives and I was thrown out of there," she reminisced, laughingly, years later. And so she and her piano moved to a suite at an ostensibly artsier establishment, the Algonquin Hotel on West Forty-fourth Street. Her rotating cast of musicians followed. "Besides Monk," Kelley writes,

a parade of pianists dropped by constantly, notably Elmo Hope, Bud Powell, Kenny Drew, Horace Silver, Hampton Hawes, Dick Katz, and Sonny Clark. Art Blakey was always there, and "Philly" Joe Jones came by on occasion, as did Charles Mingus and [the bassist] Wilbur Ware. Sonny Rollins and John Coltrane also spent a great deal of time at the Algonquin. Coltrane and Monk had grown quite close, the latter assuming the role of mentor. Coltrane had been playing Monk's tunes as part of Miles Davis's band but wanted to learn more—in particular, "Monk's Mood." So, one night at the Algonquin, Thelonious sat down with 'Trane and taught him "Monk's Mood."

He taught him well. On April 16, 1957, just days before Miles fired him, Coltrane, along with Wilbur Ware, accompanied Monk on a spare and gorgeous recording of the song, the only non-solo piece on the great Riverside album *Thelonious Himself*—and, like Trane's solo the previous fall on the Columbia "'Round Midnight," a glorious display of John Coltrane, in full lyrical form, sounding like the Coltrane his admirers would come to revere.

Inevitably, the baroness was soon banished once more ("I went to the Algonquin, because they were supposed to be broader-minded and they liked having geniuses there," Nica recalled. "But Thelonious"—who sometimes wandered the halls in a red shirt and shades, carrying a white walking stick—"turned out to be one genius too far for them"), so Coltrane's music lessons moved to Monk's apartment on West Sixty-third, and continued almost daily, in a unique fashion.

"I'd go by his apartment, and get him out of bed maybe," Coltrane told the Baltimore jazz enthusiast August Blume in a wide-ranging 1958 interview.

> And he'd wake up and go over to the piano and start playing, you know. He'd play anything, maybe just one of his tunes. He'd start playing it and he'd look at me, and when he'd look at me I'd get my horn and start trying to find what he's playing. And he'd continue to play over and over and over and over and I'd get this part, and next time he'd go over it I'd get another part. And he would stop to show me some parts that were pretty difficult, and if I had a lot of trouble, he'd get his portfolio out and show me the music. . . . He would rather a guy learn without reading, you know,

because that way you feel it better. You feel it quicker when you
memorize it, when you learn it by heart, by ear, you know. And so
when I almost had the tune down, then he would . . . leave me to
practice it alone, and he'd go out somewhere, maybe he'd go to the
store or go back to bed or something. And I'd just stay here and
run over the tune [until] I had it pretty well, and then I'd call him
and we'd play it down together. And sometimes we'd just get one
tune a day.

His firing by Miles—and maybe that gut punch, too—was the shock
that finally got Coltrane to think seriously about changing his life. He returned to Philadelphia and, as always, practiced intensely, sometimes
alone and sometimes with an old friend, the trumpeter and composer Cal
Massey. Massey was leading a quintet composed of brilliant Philadelphians: the saxophonist Clarence "C" Sharpe, bassist Jimmy Garrison,
drummer Tootie Heath, and an eighteen-year-old piano phenomenon
named McCoy Tyner. One afternoon at the Red Rooster, a club at Fifty-
second and Market, Coltrane was watching Massey's band rehearse when
the club owner asked him if he would play next week. Coltrane said that
he didn't have a band. Then he asked Massey if he could borrow his
rhythm section. Massey suggested he ask them himself.

"Naturally, we said, that would be great!" Tyner recalled. "That was the
first time I played with John. . . . We got pretty close. I used to go sit on
his mother's porch and we would talk. He was like a big brother to me, it
was more like family."

It was during that week and the next, in early May of 1957, that John
Coltrane kicked his heroin addiction cold turkey. He would have suffered
the customary agonies of withdrawal, and more: his teeth, full of cavities
from the sweets he was also addicted to, were killing him. Ordinarily,
he'd have tried to ease the pain with liquor—but he was also trying to quit
drinking.

What part Naima, the devout Muslim and steadying influence to whom
he'd been married for a year and a half, played in his reformation isn't

clear. With Miles's path out of addiction, we get every grimace and drop of sweat, every word of encouragement from his father and others; with Coltrane, the very reserved individual, we get less. Naima's faith may have inspired or driven him, though he himself never converted to Islam. It seems more likely that he was impelled by some combination of Muslim beliefs and his own spiritual and philosophical readings, along with Miles Davis's tough love and Thelonious Monk's quiet admiration. "During the year 1957," he would write in the liner notes of his great 1964 album *A Love Supreme*,

> I experienced, by the grace of God, a spiritual awakening which was to lead me to a richer, fuller, more productive life. At that time, in gratitude, I humbly asked to be given the means and privilege to make others happy through music. I feel this has been granted through His grace.

In 1958 Coltrane explained his personal code to Ira Gitler: "Live cleanly . . . Do right . . . You can improve as a player by improving as a person. It's a duty we owe to ourselves." He put it more pragmatically to Ralph Gleason in an early 1960s interview: "I went through a personal crisis, you know, and I came out of it. I felt so fortunate to have come through it successfully, that all I wanted to do, if I could, would be to play music that would make people happy."

In any case, Lewis Porter claims that when Coltrane returned to New York in mid-May, he was "rejuvenated." In April he had signed a three-album contract with Bob Weinstock and Prestige, and on Friday, May 31, at Rudy Van Gelder's studio in Hackensack, he recorded his first LP as a leader. It was an assured debut, with Trane's solo work on the standard "Violets for Your Furs" displaying his soon to be famous ability to infuse a ballad with emotion, while on an original of his own, the meaningfully titled "Straight Street," an up-tempo number that shifts between darkness and optimism, he swings with effortless Coltrane flair, the tyranny of Bird's influence far behind him.

MAY 1957 WAS A VERY BIG MONTH FOR THELONIOUS MONK. IT WAS THE month that saw the release of his great album *Brilliant Corners*, which *DownBeat*'s editor Nat Hentoff called, in a five-star review, "Riverside's most important modern jazz LP to date." And around the same time, Monk got his cabaret card back.

The restoration was the result of heroic teamwork by Nica de Koenigswarter, who hired the lawyer who got the pianist a police hearing; by Monk's manager, a Queens high school teacher named Harry Colomby (the younger brother of the trumpeter and Prestige Records gofer Jules Colomby); and by Joe Termini, the co-owner of the Bowery dive bar– artist's hangout the Five Spot Café. The State Liquor Authority had agreed to grant Monk a hearing only on the condition that a club commit to hiring him, and as a result of Harry Colomby's lobbying, Termini and the bar's co-owner, his brother Iggy, had so committed. "They not only agreed to give Monk a gig," Kelley writes, "but Joe willingly testified on Monk's behalf at the police hearing. It worked. Once approved, Monk promptly headed down to 56 Worth Street, the Police License Division, where he was fingerprinted, photographed, and relieved of two bucks (the fees went to a retirement fund for cops). He walked out with card number G7321, a license to work, and a job." He was to start, with sidemen to be determined, on July 4. He was thirty-nine years old, and it would be his first regular employment in a decade.

Buoyant in what was to be one of his biggest years, Thelonious kept his promise to John Coltrane—*you can come play with me anytime*—and hired him for his fifth Riverside album, which would begin recording on June 25. But the sessions, on the evenings of the twenty-fifth and the twenty-sixth, turned out to be more stressful than anticipated: for one thing, Monk's wife, Nellie, was suffering the emotional and physical aftereffects of a recent thyroidectomy; for another, Monk was debuting a number about which he cared a great deal and which he'd through-composed meticulously, "Crepuscule with Nellie," a tribute he'd begun writing when his wife had first fallen ill. And for yet another, he had also enlisted the great Coleman Hawkins, a hero and mentor of his, for the date. On the date as well were the trumpeter Ray Copeland, Gigi Gryce, Wilbur Ware, and Art Blakey.

After the first session had broken down over difficulties with the over-fraught "Crepuscule," the second "was a long night of recording for some of Monk's sidemen," Kelley writes. "The music challenged the musicians, and Thelonious vacillated between being an unforgiving taskmaster and a patient teacher." The difficulty of the album's creation, which had everything to do with the absolute originality of Monk's compositions, alchemized into spectacular results. On its release that November, *Monk's Music* (all its tunes, except for a prelude, a horns-only arrangement of the old hymn "Abide with Me," were Monk originals) would carry forward the momentum of *Brilliant Corners*, further erode the notion of Thelonious Monk as a mere eccentric or novelty act, and strengthen his position as one of jazz's—and America's—great composers.

———

THE FIVE SPOT, AT 5 COOPER SQUARE, THE BOWERY'S NORTHERN END, HAD begun its existence in the early 1900s as a dive called the Bowery Café, a small, nondescript bar among many other bars in the booming shadows of the Third Avenue El. The Bowery itself, all four-fifths of a mile of it, had started out innocently back in Manhattan's Arcadian days, as a country lane lined with small farms (the word "bowery" comes from an old Dutch word for farm); it wasn't until the mid-nineteenth century that the avenue began to go to seed, sprouting saloons, flophouses, whorehouses, tattoo parlors, greasy spoons, cheap clothing stores, and, of course, the bums whose very existence turned the thoroughfare's name into a synonym for dereliction. The El went up in 1878, locking in the ambient shadiness.

Salvatore Termini, Joe and Iggy's father, had bought the café in 1937, and when the two brothers came home from the war in 1946, they helped him run it. The clientele mainly consisted of drunks and blue-collar workers: the booze was cheap, overhead was low, and so were profits, but it gave the Terminis a steady income. When Sal retired in 1951, Joe and Iggy took over. Then, in 1955, the El was demolished, and everything changed.

There had been outcries to clean up the Bowery ever since it first got dirty, and with the return of sunlight, the disinfecting began. The city widened and repaved the avenue, planted trees, installed streetlights, razed flophouses. Downtown artists and musicians, always on the lookout for cheap apartments and loft space, took notice and started to move into the neighborhood. When some of the new denizens of what was now being called the East Village began to drift in for a drink—or a seventy-five-cent pitcher of beer at a poetry reading—Joe and Iggy Termini took notice. They spiffed up the place, put some art posters on the walls. A merchant marine and would-be jazz pianist named Don Shoemaker held jam sessions in his loft next door: when running schooners of brew up and down the stairs got old, he suggested that the Terminis get a piano—the musicians could play right in the bar. It made business sense. The brothers bought an old upright and applied for a cabaret license. "They received the license August 30, 1956, and a week later opened for business as the Five Spot, the newest jazz club in the Village," Robin Kelley writes. "Within weeks of the club's reincarnation, the Five Spot earned a reputation as *the* local place for cheap beer and good music."

Downtown types loved to drink, smoke reefer, and gossip: news traveled fast on the bongo-drum grapevine. Soon the little place (official seating capacity: seventy-six) was awash in painters and sculptors—names that have solid-gold Sotheby resonance in today's commoditized world, but were then mainly known to gallery goers and each other: Willem de Kooning, Grace Hartigan, Franz Kline, Joan Mitchell, Larry Rivers, Bob Thompson, Jack Tworkov—and writers: Jack Kerouac, Gregory Corso, James Baldwin, Allen Ginsberg, Ted Joans, LeRoi Jones, Frank O'Hara. And then, musicians.

The jazz musicians arrived more gradually, because the core of jazz energy was Black, and Black faces were unwelcome in what was still a largely ethnic (Italian and Polish and Ukrainian) blue-collar neighborhood. Ted Joans carried "a blackjack and a napkin filled with hot pepper to throw in their eyes in case I was attacked." LeRoi Jones had a similar strategy, carrying "a lead pipe in a manila envelope, the envelope under my arm like a good messenger, not intimidated but nevertheless ready."

The venturesome composer, arranger, and multi-instrumentalist David Amram, then studying at Manhattan School of Music under Dimitri Mitropoulos, Vittorio Giannini, and Gunther Schuller, quickly found his way to the Five Spot and soon started hipping his music friends, many of them Black, to the place. One was a twenty-seven-year-old pianist who seemed as far as possible from what the Five Spot's white habitués might have expected of a jazz musician. Cecil Taylor came from an intellectual middle-class family on Long Island; he was classically trained; he wrote poetry and read widely. (He also happened to be gay, though that was something no one talked about in those days.) And he played like nobody else. Taylor's version of Thelonious Monk and Denzil Best's "Bemsha Swing" took Monk's version—which had already sounded radical to jazz audiences when Monk first played it in 1952—and cranked its cubism a few notches forward, sometimes commenting recognizably on the tune's original lines, sometimes veering into glittering, dissonant, abstract-expressionist excursions. The poets and painters jammed shoulder to shoulder at the saloon's tiny tables took note. By the winter of 1956–57—move over, Vanguard and Bohemia—the Five Spot had become the white-hot center of experimental jazz in New York.

The spring of '57 brought the club national fame: the Magnum photographer Burt Glinn shot a photo spread there for *Esquire*; Steve Allen ran a short, respectful segment on it on *The Tonight Show*. The same period also saw the ascension of Thelonious Monk. On Thursday, July 4, he began his eight-week stand at the Five Spot with two ad hoc sidemen, bassist Michael Mattos and drummer Mack Simpkins, the musicians he wanted not being immediately available. But on July 16 he had his own band in place: Wilbur Ware, the drummer Frankie Dunlop, and, in fulfillment of Monk's promise, John Coltrane.

WORD QUICKLY GOT OUT THAT SOMETHING EXTRAORDINARY WAS HAP-pening at the Five Spot. On weekend nights that summer, long lines formed in the soft dusk. Eight weeks turned into sixteen, and then into almost six months. The long stand became historic by every measure, even while it was happening. If you loved jazz, you had to be there—and many, including many fellow musicians, returned again and again. Bud Powell is said to have attended four nights in a row. J. J. Johnson went just once, but later said, "Since Charlie Parker, the most electrifying sound that I've heard in contemporary jazz was Coltrane playing with Monk at the Five Spot. . . . I had never heard that kind of performance—it's not possible to put into words. I just heard something that I've never heard before and I haven't heard since." The critic François Postif, who frequented the club during the period, predicted Coltrane's impact on current jazz musicians would be "as great as that of Charlie Parker."

Coltrane had shifted into a new gear. A good part of his transformation had to do with a brand-new commitment to clean living. "About that time I made a decision," he told August Blume. "That's when I stopped drinking and all that shit. I was able to play better right then, you know. . . . I could play better and think better, everything. And his music, that was a *stimulant*." He laughed.

Coltrane was referring to the Monk-ness of Monk, the quantity that seemed at first like sheer musical unpredictability. Miles, as we've seen, grappled with it, unsuccessfully at first (though a good part of their early clashes, music-based as they were, would also have had something to do with the antler-locking of two alpha-male geniuses). For unfledged accompanists, Monk could be terrifying. His inner metronome gave no clear rhythmic cues, and his spare, jagged chords pointed in no obvious musical direction: those who played with him not only had to learn the unconventional structures of his compositions, but also how to *let go* and enter Monk-mind, forging new neural pathways in their musical brains.

"Opening night he was struggling with *all* the tunes," LeRoi Jones wrote of Coltrane. But, Lewis Porter writes, the saxophonist "went through a transformation during the engagement. Monk's compositions challenged Coltrane's knowledge of harmonic progressions, his spare and percussive accompaniment gave Coltrane a new-found freedom, and his motivically structured improvisations served as models from which Coltrane could learn."

And then there was the dancing. If the music was swinging and Monk's spirits were high—as they often were over the six months of the Five Spot stand—he began doing something he'd never done before in performance: get up from the piano bench while one or another of his players soloed and go into a little shuffle-tap, circling, eyes closed, returning to the keyboard at whatever moment he deemed right.

Monk's dancing was also of a piece with another custom of his at the Five Spot: "From time to time," Coltrane told Postif, "Monk went off to have a drink and left us alone, Wilbur Ware, Shadow Wilson and me. . . . And we improvised without any constraints for fifteen or twenty minutes, exploring our different instruments like madmen."

The pianist might even retire to the dressing room and stare out the window for a while—maybe a long while—still in the music in his head but in effect creating a different kind of solo, a Cage-ian silence.

"He said he wanted to hear us, he said he wanted to hear the band," Coltrane said. "When he did that, he was in the audience himself, and he was listening to the band. Then he'd come back, you know, he got something out of that thing, man."

Monk's wandering ways could be unsettling to his players at first. "I felt a little lonesome up there," Coltrane told Blume, laughing. Suddenly he had all the room in the world to solo, but what would he play over a period that, depending on Monk's mood, might last an hour or more? Everything, Coltrane said, depended on his spontaneous interaction with the bassist—and while Ware was there, there was another set of challenges. "A bass player like Wilbur Ware, he's so inventive," he said.

> Like, he doesn't always play the dominant notes. . . . Wilbur, he plays the other way sometimes. He plays things that are kind of, you know, they're foreign. If you didn't know the song, you wouldn't be able to find it. [chuckles] Because he's superimposing things. He's playing around, and under, and over—building tension, so when he comes back to it you feel everything suck in. But usually I knew the tunes—I knew the changes anyway. So we managed to come out at the end together anyway. [laughs] A lot of fun playing that way, though.

Wallace Roney described Coltrane's playing by contrasting it with that of the great, bluesy alto player Lou Donaldson: "If you heard Lou Donaldson—who played *beautiful*—you heard the chord, and you heard notes that fit right in the chord." Roney vocalized a demonstration. "When you heard Coltrane you heard"—here he sang a much wilder Coltrane run—"but it sounds *right*," he said. "It sounds like something that's taking the music—not *out*, but to the future, you know what I mean? He's playing the *extensions* of the chords. And he's playing out on the *fringes* of the chords."

Miles Davis, working across town at Café Bohemia with a new quintet—Sonny Rollins, Red Garland, Paul Chambers, and Art Taylor—quickly got wind of what was happening at the Five Spot. As Roney remembered, "He said someone would come up to him and say, 'Man! You hear Trane with Monk? Man, that's amazing!' And Miles would say, 'I know how Trane play! I was telling *you* Trane was bad before all that—' And the person would say, 'No, Miles, this is even *different*.' And then someone *else* would come back and say, 'Have you heard Monk and Trane?'

"So Miles said he went down there to the Five Spot. He said, man, he walked in and Trane was in the middle of one of his solos, and Monk was off the piano just dancin', and Trane"—Roney imitated another wild Trane solo—"and Miles said, 'Man, I found myself down there every night—late for my gig!'"

DAVIS, OF COURSE, HAD NOT LET THE GRASS GROW BENEATH HIS FEET after firing Coltrane and Philly Joe. His new quintet opened at the Bohemia in mid-June, and *DownBeat*'s reviewer, catching the gig in its second week, was effusive. Miles, he wrote, had continued to grow musically after his triumph at Newport, "making his tone purer and purer until it now is the gentlest of whispers when muted, and a subtle but somehow forceful and glowing sound on open horn."

The writer also had high praise for Rollins, Chambers, and Garland. Of Sonny, he wrote, "Perhaps it is the forceful presence of Rollins in this group which is bringing out this burst of artistry in Miles. . . . Sonny's choruses, too, are constructed with craftsmanship—now rough-edged and brimming with virility, now soft and nearly timid but always sure of footing. . . ." As for Chambers, his "fullbodied tone brings him out of the rhythm section, and his melodic voice is felt constantly in ensembles and behind the horns." Garland was "flexible and strongly rhythmic in the group, and supple in solos."

Poor Arthur Taylor, on the other hand, got just three words, noting his "often bombastic drumming."

Other than this, *DownBeat* loved everything about the quintet's Bohemia appearance: the unusually full house was "remarkably quiet, and even more remarkably attentive"; the band was "neat in appearance . . . quite businesslike, apparently absorbed in its work." And the leader? "Miles was in a buoyant mood, strolling down into the audience after his solos to chat with friends."

Miles *was* in a buoyant mood. He loved these players, had huge respect for Sonny Rollins. The group played at the Bohemia and a couple of New York jazz festivals through the summer—but Miles kept finding himself back at the Five Spot, marveling at Coltrane and Monk:

> Trane was the perfect saxophonist for Monk's music because of the space that Monk always used. Trane could fill up all that space with all them chords and sounds he was playing then. I was proud of him for having finally kicked his habit and he was showing up regularly for the gig. And as much as I always loved Sonny's playing in my band—and Art Taylor's, too—it still wasn't the same for me as when I played with Trane and Philly Joe. I found myself missing them.

He was a permanently restless soul, ever seeking, never quite satisfied with where he found himself—personally or artistically—at any given moment. Playing opposite Cannonball and Nat Adderley's quintet that summer (Cannon had quit teaching and come back north with his brother to try to make a go of it as a leader), Miles remembered how much he loved Cannonball's blues playing, and asked him to add his alto to the quintet. Adderley thanked Davis but said that he wanted to keep trying on his own.

In the meantime, George Avakian was working with a very willing Miles to broaden the trumpeter's musical palette—and his commercial appeal. An Upper West Side neighbor of Avakian's, the composer and arranger Gunther Schuller, had been collaborating for a couple of years with John Lewis of the Modern Jazz Quartet (and of Miles and Gil Evans's

1948 nonet) on a synthesis of jazz and European classical music that Schuller came to call third stream. In the fall of 1956, Schuller convinced Avakian to commission a Columbia third stream album with an orchestra Schuller and Lewis had formed, the Brass Society. Schuller then asked Davis if he might be interested in performing two pieces on the album that required a jazz trumpet soloist. Miles agreed at once. "Another musician," Avakian recalled, "might have said, 'Ah, I don't want any of that crap. It's so phony!' Miles was interested in all kinds of music. He was the perfect person. He certainly surprised me by bringing out a flugelhorn"—a valved, bugle-like instrument with a richer, warmer tone than the trumpet—"because I'd never heard him play flugelhorn. He was very effective on it."

Soon after he signed with Columbia, Miles and George Avakian had begun discussing making an album in a large orchestral jazz setting—basically, an extension of the nonet. What shape this would take, Avakian recalled, "was uncertain, beyond the conviction that Gil Evans was the arranger we wanted." Avakian told Miles he had just two conditions: that the LP be titled *Miles Ahead*, and that it would have a song of the same name, in order to promote the album.

Miles and Evans hadn't worked together since the *Birth of the Cool* sessions, and had seen each other only sporadically, primarily when Evans came to Davis's gigs. For personal and artistic reasons, the arranger was always a welcome presence: not only did he and Miles have warm feelings for each other, but Evans was one of the few musical advisers Davis trusted absolutely. "Like when he would come to hear me play, he would ease up next to me and say, 'Miles, you know you got a nice, open [non-muted] sound and tone on your trumpet. Why don't you use it more.' And then he'd be gone, just like that, and I'd be left thinking about what he had said."

In late 1956, Davis and Evans began working on the album: who would play on it, and what pieces would be included. Avakian, in high businessman mode, sold the concept hard to the higher-ups at Columbia, and came back with welcome news: "I told Gil, 'Anything goes,'" he remembered.

"He looked at me as if I were crazy. He'd gotten so used to being told that he couldn't use more than eleven musicians!"

The work went swiftly: Evans was full of pent-up ideas and thrilled to have such artistic freedom. He conceived of the LP as a suite, with each piece flowing smoothly into the next. He and Miles decided on compositions by John Carisi ("Springsville"), Léo Delibes ("The Maids of Cadiz"), Dave Brubeck ("The Duke," a tribute to Ellington), Kurt Weill and Ira Gershwin ("My Ship," from their 1941 Broadway musical *Lady in the Dark*), and more: ten pieces in all. Four recording sessions were set for May, in Columbia's Thirtieth Street Studio, a cavernous former Russian Orthodox church whose richly reverberant wooden surfaces provided magnificent acoustics. Besides Miles, no fewer than twenty musicians were hired—the best studio musicians in town, including five trumpet players (Davis would once more play flugelhorn), four trombones, three French horns, a tuba, an alto saxophone (Lee Konitz), a bass clarinet, and two players doubling on flute and clarinet. Paul Chambers would play bass; Wynton Kelly, piano; and Art Taylor, drums. Gil Evans was to conduct; Miles would be the only soloist.

The music was difficult, Evans was exacting, and the sessions were protracted, with many rehearsals and numerous takes on many of the numbers. Some of the musicians, seasoned though they were, complained of exhaustion. As a result, Avakian, in the control booth, began clandestinely recording rehearsals, fearing that Evans's perfectionism would produce no full takes acceptable to the arranger and feeling that he, Avakian, could put together what was needed with splices during the editing process. The completed album would contain many splices, and on four of the numbers, passages overdubbed by Miles on a separate session in August— overdubbing being a rarity in those days.

The technical difficulties were quickly forgotten after the LP was released in October 1957. *Miles Ahead* was an immediate hit—almost one hundred thousand LPs sold in the first few weeks, six or seven times Columbia's break-even point for its albums—but the album cover, approved and created months before release, was not a hit with Miles. For reasons best known to the label's marketing department (and all too consistently with mid-1950s masscult values), it was a color photograph of a young, pretty white woman and a little blond boy on a sailboat: an ostensible visual metaphor for the title, but to Miles, an insult. "Why'd you put that white bitch on there?" he asked Avakian (who later said that Davis made the remark in jest). "Why not a black woman?" Avakian suggested the cover be replaced with a photo of Miles, and after the first pressing it was—with a ghastly yellow design that made for one of the least prepossessing of all Davis's album covers. (Prestige and Blue Note, thus far, had it all over Columbia in this department.) The record kept selling anyway.

In his memoir, Miles speaks fondly of his work with Evans on the record and of the album itself, saying that after it came out, Dizzy Gillespie came to see him, told him the album "was the greatest," and asked him for another copy: he'd played his so much that he'd worn it out in three weeks. Quite a turnaround for the man who'd found *The Birth of the Cool* too staid and white. This new LP had the same arranger, and even with double the number of musicians, a very similar sound.

But rawness wasn't the point with *Miles Ahead*. The point was precisely Gil Evans's brilliance in finding an artistically rich middle ground between jazz and Western classical. Evans, Miles writes, once called him at 3:00 a.m. and told him that if he was ever depressed, he should listen to "Springsville." And indeed, John Carisi's composition, the first track on the LP, is (much like his great work "Israel" on *Birth*) rich, lively, and powerfully upbeat: like big-band music built on space-age harmonies. George Avakian, commercially canny yet artistically deep (he'd also recorded John Cage for Columbia), was very deliberately setting out to broaden Miles's appeal—and (the sales figures didn't lie) that was exactly what was happening.

A FOUR-WEEK ENGAGEMENT AT CAFÉ BOHEMIA THAT SEPTEMBER QUICKLY turned eventful: within a few days, Miles fired Red Garland for missing shows, Sonny Rollins left to lead his own group, and Art Taylor quit in a huff after Davis critiqued his drumming. Miles filled the gaps fast, bringing in Tommy Flanagan to replace Garland, a Belgian saxophonist named Bobby Jaspar in Rollins's stead, and, briefly, Jimmy Cobb for Taylor—until Philly Joe, the prodigal, returned. This was the way of jazz: between addictions, personality clashes, and musical tweaks, personnel could shift at a moment's notice. And far from being discouraged—after all, he was the hottest thing in jazz at the time—Miles kept hearing his ideal band in his mind's ear, and Cannonball Adderley was part of it. As soon as the Bohemia stand ended, Davis once again invited Adderley to join him, and this time—the altoist was having trouble finding bookings for his quintet—Adderley said yes.

Dizzy Gillespie had also asked Cannonball to join the small group he was leading, but as the saxophonist recalled, "Nobody was really making it except for Miles, Chico [Hamilton, the West Coast drummer and bandleader], and Brubeck. . . . [With Davis,] I figured I could learn more than with Dizzy. Not that Dizzy isn't a good teacher, but he played more commercially than Miles. Thank goodness I made the move I did."

The new quintet, with Adderley replacing Jaspar, played widely that fall: the Bohemia, Birdland, Carnegie Hall; Philadelphia, St. Louis, Chicago, Washington. Then, at the end of November, Miles put the group on hold and went to Europe.

A French producer, Marcel Romano, had booked Davis for a three-week concert tour around Europe, but by the time Miles landed at Orly, many of the dates had fallen through, and Romano offered him a substitute: besides a couple of shows at the Olympia Theater and a three-week stand at the Club St. Germain, a job creating the score for a movie by the first-time director Louis Malle, a crime thriller called *Ascenseur pour l'échafaud* (*Elevator to the Gallows*). Malle, all of twenty-five years old and a big fan of Miles, had a groundbreaking idea for the film's music: instead of writing a score, Davis—along with three outstanding French musicians: Pierre Michelot on bass, Barney Wilen on tenor sax, and René Urtréger on piano, plus Kenny Clarke, who had expatriated to Paris, on drums—would stand in a sound studio and improvise the music to a projection of the movie. The score, now dark and moody as only Miles could be, now pulse-pounding prestissimo, was a great success, the film made an international star of Jeanne Moreau, and Louis Malle went on to his own stellar career.

Miles was back in the States in the third week of December, eager to re-form his band. He asked Red Garland to come back, and Garland agreed. Then he returned to the Five Spot, where Monk and Coltrane's historic residency was winding up, to make another request. As Wallace Roney told the story, it had the resonance of a fable:

> One night he comes to Trane and says, "Trane, come on back in the band, man." Trane said, "No, Miles—I *like* it here. I'm havin' fun." Miles said, "You don't want to play this shit—we playing some *different* shit!" Coltrane said, "No, Miles, I'm *enjoying* this." Miles said, "Come on. Come on back home." He said, "Philly's back. Red's back. And we got a little boy, Cannonball." He said, "Just come on and play some with us."
>
> So Miles said he went back to Café Bohemia, and they gettin' ready to start off his set, and he looked out of the corner of his eye, and Trane was comin' in—he came in with his horn! So Miles said he saw Trane, he hurried up to count off four. And he said when he counted off four, he took his solo, he went down off the bandstand, Sonny took the next solo, and then, he said, "Wally—Trane got up there and played so much shit, took the championship belt away from Sonny. Made Sonny go to the bridge!"
>
> So that's how Trane came back in the band and it became that band with Cannonball and Trane. And soon as Trane came back, Miles said, Boom! The music took off.
>
> He said, "Wally, you couldn't *believe* how great that band was." He thinks there was no better band *ever* than that band—that's what he told me. I could understand why, because the root of

> everything that happened afterward—Cannonball's band came out of that band. Trane's band came out of that band. Wayne Shorter came out of Coltrane—you know, that was the root.

If the account is taken literally, it has a couple of chronological issues. For one thing, Sonny Rollins had left Miles's band in September, while the Monk-Coltrane stand at the Five Spot was still in full bloom. For another, Rollins's famous sabbatical from jazz, during which he practiced every day on the walkway of the Williamsburg Bridge, didn't happen until the summer of 1959, and by his own account, a cutting contest with Coltrane had nothing to do with it. And Red Garland didn't rejoin Miles until late December, at which point Rollins was long gone.

But the spirit of the legend is intact in Roney's telling. Coltrane's playing had developed exponentially during his time with Monk: "Working with Monk brought me close to a musical architect of the highest order," he told *DownBeat* editor Don DeMicheal in August 1960. "I felt I learned from him in every way—through the senses, theoretically, technically. . . . I think Monk is one of the true greats of all time. He's a real musical thinker—there's not many like him."

John Coltrane's first stint with Miles had brought him out of his musical shell; the Five Spot stand with Monk had made him a musician's musician—if still largely unknown to the jazz-listening public, a legend in the making in the close-knit circles of progressive jazz. He recorded prolifically in 1957, as a sideman to Monk and others; he also cut his second album as a leader—and the first that can be called historic.

The LP was for Blue Note, under an agreement Coltrane had made before signing with Prestige (unlike Prestige, Blue Note paid musicians for rehearsals). The session took place at Rudy Van Gelder's studio on September 15, in a sextet setting: Trane on tenor, Lee Morgan on trumpet, Curtis Fuller on trombone, Kenny Drew at the piano, and Paul Chambers and Philly Joe Jones on bass and drums. The album's bold originality was signaled by the fact that four of its five tunes were Coltrane compositions, including the standout number that would give the LP its name, "Blue Train."

Now he was ready to soar, and he sensed a sympathetic vibration in Miles's evolution: "After leaving Monk, I went back to another great musical artist, Miles," he said in 1960.

> On returning, this time to stay until I formed my own group a few months ago, I found Miles in the midst of another stage of his musical development. There was one time in his past that he devoted to multichorded structures. He was interested in chords for their own sake. But now it seemed that he was moving in the opposite direction to the use of fewer and fewer chord changes in songs. He used tunes with free-flowing lines and chordal direction. This approach allowed the soloist the choice of playing chordally (vertically) or melodically (horizontally). In fact, due to the direct and free-flowing lines in his music, I found it easy to apply the harmonic ideas that I had.

Melody was breaking loose from harmony, which meant that modal music couldn't be far behind.

IF BILL EVANS WAS DISAPPOINTED BY THE SALES OF HIS FIRST ALBUM, HE didn't say anything about it. The high standards for improvement he was setting for himself, it appeared, were far more important to him than wide acceptance. And though the public wasn't knocking at his closet door, his colleagues were: by mid-1957, by a jazz-musician's-jazz-musician standard, he was well ahead of his five-year plan. He was paying the rent and playing with people he respected.

If you don't parse the distinctions between the avant-garde and the middlebrow too finely (and if you don't look too hard at a general overemphasis on white musicians), jazz, with its Beat Generation, bongos-and-berets associations, had a small but real place in the American culture at large in the late 1950s. It was a time when every medium-sized city in the country had its own newspaper, and many of the papers ran syndicated or local music columns, and these columns took jazz seriously. Witness the *Arlington Heights* (Illinois) *Herald*, whose knowledgeable record columnist, Paul Little, could write with equal facility about Anton Bruckner, Patti Page, and, in the back pages of the June 27, 1957, paper, George Russell's *Smalltet* album:

> Russell happens to be an extremely gifted composer, as you'll find at the very outset in his "Ye Hypocrite, Ye Beelzebub," in which he takes an ancient spiritual tune and gives it a 6/4 pace with an individualistic rhythm treatment. The combo here includes Barry Galbraith's sizzling guitar, Art Farmer's mellow trumpet, Hal McKusick's alto sax, Milt Hinton's gutty bass, Bill Evans on piano and Joe Harris on drums.

True, Evans didn't rate an adjective, but he did get ink—perhaps his first in an American newspaper. He would continue to be mentioned in the press now and then, always as a sideman, always in passing, throughout '57 and '58, and yes, even in '59. His historical importance would only dawn slowly; meanwhile, he was a faint, pulsing blip on the national jazz radar. At various times he was gigging and recording with Tony Scott, the multi-instrumentalist Don Elliott, Chet Baker, vibraphonist Eddie Costa, trombonist Bob Brookmeyer, guitarist Joe Puma; with the singer Helen Merrill; with Charles Mingus and Al Cohn and Zoot Sims. He was equally comfortable playing Frank Loesser (on Costa's album *Guys and Dolls Like Vibes*), up-to-the-minute contemporary jazz (on the Mingus LP *East Coasting*), and way-beyond-the-minute avant-garde and third stream. At the June 1957 Brandeis University Festival of the Arts, Evans smoothly handled works by Schuller, George Russell, Mingus, and the serial/atonal composer Milton Babbitt.

The week before the Brandeis event, thanks to the good offices of the NBC-TV *Tonight Show*'s jazz-loving host Steve Allen, Russell previewed his contribution to the festival on the broadcast. It was a ten-minute, three-movement composition called "All About Rosie," and it was another buoyantly American Russell special: galloping, inventive, even thrilling—but far from memorable to a nonprofessional listener. It was, unapologetically, avant-garde art music. And there on national television, playing a rip-roaring right-handed solo reminiscent of "Concerto for Billy the Kid," was Bill Evans.

MILES HAD BEEN DREAMING OF PUTTING TOGETHER A JAZZ-TRANSFORMING sextet, and now he could afford to do it. Soon after Christmas of 1957, his new band began a big tour at Chicago's Sutherland Lounge. He now had three solo voices—himself, Cannonball Adderley, and the new and improved John Coltrane—along with the rhythm section he loved: Garland, Chambers, and Philly Joe. The prospect of juxtaposing Cannonball's marvelously rich, down-home blues voice on the alto with Coltrane's increasingly venturesome tenor thrilled him, and the reality was even better than he'd imagined.

With his career in high gear and family and friends around him—his brother, Vernon, came up from East St. Louis; his children, who lived in St. Louis, always spent Christmas with his sister, Dorothy, at her house in Chicago—Miles was already in good spirits, and the sounds he got from the sextet thrilled him—and, at first, baffled the genial Adderley, the only member of the group who'd never played with Coltrane before. "Right from the beginning the tour was just a motherfucker," Davis recalled.

> BANG! We hit and tore up the fucking place and that's when I knew it was going to be something else. That first night in Chicago, we started off playing the blues, and Cannonball was just standing there with his mouth open, listening to Trane playing this way-out shit on a blues. He asked me what we were playing and I told him, "the blues."
>
> He says, "Well, I ain't never heard no blues played like that!"

Adderley caught on fast, though, and the tour returned from Chicago to New York. On February 4, Miles and the band began making their first album for Columbia, at Thirtieth Street. They laid down four numbers: a blistering, beboppish version of Dizzy Gillespie and John Lewis's "Two Bass Hit" (Coltrane gave a shout-out to Monk during his solo, with a quick quote from the pianist's "Rhythm-A-Ning"); a delightful musical oddity, a rhythm-section-only take on the traditional "Billy Boy"; Monk's swinging "Straight, No Chaser"; and a propulsive new composition by the leader, "Milestones."

The tune was the first full example of the change in musical direction Coltrane referred to in that 1960 interview, Miles's moving to the use of fewer and fewer chord changes in songs. "Milestones" is based on just two changes, focusing on modes rather than chords: the heart-racing opening section, with the three horns puffing its familiar staccato four-note figure, bop-bop-BOP-bop, is in G Dorian (you can find it yourself by playing a white-keys-only scale from G to G on a piano); the tune then shifts to A Aeolian (white keys from A to A), then back to Dorian before repeating the progression.

No one else in jazz was doing this then.

In a further innovation, Miles plays flugelhorn rather than trumpet on the tune, producing a richly understated sound—cool, in the best sense. And the two other soloists are up to their task, even though, as John Szwed writes, "the two scales do not connect with each other in any obvious way, so that the improvisers [are] forced to guard against becoming comfortable with whatever [they've] been developing when the other scale [comes] along to interrupt them." Coltrane, who of course has been awaiting this musical development, plays a fluid, singing solo in both modes, and then so does Adderley, with a free-flying turn that shows how thoroughly he's assimilated Coltrane's example.

The tour moved on to Lenny Litman's Copa in Pittsburgh, a beacon of showbiz glitz at the gateway to the Midwest, where a banner newspaper ad for the sextet, with a picture of Miles ("NOW—ALL THIS WEEK—

THE TITANS OF AMERICAN JAZZ"), misspelled the tenor saxophonist's name ("Coltraine"). Then, at the beginning of March, the band
returned to New York to make its second and final recording date for the
Columbia LP. It was an eventful session.

A pair of photographs of Miles and Red Garland taken at the February 4 session tell a story. In the first image, Miles, flugelhorn held between
his legs, is leaning over Garland's shoulder, demonstrating something on
the piano keys with both hands. Garland, in a checked jacket and fedora,
has his hands on his lap, under the keyboard. He does not look happy.

The second photo, taken from the other side, probably a moment later
(Miles has now placed the flugelhorn on top of the piano), shows Davis
leaning over Garland's other shoulder, his face close to the pianist's ear,
his arms around Garland's torso, his hands on the keys. Garland again
looks unhappy.

Davis and Garland are apparently between two of the three takes of "Milestones"—the only number on the album where Miles played the flugelhorn—and Miles, never shy about telling his musicians precisely what or how he wants them to play, is clearly giving Red Garland news that Garland doesn't want to hear about this new kind of tune that the band is recording. Garland was a beautiful, fluid pianist, with a light, lyrical touch grounded in traditional jazz. Grounded, that is, in blues, standards, and jazz compositions that were either contrafacts of popular songs or originals built on multichord structures. Oddball modes and minimally chorded tunes, catnip to the likes of George Russell or Bill Evans, might not have been congenial to his ears. Moreover, Garland was older than Miles—by only three years, but now and then he had a way of talking to him as an elder. And here he was, with a photographer hovering closely by, caught being taught.

"Miles *loved* Red," Wallace Roney said. "But yeah, there could be a tension. . . . Red probably sometimes talked down to Miles, and Red boxed, too, you know. Miles wasn't *scared* of Red. At all. But I could see where he couldn't *control* Red."

John Coltrane would have relished, anytime, having the usually silent and forbidding Miles teach him anything. Cannonball Adderley, deeply schooled in music, at first resisted Davis's instructions, but came to accept and profit from them. But "Milestones," the tune, might have been a bridge too far for Red Garland, who seems to have built up a head of steam between the February 4 and March 4 record dates. At some point early in the second session, Miles says succinctly, "Red got mad at me when I was trying to tell him something and left." On the next tune, "Sid's Ahead," a slow-loping "Walkin'" soundalike, Davis himself played piano, comping with discreet block chords between his trumpet solos.

Garland returned to the sextet, briefly, for an early-April multistar concert at Town Hall. But the schism had set. Red didn't like Miles's new musical direction; Miles was eager to move ahead. He also didn't like Red's frequent absences or lateness. And Garland wanted to be a leader himself. For the next two decades he would do just that, usually in trio format, recording profusely for Prestige and other labels, playing the kind of straight-ahead music he and much of the jazz-loving public wanted to hear. But in the meantime, Miles wanted something, and someone, new. His recollection was that he called his old friend George Russell and said he was looking for a pianist who could play modally, and that Russell mentioned this guy named Evans.

Russell's story was slightly different. He recalled:

> Miles was having a problem with substance abuse in his band and asked me if I knew of any pianist who could play the job. I recommended Bill.
>
> "Is he white?" asked Miles.
>
> "Yeah," I replied.
>
> "Does he wear glasses?"
>
> "Yeah."

"I know that motherfucker. I heard him at Birdland—he can play his ass off. Bring him over to the Colony in Brooklyn on Thursday night."

Evans himself had a third version. "Although I'd never really met the man," he recalled, "the phone rang one day and I picked it up and said hello and I hear, 'Hello. Bill, this is Miles—Miles Davis. You wanna make a weekend in Philadelphia?' I almost—you know—fainted; I made that weekend and he asked me to stay with the band."

We have no record of the Colony date or the Philadelphia weekend, but we do know that the Miles Davis Sextet, with Bill Evans on piano, opened on Friday, April 25, 1958, at the Café Bohemia opposite the Jimmy Giuffre Trio. And that Evans found himself thrown into the deep end of the pool—and, to his own surprise, stayed afloat.

"I had always had a great respect for Miles Davis," he said some years later. "And when he asked me to join him I realized that I had to revise my views about my own playing. If I continued to feel inadequate as a pianist, it would be to deny my respect for Davis. So I began to accept the position in which I had been placed."

13   Fucking up the blues

On Saturday night, May 17, 1958, the Mutual Broadcast-ing System's *Bandstand USA* radio program emanated from the Café Bohemia, starring the Miles Davis Sextet (which was a quintet that night, as Cannonball Adderley was absent): Miles, Coltrane, Chambers, Philly Joe, and the band's bespectacled new pianist. Announc-ing the personnel, the show's emcee introduced "the controversial Miles Davis. We call him controversial because some people like him, some people don't. We love him, man. We're trying to get you to love him, and after you hear him tonight, if you're hearing him for the first time, we know that you will love him."

Where was the controversy? As it turned out, there would be more than enough to go around for Miles, Coltrane, and Evans.

Some of the radio audience that night would have seen Miles before in person, glowering, turning his back to clubgoers, refusing to announce songs. But the great majority of those tuning in would have known him from his recordings, and his latest LP, *Miles Ahead*, designed by George

Avakian to appeal to mass—white—audiences, was still selling. In a recent syndicated newspaper piece, Avakian had written exuberantly of an "extraordinary" boom in jazz-record sales, expressing relief at the decline of bebop, which he blamed for having driven away mass audiences, and laying out a who's who of jazz styles and musicians that was conservatively skewed, to say the least: "Dave Brubeck, of course, is the big man of jazz today." He did praise the "improvisational brilliance" of the Miles Davis Quintet, and even threw a bone to the small labels (though not mentioning any of them by name): the independents, he said, were producing "some of the best jazz . . . because their cost risks are lower than the majors'."

Just two days before the Bohemia broadcast, Prestige, trying to piggyback on Davis's Columbia successes, had finally released *Relaxin' with the Miles Davis Quintet*, which had been recorded in mid- and late 1956. *DownBeat* gave the album four stars out of five, once again docking a Davis LP for his tenor saxophone player's alleged inadequacies:

> There is a hesitancy and lack of melodic content in Coltrane's playing at times here that hampers his effectiveness for me and lowers the rating of the LP. This is particularly true on the first two tracks, on which his solos seem to be rather aimless and somewhat strident. . . .

As we've seen, Coltrane's searching solos, less ingratiating than exploratory, had sometimes tried even Davis's patience at first; but at heart, Miles knew that he'd hired him to go places other tenor players weren't going. And *Relaxin'* was a window into an earlier period in Coltrane's evolution: he'd advanced significantly since 1956.

At the Bohemia that night, the band played four tunes: "Four," "Bye Bye Blackbird," "Walkin'," and "Two Bass Hit." On "Blackbird," Miles inserted not one, but two quotations of "Maria," from *West Side Story*, into his solo—was Lenny Bernstein in the house?—and Evans, in one of his first recorded solos with Miles, offers compatibility rather than brilliance. Throughout the broadcast, the quintet sounds solid but not spectacular.

The Bohemia gig ended the following night, bringing another turbulent departure: "Everyone was tired of Philly's junkie shit by now and we just couldn't handle it any longer," Miles said. When a re-re-formed Miles Davis Sextet opened at the Village Vanguard five days later, Jimmy Cobb was in the drummer's chair. Philly Joe had left to start his own band, and the group soon to make history—Miles, Coltrane, Adderley, Evans, Chambers, and Cobb—was now in place.

ON MONDAY, MAY 26, 1958—MILES'S THIRTY-SECOND BIRTHDAY—THIS sextet made its first recording, for Columbia, at Thirtieth Street. It was a cool, pretty spring morning: the players filtered in, made small talk, took their places. In the booth in place of George Avakian, who'd gone to Los Angeles to start a record label for Warner Bros., was a new producer named Cal Lampley, a Black man who in a certain way represented Miles's road not taken—he was a Juilliard-trained pianist and composer whose job at Columbia put bread on the table. (He would also be the first Black producer to work with white musicians.)

An ordinary Monday record date; yet, Peter Pettinger writes, "no one could have anticipated the outcome of this session, which produced playing of such intensity, spirituality, and Olympian beauty that it ranked as one of those crucial moments in the history of art after which things were never quite the same again."

The band recorded three ballads that day: the Polish composer Bronisław Kaper's "On Green Dolphin Street," a Miles sort-of original called "Fran-Dance," and Ned Washington and Victor Young's standard "Stella by Starlight." The ballads would take up the entire second side of an LP, *Jazz Track*, that Columbia would issue in late 1959. Side 1 contained the soundtrack Miles had recorded for *Elevator to the Gallows*.

The Kaper and Young tunes both had cinematic origins: "On Green

Dolphin Street" came, rather improbably, from *Green Dolphin Street*, a 1947 MGM historical disaster movie (based on a nineteenth-century earthquake and tsunami in New Zealand), for which Kaper had written the score. Similarly, Victor Young had scored a 1944 horror film, *The Uninvited*, which contained a played-but-not-sung song within the story titled "Stella by Starlight." Two years later Washington wrote lyrics for it, and it caught on both as a popular song and as a basis for jazz instrumentals.

"On Green Dolphin Street" hadn't been much recorded before Miles came to it—some say Cannonball Adderley brought the tune to his attention. Jimmy Dorsey and his orchestra did the movie soundtrack, including a vocal version of the number; Ahmad Jamal and the guitarist Barney Kessel had each recorded the song in trio settings. Yet the Davis sextet's reading stands alone as a thing of magnificence: it would turn the tune into a jazz standard.

Miles muffs the melody almost immediately, as he so often did to lay claim to a song, then continues his solo, which proceeds in different weathers, like an early-spring day with dark clouds swiftly scudding across a clear sky: by turns haunting, melancholy, joyous. Adderley solos, Coltrane solos (one blending seamlessly into the next, Adderley astonishingly fluid, Coltrane equally so, only wilder and stranger), Evans solos, all gorgeously. Chambers guides them with quiet urgency, often standing on a single note in pedal point to convey hushed suspense. Cobb swings happily throughout.

Miles's new pianist brought far more to the party than virtuosity. "Touch is everything," the pianist and bandleader Jon Batiste told me. "Touch is the thing that most people will recognize. Touch is your voice."

Evans's voice, fully realized on the first song recorded at this historic session, was one altogether new in jazz. "With the very first chord [on 'On Green Dolphin Street'],

> he hit his true vein, refuting those piano technicians who maintain that the instrument is incapable of individual expression.

There *is* a way of weighting the touch, distributing the timbre, and breathing the approach that says, *listen*. The imagination *can* manipulate ivory, felt, steel, and spruce to sublime ends. Evans called it putting emotion into the piano, and he proved that it can be done; it is the artist's mind over matter. The sounds he created on this date were so incredible that he might have invented a new instrument. This was no ordinary piano but a new breed of animal, the familiar instrument transcended. As a matter of fact, the studio piano was sadly out of tune, but we hardly notice; on the contrary, the enduring impression is of beautiful piano sound, such is the depth of the player's message.

It was a message that Evans had only recently found himself capable of delivering. Like Bird, like Miles, like Coltrane, he'd discovered that technical facility was only a way station on the road to the summit of the art: "You have to spend a lot of years at the keyboard before what's inside can get through your hands and into the piano," he said.

> For years and years that was a constant frustration to me. I wanted to get that expressive thing in, but somehow it didn't happen. When I was about twenty-six—about a year before I went with Miles—that was the first time I had attained a certain degree of expressiveness in my playing. Believe me, I had played a lot of jazz before then. I started when I was thirteen. I was putting some of the feelings I had into the piano. Of course, having the feelings is another thing, another matter.

On "Green Dolphin Street," Evans's hard-won lyricism met Miles's and began a brand-new conversation. "Fran-Dance" (Davis's take on the old children's song "Put Your Little Foot Right In") and "Stella by Starlight" continued it. Miles was in love again that spring, having recently run into Frances Taylor, who was performing on Broadway in *West Side Story*, and started seeing her regularly. By May she had moved into his big loft at 881 Tenth Avenue, between Fifty-seventh and Fifty-eighth Streets; they would marry the following year.

Part of the quiet revolution that Miles was engineering was a new emphasis on solos. "I used to use the solo as a secondary thing, more or less, to the band," Cannonball Adderley would later tell Ira Gitler, in an interview for the magazine *Jazz*.

> The ensembles were the thing; cleanliness, the ensembles, all the fundamentals of music. And listening to Miles—who is not a good trumpet player but a great soloist—you know what I mean. All of a sudden the fundamentals don't mean that much to me because he's so brilliant otherwise. A solo is like the way he thinks about the composition and the solo became *the* thing . . . he's tired of *tunes*. You know, he says, "You play the melody, then everybody blows and you play the melody and the tune is ended and that's a jazz performance." He thinks a solo can be a composition if it's expressed the right way.

Adderley came to this understanding gradually; Coltrane got it immediately. And there was immediate blowback. "When *Jazz Track* reached France," Szwed writes, "a letter from CBS International complained that on side 2, tracks 1 and 2 ["Green Dolphin Street" and "Fran-Dance"], one of the saxophone solos was 'off,' and that the quality control department had checked to make sure that there was no mechanical distortion in the tracks. [Columbia producer] Teo Macero wrote back that 'nothing was wrong, and John Coltrane is a great musician.'"

And great is how his May 26 solos sound—to our ears. But it's useful to remember, as Szwed tells us, that while "today, this music has the sound of classic ballads, coming straight from the roots of jazz . . . at the time, these recordings had the power to shock." And the shock of the new—as the art critic Robert Hughes would later describe the unsettling power of American abstract expressionist painting, which was evolving along a postwar arc similar to that of American jazz—would keep getting more shocking.

TIRED BY THE TIME THE BAND CAME TO THE THIRD SONG OF THE SESSION, "Stella by Starlight," Cannonball laid out—and then fell asleep in the studio as the five other players went through take after take of the number, stymied at first by a technical difficulty in the control booth and then by a frustrating inability to get the tune exactly right. By take 5, Miles's patience was fraying: "Paul, what's wrong with you?" he snapped at Chambers after a false start. Another brief take came to a halt with the intrusion of a loud, startling sound in the studio: Adderley's snoring. "Hey, man, wake Cannonball up," Miles said. Someone woke him up. "Don't snore on my solo, bitch," Miles told him, as loud laughter broke out.

MILES WAS CONTROVERSIAL, COLTRANE WAS CONTROVERSIAL; EVANS WAS, too. Everywhere the sextet played—and they were very busy on the road and in the recording studio throughout most of the rest of 1958—there were mutterings, and worse, from Black audiences and musicians: What was this square-looking ofay doing in Miles Davis's band? Why was Miles depriving brothers of work?

Chick Corea remembered the first time he saw Evans, playing with Miles's sextet at Storyville in Corea's hometown, Boston: "Me and my drummer friend Lenny," he told me, "we sat up at the first table, right next to the stage, which was, like, one of those eight-inch-high platforms. And out came the band. Paul Chambers, Jimmy Cobb, Cannonball, Trane. Miles. And then this white piano player with horn-rimmed glasses walks out and sits behind the piano. And I was so fucking disappointed."

Many audiences were disappointed, especially Black audiences. And many fans were vocal about their disappointment. "Many blacks felt that since I had the top small group in jazz and was paying the most money that I should have a black piano player," Miles remembered. "Now, I don't go for that kind of shit; I have always just wanted the best players in my group and I don't care about whether they're black, white, blue, red, or yellow. As long as they can play what I want, that's it."

Yet Davis was keenly aware of Bill Evans's color, from the start. With his shy, professorial mien, this man was as white as could be, from his horn-rimmed glasses and slicked-back hair to his fascination with William Blake and Thomas Hardy and his readings in Zen and Krishnamurti, to his love of Stravinsky and Ravel and Rachmaninoff and Khachaturian. It was the last that snagged Miles: his own incomparable ear and endless musical curiosity told him at once that Evans could not only enrich his band but teach him things. And his finely tuned racial antennae instantly detected the pianist's deep respect for him.

A kind of romance began. It started spikily: in his closest relationships, Miles tended to combine the rough with the smooth. Having declared his own color-blindness, he would sometimes zing Evans—"Jimmy [Cobb] told me," Wallace Roney said, "when they would talk about music and stuff, Miles would say, when Bill would say something, 'We don't want no white opinions!'"

Next came the nickname, often a crucial part of the jazz life: early in Miles's apprenticeship with Billy Eckstine, Eckstine, for his own reasons, took to calling Davis Dick. Now Miles, for *his* own reasons—it couldn't have been a physical resemblance—took to calling Evans Moe, after the bowl-coiffed leader of the Three Stooges.

Then came word of a startling initiation rite. Soon after Evans joined the sextet, Miles took him aside:

> "Bill, you know what you have to do, don't you, to be in this band?"
>
> He looked at me all puzzled and shit and shook his head and said, "No, Miles, what do I have to do?"
>
> I said, "Bill, now you know we all brothers and shit and everybody's in this thing together and so what I came up with for you is that you got to make it with everybody, you know what I mean? You got to fuck the band." Now, I was kidding, but Bill was real serious, like Trane.
>
> He thought about it for about fifteen minutes and then came back and told me, "Miles, I thought about what you said and I just can't do that. I'd like to please everyone and make everyone happy here, but I just can't do that."
>
> I looked at him and smiled and said, "My man!" and then he knew I was teasing.

Mostly. Bill was real serious, like Trane—but Miles never pulled the fuck-the-band joke on Trane. Did the jest come from an unconscious (or conscious) wish on Miles's part? Evans was slim and graceful: as a boy he had been a good athlete, and an early life spent around his father's driving range had made him, of all things, a skillful golfer. His all-American good looks and professorial intensity were attractive to women—and to

Miles Davis. Miles had, at the very least, a musical crush on Evans ("Bill had this quiet fire that I loved on piano. . . . [T]he sound he got was like crystal notes or sparkling water cascading down from some clear waterfall"). Archie Shepp remembered a touching moment he'd witnessed at a Philadelphia nightclub in 1958, soon after the pianist had joined the band: "Bill Evans was sitting with his arms folded together and Miles was behind him, his arms cloaked around Bill's shoulders showing him some voicings at the piano." It's exactly the posture Miles had foisted on an unhappy Red Garland just before Garland left the band—except that here it reflects a nascent musical intimacy, one that will produce extraordinary results.

Evans and Davis spent time together at Miles's place, talking about music for hours: listening to classical records, working things out on the piano. Sometimes at night, Miles would telephone Evans and ask him simply to leave the phone off the hook so he could listen to him play. "Miles *loved* Bill," Roney said.

Evans was thrilled to be holding the piano seat in the best small jazz band in America, a position that made him the envy of every pianist in the land, but his excitement was underlaid with insecurity. He had heard, loudly, the grumblings of Black musicians; he'd heard, loudly, the voice of his own self-discontent. He had determined to make it as a *jazz musician*— yet he looked the way he looked and came from the place he came from. He was a white piano player from New Jersey. He was of a rigorous and orderly mindset (in good part as a reaction to the chaos of his family background), thoughtful and articulate at all times; but he yearned to shake himself up—and to fit in.

"In his army days Evans had tried marijuana and had continued to smoke it even though it interfered with his memory," Pettinger writes.

> Contrary to most current medical evidence, he believed that marijuana led to heroin—and, as if to prove his point, he tried that, too. Not until he played with Miles, though, was his heroin use more than experimental; he was determined not to isolate himself from the drug-grounded fellowship of that band.

"I think for Bill, the white guy from Plainfield, New Jersey, who looked every bit the part of the white guy from Plainfield, New Jersey, he really felt that to get into that world he needed to become a junkie," the drummer Eliot Zigmund, who played in Evans's trio in the seventies, told me. "And boy, did he become a junkie."

The sextet really was a fellowship, even capable of closing ranks to defend Evans, but were they really drug-grounded? Coltrane seems to have beaten his addictions to heroin and alcohol (though not to sweets) entirely; Adderley appears never to have used hard drugs at all. Philly Joe and Evans had been in the band together for just three weeks before Jones left (though the two had bonded instantly over music and drugs, and would stay friends—junkie-buddies, in Pettinger's formulation—for the rest of Evans's life). Jimmy Cobb, by contrast, had seen so many young jazz players ruined by the Bird Fallacy that he said, early in his career, "That will never be me." Paul Chambers, a severe alcoholic and periodic heroin user, was the band's one active addict after Philly Joe's departure. And then there was Miles.

Heroin was in his past; cocaine and alcohol were not. Cocaine (which he could now afford) often helped fuel a grueling schedule of late-night gigs and long recording sessions, and as it is wont to do with frequent users, it may have aggravated his temper outbursts. For all the euphoria of his new relationship with Frances Taylor, Miles admitted that their love affair was not immune to what seems to have been his lifelong habit of hitting women. Taylor's first infraction was to remark on Quincy Jones's handsomeness—in a jealous rage, Miles "knocked her down and she ran out of the apartment over to Monte Kay and Diahann Carroll's place buck naked. . . . I told her not to ever mention Quincy Jones's name to me again, and she never did."

Meanwhile, Evans's girlfriend, a young Black woman named Peri Cousins, observed his growing heroin addiction with helpless sorrow. "Of course, that was the bane of our existence," she said. She had a theory about why he wouldn't stop: "When he came down, when he kicked it, which he did on numerous occasions, the world was—I don't know how to say it—too beautiful. It was too sharp for him. It's almost as if he had to blur the world for himself by being strung out."

This has an almost holy sound, but it wasn't just beauty that he was blurring. Besides the reverse racism of Black musicians and audiences—"Crow Jim"—he even met intolerance within the sextet: "Coltrane never quite approved his presence," Pettinger writes. There were also Evans's own easily tapped feelings of musical insufficiency, a familial tendency to depression, and the exhaustion of touring. And to help him do the blurring, there were pushers wherever the band went. He soon graduated from snorting heroin to injecting it, and the horn-rims and slicked-back hair took on a new, faintly ratty valence: he had joined the great doomed brotherhood of junkie jazz musicians, and from here to the end of his life, evidence would accumulate that he was delighted to be there.

IN FEBRUARY 1958 COLTRANE HAD RECORDED HIS FOURTH ALBUM AS A leader, with Red Garland's trio—Garland, Paul Chambers, and Art Taylor. In customary Prestige style, the LP was recorded in one session, at Van Gelder's studio, with no rehearsals; Bob Weinstock produced. The album would be called *Soultrane*.

The quartet laid down four ballads—Tadd Dameron's "Good Bait," Billy Eckstine's "I Want to Talk About You," Leo Robin and Jule Styne's "You Say You Care," and an elegy for the recently deceased saxophonist Ernie Henry, "Theme for Ernie"—when Weinstock realized they didn't have quite enough for an LP. "We were hung for a tune," he remembered,

> and I said, "Trane, why don't you think up some old standard?"
> He said, "OK, I got it. Ready, Rudy?" They always said, "Ready, Rudy?" And they played "Russian Lullaby" at a real fast tempo. At the end I asked, "Trane, what was the name of that tune?" And he said, "Rushin' Lullaby." I cracked up. He had that type of sense of humor—riddles and cute things.

Despite the breakneck tempo, Coltrane was able to preserve the poignant beauty of Irving Berlin's plaintive 1927 song. But his soloing might have made Berlin blanch. As Ira Gitler wrote on the album's liner notes:

> Red begins *Russian Lullaby* with an out-of-tempo introduction before Trane comes ripping in. Taking this and *Soft Lights and Sweet Music* [recorded with the Garland trio on a previous date] as evidence, it would seem that the boys like to play their Irving Berlin at high velocity. I'm sure this Lullaby would keep Nikita [Khrushchev] awake and swinging all night. Trane's "sheets of sound," which he has since put to wider use, are demonstrated in the beginning of the tag [final solo].

Sheets of sound. In much the same way as the critic Harold Rosenberg's term "action painting" defined both a branch of abstract expressionism and the dynamic New York art scene of the 1950s, Gitler's term of art quickly caught on, not just as a descriptor of Coltrane's blazing vertical solos but as a kind of compass needle pointing toward a new way of jazz at the end of the decade. As John Coltrane played them, sheets of sound were rapid-fire investigations of the scales suggested by given chords in a song, each lightning arpeggio quickly succeeded by another—hence the (almost abstract-expressionist) image of sheets, one falling on another. (Coltrane was also inspired by an interest in the harp that he developed around the same time.)

The approach didn't always jibe with the customary rhythmic patterns of jazz. As Coltrane would later tell an interviewer,

> About this time, I was trying for a sweeping sound. I started experimenting because I was striving for more individual development. I even tried long, rapid lines that Ira Gitler termed "sheets of sound." . . . The tendency was to play the entire scale of each chord. Therefore, they were usually played fast and sometimes sounded like glisses [glissandos].

I found there were a certain number of chord progressions to play in a given time, and sometimes what I played didn't work out in eighth notes, sixteenth notes, or triplets. I had to put the notes in uneven groups like fives and sevens in order to get them all in.

The solos can sound thrilling to modern ears, but at the time, many heard them as discordant, self-indulgent, even hostile. Miles took the sextet to Newport that summer, his first return to the festival since his 1955 breakthrough. In worldly terms it was a triumphant homecoming: Davis, now a big star on a major record label, had risen to jazz's pantheon. But *DownBeat*'s review rained on his halo:

> Unfortunately, the group did not perform effectively. Although Miles continues to play with delicacy and infinite grace, his group's solidarity is hampered by the angry young tenor of Coltrane. Backing himself into rhythmic corners on flurries of notes, Coltrane sounded like the personification of motion-without-progress in jazz. What is equally important, Coltrane's playing apparently has influenced Adderley. The latter's playing indicated less concern for melodic structure than he has illustrated in the past.
>
> Although Chambers continues to be one of jazz's most agile bassists, he was drowned often by Cobb's oppressive support. Evans, too, had little opportunity to speak as authoritatively as he has indicated he can speak.
>
> With the exception of Miles' vital contribution, then, the group proved more confusing to listeners than educational.

Coltrane was finally coming into his own, filled with confidence (largely thanks to Miles) in his experiments. His record label and his fellow musicians got it at once: from the moment he rejoined Davis, he recorded abundantly, both as a leader and a sideman. Miles's booking agent, Jack Whittemore, also started finding Coltrane leader gigs in between his engagements with Davis; and Miles's attorney Harold Lovett took the saxophonist on as a client, moving his recording contract from Prestige to Atlantic in a deal that guaranteed him seven thousand dollars a year, with a new Lincoln Continental thrown in.

But the world would catch on only gradually.

Meanwhile, as Coltrane's influence on Cannonball deepened (though Adderley would always remain a great soul player at heart), Evans, Pettinger writes, "had put his own stamp on the band and had steered its repertoire into new lyrical paths, becoming in the process one of the few white jazzmen ever to influence Black colleagues. Great music had been made, and he had catalyzed new depths in Davis's own playing." And Miles himself continued to catalyze new musical depths in all his men's playing—and new heights, and economies. When Cannonball first joined the band, he later told Ira Gitler,

> There were certain things that I did that Miles didn't like and he is outspoken enough to tell you when he doesn't like something. . . . At first it didn't hurt me but it shocked me. I'd think I played something that was nice and he'd say, "Yeah, why you got to play all that? That ain't got nothing to do with it. Man, you playin' all them notes that don't mean nothin'." When you play a note it should mean something.

Earlier in the year, Cal Lampley had phoned Miles with an idea for a follow-up to *Miles Ahead*: an instrumental version of George Gershwin's 1935 opera *Porgy and Bess*, to be scored by Gil Evans. Davis shut Lampley down abruptly. Gershwin's great and controversial work was much in the air in 1958: a Samuel Goldwyn film adaptation, starring Sidney Poitier, Dorothy Dandridge, and Sammy Davis, Jr., was in production, and several jazz interpretations of the opera had come out recently: a 1956 version with Duke Ellington's orchestra and the (white) singers Mel Tormé and Frances Faye; a 1957 instrumental LP with the saxophonist Buddy Collette leading a sextet; a 1958 recording by Louis Armstrong and Ella Fitzgerald singing all the parts and backed by a full orchestra. Possibly it all seemed to Miles like too much *Porgy and Bess*. But then something—the chance to work with Gil again, the opportunity to put his stamp on a piece that had entered the jazz canon—changed his mind.

A couple of weeks after Newport, at the Thirtieth Street Studio, Davis joined Gil Evans and a nineteen-piece orchestra (mostly brass, and including Cannonball and Paul Chambers, as well as Philly Joe) to begin making the album. Evans's arrangements were rich and strange, and extremely complex: "Gil reconstructed *Porgy and Bess* both narratively and musically," Stephanie Stein Crease writes. "He reordered Gershwin's songs almost completely, stayed close to some, considerably recomposed others, and left out those that didn't fit well in this rendering." It was post-bop big-band music as only Gil Evans could arrange it. And much of the writing reflected Miles's own shift toward modality—fewer chords, more solos, new scales with notes that, to unaccustomed ears, sound wrong.

The album was purely instrumental, but with Miles's trumpet and flugelhorn—now cracked and now flowing; plaintive, haunting, and at times purposely discordant—playing all the opera's voices, male and female, it achieved something entirely new and different, and became Davis's top-selling LP to date, the epitome of George Avakian's plan to make him a jazz star transcending jazz, with an odd side effect: the strangeness of a Black artist presenting a white composer's work about Black people to a white audience.

The album would be released the following March with a stunner of a cover, Miles's best to date: a gorgeous, mysterious color photo by the great Harlem-born photographer Roy DeCarava shows, against a black background, just the midsection of a Black man in a white shirt holding a trumpet on his lap, and just one green-skirted leg of a woman of indeterminate race, her gold-braceleted hand poised questingly over the trumpet's mouthpiece. In color and tonality, the image looks like a slightly blurred detail of a Vermeer. The LP's title, in white print on a red banner above, reads: MILES DAVIS—PORGY AND BESS, with George Gershwin's and Gil Evans's names, in all but subliminal black italic, appearing over and underneath. Miles, now a legitimate superstar, is the main event.

Meanwhile, centrifugal forces threatened the great sextet. Both Coltrane and Adderley were itching to leave the nest and lead, to play their own material rather than Miles's. Bill Evans was under continuous pressure to justify his presence, and nightclubs rarely provided an atmosphere congenial to his demonstrating his lyrical sensitivity. Audiences were especially skeptical when the band played the kind of up-tempo numbers they associated with Red Garland: their unresponsiveness stoked his insecurity. "At the time I thought I was inadequate," Evans recalled.

> I wanted to play more so that I could see where I was going. I felt exhausted in every way—physically, mentally, and spiritually. I don't know why. Maybe it was the road. But I think the time I worked with Miles was probably the most beneficial I've spent in years, not only musically but personally. It did me a lot of good.

But he said this in retrospect. At the time, he had just had it.

THAT SEPTEMBER, COLUMBIA THREW ITSELF A PRESS PARTY AT THE EL-egant Persian Room of the Plaza Hotel, celebrating the label's success with jazz records. The afternoon event was the brainchild of Irving Townsend, a former bandleader who'd started as an advertising copywriter at Columbia and worked his way up to becoming a full-time producer. Now, with the departure of Cal Lampley, whom George Avakian had just wooed out to L.A. to work at Warner Records, Townsend had been tapped to produce Miles Davis.

Miles's sextet was on the bill that afternoon, along with Duke Ellington's Orchestra and the singers Jimmy Rushing and Billie Holiday. And Columbia had thought to bring along recording equipment, for archival rather than commercial purposes—and so, because many years later the label issued a record of the event, we can hear what went on. The band was in fine form all around, and though the Persian Room, for all its uptown airs, had an out-of-tune piano, Evans was able to bewitch it into beauty, especially on an exquisite musical conversation with Miles on "My Funny Valentine." On a ten-and-a-half-minute version of Sonny Rollins's rousing bebopper "Oleo," Coltrane worked his by now customary vertical magic, running his sheets of sound up and down scale after scale—and then handing off to Cannonball, who, with more respect to Trane than ever, waxed equally alpinistic—yet somehow, characteristically mellow and tuneful at the same time. And then Evans channeled Bud Powell with some breakneck bebop runs and clusters on that bushwhacked piano.

Ralph Ellison was there that day as Columbia Records' guest, and, thrilled though he was by the offerings of Duke, Mr. Five by Five (about whom Ellison had just published an encomium in *Saturday Review*), and Lady Day, the playing of Miles and his band did not fall sweetly on his ears. He later wrote to his friend the writer Albert Murray:

> I finally saw that . . . poor, evil, lost little Miles Davis, who on this occasion sounded like he just couldn't get it together. Nor did Coltrane help with his badly executed velocity exercises. These cats have gotten lost, man. They're trying to get hold of something by fucking up the blues.

For the supremely literate and sensitive Ellison, who had been much taken with "the complexity of sound and rhythm and self-assertive passion" of bebop, this new thing—whatever it was—sounded like so much noise. Jazz was plainly going off the rails.

Murray wrote back with a related bone to pick:

> I cannot understand for the life of me what these guys are finding so revolutionary in Gil Evans–Miles Davis' Miles Ahead and Porgy and Bess. It's nice and pleasant but other than that all I can hear is a bunch of studio musicians playing decadent exercises in orchestration based on Ellington's old pastel period. . . . Gil Evans, my ass. This guy caint even beat Lenny Bernstein.

These two men, in the prime of their lives, filled with vigor and opinions, were nonetheless, at forty-five and forty-two respectively, middle-aged. For Ralph Ellison and Albert Murray, the true thrill of jazz lay back in Kansas City and Harlem in the prewar years, in the railroad rhythms of Duke and the Count and Jimmie Lunceford and Pete Johnson and Meade Lux Lewis. In the blues, before the blues got fucked up. These new winds, blowing in hard from somewhere out ahead, just didn't smell right.

THE BAND PLAYED ON FOR THE NEXT TWO MONTHS—AT THE APOLLO IN Harlem and the Spotlite Lounge in D.C. and, back in New York, at the Village Vanguard. But in October, Evans gave Miles his notice. He was burned out, he said, and his father was sick in Florida. He needed a break, and not a short one. Sunday, November 16, 1958, closing night at the Vanguard, was the last time he would ever perform in public with Miles.

14 Outside of time

The new year dawned gray and slushy in New York City: the last year of the fifties, good riddance. A quiet Thursday: most offices in Manhattan were closed until Monday. Anyone wanting to risk wet feet and usher in 1959, or maybe just chase off a hangover with a little hair of the dog, had many going-out options—you could catch Freddie Alonso's rumba group at El Morocco, or the sublime Eartha Kitt at the Waldorf-Astoria's Empire Room, or even Guy Lombardo, still vibrating from the night before, at the Roosevelt Hotel. The more adventurous might venture down to the Village Vanguard, where Dizzy Gillespie's quintet was holding forth, or over to Birdland to hear the Miles Davis sextet, which, according to *The New Yorker*'s always wry Goings On About Town section, "has split into two or maybe three personalities since the saxophones of John Coltrane and Cannonball Adderley have been attached."

Was this true? The characterization bore the unmistakable stylistic fingerprint of the magazine's jazz critic Whitney Balliett, who, as great as he was, was not infallible. It was Balliett, after all, who as recently as the previous May had referred to Coltrane as "a student of Sonny Rollins." Admittedly, the assessment appeared in Balliett's review of Miles's just-released but almost two-year-old LP *Relaxin'*, made when Coltrane was still finding his musical footing.

But the charge of multiple personalities was not without merit. Miles himself noted that "in 1959 we had three bandleaders in the group, and things started getting difficult." Between gigs with Davis, both Coltrane and Cannonball continued to front their own groups and make significant recordings. On the day after Christmas 1958, Coltrane led a date for Prestige with Red Garland, Paul Chambers, and two alternating trumpeters, Donald Byrd and a twenty-year-old phenom from Indianapolis named Freddie Hubbard. The first number the band laid down was "The Believer," a blues with modal ambitions written by another precocious twenty-year-old, McCoy Tyner—who wasn't on this session, but by the time the album named after the song was released, in 1964, would hold the piano chair in Coltrane's great quartet. And in early February, on the day after Miles's sextet closed at Chicago's Sutherland Lounge, Cannonball made an LP with a quintet that included Coltrane, Chambers, Jimmy Cobb, and Davis's new piano player, Wynton Kelly.

The son of Jamaican immigrants, the genial twenty-seven-year-old Kelly was a popular and versatile accompanist, comfortable in both big- and small-band settings; he'd played with Charles Mingus and Dizzy Gillespie and had also backed Dinah Washington and Billie Holiday. He had a sparkling, blues-tinged technique that somehow managed to be assertive and supportive at the same time. "I loved the way Wynton played," Miles said, "because he was a combination of Red Garland and Bill Evans; he could play almost anything. Plus, he could play behind a soloist like a motherfucker, man. Cannonball and Trane loved him, and so did I."

The Adderley album, *Cannonball Adderley in Chicago*, was a declaration of independence, the Miles Davis Sextet without Miles. And on the rousing opening track, the 1921 standard "Limehouse Blues," Cannonball's solo is so jubilant that it's hard to escape the impression that he's feeling liberated—and so fast and free that you can practically see Coltrane stand-ing nearby, nodding with approval. Then Coltrane solos, and within sec-onds you realize that as adventurous as the alto solo had been, it had *followed the chords of the song*, and now the tenor player has led you off the map into his own rich and humid chordal territory, draped with sheets of sound like hanging jungle vines, a region that "Limehouse"'s English writers, Douglas Furber and Philip Braham, twin pillars of West End musical theater in the twenties, would have found unrecognizable. It's Coltrane Coltraning, and 1959—which by year's end will have heard a lot of things jazz has never heard before—is just starting to get used to it.

BILL EVANS SPENT THE REST OF NOVEMBER 1958 IN THE SOUTH, DECOM-pressing: visiting with his parents in Ormond Beach, Florida, hitting drives on his father's driving range, playing golf—he proudly carded a 41 for nine holes—and thinking. Visiting his brother, Harry, in Louisiana proved inspirational. "While I was staying with my brother in Baton Rouge," he later recalled, "I remember finding that somehow I had reached a new inner level of expression in my playing. It had come almost auto-matically, and I was very anxious about it, afraid I might lose it—I thought maybe I'd wake up tomorrow and it wouldn't be there."

Nothing he had done since making *New Jazz Conceptions* had con-vinced the endlessly self-critical and analytical Evans of his potential as a leader. While he demonstrated his highly valued adaptability as a sideman on literally dozens of record dates, Riverside's Orrin Keepnews kept try-ing to persuade him to make another trio album. But "before joining Miles," Pettinger writes, "the pianist felt that he hadn't anything fresh to say; by the time he knew that he had, he was too busy traveling with the band."

The single exception had been one number on Adderley's first River-side LP, *Portrait of Cannonball*, recorded in July and released that fall. Miles was present at the date, not as a musician but as a gift-giver, having brought his alto player a song he'd written, "Nardis." It was an enigmatic, winding melody with a Middle Eastern tonality, a little like a less resolute "Caravan": it scrolled and furled hypnotically, without a strong rhythmic pulse, and Cannonball and the other musicians—Blue Mitchell on trumpet, Sam Jones on bass, Philly Joe on drums—struggled to make jazz out of it. Everyone had trouble with it, in Miles's estimation, except Evans, who latched onto the song as a showpiece, continuing to plumb its depths and mysteries for years to come. Many other musicians came to love it, too. Davis never recorded it.

Now Evans had breathing room, a new inner outlook, and some fresh ideas. On December 15, he returned to Reeves Sound Studios with his *Portrait of Cannonball* colleagues Sam Jones and Philly Joe and, in a single long session, recorded the ten songs that would compose his second album as a leader, *Everybody Digs Bill Evans*. The material ran the gamut, from standards (Cole Porter's "Night and Day"; Jack Lawrence and Walter Gross's "Tenderly") to show tunes (Leonard Bernstein, Betty Comden, and Adolph Green's "Lucky to Be Me" and "Some Other Time," from the 1944 musical *On the Town*) to ur–hard bop (Gigi Gryce's "Minority" and Sonny Rollins's "Oleo"). Evans contributed a dreamy, meditative original, "Peace Piece," based on the opening vamp to "Some Other Time" and wreathing lyrical garlands along a single chord: it too would become a staple in his trio repertoire.

His treatments of the songs also varied, from pensive to sprightly, giving the lie to the charge that he couldn't swing. But, even at faster tempos, he produced harmonic colors the likes of which jazz had never seen before. In the space of a single album—note, especially, his "Night and Day"—Evans completely overhauled the traditional piano-bass-drums trio concept, elevating his sidemen from timekeeping accompanists to equal participants in a three-way musical conversation. The great Porter standard was a special showpiece of Philly Joe's—you can hear his indelible personality as you listen to his mesmerizing stickwork.

And the chance to work once more with his favorite drummer gave Evans the chance to strengthen his bond with his junkie-buddy.

Reenergized by the break and the thrill of his new record, Evans went on a tear in late '58 and early '59, accompanying Chet Baker on a ballad album, playing on a multimusician LP called *The Jazz Soul of Porgy and Bess*, sitting in a couple of times for Lennie Tristano at the Half Note on lower Hudson Street (with Lee Konitz, Warne Marsh, Jimmy Garrison, and Paul Motian), then returning to the club with two more quintets, both led by old friends, Tony Scott and the valve trombonist Bob Brookmeyer.

Then Miles called once more.

IN FEBRUARY, THE NATIONAL DANCE COMPANY OF GUINEA, LES BALLETS Africaines, opened at Broadway's Martin Beck Theatre, and Frances Taylor (perhaps looking for a whiff of freedom, since Miles seemed determined to clamp down on her career ambitions as he maximized his own) insisted that they get right down to Forty-fifth Street to see the show. Miles was bowled over by what he saw and heard: "It just fucked me up what they was doing, the steps and all them flying leaps and shit," he said. "And when I first heard them play the finger piano that night and sing this song with this other guy dancing, man, that was some powerful stuff."

He was entranced by the rhythms of the dancers and the drummers that accompanied them; he counted them off as he watched: "rhythms like 5/4 and 6/8 and 4/4 . . . changing and popping. That's the thing, that secret, inner thing that they had. . . . I knew I couldn't do it from just watching them dance because I'm not African, but I loved what they were doing. I didn't want to copy that, but I got a concept from it."

It might be more accurate to say that the show reflected certain concepts he'd been considering for a long time. Miles had been thinking modally for at least five years: witness 1954's "Swing Spring." Much further back, as early as Juilliard, he'd been looking into advanced notions in modern Western classical. Gil Evans and George Russell showed him lands beyond blues and American Songbook chord structures, and then his other Evans came along with his Ravel and Rachmaninoff and those *chords*.

And now there was something else. The African finger piano—variously known as mbira, kalimba, or gongoma, among other names—was often tuned to scales similar (but not identical) to modes such as the Dorian, the Phrygian, and the Mixolydian, with random (to Western ears) partial tones thrown in. The defiantly un-Western sound of that instrument, and of those drums—DA DA DA DA POW!—goading those leaping dancers along; the whole gloriously riotous (by Western standards) spectacle—all of it stirred him powerfully. He went back to the show twice, at least once with Gil Evans.

Miles started writing a piece that would capture some of the feeling that finger piano gave him, a blues that would also harken back to a sense memory of being a small boy visiting his grandparents in Arkansas. His family used to go to church when they were down there, and Miles remembered the gospel music sung by that rustic congregation, and remembered how it felt, while the music was still echoing in his mind, to walk back home along a dark country road. He wrote about five bars of a song, then recorded it—whether on trumpet or piano he doesn't say—"and added a kind of running sound into the mix"—nor does he explain what this means—"because that was the only way I could get in the sound of the finger piano."

Davis had a feeling about the album he wanted to make next, a feeling he hadn't entirely worked out yet, and he wanted Evans to help him find what he wanted. The music he'd been playing, and the musicians he'd been playing it with, were mostly going in the wrong direction, he felt: there were too many chords, and he didn't want to play them. "The music was too thick."

Bill Evans had introduced him to works by Ravel, Rachmaninoff, and Khatchaturian; "once [Davis] had listened to them," Szwed writes, "they often spent hours analyzing the scores." One piece that Miles became almost obsessed with was Arturo Benedetti Michelangeli's 1957 recording of Ravel's Piano Concerto in G, a great work that resulted from the composer's triumphant tour of the U.S. in 1928. It was only the second concerto written by Ravel, then in his fifties and close to the end of his career, and, clearly influenced by the fast pace and openness of America—and unmistakably, in several passages, by the blue notes and ardent drive of Gershwin's *An American in Paris*—the piece, a reaction against the heavy furniture of nineteenth-century classical, is the opposite of thick: rather, it starts with a whip crack, then gallops like Pegasus, shimmering with piccolo and trumpet sounds, and takes its own time modulating from chord to chord, never landing where an ear accustomed to blues and Songbook standards expects.

And then the second movement, the adagio assai, begins with just the piano, in the most profound quiet.

Miles wanted to put wide-open space into his music the way Ravel did. He wanted to use different scales the way Khatchaturian, with his love for Asian music, did. He sought, Pettinger writes,

> to tap the possibilities latent in any one mode: he would improvise on its scale and the chords derived from that scale rather than relying for interest and stimulation on a progression of related chords (or chord sequence). Evans, through the George Russell connection, was able to embrace this concept in his own playing, as Davis well knew, and his presence became crucial to the character of the album.

More than crucial; central. "I planned that album around the piano playing of Bill Evans," he said. If you have to call the record something, he said, call it "Moe's music."

"I had been out of the group for a few months," Evans recalled, "but Miles called me to make this date." Davis told Evans that the new album he had in mind would make use of some of the Western classical themes they'd analyzed together, along with the sound of the mbira, and the echo of those gospel voices in his mind as he walked that dark back road in Arkansas as a boy. Evans thought he knew just what Miles meant.

At the end of February they began to meet at Davis's place to rough out some ideas for a record that would explore a modal language. The "brooding masterpiece" "Blue in Green" began at one of these meetings: "One day at Miles's apartment," Evans recalled, "he wrote on some manuscript paper the symbols for G-minor and A-augmented. And he said, 'What would you do with that?' I didn't really know, but I went home and wrote 'Blue in Green.'"

"Their thought was to keep it simple, play music of the most basic order, and try to make each first take work," Szwed writes. In making records, Miles had much the same philosophy Frank Sinatra brought to acting in movies: first take, best take. "First-take feelings, if they're anywhere near right, they're generally the best," Bill Evans said. In a radio interview twenty years after recording *Kind of Blue*, Evans elaborated on the album's freshness. "There was a simplicity about the charts that was remarkable," he remembered.

> Like "Freddie Freeloader," "So What," and "All Blues"—there was nothing written out on. Oh, on "So What" I think the introduction was written out single line, and Paul [Chambers] and I played it—and added, you know, a little harmony to it. Other than that, the charts were just spoken, just [Miles] saying like, "Play this pretty." "*You* play this note." "You play *this* note."

Miles believed that playing from bare sketches ("It could have been done on a napkin, the forms were so simple," the bandleader and producer Bob Belden said), or even spoken guidelines, would inspire his musicians to the kind of spontaneity he'd thrilled to in Les Ballets Africaines: "the interplay between those dancers and those drummers and that finger piano player."

A LATE-WINTER MONDAY AFTERNOON, SOFT BLUE SKIES, MILD FOR EARLY March. Irving Townsend had booked the Thirtieth Street Studio for Columbia Project B 43079: two consecutive Miles Davis sessions, from 2:30 to 5:30 p.m. and from 7:00 to 10:00 p.m. The studio had been vacant since the previous Saturday, when the pop singer Jerry Vale laid down several tunes for a moon-themed album produced by Mitch Miller. After the end of Miles's session this Monday night, the trumpeter-bandleader Lee Castle and the Jimmy Dorsey Orchestra (Dorsey himself had died in 1957) were scheduled to record from 11:30 p.m. till 2:30 in the morning. The smoothly running machine that was Columbia Records was turning out product to satisfy its various markets.

No musician ever goes into a record date expecting to make history; every man in Miles's band had recorded dozens of times before. "Professionals," Bill Evans said, "have to go in at 10 o'clock on a Wednesday and make a record and hope to catch a really good day." On the face of it, there was nothing remarkable about Project B 43079. "Jimmy Cobb arrived early, to give himself time to set up his drum kit and the engineers time to deal with its placement in the studio," Ashley Kahn writes. "As Cobb set up his kit, the others arrived, hung their coats on the rack near the door, and arranged themselves and their instruments on various stools and chairs in the studio."

Two of those others were surprised to see each other. Davis's current pianist, Wynton Kelly, had taken a cab from Brooklyn because he hated the subway. "So he saw Bill sitting at the piano and was flabbergasted!" Jimmy Cobb recalled. "He said, 'Damn, I rushed all the way over here and someone else is sitting at the piano!' I said, 'Hold it before you go off, you're on the date too.'"

The control booth at Thirtieth Street was up a flight of stairs from the studio floor, in what had once been the balcony of the old church: Townsend, recording engineer Fred Plaut, and Plaut's assistant Bob Waller looked down from above as Miles talked to the musicians, who were placed around the open floor much as they'd stand onstage in a concert. On some recording sessions, Columbia producers used rolling baffles to isolate musicians or singers and eliminate sound leakage; at Davis's direction, this session would proceed baffle-free, all musicians constantly aware of, and inspired by, each other's playing. Sound leakage from one player's mike to another's was not only expected but essential. Each man had his own Telefunken U-49 microphone, except for Cobb, who had two, one pointed at the snare and one overhead to pick up the cymbals. The state of studio recording in 1959 was such that the musicians rather than the engineer were responsible for regulating the loudness or softness of their instruments, by dynamics or distance from the mike. As Davis picked up his horn, Waller started the tapes rolling—one master and one safety—on the Ampex reel-to-reel recorders, and Townsend pushed the intercom button. "The machine's on," he said. "Here we go. CO 62290, no title, take one."

CO 62290 was the straight-ahead blues that Miles would later title "Freddie Freeloader," with Wynton Kelly on the piano. In putting this number first, Davis may have had some thought of placating Kelly, but he also would have known that the relatively simple form of a blues would let the musicians limber up. (The blues was also a form in which Bill Evans was never completely comfortable, feeling he "was not at his best playing [it].") Davis pointed to Kelly, Coltrane, and Adderley and indicated the order of solos: "Him, me, him, and you," he said. Then: "Hey, Wynton— after Cannonball, you play again and then we'll come in and end it."

Miles counted off with a light foot-tap and the sextet began to play. After eight seconds, he stopped the take with a whistle and a wave of his hand. "It was too fast," he rasped, putting an encyclopedia of meaning into the four words: what they had played was not in keeping with his idea of the album's serene tone.

Now Townsend clicked on the intercom. "Miles, where are you gonna work now?" he asked. The producer was referring to Davis's position in relation to the microphone, from which he had apparently stepped back momentarily.

"Right here," Miles said.

"Okay," the producer said, "'cause if you move back we don't get you. You were right when you played before."

"When I play it I'm gonna raise my horn a little bit," Miles said. His customary playing stance, onstage or in the recording studio, was to point his trumpet straight at the floor as he played, a position that communi-

cated contemplation and moodiness, though it was primarily a way of regulating his tone. "Can I move this down a little bit?" He indicated the
mike.

"It's against policy to move a microphone," Townsend said, deadpan.
The old church echoed with laughter.

THERE WERE THREE MORE FALSE STARTS, OF FIFTY-ONE SECONDS, A MIN-
ute twenty-one, and four seconds respectively, and then there was a full
take of nearly ten minutes. First the three horns in unison set the mood,
soft and mellow and just behind the beat. Then Wynton Kelly soloed,
and—given that he was that rare jazz pianist who far preferred comping
to parading his playing—he produced a sparkling, tasty beauty. Miles's
two-chorus solo, on open horn, now meditative, now the slightest bit hesitant, was unmistakably expressive—cool, yet packed with barely sup-
pressed emotion—and masterly. "I think Miles's blues solo on that track
is one of my favorites," Evans said in an interview two decades later.
"There are a couple of places where just one note contains so much meaning that you can hardly believe it."

Coltrane came next, entering with a bang. "Trane was the loudest,
fastest saxophonist I've ever heard," Miles once said. "It was like he was
possessed when he put that horn in his mouth." On "Freddie," the fast and
daring runs he played, though keeping within the framework of the song's
mellow volume and laid-back pulse, harkened back to the saxophonist's
walking-the-bar, Cleanhead Vinson days, showing he could still wail like
the blues musician he had once been, albeit one who had evolved into John
Coltrane.

And after the nearly imperceptible handoff ("It was sometimes difficult to tell when one instrument stopped and the other started," Adderley
later recalled, of his work with Coltrane; "it sounded like a continual
phrase"), Cannonball, too, conjured the bluesman he had been, back when
he and his brother were gigging at Florida dive bars. His solo was more
melodic than Coltrane's, and more classically bluesy—at one point he

even threw in a quote from a recent R&B hit by Junior Parker, "Next Time You See Me." Like Charlie Parker, like Sonny Rollins and Dexter Gordon, Adderley was a jazz magpie, fond of inserting bits and scraps of familiar melodies into his solos; Coltrane seemed to quote only from God.

OUTSIDE THE THIRTIETH STREET STUDIO, MANHATTAN WAS MANHAT-taning: rounded buses and big yellow cabs grinding up and down the avenues; car horns and scraps of radio music and pedestrians' voices echoing in the deep-shadowed side streets. Outside, the everyday clamor and clash of a city afternoon in late-winter 1959; inside, the densest quiet as a passage apart from time proceeded: the recording of CO 62291, the number that would come to be titled "So What," leading off the album soon to be known as *Kind of Blue*.

The first take began. There was a false start of four seconds, followed by an incomplete take of forty-nine seconds. Townsend interrupted from the booth: something was interfering with the song's profound hush. "Hold it," the producer said. "Sorry—listen, we gotta watch it because, ah, there's noises all the way through this. This is so quiet to begin with, and every click—watch the snare too, we're picking up some of the vibrations on it—"

Miles, ever on the lookout for meaningful accidentals, demurred. "Well, that goes with it," he said. "*All* that goes with it."

"All right," Townsend allowed. "Not all the other noises, though . . ."

Another false start, seventeen seconds. An incomplete take, a minute eleven. A telephone rang in the control booth. Once quiet was restored, three more false starts, of sixteen, seven, and fifteen seconds.

Then, history.

Someone—some say it was Gil Evans; Peter Pettinger and Wallace Roney asserted it was Bill Evans—had sketched out a single-line introduction to the piece, a hushed dialogue between piano and bass, proceeding at its own dreamy pace and built on meditative, European art song–esque chords (the fourth, with two white piano keys between the lower and upper notes, being an interval that, enigmatically, presents as neither major nor minor), then on skipping single notes played in unison by the two instruments. Paul Chambers then set the rhythm, plucking the eight-note figure that was to become immortal, the call that began the rhythmic call-and-response of "So What." Evans then answered, followed by the rest of the sextet.

"The piano's (and then the band's) answering 'amen' (or 'so what') riffs," Pettinger writes, "were built up largely in fourths, as opposed to the thirds that are basic to the tonal system, as exemplified by Bobby Timmons's comparable composition 'Moanin',' recorded by him some four months earlier."

Timmons, the pianist for Art Blakey's Jazz Messengers, was all of twenty-two when he wrote "Moanin'," a call-and-response number that, unlike Miles's, had a strong, foursquare gospel feeling. Call-and-response was an ancient form, with roots in African ritual, civics, and music; it traveled to America and underlaid African American work songs and religious rituals from 1619 on. Timmons's song, like Blakey's quintet and Horace Silver's compositions and bands, was hugely influential in pointing jazz in a more soulful direction. Miles would have known the tune well—would he have enjoyed its old-fashioned wholeheartedness? been impatient with it? It didn't matter: he was proceeding on his own musical path, channeling strong emotions through the prisms and filters of his biting intelligence and contrary spirit. Some people called this Cool; under the surface it was anything but.

The full take 3 was nine minutes and thirty-five seconds of musical transcendence. Miles's solo, an impromptu composition in itself, would gain its own immortality: generations of musicians would memorize it note for note. Miles is talking to you in that solo, playing in the middle sonic range of the human voice, and he's got all kinds of things to say, in brief and at length. He starts and stops; he starts again and goes on. And we're freshly astonished at how very much he can express, in so few notes, *in the moment.* In the liner notes he eventually wrote for *Kind of Blue,* Bill Evans compared the album's spontaneity to the Japanese art of ink painting, *suibokuga,* in which the artist must paint on a thin stretched parchment with a special brush and black water paint in such a way that an unnatural or interrupted stroke will destroy the line. . . . Erasures or changes are impossible. These artists must practice a particular discipline, that of allowing the idea to express itself in communication with their hands in such a direct way that deliberation cannot interfere.

The resulting pictures lack the complex composition and textures of ordinary painting, but it is said that those who see will find something captured that escapes explanation.

The richness each of the soloists was able to create improvising over just two chords, D and E♭ Dorian, vindicates Miles's modal concept. Coltrane was in exploratory rather than loud and fast form, traveling up and down each scale to find astringent delights. Cannonball was no less seeking, but lush toned as always, and unable not to find melodies and tuneful fillips, even in this minimalist frame. And Evans's solo was perhaps most in sync with the tune's hushed simplicity: playing quiet arpeggios and complex chords a little shyly at first, but then growing more assertive—and surprising: "I'm thinking of the end of Bill's solo on 'So What,'" Herbie Hancock told Ashley Kahn. "He plays these phrases, a second apart. He plays seconds." Still filled with wonderment forty years after the fact, Hancock was talking about an interval on the piano that's barely an interval—two adjacent keys played simultaneously. By itself, the sound is dissonant; in this context it's startlingly expressive. "I had never heard anybody do that before," Hancock said. "He's following the modal concept maybe more than anybody else. That just opened up a whole vista for me."

CO 62291 wasn't yet officially named on the day it was recorded, but in the years after *Kind of Blue*'s release, more than one person would take credit for its title: John Szwed writes that it "may have been suggested to [Davis] by Beverly Bentley [a girlfriend of Miles's, later Norman Mailer's fourth wife], who said it sounded like his favorite dismissive remark, but folks in East St. Louis were more likely to believe that it came from Miles's brother-in-law's retort when Miles told him in 1944 that he was leaving for New York: 'So what?'" And the actor Dennis Hopper, who said he was a close friend of Davis's, recalled that the phrase was a comeback he, Hopper, used to deploy, jablike, when Miles ran his mouth while the two of them sparred together: "Oh come on, Miles, so what?" "So one time I came into the [jazz] club," Hopper remembered, "and he said, 'I wrote a little song for you'—and he played 'So What.'"

THE WORD "TIMELESS" HAS BECOME A CLICHÉ, A SELLING TOOL FOR LUX-ury goods. And yet *Kind of Blue* is a timeless album, and "So What" arguably its signature number. What is this about? For sixty years and more, jazz and popular music had consisted of songs that told stories, either explicitly—in lyrics—or in their construction. The most common song framework in both genres was known as AABA: two choruses followed by a bridge (aka channel, release, or middle eight), followed by an out-chorus. (Popular songs of the first half of the twentieth century also typically began with a verse: a brief, explanatory introduction that might or might not be included in performance or on recordings.) The sound of tunes made this way was a satisfying blend of exposition and resolution. Popular songs, which often became the explicit or implicit basis for jazz tunes, were written in a given key, and while they might wander chordally—see Oscar Hammerstein and Jerome Kern's "All the Things You Are" or the bridge of Richard Rodgers and Lorenz Hart's "Have You Met Miss Jones?"—they tended, satisfyingly, to come back home to that first chord. This was even truer of the blues, with its intrinsic I-IV-V format, a structure that was restrictive but deeply pleasing. A story was told and you learned the outcome, even if it was sad. (See: "Moanin'.") You knew how it turned out—maybe you knew before the song started—but hearing about it could make you forget your troubles for a while, or identify with the singer's or the musician's troubles.

But with Miles, in life and in art, it was always the thing withheld. And the essence of modal music—the essence of "So What"—was that you had no idea how it turned out, or if it turned out. Which was pretty much the way the world was looking at that moment, and maybe the way (you had to think) it was going to look from then on.

It was 1959; the world jostled and rocked. American automobiles sprouted double headlights and fins. Batista fled Havana; Castro entered. Khrushchev met Mao, visited Disneyland, debated Nixon in a model kitchen at the American National Exhibition in Moscow. Alaska and Hawaii joined the Union; the flag gained two stars. The crashes of commercial airliners were a depressingly regular event. The music died in Clear Lake, Iowa; the Clutters died in Holcomb, Kansas. Johnny and the Moondogs, a British guitar trio led by the eighteen-year-old art student John Lennon (his bandmates were the seventeen-year-old Paul McCartney and sixteen-year-old George Harrison), played gigs around Liverpool whenever they could find a drummer. *Rocky and Bullwinkle* and *Bonanza*—in color—debuted. As did the Xerox machine. As did the Barbie doll. NASA named the seven original astronauts, and the Space Age began. *Gypsy* and *The Sound of Music* and *A Raisin in the Sun* premiered on Broadway. The Boeing 707 and the ICBM were introduced: travelers could now fly to far-off destinations at unprecedented speeds, as could nuclear bombs.

So what.

TWO SONGS IN THE CAN, ONE LEFT TO RECORD: THE BAND WOULD HAVE taken a dinner break at five thirty. Did they leave the studio's quiet little world for Manhattan's blare and clatter? Close to sunset on this early-March late afternoon, the city's river light would have been soft, the air rich with car and bus fumes and a slight promise of spring. It was the time of day when, as Willa Cather once wrote, everything goes home. The streets would have been filled with outbound workers, while these six would soon be headed back to the job.

A certain amount of controversy has accrued to the album's third number. "Some people went around saying that Bill was co-composer of the music on *Kind of Blue*," Miles said in his memoir.

That isn't true; it's all mine and the concept was mine. What he did do was turn me on to some classical composers, and they influenced me. But the first time Bill saw any of that music was when I gave him a sketch to look at just like everyone else.

Evans begged to differ on one count. "I sketched out 'Blue in Green,' which was my tune," he said, years later. "I sketched out the melody and the changes to it for the guys."

Yet on the album, it's credited to Davis, who also copyrighted it. Why, almost a decade after Evans's death, would Miles lie about this, undercutting his old friend Moe, the man who had taught him so much?

Years later, a radio interviewer asked a friend of Evans's, the composer and arranger Earl Zindars, if the tune belonged to Bill alone. "Definitely," Zindars said. "I know it . . . because he wrote it over at my pad where I was staying in East Harlem, fifth-floor walk-up, and he stayed up until three o'clock in the morning playing those six bars over and over."

"I know that on the album it is credited to Miles," Evans told the jazz journalist Brian Hennessey, "but he did the same thing with two of Eddie Vinson's tunes, 'Tune Up' and 'Four.' It's a small matter to me, but when someone asks me about it I tell the truth." In 1978, when Evans was a guest on Marian McPartland's National Public Radio show *Piano Jazz*, McPartland put the question to him directly: had he written "Blue in Green"? "The truth is I did," Evans said. "I don't want to make a federal case out of it, [but] the music exists, and Miles is getting the royalties." Late in his life, Evans told a friend that when he suggested to Miles that he was entitled to a share of the royalties, Davis wrote him a check for twenty-five dollars.

At just over five and a half minutes, the shortest song on the album (by far) is more mood piece than tune, and the mood is pensive and sad: only the number's beauty rescues it from lugubriousness. It's built on chords, but there's no sense of thrust or resolution—it ambles, slowly, hypnotically. Solos by Evans and Miles, then Miles and Evans, form a symmetrical bracket around Coltrane's forty-one-second central solo. It seems doubly appropriate that Adderley lays out here: not only would his natural exuberance be misplaced, but melancholy is so deeply engraved in all three of *Kind of Blue*'s central geniuses that "Blue in Green" feels like a kind of group character statement.

A MONTH LATER, MOST OF THE SEXTET—CANNONBALL WAS OUT WITH A migraine; Wynton Kelly replaced Evans—performed on the CBS telecast *The Robert Herridge Theater*. Herridge was a serious cultural type who had presented both Western classical and jazz on his weekly show. Against the bare-bones industrial backdrop of CBS Stage 61, on Manhattan's West Side, Miles, elegant in a light-colored suit, dark sweater, and neck bandanna, led the band in a superbly cool, slightly up-tempo version of "So What." The show wouldn't air for more than a year, but when it was broadcast, in July 1960, it impressed a broad swath of the television-watching public who had had little or no experience of jazz, "[providing] invaluable promotional support for *Kind of Blue* and the rest of Miles's catalog," Ashley Kahn writes, "[and adding] several degrees to the steep angle of his career ascent. . . . Miles Davis the jazz phenomenon was becoming simply Miles the star."

KIND OF BLUE'S SECOND AND FINAL RECORDING SESSION WAS A MUCH shorter affair than the first: the sextet laid down just two tracks between 2:30 and 5:30 p.m. on Wednesday, April 22, and though "Flamenco Sketches" required six takes, two of them full versions of the number, the band achieved the final, quite beautiful version of "All Blues" in a single try.

"Flamenco Sketches" was born on the morning of March 2, when Bill Evans went over to Miles's place to prepare for the album's first session. Davis had heard Evans play his composition "Peace Piece"—a serene and pensive ramble over the haunting two-chord vamp that begins Betty Comden, Adolph Green, and Leonard Bernstein's tune "Some Other Time," from the musical *On the Town*—and wanted to include the number on the LP. Having already recorded the tune with Cannonball, Evans had another idea. You could, he told Miles, construct a song that started out from the "Peace Piece" vamp but then journeyed through five different modes. Working together at the piano, the two sketched out a similarly ethereal number, the most collaborative Davis-Evans piece on *Kind of Blue*—and the only other one besides "Blue in Green" with a written-out road map. The fourth, Spanish-style, mode gave the tune its title.

The first session had begun with a blues; the last ended with one that both graces and transcends the form that Miles is about to leave behind. "All Blues" contains two inventions by him that, characteristically, are seemingly simple but subtly powerful. A normal blues in G would change to the IV chord—C—after the first four bars. Davis's blues in G stays in G for the first eight bars: the change is in shifting from G7 to what Jimmy Heath called "a G minor sound . . . [making Miles's] improvisation sound a little dissonant, and a little more sophisticated." Less chordal, more modal. Kind of blue.

The other subtle touch was putting more space between the solos: Miles, as we've seen, loved space. "On 'All Blues,'" Evans remembered, "he said, 'Play the chart, and then before each soloist, the [musical] figure will serve as a little vamp to enter the next soloist.'"

From Evans's opening piano tremolo to Miles's muted fadeout, the tune is warm and serene, yet in its "waltz-like bounce," quietly joyous. And unexpected throughout. After stating the Harmon-muted theme, Miles switches to open horn for his solo; Adderley, rather than Coltrane, plays the first solo after Miles, and both saxophonists invoke their R&B days in the mellowest way possible. And when Evans's turn comes, he finds pleasure in a form he'd never been comfortable with before, even throwing in a bright spray of fourths that prefigures McCoy Tyner's later work with Trane.

Fourths, neither major nor minor, are about ambiguity. They're unresolved, questioning. As is *Kind of Blue* itself—starting with the album's title itself. In the mid- to late fifties, the music that some called hard bop enlisted elements of blues and gospel to restore emotion to jazz: the music sang out joyously and hit out powerfully, calling forth the incipient power of Black liberation. *Kind of Blue*, on the other hand, marked a kind of fermata in the onrushing torrent of jazz: "It sounds reflective, it sounds relaxed, at a time when most jazz had a more aggressive stance," Loren Schoenberg said. It was an island of quiet mystery in a world growing faster and louder by the day. It was Miles, Coltrane, and Evans leaving the blues behind and heading for parts unknown.

It was the last time this sextet would ever play together.

Ornette Coleman, 1959.

15 Annus mirabilis

Less than two weeks after the second and final record date for *Kind of Blue*, John Coltrane began making his first Atlantic album, *Giant Steps*. The aptly named LP was also the first by Coltrane to consist exclusively of his own compositions. Trane, though still part of Davis's sextet, was spreading his wings, taking the artistic autonomy Miles had granted him—more than granted, insisted on ("I've been so free here," the saxophonist told an interviewer, of his time in the sextet, "that almost anything I want to try is—I'm welcome to do it, you know?")—and turning it into his own brand.

Giant Steps' title track was a genial monster, a romp in verticality: a sunny, sizzlingly fast excursion through three keys, B major, G major, and E♭ major, in chords separated by major thirds—a sequence, similar to the bridge of "Have You Met Miss Jones?," that would soon be known as *Coltrane changes*. The tune would become an instant classic upon the record's release in early 1960, and a beyond-challenging practice piece for generations of saxophonists to come.

The record's other classic-to-be (it would be recorded that December) was "Naima": a slow, mist-wreathed love ballad for his wife, a song that stood as an answer to those who, within recent memory, had called Coltrane an angry young tenor. "While it's true," Nat Hentoff would write in the album's liner notes,

> that to musicians especially, Coltrane's fiercely adventurous harmonic imagination is the most absorbing aspect of his developing style, the more basic point is that for many non-musician listeners, Coltrane at his best has an unusually striking emotional impact. . . . Part of the fury in much of his playing is the fury of the search, the obsession Coltrane has to play all he can hear or would like to hear—often all at once—and yet at the same time make his music, as he puts it, "more presentable."

Coltrane clarified this. "Tonewise, I would like to be able to produce a more beautiful sound," he said. "But now I'm primarily interested in trying to work what I have, what I know, down into a more *lyrical* line. That's what I mean by beautiful; more lyrical. So it'd be, you know, easily understood."

For all too long in his early career, he had been all too easily understood: a musical chameleon, trying to lose Charlie Parker's influence, playing only what was asked of him, until Miles asked him to play more. Now, just in his thirty-third year, he had become *John Coltrane*—such a towering influence that jazz writers around the country (there were jazz writers around the country then) could speak of Coltrane disciples, and even worry that his outsize effect on younger musicians was hampering their own questing for originality. A January review of Art Blakey and the Jazz Messengers' latest album praised the playing of Blakey's tenor man, Coltrane's close friend and old running buddy Benny Golson, but added: "At times we had the feeling that he'd been listening quite a bit to John Coltrane lately."

Golson, if possible an even humbler great player (and great composer) than Coltrane himself, never worried, then or later, about admiring Trane's greatness: "Everybody finally had to acknowledge that John was a phenomenon walking in nobody else's footsteps," he wrote in his graceful memoir. "John searched in places never before visited musically, uncharted musical territory that contained ideas defying the banality of names. No one walked with him; we all merely followed if we could, or watched him forge ahead by himself."

Nineteen fifty-nine was bringing on jazz's future with ruthless speed. In part this meant the sunset of the music's past. On March 15, Lester Young died at age forty-nine—officially of a heart attack, but more accurately of the Life—the condition of being a Black jazz musician in the United States. Young had his own way of thinking about the world, and his own way of talking about it, too: he may have been the first person to call money *bread*, and he named Billie Holiday Lady Day, a favor she returned by dubbing him Prez. The president of jazz. (Holiday herself would outlive Young by just four months: on July 17 she too would die of the Life, at age forty-four, handcuffed to a bed in Harlem Hospital, under arrest for possession of the drug that was both killing her and just barely keeping her alive.) In an era when men wore fedoras, Lester Young favored a strikingly different kind of headgear, one with a flat crown and a wide brim. No one looked like him; no one talked like him; many played like him—but only because he'd taught them to.

That spring Charles Mingus wrote a haunting musical elegy to Young. "Goodbye Pork Pie Hat" would be the second track on *Mingus Ah Um*, the Columbia album the bassist recorded in the Thirtieth Street Studio in early May. It was an LP that, Janus-like, looked back to Mingus's musical roots ("Jelly Roll," "Open Letter to Duke," "Boogie Stop Shuffle") and ahead to the dark and complexified days of the present and future ("Better Git It in Your Soul," "Fables of Faubus"). The brilliant and irascible Mingus, who unlike Coltrane really was an angry young jazz musician, assembled a superb cadre of spirited players (saxophonists John Handy, Booker Ervin, and Shafi Hadi; trombonists Willie Dennis and Jimmy Knepper; pianist Horace Parlan; and drummer Dannie Richmond) and

put all his lyrical, clapping, stomping, contrary soul into the album—
which was, at once, both a thing of great beauty and the ecstatic and ag-
onized cry of a Black soul in an implacably racist America. Mingus, a
polemicist at heart, soon found that unlike Miles, he was not prepared to
hitch his wagon to the star-making machinery of Columbia Records.
Mingus Ah Um, however, has held up as one of the artistically revolutionary signposts of the remarkable year of 1959. And other, even more radical,
changes in the music were afoot.

RANDOLPH DENARD ORNETTE COLEMAN, A SHY, THOUGHTFUL, ARTISTI-
cally questing saxophonist, was Texas-born and, like his idol Charlie
Parker, largely self-taught. Like John Coltrane, Coleman served appren-
ticeships in blues and R&B bands—around the South and Southwest in
Coleman's case. He even did time in a ragtag traveling minstrel show,
Silas Green from New Orleans. Once, at a Baton Rouge dance gig, after
Coleman played some Parker licks that stopped the dancing, a half dozen
young Black men, unhappy with the way he played and unhappy, too,
with the way he looked and acted—at nineteen, Coleman was a vegetar-
ian proto-hippie, with long hair and a beard—beat him up and destroyed
his tenor sax. The only replacement he could (eventually) afford was a
cream-colored Grafton plastic alto, an instrument the ceaselessly idiosyncratic Ornette Coleman would stick with for the rest of his career. The
horn had a warm nonmetallic tone, which Coleman could make sound
uncannily like a human voice.

    In the early fifties he landed in Los Angeles, where most of the tal-
ented musicians were, like him, heavily under the influence of Bird. This
quickly palled: "I could play and sound like Charlie Parker note-for-note,
but I was only playing it from method," Coleman later said. "So I tried to
figure out where to go from there."

    His figuring led to a style he called harmolodics, or as it would come
to be known, mostly by nonmusicians, free jazz. Unlike bebop, hard bop,
or even modal jazz, Coleman's new music often began and ended with a

melody or the suggestion of one, but in between was improvised by all instruments (usually in a quartet format), according to each player's mood at the moment, without regard to chordal construction, recognizable harmony, or conventional rhythm.

In a certain way this was a predictable, even late-arriving, advance: European classical composers such as Arnold Schoenberg, Alban Berg, and Anton Webern had begun experimenting with atonal music more than fifty years earlier. The reaction against their innovations among listeners with more conventionally tuned ears was often violent, and Coleman's work would provoke similar outrage in the world of jazz, which had its own set of conventions and intolerances. His explorations (among them his realization that "you could play sharp or flat in tune") caused more than a few musicians to walk out when he tried to sit in. The white plastic saxophone (despite the fact that Bird, too, had played one for a time)

signaled to some that he couldn't be taken seriously. "The rejection of Coleman by Los Angeles musicians was massive," his biographer John Litweiler writes. "One night he was playing with Dexter Gordon's rhythm section when Gordon showed up at the club late and ordered him to immediately finish the song and get off the stage." Coleman eked out a living as best he could, sometimes in music, more often not.

By the late fifties Coleman, now working as an elevator operator in the Los Angeles department store Bullock's, had assembled a core of players who did like what he was doing: the trumpeter Don Cherry, bassist Charlie Haden, and the drummers Ed Blackwell and Billy Higgins. Soon he formed a quartet with Cherry, Haden, and Higgins. (The absence of a pianist was notable: Gerry Mulligan had worked with a pianoless quartet, and Sonny Rollins sometimes played with just a bassist and drummer; but Mulligan and Rollins were making a very different kind of jazz from Coleman's.) In the absence of paying gigs, the group rehearsed steadily.

In early 1958, the bebop bassist Red Mitchell told Lester Koenig, the founder of the West Coast label Contemporary, about Coleman. Koenig, who'd recorded Rollins's great (pianoless) 1957 album *Way Out West*, as well as LPs by Chet Baker, Art Pepper, and André Previn, among others, had big ears: he counted Arnold Schoenberg as a friend. He listened to Coleman and Cherry audition and, excited by this completely new sound, signed the saxophonist to a two-record deal—with conditions. That February and March, Coleman, along with Cherry, Higgins, the bassist Don Payne instead of Haden—and as Koenig apparently required, a pianist, Walter Norris—recorded the album that would be titled, with exclamatory emphasis on its novelty, *Something Else!!!! The Music of Ornette Coleman*.

It's an odd record—or more pointedly, one that seems at odds with itself, locked in a struggle between spiky unconventionality and cheery accessibility. Some of the blame can be laid on Lester Koenig, who produced the session. Norris was a skillful and adaptable player, who might have been able to reflect Coleman's purposefully aleatory approach; instead, the LP's tunes, all Coleman compositions, often sounded as though the bebop-style piano and the inimitably strange saxophone were on two different pages. ("As much as he knew about harmony," Charlie Haden later said, "Norris couldn't forget it when he was playing with Ornette.") On its release in September 1958, *Something Else!!!!* made a small stir—and produced very small sales—but gave no hint of the seismic changes Coleman would soon bring to jazz.

In early 1959—as Miles and Bill Evans were starting to work on the modal innovations that would lead to *Kind of Blue*—Ornette managed to convince Lester Koenig to let him go pianoless on his next album. Like the previous LP, *Tomorrow Is the Question! The New Music of Ornette Coleman!* consisted exclusively of Coleman compositions. Don Cherry was back, now playing a Turkish pocket trumpet; the well-traveled Shelly Manne was at the drums. But after Red Mitchell played on some tracks, Coleman and Cherry decided they needed a different bassist. With Charlie Haden not available (or not approved by Koenig), they drove up to San Francisco, where the Modern Jazz Quartet was playing at the Black Hawk, to try and enlist the MJQ's Percy Heath. They wound up not just snagging Heath but sitting in with the band—and mightily impressing its leader, John Lewis. "I've never heard anything like Ornette Coleman and Don Cherry before," Lewis later said. "Ornette is the driving force of the two. They're almost like twins; they play together like I've never heard anybody play together."

A liberation from rhythm's conventional constraints was a great part of Coleman's overall conception: Cherry understood it completely, but on *Tomorrow Is the Question!* Mitchell, Heath, and Manne seemed unwilling or unable to improvise as freely as Coleman wanted. The three "all made up their own parts and played what they wanted," the jazz pianist and commentator Ethan Iverson writes. "Their solutions are interesting but not ideal. . . . These are *not* musicians in the mystic circle." Yet apart from Don Cherry, Coleman still couldn't bring his circle into a recording studio.

John Lewis's enthusiasm for Coleman and Cherry was somewhat paradoxical. Lewis's determinedly formal, European-classical-influenced (and commercially very successful) Modern Jazz Quartet exemplified his ambivalent feelings about the directions the music had taken since the advent of bebop. Many years later, Kenny Clarke told Loren Schoenberg that he left the group in 1955 because Lewis hated jazz. But in 1959 Ornette Coleman seemed like such a breath of fresh life to John Lewis that Lewis recommended him to Nesuhi Ertegun, head of the jazz division at MJQ's (and Coltrane's) label, Atlantic, and brother of the label's co-founder, Ahmet Ertegun. After getting the approval of his old friend Koenig (Nesuhi had briefly worked at Contemporary before joining Atlantic), who admitted that he'd been unable to get anything going for Coleman commercially, Ertegun signed him.

Thus it was that in that same eventful May, the birth month of both *Giant Steps* and *Mingus Ah Um*, Ornette Coleman made his third album, *The Shape of Jazz to Come*, at Radio Recorders studio in Hollywood. It was a provocative, almost laughably bold title—in fact it had been thought up not by Coleman but by Ertegun—but it was one to which, as would soon be seen, Coleman could lay a fair claim. Just twenty-nine, he had already made an indelible stamp on the genre, and when *The Shape of Jazz to Come* was released that November, the impact of his art would become as powerful in its way as that made by Miles, Coltrane, or Bill Evans.

THAT SUMMER, WHILE ORNETTE COLEMAN WAS STILL LABORING IN OBscurity in Los Angeles, the much-lionized, three-quarters-white Dave Brubeck Quartet—Brubeck, the alto saxophonist Paul Desmond, the bassist Eugene Wright, and the drummer Joe Morello—recorded the pianist's twenty-ninth album, *Time Out*, in Columbia's Thirtieth Street Studio. Inspired by the band's recent State Department-sponsored tour through Europe and Asia, Brubeck had conceived an experimental LP of songs in exotic tempos, like the folk tune he'd heard played by Turkish street musicians in 9/8 time. The pianist wrote all the numbers on the record—except for the one that would become its biggest hit, Desmond's excursion in 5/4, "Take Five."

Time Out would become the first jazz album to sell a million copies, and "Take Five" would be the first jazz single to reach the same plateau. The LP remains a well-loved classic, in good part because for all Brubeck's innovative intentions, *Time Out* never bit deep or challenged. "It was experimental music, but mildly so," Szwed writes, "and his quartet still sounded friendly to those who followed him." If many of those followers were (and still are) white, does that diminish the album's importance? Those with ears big enough to appreciate music across jazz's wide spectrum, including musicians both Black and white, respected and continue to respect Brubeck: Miles Davis, who recorded beautiful versions of two of the pianist's numbers, "In Your Own Sweet Way" and Brubeck's tribute to Ellington, "The Duke," was one of them.

There's a story, perhaps too good to be entirely apocryphal: One night in the early sixties, Brubeck went to hear Miles's quintet at the Black Hawk. In the wee hours of the morning, as the band was finishing its last set, Ella Fitzgerald stopped by. She told Brubeck she felt like doing some singing, and asked him to accompany her. Afterward, Miles said, "Dave, *you* swing. Your fucking *band* don't swing."

The ability to swing was, as we've seen, one of Miles's highest musical values. But how would he feel when he encountered a jazz musician, and a band, for whom the very concept of rhythm was up for grabs?

IN AUGUST, ORNETTE COLEMAN AND DON CHERRY ATTENDED THE THIRD annual session of the School of Jazz, at the Music Inn in Lenox, Massachusetts. John Lewis and Gunther Schuller ran the school, whose purpose was to mentor young musicians as they began their careers; faculty included Lewis's bandmates in the Modern Jazz Quartet, as well as George Russell, Kenny Dorham, Max Roach, J. J. Johnson, Bob Brookmeyer, Jimmy Giuffre, Jim Hall, and Bill Evans. Jazz writers from New York—in particular, the cofounders of the (short-lived) magazine *The Jazz Review*, Nat Hentoff and Martin Williams—came up to scout new talent.

Though such soon-to-be stars as Freddie Hubbard, the pianist Steve Kuhn, and vibraphonist Gary McFarland had matriculated, in the eyes of many at the school Coleman and Cherry were on a different level: "In some deep sense [Ornette] wasn't a student there—he could have taught any of the faculty at Lenox," Schuller recalled. "He burst on the scene completely intact." And split the faculty in two: some, wrote *The Berkshire Eagle*'s culture columnist Milton R. Bass, "regarded [Coleman's playing] as the new slipstream off the mainstream of jazz, speaking in tones that had formerly been reserved only for the late Charlie 'Yardbird' Parker. Other faculty members decried the seeming formlessness which ripped down all standards and the surging bitterness that dominated the sound."

After jamming with Coleman, Jimmy Giuffre, whom Ornette had gently needled for playing in too structured a way, wound up "[playing] the wildest, craziest music," Schuller said. "I remember him lying with his back on the floor playing his tenor saxophone, just playing altissimo notes and screaming and all this wailing—he was trying to play a kind of Ornette Coleman on tenor." Bob Brookmeyer, on the other hand, "screamed, 'Damn it, tune up!' and then left the faculty in protest of the attention paid Ornette."

"The students at the school were terribly shook," Bass wrote. "They came to hear pronouncements and encyclicals from their idols, and they found instead several sects fighting a battle which had no beginning, middle or end. It was exciting to be in the middle of it, but they never knew from which direction they might be clobbered."

In truth, John Lewis had craftily engineered Coleman and Cherry's attendance at Lenox—Nesuhi Ertegun paid for their trip from L.A., as well as their tuition—to raise their profile on the East Coast. The ploy worked: nobody was neutral about Ornette. After hearing him play, not to mention witnessing the brouhaha at Lenox, the influential Martin Williams, who also wrote about jazz for *The New York Times* and *Saturday Review*, began to lobby his friends Joe and Iggy Termini to give Coleman and his band their first East Coast engagement, a spot on the Five Spot's schedule. The Terminis hired the quartet for a two-week stand, to start on Tuesday, November 17.

THE COLUMBIA RECORDS PUBLICIST DEBORAH ISHLON HAD RAISED MILES'S already high profile considerably over the past year, landing features on the trumpeter in *Time*, *The New York Times*, and *Esquire*. A heavy publicity push for *Kind of Blue* over the summer of '59, along with the producer Teo Macero's word of mouth to jazz DJs, sent the jazz community into a tizzy about the August 17 release date: "I remember standing at the record store, a little tiny place under the railroad tracks on the South Side," the pianist Warren Bernhardt, then an undergrad at the University of Chicago, told Ashley Kahn. "I was waiting with a bunch of other guys for the records to come in off the truck."

Yet *Kind of Blue*'s release did not make the earth move. *Billboard*'s comment was measured: Miles, the trade magazine said, was "staying within the confines of what might be called the 'interior' style of cool jazz. . . ." And while *Metronome*'s October review praised the LP's "fine ensemble playing" and "neat, simple charts," it complained, similarly, that "Miles seems to be limiting himself more and more all the time . . . playing within a smaller and smaller limit all the time, taking no chances at all." The music columnist Jack Coffman lauded the sextet's integrated thought and "ultra-subtle sounds," but added, oddly: "technical perfection has sold very few records and one of the troubles with this performance is that it just doesn't swing."

From a present-day perspective it's easy to overlook how new and strange this material was in 1959, even to jazz insiders. The singer and pianist Shirley Horn, a fan and friend of Miles, recalled running into Stan Getz at Birdland in April, when the sextet was playing material from the album: she and Getz "hugged and then we stood there and listened. I said, 'What do you think?' He said, 'I don't know. . . .' I said, 'I don't either.' It was beautiful but confusing."

The *San Francisco Examiner* columnist C. H. Garrigues sounded a lonely and perhaps quixotic note:

> This is one of Miles's great records . . . it is perhaps his greatest record since his days with Bird. . . . Buy it and play it, quietly, around about midnight . . . you will agree that this is jazz which, in all likelihood, will never be duplicated.

It was true, but nobody knew just why. *Kind of Blue* was like a stone tossed into a dark lake, the concentric waves of its power radiating smoothly, silently, in all directions.

In concrete affirmation of the album's immaterial force, it kept selling. Unlike *Porgy and Bess*, which was an immediate smash, *Kind of Blue*'s popularity built slowly, but with gathering strength. "A comparative sales study from Columbia's files," Kahn writes, "reveals that of all Davis's LPs to January 1962, *Kind of Blue* was his leading seller by far, with over 87,000 copies sold. *Porgy & Bess* was the only album that came close." The record's sales would continue to rise, ever more steeply, through the decades.

IN JUNE, AN ODD ITEM IN DOROTHY KILGALLEN'S GOSSIP COLUMN NOTED that "Sonny Rollins, one of the biggest names in modern jazz, bids fair to become one of the biggest problems to his record company." After Metro-Jazz (a division of MGM Records) sent Leonard Feather to Los Angeles to prepare and produce a new album by Rollins, the columnist said, and after Feather had engaged a studio and hired sidemen, the saxophonist had simply never appeared. Reached for comment, Rollins said, "I've decided not to show up for the date, that's all."

This was likely the first indication of an artistic/spiritual crisis Sonny Rollins suffered in the summer of 1959, one that led to his famous sabbatical: the two-year period in which Rollins, rather than recording or performing, left his Lower East Side apartment every morning and went out to practice all day, every day, in every kind of weather, on the Williamsburg Bridge. Some have said—Wallace Roney asserted it as fact—that Rollins's hiatus was the result of a breakdown he suffered after hearing John Coltrane play the latest iteration of his rapidly advancing style. It's been suggested that the emergence of Ornette Coleman might also have rocked him. But when I spoke to Rollins in 2019, he said the cause was more internal than external.

"I certainly heard Ornette," he told me. "I heard the modal stuff exemplified in *Kind of Blue*. But I never was trying to learn to play modally; I never was trying to learn to play free jazz. My thing was getting inside of me, developing what was inside of myself. It might have [also] been to be as accepted as everything that was going on. But it wasn't to emulate them.

"People were expecting so much from me," he said. "It was Sonny Rollins, Sonny Rollins, Sonny Rollins. Elvin Jones and I played one job in particular, and I didn't give the people what they needed, what they wanted to hear. I said, 'Okay, somehow I'm not getting across. I'm not going to be out here, a big name, and then disappointing the people.' I mean, I couldn't live like that. What was I there for? To make the little bit of money that a top jazz player was getting at that time? Money didn't even enter into it. The idea was that if I wasn't satisfying the people, then I was being a fraud. I felt that I just needed to get myself together, regroup, do more practicing."

Far from being a rival, Coltrane was a close friend. (He named a song, "Like Sonny," on an album he recorded that year, after Rollins.) He was also a frequent visitor to Rollins during the period, a comfort, a support, and even a kind of spiritual adviser. "He used to come by my house," Rollins said, "and we'd talk about music, but he also introduced me to Sufism. At the time, I was getting into yoga. Really, it's the same. It's a distinction without a difference, Sufism and yoga."

REMARKABLY, WHEN *THE SHAPE OF JAZZ TO COME* WAS RELEASED IN early November, *Billboard*—on a page that also included capsule reviews of LPs by Kate Smith, Johnny Puleo & His Harmonica Gang, and the Columbus Boychoir—gave the album three stars for Good Sales Potential. "Ornette Coleman is one of the controversial new artists to spring from the modern jazz scene," the notice began.

> By some he is considered an important new innovator and creator; by others too far out for serious consideration. He is heard here, with Donald Cherry on cornet, Charlie Hadden [*sic*] on bass and Billy Higgins on drums, performing a group of selections written by himself. Coleman's alto work is self-consciously original and

won't have mass appeal. But its uniqueness will interest many avant garde jazz buffs. Best sides are "Peace," and "Lonely Woman."

It's funny—funny both ha-ha and strange—to hear two Ornette Coleman songs, nine minutes and five seconds and five minutes two seconds long respectively, described as "sides," in the same sense as, say, Perry Como's contemporaneous "Catch a Falling Star" or Connie Francis's "Lipstick on Your Collar"—or even, for that matter, "So What." "Sides" was a term from the pre-LP days, when recorded songs could last only three minutes, the length of one side of a 78 rpm phonograph record. A side was a number you could dance to, or sing along to, or snap your fingers to, or swoon romantically to.

"Peace" and "Lonely Woman," along with the other four tunes on *The Shape of Jazz*, were none of the above—or maybe they were all of them put together. Mainly, the album, like Ornette's band's live performances, demanded to be *listened* to, and reactions among listeners varied—and can still vary—wildly, even explosively, from the ecstatic to the incredulous. Heard more than sixty years later, the album still has the power to provoke. "Lonely Woman," its greatest hit, is goose bump raising: at once a cry of pain, a human-voiced wail in a dark sonic landscape (its echo of Monk's "'Round Midnight" can't have been accidental), a thing of great beauty and a reminder of Ornette's roots as a Texas blues musician. But recognizable rhythmic pulse and singable melody are strongly desirable quantities: both are certainly present throughout in *Kind of Blue* and *Giant Steps*—and yes, in *Time Out*. Their relative absence on *The Shape of Jazz to Come* makes most of the album, for some listeners, an intellectual rather than a visceral pleasure.

Yet intellectual pleasure is no small thing! And intellectuals have, from time to time, the power to teach even the most mulishly retrograde of us.

OF COURSE, WHAT WAS AT PLAY WITH ORNETTE COLEMAN'S MUSIC IN 1959 was more than provocation—it was shock. On the cold and rainy Tuesday night of November 17, the Five Spot gave a press preview of the Coleman quartet: attendance was de rigueur for all of New York's jazz-writing establishment. As the *DownBeat* columnist George Hoefer wrote soon afterward,

> some walked in and out before they could finish a drink, some sat mesmerized by the sound, others talked constantly to their neighbors at the table or argued with drink in hand at the bar. It was, for all this, the largest collection of VIP's the jazz world has seen in many a year. . . .

The controversy instantly created sellout business at the club, and the Terminis extended the quartet's engagement from two weeks to two and a half months. Suddenly it was like the summer of '57 all over again, with Ornette instead of Monk rising as the prophet of jazz's, and American culture's, new age. The hip and the wannabes beat a path to 5 Cooper Square, happily queuing up for the chance to be mystified by the strange sounds within. "The public at the Five Spot," wrote the British historian Eric Hobsbawm, under his jazz-journalist pen name Francis Newton,

> is overwhelmingly young, white, and intellectual or bohemian. Here are the jazz fans (white or colored) with the "Draft Stevenson" buttons, lost over their $1.50 beer. If Coleman were to blow in Small's Paradise in Harlem, it would clear the place in five minutes. Musicians such as he are, it seems, as cut off from the common listeners among their people as Webern is from the public at the [English middle-class holiday camp] Filey Butlin's. They depend on those who are themselves alienated, the internal emigrants of America.

Those other internal emigrants, the painters and poets and musicians, also returned to pay homage. There were surprises. Though playing with Coleman had made Charlie Haden a master of improvising in the moment, during one show he found himself flummoxed by an unexpected occurrence: "One night I was playing with my eyes closed again," he remembered, "and all of a sudden, I open my eyes, and somebody's up on the stage with his ear to the 'F' hole of my bass. And I said, 'Coleman, who is this? Man, get him off this bandstand.' He says, 'That's Leonard Bernstein.'"

Bernstein, who pronounced Ornette a genius, subsequently sat in with the quartet on piano, as did Charles Mingus, whose spikiness about the world in general and his jazz colleagues in particular extended to Ornette. "I'm not saying that everybody's going to have to play like Coleman," Mingus wrote in *DownBeat*, "but they're going to have to stop copying Bird. . . . [Coleman's music is] like organized disorganization, or playing wrong right. . . . And it gets to you emotionally, like a drummer." It was hedged praise, but praise the remorselessly honest bassist couldn't help giving. Mingus, too, was a genius, but he was also a master communicator: his revolution took place within established boundaries of tone and rhythm. His gut punches were immediately comprehensible to even the most unsophisticated listener. Coleman was on a different plane altogether.

Coleman's jazz colleagues were divided on the subject, and not necessarily by age. The forty-eight-year-old Roy Eldridge said, "I listened to him all kinds of ways. I listened to him high and I listened to him cold sober. I even played with him. I think he's jiving, baby." Yet Lionel Hampton, fifty-one, who, as Dizzy Gillespie once noted, was always searching for something new, was captivated. Dizzy himself, however, was not. "I didn't dig Ornette Coleman at the beginning," he said. "I imagine I was just like the older guys, how they treated me when they first listened to me." He would eventually come around.

Max Roach in particular did not dig Coleman at the beginning. Ornette later told the record producer John Snyder that Roach came to the Five Spot to hear "what the fuss was all about," and at the end of the set walked up to Coleman and punched him in the mouth. And that wasn't the end of it. At four o'clock the next morning, Ornette said, Roach appeared on the street where he lived and screamed, "I know you're up there, motherfucker! Come on down here and I'll kick your ass!"

But his greatest fellow saxophonists were intrigued from the start. "When I first heard Ornette on this Contemporary record, *Something Else!!!!*, I liked it," Sonny Rollins told me. "I didn't say, 'Oh, this is different.' In fact, it did not sound different. It sounded just like Charlie Parker, in a way. To me it sounded more the same than different."

When an interviewer asked John Coltrane a year or so later what he thought of Coleman, Coltrane said, "I love him." He laughed. "Yeah, I love him. I'm following his lead. He's done a lot to open my eyes to what can be done. . . . I feel indebted to him, myself. Because, actually, when he came along, I was so far in this thing I didn't know where I was going to go next, you know. I don't know whether I would have thought about just abandoning the chord system or not. I probably wouldn't have thought of that at all. And he came along doing it, and I heard it, I said, 'Well, you know, that must be the answer.'"

Though he had no intention of abandoning the chord system, Bill Evans, too, was listening—and soon, dipping his oar in: at the end of 1960 Evans—who by now had been touring and recording for a year with Paul Motian and the bassist Scott LaFaro—played on an Atlantic album produced by John Lewis and Nesuhi Ertegun and arranged by Gunther Schuller, *Jazz Abstractions*. On Schuller's composition "Variants on a Theme of Thelonious Monk (Criss-Cross)," Evans accompanied Ornette (and nine other musicians, including a vibraphonist, a violinist, a violist, and a cellist) perfectly with sparse, sweetly dissonant chords that were first cousins to the seconds he'd played on "So What."

And then there was Miles.

Less than three months elapsed between the releases of *Kind of Blue* and *The Shape of Jazz to Come*, and between the uproar over Ornette's album and the hullabaloo around his residency at the Five Spot, Davis, so often the center of attention in jazz culture and as the Black avatar of jazz in the American culture at large—he'd garnered huge publicity in August when a New York cop beat him bloody outside Birdland after he refused to "move along"—had become somewhat eclipsed in the public eye. He didn't like it. "Hell, just listen to what he writes and how he plays," he said of Coleman at the time. "If you're talking psychologically, the man is all screwed up inside." Other sources have him putting it more pungently.

Speaking to Quincy Troupe decades later, Miles was both scathing and self-contradicting about this pretender to the throne. Coleman, he admitted, had "[come] to New York City and [turned] the jazz world all the way around. He just came and fucked up everybody." Back in the day he had said much the same about Bird, but Parker's bandwagon had been one that the young Miles had been eager to jump on. Now he was well into his thirties, and something crucial was rolling on without him. Worse still, "a lot of the 'star' people who used to come and see me—like Dorothy Kilgallen and Leonard Bernstein (who, they tell me, jumped up one night and said, 'This is the greatest thing that has ever happened to jazz!')—were now going to see Ornette."

By Miles's lights, Coleman's music was at once screwed up and negligible: "I liked Ornette and Don [Cherry] as people," he said,

> and I thought Ornette was playing more than Don was. But I didn't see or hear anything in their playing that was all that revolutionary, and I said so. Trane was there a lot more than I was, watching and listening, but he didn't say nothing like I did. A whole lot of the younger players and critics jumped down my throat after I put down Ornette, called me "old-fashioned" and shit. But I didn't like what they were playing, especially Don Cherry on that little horn he had. It just looked to me like he was playing a lot of notes and looking real serious, and people went for that because people will go for anything they don't understand if it's got enough hype. They want to be hip, want always to be in on the new thing so they don't look unhip. White people are especially like that, particularly when a black person is doing something they don't understand.

This is not without merit, but the fact is that it wasn't just white wannabes and trend followers who liked, or even loved, what Coleman was doing; it wasn't just the seigneurial Leonard Bernstein, who carried down to the Five Spot the faint but unavoidable air of slumming, or at best, anthropological investigation. It was Sonny and Trane and Hamp and John Lewis. Even Bob Brookmeyer came around.

And, like Bernstein and Mingus and Eldridge and Hampton and Percy Heath, Miles also sat in with Coleman's quartet—in his case, at the request of Don Cherry, "a nice guy." There wasn't much to the experience, he recalled: he could play "with anybody, in any style," so he "just sat in and played what they played."

After writing off Ornette as a musician (Coleman "could play only one way back then," Miles charged), then waxing envious at length about him, Davis had the nerve to call Coleman "a jealous kind of dude, man. Jealous of other musicians' success. I don't know what's wrong with him." But there is some evidence that Miles was at least partly right, and that Ornette was just as human as he was. Speaking to a journalist decades later, Coleman put a different—and pointed—spin on Davis's sitting-in story: "I'm not mentioning names, but I remember one trumpet player who came up to me and said, 'I don't know what you're doing, but I want to let the people see me playing with you. Why don't you play some blues and let me come up and play.' So I said, 'OK,' and we did some song that he had played with Charlie Parker. Then when they asked him what he thought of my music, he said, 'Oh, the guy's all messed up—you can tell that just by listening to him.' And it wasn't true."

"The bop revolution of the 1940s was a successful coup d'état," the jazz critic and essayist Francis Davis wrote in 1985. "The revolution that Ornette Coleman started is never wholly going to succeed or fail. Coleman's revolution has proved to be permanent. Its skirmishes have marked the emergence of jazz as a full-fledged modern art, with all of modernism's dualities and contradictions."

And with modernism's limited audience.

In 2011 the trumpeter and provocative jazz commentator Nicholas Payton wrote a famous/infamous essay, "On Why Jazz Isn't Cool Anymore." The piece was framed not in paragraph form but as a series of pungent

Wittgensteinian propositions—arguable, if not irrefutable, assertions about the music. The first was an attention-getter:

Jazz died in 1959.

Then,

Jazz separated itself from American popular music.
   Big mistake.
   The music never recovered.
   Ornette tried to save Jazz from itself by taking the music back to its New Orleanian roots,
      but his efforts were too esoteric.
   Jazz died in 1959, that's why Ornette tried to "Free Jazz" in 1960. . . .
      John Coltrane is a bad cat, but Jazz stopped being cool in 1959.
      The very fact that so many people are holding on to this idea of what Jazz is supposed to
      be is exactly what makes it not cool. . . .
   Jazz, like the Buddha, is dead.
   Let it go, people, let it go. . . .
   Stop fucking the dead and embrace the living.
   Jazz worries way too much about itself for it to be cool.
   Jazz died in 1959.
   The number one Jazz record is Miles Davis' Kind of Blue.
   1959 was the coolest year in Jazz.
   Jazz is haunted by its own hungry ghosts.
   Let it die.

16   After

I f jazz really had died in 1959, then it was a very lively corpse. The dawn of the sixties saw jazz clubs, concerts, and festivals continuing to flourish around the country. Record labels great and small kept issuing and selling jazz albums; jazz writers and record reviewers rated column inches in the nation's many newspapers. Jazz was still the essence, and the soundtrack, of hipness. Somewhere a figurative Vesuvius was spouting ominous fumes, but no one paid it any mind. A February 1960 piece in the *San Mateo Times* heralded upcoming performances by the Miles Davis Quintet at the San Jose Civic Auditorium and the San Francisco Civic Auditorium—not small venues—and praised the thirty-three-year-old trumpeter, not just as a jazz musician but as an American institution, with

> enormous appeal for non-jazz audiences as well. He belongs to that extremely rare company of jazz innovators—like Louis Armstrong and Duke Ellington—who have attracted a mass following with-

out diluting the quality of their musical product or compromising their standards. . . .

Appearing with him will be the all-star group that made the historic records which established the Miles Davis quintet as an innovating force in modern jazz—John Coltrane, tenor sax; Wynton Kelly, piano; Paul Chambers, bass; James Cobb, drums.

Two names are missing from the list. Bill Evans, hankering to start his own trio, with a fresh format—one that would allow a bassist and drummer creative autonomy equal to the pianist's, rather than mere timekeeping duties—had parted ways with Miles ten months earlier, after the second *Kind of Blue* session in April of '59. The split was amicable, although Davis would later give it the kind of cold stare he reserved for the failed relationships that had hurt him most: Evans, he told Quincy Troupe, "was a great little piano player, but I don't think he ever sounded as good after that as he did when he played with me."

Cannonball, sweet, brilliant Cannonball, had moved on in September, leaving Miles more bereft than bitter: "He never came back," the eternally lonely Davis wrote, with the terse plangency of one of his trumpet passages. Adderley left to form a band once again with his brother Nat, and this time around they caught fire. A Riverside LP they made in October, *The Cannonball Adderley Quintet in San Francisco*, was groundbreaking, marking one of the first times an album recorded live in a noisy club (The Jazz Workshop) proved artistically and commercially viable, and setting an infectious new style, one that Cannonball laid out in his prefatory comments to the audience—comments that the producer, Orrin Keepnews, wisely opted to leave on the record. "If we could have the lights out, please, for at-mo-spheah," Adderley said, leaning hard on his deep Florida accent,

now we're about to play a little composition by our pianist, Bobby Timmons. This one is a jazz waltz, however it has all sorts of *prop-*

erties. It's simultaneously a shout and a chant. Depending on whether you know anything about the roots of church music and all that kind of stuff. Meaning *soul* church music—I don't mean Bach chorales. That's *different*, you know what I mean? This is *soul*.

Now we're going to play this by Bobby Timmons. It's really called "This Here." However, for reasons of soul and description, we have corrupted it to become "Dish Heah."

This was a very far cry from playing with Miles, in terms of both material and presentation. Timmons, who'd recently left Art Blakey to join Cannonball, was a joyous player, and as we've seen, his roots were in gospel. And Adderley, as a bandleader and a great musician in his own right, was an irrepressibly sunny and charming extrovert, qualities he would take to the bank through the rest of his tragically brief career—he would die in 1975, at age forty-six, of a cerebral hemorrhage.

Adderley's showmanship had nothing to do with ingratiation. He was a friendly presence onstage but also a commanding one, with aspects of both the preacher and the teacher. And his music was unabashedly warm and soulful, rather than cool: qualities that would keep him commercially and artistically viable through the turbulent times ahead, as younger audiences looked for music that made their bodies move. The soul-stirring Timmons composition would go on to become a jazz classic, as would several other ebullient numbers associated with Cannonball—including, and especially, the 1967 tune written by Adderley's latter-day pianist Joe Zawinul, "Mercy, Mercy, Mercy," which became a huge hit single, and which Miles, for reasons of his own (one of which, no doubt, was sharp envy), insistently referred to as "Country Joe."

Adderley's departure in September 1959, leaving Miles without a saxophone voice complementary to Coltrane's, cut deep. The quintet now had to go back to "the style before we had gone into the modal thing." This was a regression, an artistic retreat—a defeat for this proudest and most forward thinking of great artists. "Without Cannon's alto voice up in the mix," Davis wrote, "I kind of reached a dead end of ideas for what I wanted a small group to sound like. I just felt I needed to take a rest."

Miles's idea of a rest was making another album with Gil Evans. *Sketches of Spain*, inspired by Joaquín Rodrigo's 1939 classical-guitar work *Concierto de Aranjuez*, was the third and final third-stream work Davis and Evans would create together, though unlike both *Birth of the Cool* and *Porgy and Bess*, it spoke more to the European classical tradition than to jazz. It's a quiet, moody, often starkly beautiful album, a meaningful excursion for Miles that provoked passionate—and divided—responses. *DownBeat*'s reviewer effused at length: "This record is one of the most important musical triumphs that this century has yet produced," Bill Mathieu wrote. In London, the fourteen-year-old future British Invasion star Marianne Faithfull preferred *Sketches* to pop records. In New York, on the other hand, the eighteen-year-old future music critic Robert Christgau was severely disappointed. "In 1960," he later wrote, the album "catapulted Davis into the favor of the kind of man who reads *Playboy* and initiated in me one phase of the disillusionment with jazz that resulted in my return to rock and roll."

Sketches of Spain, a Miles Davis album first and foremost, went gold. Was jazz expanding, or was it redefining itself out of existence?

Nor were Evans and Adderley Miles's only losses. He'd known for a while that Coltrane wanted to strike out on his own, but, ever the autocrat, demanded that the transition be on his terms rather than Coltrane's. This was easier demanded than obtained. Not long after *Kind of Blue* was finished, the saxophonist had infuriated Davis by talking to the West Coast jazz writer Russ Wilson, a "white boy," about his bandleader plans, and even revealing that Jimmy Heath was the player with whom Miles intended to replace him.

Coltrane would spend the rest of 1959 and almost half of 1960 agonizing over what to do next. He was making good money working for Miles—$350 a week, the equivalent of roughly ten times as much today—and as a husband, stepfather, and homeowner, he had responsibilities. But the Five Spot's Joe Termini, who with his brother Iggy had just opened a new club, the Jazz Gallery on St. Marks Place, kept at him. "Everybody was talking about him," Termini later told Lewis Porter. I said, 'John, make your own group. It's time.'"

Termini promised him that between the Five Spot and the Jazz Gallery, he could guarantee Coltrane at least ten weeks' work a year and match what Miles was paying him. And so, while on a European tour with Davis that spring, the saxophonist gave his notice—with his blessing, Miles later said—and opened at the Jazz Gallery on Tuesday, May 3, 1960, with Steve Kuhn on piano, Coltrane's old Philadelphia friend Steve Davis on bass, and Pete La Roca on drums. It was an excellent rhythm section, and Coltrane's name by itself was enough to draw crowds, but the band he opened with wasn't the band he truly wanted.

The players Coltrane really wanted all happened to be otherwise engaged. McCoy Tyner, not yet twenty-one but Trane's close friend and musical confidant since 1957, was touring with the Jazztet, a group co-led by Art Farmer and Benny Golson. (The band had played opposite Ornette Coleman at his Five Spot opening in November.) The bassist Art Davis was traveling with Dizzy Gillespie. And the great Elvin Jones, recently arrested for possession of heroin, was temporarily residing at Rikers Island.

At first it barely seemed to matter whom Coltrane was playing with. As had happened with Monk and Trane at the Five Spot, the Gallery instantly became a scene. Even Coltrane's temporary sidemen stood in awe of him. "He was and still is like a God to me," Kuhn said.

> He was only ten years older than I was, but he could have been a hundred years older. He had really gotten himself together musically and it was a real education to be there with him on the bandstand. It was like electricity. The people in the audience were just going crazy—it was like a revival meeting. . . . The energy he brought to the bandstand every night was incredible.

The quartet's repertoire included the Coltrane compositions "Giant Steps," "Countdown" (aka "Tune Up"), "Naima," "Straight Street," "Spiral," "Cousin Mary," and "Like Sonny," as well as Billy Eckstine's ballad "I Want to Talk About You," the Gershwins' "Summertime," and two jazz chestnuts Trane had reharmonized with "Giant Steps" chords, "How High the Moon" and Charlie Parker's "Confirmation." Coltrane could play as ebulliently as Cannonball, but the energy was different: the ecstasy of Coltrane's music was more spiritual than physical. And Coltrane, eyes closed, unsmiling, was more serious than ever. He might've walked some bars in his early days, but he discovered early on that in performance, he could only be who he really was. "I realize I'm in the entertainment business, and I'd like to be [the] sort of guy who can set audiences at ease," he told a British journalist.

> If you go about music without a smile, people think you're not happy. I don't make a habit of wishing for what I don't have, but I often wish I had a lighter nature. Dizzy has that beautiful gift—I can't say "Be happy, people"—it's something I can't command. But you have to be true to your own nature. May I say, though, that when I go to hear a man, as long as he conducts himself properly, and moves me with his music, I am satisfied. If he should happen to smile, I consider it something added to what I have received already; if not, I don't worry because I know it is not wholly essential to the music.

"I never met anybody so 100 percent dedicated to just dealing with music," Kuhn remembered.

A month after the opening, McCoy Tyner's Jazztet gig ended, and Coltrane—after telling Steve Kuhn in the kindest way that his services were no longer needed—snapped up his old Philadelphia friend. Tyner brought a new and revolutionary musical element to the mix: the percussive use of fourths, fluidly deployed with both hands—like Bill Evans,

Tyner was left-handed—and with what McCoy himself (he was never shy about discussing his strengths) called "metronomic rhythmic accuracy."

"Whereas triads [thirds] have a certain earthy familiarity," Lewis Porter writes, "fourth chords are abstract. Perhaps because they avoid the familiar ring of popular songs, which are based on triads, fourth chords seem to add to the spiritual quality of Coltrane's music."

Another piece of the puzzle got filled in at the end of September, when Elvin Jones called to say he was available. "That first night Elvin was in the band," Steve Davis remembered, "he was playing so strong and so loud you could hear him outside and down the block. Trane wanted it that way. He wanted a drummer who could really kick, and Elvin was one of the strongest, wildest drummers in the world. After the gig, Trane put his arm around Elvin, took him to a barbecue around the corner, and bought him some ribs."

Elvin Jones was, much as Coltrane had been when Miles hired him, "quite unknown and underestimated," Coltrane said. That would soon change. Built like a linebacker, with ebony skin and rugged features, Jones was a great drummer and a legendarily powerful presence. Yet Jones brought not just physical strength, but an "ability to mix and juggle rhythms," Coltrane said. "He's always aware of everything else that's happening. I guess you could say he has the ability to be in three places at the same time."

But because of his addiction, what Jones sometimes lacked was the ability to be in one place at the appointed time. This often left Coltrane in the position of having to pick up last-minute substitutes who weren't remotely in Elvin's league. It annoyed him, but he always forgave the drummer. On one such occasion, at a Detroit club in 1961, the sub had played the first couple of sets when, late in the evening, Jones appeared out of nowhere, sat at the drum kit, and proceeded to burn the house down. Afterward, Coltrane went to the microphone and said, "See, he's a genius, what can I say? He's just a genius."

Genius times three, Coltrane and Tyner and Jones (and Steve Davis), went on an incomparable recording streak in late October of 1960, laying down, in three sessions, nineteen extraordinary tracks, eighteen of which would make up two monumental Atlantic albums, *My Favorite Things* and *Coltrane's Sound*, and one quirky and delightful one, *Coltrane Plays the Blues*.

Coltrane seems to have experimented as early as 1958 with the soprano saxophone, an instrument pioneered in early-twentieth-century jazz by the great New Orleans player Sidney Bechet, but latterly out of favor. On Trane's farewell tour with Miles, in Europe in the spring of 1960, Davis presented him with an antique soprano—probably, in Miles's oblique way, a parting gift—and Coltrane quickly became fascinated with it. "It had an effect on his tenor playing," Miles contended.

> Before he got that soprano, he was still playing like Dexter Gordon, Eddie "Lockjaw" Davis, Sonny Stitt, and Bird. After he got that horn, his style changed. After that, he didn't sound like nobody but himself. He found out that he could play lighter and faster on the soprano than he could on the tenor. And this really turned him on . . . he found he could . . . think and hear better with the soprano than he could with the tenor. When he played the soprano, after a while, it sounded almost like a human voice, wailing.

Coltrane, both of whose grandfathers were ordained ministers in the African Methodist Episcopal Zion Church, was in the midst of a spiritual search, a quest to find, through the religions of the world—principally those in Africa and India—what the musicologist Michael Budds called "a universal concept unifying all faiths," and to somehow integrate it into his music. With this new horn, he'd found a voice, and perhaps a path.

Coltrane had been playing the soprano in public since the beginning of the Jazz Gallery stand; he had even performed Rodgers and Hammerstein's "My Favorite Things" on it that summer. But he'd never recorded with the instrument before October 21, 1960, the day he, Tyner, Davis, and Jones turned *The Sound of Music*'s perky song of uplift into a jazz classic.

As written by Richard Rodgers, the melody is a waltz. And while Coltrane refers to his version as a waltz, his rendering quickens the tempo considerably, changing it from ¾ time to ⁶⁄₈. Rodgers and Hammerstein's original version is written in AAAB form, the A sections contrasting the great lyricist's sparklingly sensuous evocations of the good things— kittens' whiskers, bright copper kettles, "wild geese that fly with the moon on their wings"—with the bad, spelled out in the B section: dog bites, bee stings, sadness.

It's Coltrane's genius—inspired by Miles's impulse to radically simplify the chord structure of his tunes—to base nearly the entirety of his thirteen-minute forty-six-second version of "My Favorite Things" on the two harmonies of the A section: harmonies that, Coltrane later said, "we've stretched . . . through the whole piece." In his version, the B section is given precisely eleven seconds in the entire song, played just seconds before the track winds up. His improvisation throughout the A sections is as audacious as any he has recorded to date: at times his lightning runs up and down the E-minor scale, set against the dronelike effect of Tyner and Davis's pedal point, resemble the Indian ragas played by the great Ravi Shankar that Coltrane was studying at the time.

Longer and even bolder solos were to come.

TEN DAYS BEFORE COLTRANE RECORDED "MY FAVORITE THINGS," MILES was back at the Olympia in Paris with his *Kind of Blue*–period rhythm section—Wynton Kelly, Paul Chambers, Jimmy Cobb—and Coltrane's replacement, Sonny Stitt, on tenor saxophone. Stitt, a couple of years older than Davis, was a highly skilled and adaptable musician whose early alto work had drawn so many comparisons to Charlie Parker that he took up tenor in self-defense. To say that his playing was still anchored in bebop is to take little away from it: Stitt was brilliant, but only Coltrane was Coltrane. And though the version of "So What" that the new quintet played at the Olympia, at a barreling, "Milestones"-like tempo, was a lovely thing, would it be churlish to say that it lacked depth and introspection—meaning, more pointedly, that it lacked Coltrane and Evans?

"Coltrane's departure," Davis biographer Ian Carr writes,

> was a devastating loss to Miles, who almost broke down and wept during their last gig together, in Philadelphia. So strongly did he feel that he even went to the microphone and made a brief announcement about the saxophonist's imminent departure from the group. And, as Jimmy Cobb commented: "He never talks with nobody about nothing, so you know, he really must have felt something for Coltrane." The saxophonist's departure left a gap that, in some ways, Miles was never able to fill again.

He'd tried to hire the newest young genius, the Newark saxophonist-composer Wayne Shorter, but Shorter was ensconced with Art Blakey and the Jazz Messengers, and would remain so for the next four years, ultimately becoming the band's musical director. At the end of 1960 Stitt moved on—some sources say Miles fired him for drinking, though that wouldn't explain why he kept Chambers, an alcoholic and a heroin addict—and Davis hired Hank Mobley.

Meanwhile there was the mixed consolation of success, as George Avakian's grand plan to make him a cross-genre star continued to bear fruit. "Miles today is a wealthy man, owning some $50,000 worth of stock," Leonard Feather wrote, with ringing crassness, in a long profile in London's *Melody Maker*.

> He just bought an entire building in a good section of Manhattan, where he lives on the first two floors renting out the rest of the building as apartments. He drives a Ferrari that cost $12,500 and he likes to drive fast. He has a substantial five-figure annual income from Columbia Records. Miles' apparent aloofness on the

stand has a devastating effect on women, who often find his good looks more irresistible than his most lyrical solo. Recently he was married to a lovely, petite girl named Frances Taylor, who teaches dancing. He has remained close to his daughter and two sons (seventeen, fourteen, and ten) by an early marriage.

The building was a five-story brownstone, a converted Russian Orthodox church, at 312 West Seventy-seventh Street; Miles would live there, in good times and bad, for the next two decades. In the basement he installed a gym and a music room where he could practice without disturbing anybody; the first floor contained a big kitchen and living room, and the bedrooms were upstairs. There was a small garden in the backyard. "We were very comfortable by this time," Miles said.

This was both true and not true, as were Leonard Feather's assertions. Miles was supremely well off for a jazz musician: he later claimed to have been making substantially more than five figures at that point—two hundred thousand dollars a year—and admitted to checking the newspapers frequently to see how his stock portfolio was doing. But he might have been doing so out of anxiety, since he had a big nut to cover, and moreover tended to spend money as fast as it came in, if not faster. He had never been married to Irene, the mother of his three children—who were not only close to him, but living with him, as was Frances Taylor's son. And he and Taylor weren't yet married when the *Melody Maker* piece came out, but would be that December. This "lovely, petite girl"—she had just turned thirty—had been (at nineteen) the first African American ballerina to perform with the Paris Opera Ballet, a principal dancer with the Katherine Dunham Company, and a member of the original cast of one of Broadway's greatest musicals—until Miles forced her to quit in March 1958, because, he said, "a woman should be with her man. I want you out of *West Side Story*." Taking private dancing pupils was the only profession Davis would allow her.

Yet she could have left, and didn't. Every marriage is a mystery, and Frances and Miles seemed in love, at least for the moment. Miles loved to prepare and eat both French cuisine and traditional Black dishes, and he taught her to cook: both of them regularly prepared family meals. As a memento of Bill Evans's influence, classical music ("Stravinsky, Arturo Michelangeli, Rachmaninoff, Isaac Stern") rather than jazz played constantly over the house's state-of-the-art sound system. It was, as Carr writes, "perhaps the only period of conventional family life Miles would enjoy as a husband and father."

But all was far from well. He had recently been diagnosed with sickle-cell anemia and was suffering from continuous pain in his joints, especially his left hip. Although he was no longer using heroin, he became more and more dependent on other palliatives—alcohol and, increasingly, cocaine, which both numbed his discomfort and gave him energy. Yet the drug was also causing long-term damage to his kidneys, liver, and digestive system, and triggering immediate side effects such as insomnia, mood swings, irritability, paranoia, and depression, all of which threw his already dark disposition into deeper shadow.

Worst of all, his music, the root of his existence, was in disarray. Hank Mobley was a world-class saxophonist, but to Miles's ultra-demanding ear, he was just a pitifully inadequate substitute for John Coltrane. "Playing with Hank just wasn't fun for me; he didn't stimulate my imagination," he said. Coming from almost anyone else, it would have sounded high-handed; coming from the ever-restless Miles, it was simply a statement of fact.

In November 1960, a week to the day after John F. Kennedy was elected president, personifying what Norman Mailer had presciently called America's "subterranean river of untapped, ferocious, lonely and romantic desires, that concentration of ecstasy and violence which is the dream life of a nation," Miles's quintet opened for a two-week stand at the Village Vanguard, opposite the Bill Evans trio. Over the course of the engagement, Evans regularly played a suddenly topical-feeling tune, one he'd recorded the previous year on *Portrait in Jazz*, his first album with Scott LaFaro and Paul Motian: Frank Churchill and Larry Morey's "Someday My

Prince Will Come," from the 1937 Walt Disney animated feature *Snow White and the Seven Dwarfs*. Dave Brubeck had been first to see the jazz possibilities of the number, including it on an LP of Disney tunes he made in 1957. Evans, Pettinger writes, also saw in it "a freshness and a strength fit for probing." Miles felt his own pull to the song.

On March 7, 1961—two years almost to the day after the first *Kind of Blue* session, and once again in the Thirtieth Street Studio—Davis began making a new LP based around (and to be named after) the Disney tune. On the second session, two weeks later, John Coltrane, who was under contract to Atlantic, appeared in the studio ("I sneaked down one afternoon and made [the recording]," he later recalled) and, at Davis's direction, replaced Mobley on "Someday My Prince Will Come"—in the process producing a supremely graceful, liltingly lovely solo that contributed mightily to making the track one of Miles's greatest ballads.

However discontented Davis could be with the music he was playing and the stardom Columbia really hadn't had to foist on him ("people were coming just to look at me, to see what I was going to do, what I had on, whether I would say anything or cuss somebody out, like I was some kind of freak in a glass cage at the motherfucking zoo"), you wouldn't know it from the live recordings he, Mobley, Kelley, Chambers, and Cobb made the following month at San Francisco's Black Hawk. This was magnificent jazz, by turns tender ("Fran-Dance," named after his wife; "I Thought About You"), infectiously upbeat ("All of You"; "Bye Bye Blackbird"), and electric ("Walkin'"). And that very enthusiastic crowd clearly hadn't come just to look.

AND AT THE SAME TIME, HE WAS HURTING, AND TIRED. DURING THE Black Hawk stand he told Russ Wilson—the same "white boy" to whom Coltrane had given that indiscreet interview—that he was going to retire. "I've got $1,000 a week coming in now so I don't have to work. And I've been playing for twenty-two years—a long time." The next month, the critic Gilbert Millstein found him in fainting-couch mode at 312 West Seventy-seventh:

> Lying on a bed in his home . . . , an arm over his eyes against the light, he remarked that he feels weak and irritable until he gets on the stand to perform. "Music is like having a habit," he said. "Only this one you can't break. You never feel like other people." He raised himself on an elbow and rolled over. "I know one of these days I'm going to walk off the stand and never play again. Something's going to touch me. And when that happens, I'll divorce myself from the trumpet."

BACK IN NEW YORK, MILES FOUND FAMILIAR COMFORTS, AND WOES BOTH familiar and new. He was cheered by visits from Cannonball and Coltrane, who jammed with him in the basement; he worried about Evans, who didn't come around anymore—and who, he knew, was now fully in

the grip of heroin addiction. "That just made me sick, man, because I had talked to Bill when he first started to experiment with it, but I guess he didn't pay me no attention. . . . He was such a beautiful musician and here he was getting a habit when everyone else, even Sonny Rollins and Jackie McLean, were cleaning themselves up."

Addicted though he was, Evans was—like Coltrane, unlike Miles—at an artistic zenith at the turn of the year. He'd formed the trio with La-Faro and Motian after much trial and error, having finally found a bassist and a drummer who were thoroughly in sync with his singular concept: "I'm hoping the trio will grow in the direction of simultaneous improvisation rather than just one guy blowing followed by another guy blowing," he said. "If the bass player, for example, hears an idea that he wants to answer, why should he just keep playing a ¼ background? The men I'll work with have learned how to do the regular kind of playing, and so I think we now have the license to change it."

His bassist had little patience with the regular kind of playing. Evans had first heard Scott LaFaro in Los Angeles in 1956, when LaFaro, just turned twenty, was auditioning for Chet Baker. His initial impression, he remembered, "was that he was a marvelous bass player and talent, but it was bubbling out of him almost like a gusher. Ideas were rolling out on top of each other; he could barely handle it. It was like a bucking horse."

By the ripe old age of twenty-three, when LaFaro, Evans, and Motian made *Portrait in Jazz*, the bassist was thoroughly in control of his playing, and doing extraordinary things. Listen to the trio's version of Carolyn Leigh and Cy Coleman's "Witchcraft," and you'll hear one of the most innovative approaches to the jazz double bass since Jimmy Blanton played with Duke Ellington in the swing era: far from being a mere timekeeper (and instead of waiting for his solo), LaFaro sets up from the outset a vigorous, rhythmically and melodically daring counter-tune to Evans's line. The bass line is almost aggressive, yet the pianist is clearly exhilarated by it.

The three advanced Evans's concept even further on their second album, *Explorations*, laid down on a single day, February 2, 1961. But the truest embodiment of this revolution in the art of the jazz trio did not occur in the recording studio. "What gave that trio its character," Evans recalled, "was a common aim and a feeling of potential. The music developed as we performed, and what you heard came through actual performance."

Evans's new home for performance was the tiny temple of jazz on lower Seventh Avenue where, as the Village Vanguard's owner Max Gordon wrote in his memoir, the pianist had started out, just a few years earlier, "filling space between sets for the star attraction." In 1961, Evans was fast becoming the star attraction.

On Sunday, June 25, toward the end of the group's Vanguard stand, Riverside's Orrin Keepnews had recording equipment brought in to try to capture the trio's elusive essence over two half-hour sets in the afternoon and three in the evening. The result was the triumphant LP *Sunday at the Village Vanguard*—reissued in 2005 as a historic three-CD set, *The Complete Village Vanguard Recordings, 1961*. The new recording was remastered to give a greater sense of the ambience in the club, including the sound of Evans quietly calling the numbers.

After Keepnews tells the audience that the proceedings are to be recorded, Evans turns to LaFaro. "Let's start with your tune, that one we were just playing," he says.

"Hmm, nasty," the bassist says. His voice is youthful, irreverent. Evans laughs.

The song is "Gloria's Step," a questioning, minor-toned, "Nardis"-esque composition by LaFaro, and not only is the performance lovely, but the audience is reverentially silent, as Evans's early audiences were not. And not only is the performance lovely, but—as is not the case with the vast majority of piano-based jazz trios—each of the three musicians is somehow able to play expressively and independently, yet in absolute sync with the other two: "with perfect empathy and telepathy," as one writer put it.

Eleven days later, Scott LaFaro would be dead at twenty-five.

Late in the night of July 6, four days after accompanying Stan Getz at the Newport Jazz Festival, LaFaro was driving with a high-school friend back to his parents' house in western New York State when his car veered off an unlit rural road and hit a tree. In all likelihood he fell asleep at the wheel. Both young men were killed instantly.

Evans was devastated by the news, which hit him both personally and artistically. He had loved the boyish bassist, not just for his brilliance and youthful effervescence, but for his irreplaceable ability to invent abundantly while melding into the trio's magical synergy. "When you have evolved a concept of playing which depends on the specific personalities of outstanding players," he said later, "how do you start again when they are gone?"

For months afterward, Evans was unable to answer the question. "Musically everything seemed to stop," he later said. "I didn't even play at home." By other accounts, he played the Gershwins' haunting "I Loves You Porgy" over and over, obsessively. It's hard to listen to the trio's performance of the tune on the Village Vanguard recording without tearing up.

Shortly before LaFaro's death, Evans broke up with Peri Cousins. It was hard enough being an interracial couple in early-sixties America, and the pianist's addiction caused endless tensions between the two. Around this time, while tripping on mescaline at a party, he spotted a petite, intense-looking woman across the room and, as he later told friends, felt a kind of mind explosion: the psychedelic version of love at first sight. Her name was Ellaine Schultz. "She was small, dark, Jewish—full of nervous energy, always smoking," Harry Evans's wife, Pat, recalled. From the moment they began talking with each other, Schultz and Evans recognized each other as addicts. They would be together for the next twelve years.

JOHN COLTRANE MET ERIC DOLPHY IN THE LATTER'S NATIVE LOS ANGE-les in 1954, when Trane was touring with (and getting fired by) Johnny Hodges. Dolphy, who played alto sax, bass clarinet, and flute, was both deeply schooled and experimentally minded, and he and Coltrane became fast friends, frequently exchanging musical ideas. In early 1961, as the release of *My Favorite Things* (and the titular single) rocketed Coltrane to prominence, he asked Dolphy to join his band, and the music they began to play together—modal, questing music, veering sharply from chordal structure and melody—attracted instant hostility.

"At Hollywood's Renaissance Club recently," *DownBeat*'s associate editor John Tynan wrote,

> I listened to a horrifying demonstration of what appears to be a growing anti-jazz trend exemplified by these foremost proponents [Coltrane and Dolphy] of what is termed avant-garde music.
>
> I heard a good rhythm section . . . go to waste behind the nihilistic exercises of the two horns . . . Coltrane and Dolphy seem intent on deliberately destroying [swing]. . . . They seem bent on pursuing an anarchistic course in their music that can but be termed anti-jazz.

The term "anti-jazz" caught on at once, critical pressure mounting so fiercely that Coltrane would soon feel forced to let Dolphy go. In the meantime, though, the producer Creed Taylor, founder of the new all-jazz record label Impulse! bought out Coltrane's Atlantic contract, and the saxophonist began to make a series of albums that would cement his reputation as a composer, an exquisitely sensitive player of ballads, and a fearless explorer, on both the tenor and soprano horns, of abstruse musical realms.

He continued to explore onstage, where his solos still sometimes seemed, even to educated ears, to go on forever. "They're long because all the soloists try to explore all the avenues that the tune offers," he said, in defense. "They try to use all their resources in their solos. Everybody has quite a bit to work on."

Especially the leader. The pianist/psychiatrist Denny Zeitlin recalled attending a performance by the Coltrane quartet at the Five Spot one night in 1963: "He played an extended coda on a song that, for the first two or three minutes, I was interested," he told me. "And then it seemed to me, Hey, this guy's back in his pad and he's practicing! He's just working on some shit! And for about a half-hour he stood there playing licks and riffs and scales and alternative things, and I was thinking, What the hell is *this*, man? Where's your perspective? I love what you do, but this is not a place to be doing that! So that's a rare example where I remember just feeling totally put off. Otherwise, hearing him was *galvanizing*, man. The live experience of hearing what he and Elvin would do together— just, God *damn*."

Many others felt this duality. In a *DownBeat* review of the 1962 album *"Live" at the Village Vanguard*, Pete Welding called Coltrane's long blues solo on "Chasin' the Trane" "a torrential and anguished outpouring, delivered with unmistakable power, conviction, and near-demoniac ferocity." It was "a remarkable human document," Welding wrote, but "the very intensity of the feelings that prompt it militate against its effectiveness as a musical experience." Ira Gitler, long one of Coltrane's most crucial advocates, was more pointed: "Coltrane may be searching for new avenues of expression," he said, "but if it is going to take this form of yawps, squawks, and countless repetitive runs, then it should be confined to the woodshed."

The saxophonist's first albums for Impulse! failed to build on the huge popularity of *Giant Steps* and *My Favorite Things*—Coltrane had effectively moved into ahead-of-his-time territory. The big-band settings of *Africa/Brass* were beautiful but challenging: with puckering ambivalence, Martin Williams wrote, "In these pieces, Coltrane has done on record what he has done so often in person lately, make everything into a handful of chords, frequently only two or three, turning them in every conceivable way." When the storm of critical outrage over the Vanguard recordings overshadowed the July release of *Coltrane*—a modal masterpiece that contained definitive renditions of Harold Arlen and Johnny Mercer's "Out of This World," Mal Waldron's "Soul Eyes," and Frank Loesser's "The Inch Worm," another movie theme (from the 1952 musical *Hans Christian Andersen*) transformed by Trane into great jazz—Bob Thiele, Coltrane's producer at Impulse!, shifted into damage control, in quick succession teeing up three albums that would be certain not to ruffle anyone's feathers.

The funny thing about the three, *Duke Ellington & John Coltrane* (released in February 1963), *Ballads* (March 1963), and *John Coltrane and Johnny Hartman* (July 1963), is that they were anything but artistic compromises: each was important in its own way.

The co-led album with Ellington paired Duke (on piano) and Coltrane backed by just bass and drums: the results were as potent with four pieces as they would've been with two dozen. Though in his sixties and written off by many as passé, Duke (who just the week before had made the towering album *Money Jungle* with Charles Mingus and Max Roach) was and would be until his death in 1974 every bit as harmonically venturesome as Coltrane—and, having been recording since before Trane was born, far wiser about both the poetics and the realities of music-making. At one point during the session, when Thiele asked if another take was necessary, Ellington spoke with cautionary wisdom: "Don't ask him to do another. He'll just end up imitating himself."

Coltrane wasn't, and would never be, his own best editor.

With one exception, the ballads on the eponymous LP were all American Songbook standards, from Jimmy McHugh and Frank Loesser's "Say It (Over and Over Again)" to Arthur Altman and Jack Lawrence's "All or Nothing at All," indelibly associated with Frank Sinatra, to Rodgers and Hart's "It's Easy to Remember." Coltrane played each with loving attentiveness and unironic beauty—even lending dignity to a McHugh and Harold Adamson obscurity called "Too Young to Go Steady." "I chose them," he later told an interviewer. The songs "seemed to be something that was laying around in my mind—from my youth or somewhere—and I just had to do them."

But his collaboration with the silken-voiced baritone Johnny Hartman, whose singing Coltrane had admired since 1950, when both were members of Dizzy Gillespie's band, rose to a different level. The tunes on the album were also mostly standards, including the famously difficult "Lush Life," which Hartman conquered with consummate grace. And then there was Peter DeRose and Sammy Gallop's "Autumn Serenade," a little-known 1945 dance number, a catchy minor-toned trifle Coltrane probably remembered from his teens. In the interplay of his tenor and Hartman's gorgeous baritone, the corny lyrics fade and the song becomes a thing of timeless magnificence.

NINETEEN SIXTY-TWO MARKED A PERIOD OF DISORDER AND TRANSITION for Miles. In May his father died, felled by neurological problems that had begun after his car was hit by a train at a railroad crossing months earlier. His professional life was also in flux. A fourth (and, it would turn out, final) studio collaboration with Gil Evans, a Latin American–themed album meant to capitalize on the bossa nova craze recently ignited by Stan Getz's LP *Jazz Samba* and its wildly successful single "Desafinado," petered out, a victim of Miles's lack of interest in the material: "I didn't really feel nothing about the music we did on this album. . . . We were trying to get some bossa nova shit on to that record."

Arguments can be made up and down about the ultimate musical worth of this Brazilian genre, but based on Miles's utter lack of connection with the one Antonio Carlos Jobim composition on the record, "Corcovado," there was a basic incompatibility between Jobim's *saudade*, the indefinable quantity whose closest translation is nostalgia, and Davis's lonesome cool. Hoping to recoup some of the buckets of money Columbia had spent on several recording sessions with full orchestras—which had produced a grand total of twenty minutes of usable music—Teo Macero cobbled together an album, *Quiet Nights*, by grafting in "Summer Night," an outtake from a quintet record date for another Davis project, *Seven Steps to Heaven*. Infuriated by the label's release of what he considered incomplete work, Miles refused to speak to Macero for three years.

In his memoir, Davis and Troupe imply that the sole reason Miles had to withdraw from lucrative bookings in 1962 and early 1963 (and pay club owners tens of thousands of dollars in compensation for the last-minute cancellations) was personnel problems. These were considerable in themselves: Sonny Rollins, who'd played a bit with Davis after his Williams-burg Bridge sojourn, had left to form his own group; Wynton Kelly and Paul Chambers were agitating for more money and making noises about also going out on their own. But at the same time, Miles's medical issues started to become more acute, and his marriage was falling apart. His hip was giving him more trouble than ever, he was self-medicating with alcohol and cocaine, and, as Szwed writes,

> His paranoia was growing. When he and Frances went anywhere that he wasn't known, it was she who had to go in and see to reservations or a table; he wanted to avoid being turned away because of his color. He became difficult to talk to, and when she said anything that he said sounded like something his mother had said to him a long time ago ("when he couldn't do anything about it," as he put it), he'd slap her.

At the beginning of 1963 Wynton Kelly left to form his own trio, taking Paul Chambers and then Jimmy Cobb with him. Miles had to start again from scratch, at first hiring a trio of Memphis musicians—tenor player George Coleman, alto Frank Strozier, and pianist Harold Mabern—as well as the young Detroit native Ron Carter on bass and, on the recommendation of Jackie McLean, the very young (seventeen-year-old!) powerhouse Tony Williams on drums.

Mabern and Strozier, Miles quickly realized, "were very good musicians, but they just belonged in another kind of band." Davis could go altoless, fielding a quintet rather than a sextet, but he needed a pianist. While gigging on the West Coast, he found one in the person of a brilliant English player named Victor Feldman—then Feldman realized he could make far more money as a Los Angeles studio musician than as a sideman, even for Miles Davis. On his return to New York, Miles called Herbie Hancock.

Hancock, just twenty-three, was a classically trained former child prodigy, a college graduate (Grinnell, 1960) with a degree in music and

electrical engineering, and, on the basis of his 1962 debut album *Takin'
Off*, whose first track, "Watermelon Man," charted in Billboard's Top 100,
a superstar in the making. Miles asked him over to his house to work out
with Carter and Williams, surreptitiously listening to the three over his
intercom system, and was delighted with what he heard. He invited Hancock to the Thirtieth Street Studio for the final sessions of *Seven Steps to
Heaven*, where, excited by his new players, Davis decided to rerecord the
up-tempo numbers from the April date in Hollywood. "So does that
mean I'm in the group?" Hancock asked, between takes.

"You're making the record with me, ain't you?" Miles said.

He took the new band on the road—to Bowdoin College in Maine and
the Jazz Villa in St. Louis and Sutherland Lounge in Chicago and the
Jazz Temple in Cleveland and back to the Vanguard in New York—and
he stayed excited. Williams, he said, was the reason: not only was the
young drummer preternaturally self-assured, but there was a quality of
magic about him.

> He just lit a big fire under everyone in the group. He made me play
> so much that I forgot about all the pain in my joints which had
> been bothering me a lot. I was beginning to realize that Tony and
> this group could play anything they wanted to. Tony was always
> the center that the group's sound revolved around. He was some-
> thing else, man. . . . I just loved him like a son.

Between Miles and Tony, the age-old bond between trumpet and
drums—the two loudest instruments in a band and natural partners since
the origins of jazz—flourished. And maybe more. Though gayness in jazz
was then and would remain—perhaps to this day—a taboo, Miles, by the
testimony of friends and former bandmates projected (and may have acted
on) a certain air of omnisexuality. And he seems to have understood from
the beginning that Williams was similarly disposed ("He wouldn't need
to have any girlfriends," Davis later said, oddly but pointedly, "so his head
was open"), and wanted to protect him. After all, the drummer hadn't

even attained legal majority. (In September 1963 the local constabulary shut down the new quintet's stand at San Francisco's Jazz Workshop, charging the owner with "employing a minor.") Williams brought an unprecedented quality and quantity of energy to the band, and a level of drumming that none of the others had ever experienced before. He was loud (he used extra-heavy sticks), he was fluid, and he was *fast*. He played polyrhythms—two different rhythms at once—and he changed the pulse at will, forcing the other musicians to pay intense attention at every moment: in effect, leading the band. He was, and for the rest of his brief life (he would die at fifty-one, in 1997) would remain, a singular force: by 1970 Robert Christgau could assert, only slightly hyperbolically, that Williams was "probably the best drummer in the world."

"I could feel that we were making a new statement, we were breaking ground," Williams recalled. "Before I joined Miles, Ornette Coleman's music had become very important. And so I was very much influenced by what was known then as the avant-garde. . . . I was interested in expressing the drums, the drum set, in a different way."

"What we were trying to do in Miles's band—at least what I was trying to do, and what I *feel* they were trying to do," Herbie Hancock said, "was to take these influences that were happening to all of us at the time and amalgamate them. Personalize them in such a way that when people were hearing us, they were hearing the avant-garde on one hand, and they were hearing the history of jazz that led up to it on the other hand, 'cause Miles *was* that history. And he was that link."

To listen to the new band's excitingly quick-paced rerecording of Victor Feldman's composition "Joshua," with Hancock at the piano instead of Feldman, is to hear an inspired and revitalized Miles, with one foot in the modal near-past of *Kind of Blue* and the other in a dynamic (and rapid) future.

"When I came in the band," George Coleman recalled, "they upped everything—all the tempos. Miles knew I could play fast, so he pushed them up. With Miles I got everything—up tempos, harmonic situations, taking chances . . . and I began to get this adventurous spirit."

But not adventurous enough for Tony Williams, who began to complain that Coleman wasn't hip enough for him. After Miles heard the saxophonist practicing "some tricky little figures in his hotel room," he got angry. In an outburst that became famous, he told Coleman, "I pay you to practice *on* the bandstand."

George Coleman, still alive as of this writing, is one of the greats, an NEA Jazz Master, a player of power and lyrical imagination and superb musicianship much in demand across the decades by many of the genre's immortals. But Tony Williams, young and besotted by the free-flying explorations of Ornette and Coltrane and Archie Shepp, found Coleman—whom Miles called "a hell of a musician" who "played everything almost perfectly"—too correct for his liking. Williams "liked musicians who made mistakes, like being out of key," Davis said. This was not George Coleman. And Coleman, who'd been elated at first to be asked by Miles to join him, had grown disenchanted by the leader's grandiosity, especially when the group played Paris and the Antibes Jazz Festival in the summer of 1963: "Miles was living too fast for me. . . . He was centering on his own ego, rather than on the music. . . . He demanded a lot for himself—champagne, women, cars . . . or whatever else he might want."

And his hip problems were getting worse and worse. He was often absent from the bandstand, and when he was gone the inmates—Hancock and Carter and Williams—took over the asylum, shifting into Williams's beloved free-jazz mode and boxing out Coleman, who could play free, as the expression went, but just preferred not to. When Miles told the band they'd be playing Japan in July of 1964—it would be his first tour there—Coleman said he wouldn't be going with them. Sam Rivers, an innovative Boston tenor whom Tony Williams had been urging on Miles, joined the group in his stead. But in the meantime, everything had changed.

ON SUNDAY NIGHT, FEBRUARY 9, 1964, FOUR YOUNG MUSICIANS FROM LIV-erpool appeared on *The Ed Sullivan Show* and, in a joyous few minutes (joyous for white America, at any rate), not only dispelled the pall of mourning that had followed the Kennedy assassination, but also sent millions of (white) adolescent boys, potential jazz fans, racing out to buy electric guitars.

And three chords on a guitar were a lot easier to learn than even the basics of a tenor saxophone.

Suddenly, the 1964 counterparts of all those "beards, lasses with pale pink lipstick, and . . . Ivy Leaguers" that Dorothy Kilgallen had observed enjoying jazz at Café Bohemia in the mid-fifties were buying Beatles records. And no longer queuing up outside the Bohemia or the Half Note or the Five Spot. Within a year, Art Farmer would tell Whitney Balliett, "rock was beginning to be felt, and the bottom was falling out of jazz in New York."

If the bottom was falling out in the Apple, it was much worse everywhere else. And the effects of the rock revolution were felt most acutely by the brilliant jazz artists of the second tier: the Art Farmers and Hank Mobleys and Sonny Stitts and Duke Jordans; the Kenny Dorhams and the Gene Ammonses and the Booker Ervins. "Good jazz musicians found work as sidemen in recording studios and on TV talk shows," wrote the Associated Press's Mary Campbell. (The ones, that is, who could read music.) The superstars—Dizzy and Duke and Louis Armstrong; and yes, Miles and Coltrane and to a lesser extent Bill Evans—lived in a kind of parallel universe, albeit a somewhat reduced one, where what they did still mattered intensely to their fans, and they could still earn real money.

When Miles returned from Japan, he got the welcome news that Wayne Shorter was growing impatient with working for Art Blakey. To a listener, Blakey's Jazz Messengers exemplified the exhilaration of hard bop, but seen from the inside, their act had a prefabricated character: "Playing with Blakey was something like being in a show," Shorter said. "There was a fixed structure to every piece, with no room for variation except in the solos, and even they were determined by structure."

Shorter had admired the freedom and mystery of Miles's *Kind of Blue* sextet one night several years before, when the Messengers had opened for them at the Regal Theater in Chicago:

> I was listening to the power of individualism and subjectivity that was going on with all the players. Cannonball, Coltrane, and whoever was playing piano at the time, probably Wynton Kelly, and Paul Chambers on bass. They opened with . . . "All Blues" and what I heard and felt was this penetrating . . . it was not a sudden blast with a showlike . . . bang! . . . you know. Instead they opened with a tremolo on the piano. The tremolo sounded like a Ravel thing. This tremolo threw a hush over the audience that was different from the Messengers' kind of opening impact sound of "bang!" . . . The music seemed to transport the audience to some place they don't usually go in their everyday life.

That tremolo, of course, had been the invention of Bill Evans, whose deep artistic impact on Miles and Miles's bands would endure. When Wayne Shorter joined Davis in September of 1964, he brought another capacious artistic sensibility, the soul of a composer, and the power to both teach and learn. His arrival marked the beginning of Miles's second great quintet, "the all-time classical hydrogen bomb and switchblade band," in Amiri Baraka's memorable formulation. Davis's new quintet would thrive and thrill for the next four years, at which point the far more powerful explosion set off on *The Ed Sullivan Show* would affect even him.

AT THE END OF THE STRANGE MONTH OF FEBRUARY 1964, A PERIOD THAT encompassed the Beatles' appearance on *Ed Sullivan* and Thelonious Monk's appearance on the cover of *Time*, Cleota Davis died in St. Louis. Miles and Frances got on a plane to go to his mother's funeral, but when the plane returned to the gate with an engine problem, Davis, feeling superstitious, debarked and went home, leaving his wife to fate—and to attend his mother's funeral without him. "I . . . cried like a motherfucker all night, cried until I was almost sick," he said. "I really didn't know just how much I loved my mother until I knew she was dead." This has a double-edged sound to it, as though it wasn't safe for him to love the woman who used to "whip the shit out of me at the drop of a hat" until she was in the ground. "I loved her and learned a lot from her," he said. Including, no doubt, the whipping part.

KENNY DORHAM—THE VERSATILE, HIGHLY REGARDED TRUMPETER WHO'D replaced Miles in Charlie Parker's band and gone on to accompany almost every player of importance in jazz as well as lead his own groups—didn't like the quintet's first record, *E.S.P.* (The title referred to the telepathic compatibility Miles felt this band, like Bill Evans's trio with LaFaro and Motian, shared.) "Emotionally, as a whole, this one is lacking," Dorham wrote in a *DownBeat* review. "It's mostly brain music. . . . [The] music in general is monotonous—one long drone."

It's an odd way to describe an album of such vivacity, one on which Miles was clearly so excited, intellectually and viscerally, to be playing. He loved his new players, all of whom were significantly younger than he: as proof of his affection and connection, for the first time since *Kind of Blue*, all the material on the record was original, generated from within the band. Wayne Shorter's fast-moving, melodically indeterminate title tune, a kind of response to the call of Coltrane's "Giant Steps," seemed to lead the way into a new era, one in which jazz was, all at once, expanding in its artistic ambitions, contracting in its influence on the culture at large, and exploding into dozens of different stylistic shards.

Was *E.S.P.*, the album, music for the head, not the heart? It might not have been to Kenny Dorham's lyrical taste, but it also wasn't free jazz of the kind Ornette Coleman, Albert Ayler, and Cecil Taylor were playing: it hadn't abandoned chordal structure and steady percussive pulse; rather, it built on the advances of *Seven Steps to Heaven*, combining, in John Szwed's formulation, the abstract and the earthy. It was fewer chords, less-conventional modulations, but it *felt* like Miles Davis music. It might not have been hummable, but it was highly listenable. And whatever Kenny Dorham said, it made the body move.

E.S.P. was recorded in Hollywood in January 1965; after the band returned to New York, the trumpeter's hip pain became so bad that he had to cancel several lucrative engagements. In April he had replacement surgery; it was not successful. In August he broke the hip while horsing around with his sons, and had another operation, this time to implant a plastic joint. He returned from the hospital in intense pain, which he medicated with cocaine, with the expectable side effects of aggression and paranoia. That month—the month of *E.S.P.*'s release—he vanished on a days-long binge, and returned hallucinating. "There was nothing more frightening than hearing crutches coming after you," Frances Taylor Davis recalled.

> I mean, he came into the house and he was looking for this imaginary man that he said I was supposed to be sleeping with. Under the bed, in the closet. But, of course, there was no one there. He had a butcher knife and he took me downstairs in the basement because he thought he heard someone. And there was no one there. He had me by my wrists. We came upstairs, and . . . something came to me at this moment, and I said to him, "There is somebody in

this house! Let me call the police!" And I tried to make it to the door. But he said, "You're not going anywhere."

The cover of *E.S.P.*, Miles's second Columbia album with a picture of Frances on the sleeve, was an odd image, a Bob Cato photograph of Davis, seated in the back garden of his town house, gazing up at the beautiful Taylor, who stands, in a black top and floral print skirt, looking at the photographer with an enigmatic, wide-eyed expression, her lips parted as if about to say something. ("Help"?)

The irony of the image—that an album named after an intimate and mysterious form of communication shows a married pair not even looking at each other—need hardly be mentioned.

Miles's expression is less mysterious: it's almost theatrical. A pensive finger to his lips, brow furrowed, he looks up at her, evaluative, concerned. Is this gorgeous prize about to escape his grasp? As it turned out, she was. The next time her husband attacked her, Frances really did call the police. Amid the official bustle inside 312 West Seventy-seventh, she slipped out and made her escape. She never returned.

SOMETIME IN THE EARLY SIXTIES, WE CAN'T BE SURE EXACTLY WHEN, the Jazz Baroness, Nica de Koenigswarter, began compiling a book that consisted exclusively of jazz musicians' answers to the question: What three wishes would you most like to have granted?

John Coltrane's responses were deeply self-revealing, if not prescient:

1. To have an inexhaustible freshness in my music. I'm stale right now.

2. Immunity from sickness of [*sic*] ill health.

3. Three times the sexual power I have now. And something else too: more natural love for people. You can add that on to the other.

For all his quiet and apparently pure ways, for all his colleagues' claims that John Coltrane lived in a world of his own devoted to music and little else, the saxophonist had succumbed early in his life with Naima to one of the chief temptations facing traveling musicians, especially celebrated ones. In 1958, not long after Coltrane's wife had helped him kick drugs and alcohol, a New Jersey woman gave birth to a daughter he had fathered. "She was somebody who was blamed on John and he accepted it and helped take care of her," his cousin Mary Alexander told Lewis Porter. But his involvement with the baby, Sheila, went beyond support: the child (whether with her mother or without is unclear) seems to have visited the Coltrane household on at least a couple of occasions. "Naima appears to have handled the situation with grace and understanding," Porter writes, not completely persuasively.

Not long afterward, while playing a date in Detroit, Coltrane met a tall, pretty, extremely shy young woman named Alice McLeod. At a party he overheard someone say, "I thought you were working tonight, Alice. I wanted to hear you play." Coltrane trained his intense gaze on the shy young woman—who, it turned out, was a local pianist with a flair for bebop—and said, "I didn't know you were a musician; tell me more."

"From the way he looked at me," she later recalled, "I knew we would be meeting again."

McLeod next saw Coltrane in March of 1960, from the audience of the Olympia in Paris, when he was playing there with Miles. Whether he knew of her presence or not, she said, "I felt I was receiving a message from John through his music, as if he was talking to me personally."

Two months later, when Coltrane left Miles and opened at the Jazz Gallery, he began an affair with still another woman—a white woman, whatever this signified and still signifies. "Trane's Lady," as the saxophonist's first biographer, J. C. Thomas, called her, seems to have set her cap for him: she took a homemade sweet potato pie, his favorite, to the club and handed it to him after his first set. "I've brought you a present," she's said to have said.

"You?" Coltrane teased.

"Me," she affirmed.

This was a very different Coltrane from the bashful and retiring person his colleagues describe—the one who, Miles claimed, wouldn't have noticed a naked woman standing in front of him while he was on the bandstand. The relationship would continue for the rest of 1960 and throughout 1961; during the same period, Naima suffered a second miscarriage (the first had happened in 1957).

In the summer of 1962, Coltrane took his wife along when the quartet toured Europe, but, Naima noticed, he seemed to have grown painfully remote. She asked her husband whether his distance had anything to do with the miscarriages—or with anything at all that she had or hadn't said or done. He brushed her off with a curt "No."

In truth, Coltrane was in a painful personal and professional whirl at the time, his affections diverted, his musical reputation suffering from the sniping of the "anti-jazz" accusers in the critical establishment. He would come to forgive the critics, who, he realized, were just trying to make a living but having to write about music they didn't really understand: "There was a time I kind of froze up on the people at *DownBeat*," he later told the writer Frank Kofsky. "I felt that they were letting their weakness direct their actions. . . . [But] the test was for me. . . . They could do what they wanted to do. The thing was for me to remain firm in what I was doing. That was a funny time—a period in my life, because I went through quite a few changes, you know, like the home life—*everything*, man."

Or, as he would put it more stiltedly in the liner notes to *A Love Supreme*: "A period of irresolution did prevail. I entered into a phase which was contradictory to the pledge and away from the esteemed path."

In late July 1963 the John Coltrane Quartet (with Louis Hayes subbing for Elvin Jones, who was trying to beat his addiction at the Lexington federal facility) shared a bill at Birdland with the vibraphonist Terry Gibbs's quartet. From the diary of "Trane's Lady":

> 7/18: John working at Birdland opposite Terry Gibbs. Stopped by later, told me he'd talked with Alice McLeod, who's playing piano with Gibbs. Said he had a headache, then we had a spat about him standing in front of my air conditioner which wasn't good for him.

McLeod didn't just play piano. Terry Gibbs had a showstopping bit, "two vibes," in which his pianist would switch to vibraphone and he and she would trade fours. Afterward, Coltrane came up to McLeod, and the two formerly shy people instantly shucked their inhibitions.

"I never knew you could play vibes," he said.

"You never knew a lot of things about me," she told him.

"Well, I'm going to make it my business to find out all I can about you," he told her.

Many years later, Alice Coltrane recalled the encounter:

> When we really actually met, it was really like two friends that had known each other many, many years, like meeting again. It was so beautiful. And so everything on my agenda stopped. He said, "You are concertizing with this group, but I would like you

to get permission from your mother to travel with me wherever I'm going around the world." So I told him that if I got my mother's permission and blessings that I would leave that group and I would travel with him. So I called her and she gave her permission. . . .

No wonder he had a headache.

"Naima, I'm going to make a change," was all Coltrane told his wife on the summer day he left her. She was saddened but not surprised. "I could feel it was going to happen sooner or later," she said. "He didn't offer any explanation. He just told me there were some things he had to do, and he left with only his clothes and his horns. He stayed in a hotel sometimes, other times with his mother in Philadelphia."

And soon, with Alice McLeod. "We were both traveling in a particular spiritual direction, John and myself, so it seemed only natural for us to join forces," she later said.

It was like God uniting two souls together. I think John could have just as easily married another woman, though. Not myself and not because I was a musician, but any woman who had the particular attributes or qualities to help him fulfill his life mission as God wanted him to.

Why does it seem so definitive of Miles Davis that the single time he mentions religion in his lengthy memoir, it's to talk of "being spiritual and [believing] in spirits"? He doesn't elaborate on what being spiritual might mean. Of yielding to a higher power, he says nothing. Of the spirits, he says much. The dead—his mother and father; deceased musicians (as of the late eighties, when he and Quincy Troupe were putting together the book) such as "Monk, Mingus, Freddie Webster, and Fat Girl. . . . Trane or Gil or Philly"—come to visit him; he can even summon them at will! They materialize; in effect, they dance attendance. As always, Miles is the one in charge.

John Coltrane, unsurprisingly, had a very different take on religion. Humility guided him in all things: "When there's something you don't understand, you have to go humbly to it," he said. He had refound his faith several years earlier, he told a French journalist in the summer of 1965. "I had already found it and lost it several times. I was brought up in a religious family. I had the seeds of it in me, and, at certain moments, I find my faith again. All of that is connected to the life one leads."

"Does religion help you in living, in playing?" the writer asked.

"It's everything for me," Coltrane said. "My music is a way of giving thanks to God."

Or of addressing God. Two months after the Birmingham church bombing (and four months after his switch from Naima to Alice), he recorded, for a part-live, part-studio album, *Live at Birdland*, an original song dramatically different from any he had written before. "Alabama" begins with a kind of invocation, a mournful tenor prelude played over McCoy Tyner's dramatic, almost menacing tremolo, then shifts to an oddly swinging middle section with the whole quartet, a passage packed with mixed emotions: sorrow, anger, resignation—and then returns to Coltrane's somber tune within a tune. The total effect is devastating. "If anyone wants to begin to understand how Coltrane could inspire so much awe so quickly," Ben Ratliff writes, "the reason is probably inside 'Alabama.' The incantational tumult he could raise in a long improvisation, the steel-trap knowledge of harmony, the writing—that's all very impressive. But 'Alabama' is also an accurate psychological portrait of a time, a complicated mood that nobody else could render so well."

Coltrane's mood was also complicated. In the early sixties he'd been feeling stalled—stuck in a pattern of performing "My Favorite Things" over and over; stuck, too, in a marriage that was coming undone. And the undoing was chiefly his doing.

His irritation with himself goaded him into an extended period of writing, in which he produced gems like 1961's "Impressions" and 1963's "Alabama" and "After the Rain." In the spring of 1964, the quartet recorded a great, under-recognized album, *Crescent*, which represented, in

Ashley Kahn's formulation, "a stylistic resting point"—a stop on the mountainside with a suddenly clear view of the peak ahead.

Crescent had two standout numbers, the slow, pensive title song and "Wise One," a haunting and melancholy ballad that may have been inspired by Naima or Alice (or both), but seems to speak to the sadness of his transition from one woman to the other. It was a contemplative record, a still point in the midst of a furiously hectic time. While the quartet played a packed concert schedule, Coltrane suffered the death of his best friend (Eric Dolphy, critically ill with undiagnosed diabetes, succumbed to insulin shock in June, at age thirty-six) and celebrated the birth of his first child (John William Coltrane, Jr., was born in August)—all against the backdrop of rock 'n' roll's rocket rise and the acceleration of the Vietnam War and the protest movement, as well as the Black Power movement, Freedom Summer, the Civil Rights Act, and the Harlem riots. And in an island of tranquility in this tempest-tossed period—Coltrane and Alice McLeod, along with her young daughter, Michelle, moved into a large and handsome brick ranch house on four acres in a prosperous Black enclave of suburban Dix Hills, Long Island, in the summer of '64—John Coltrane created his greatest composition, a work of transcendent beauty and serenity expressed in the form of gratitude to God.

It would be easy, in light of Coltrane's all too human peccadillos—flaws that sprang, as we've seen time and again, from a deep, dark maw of loss and neediness—to dismiss such an enterprise as mildly (or not so mildly) hypocritical, or at the very least overblown, a sinner's grandstanding compensation for wrongs committed. In fact *A Love Supreme* is nothing less than a great work of art, a through-written suite paradoxically created, much like *Kind of Blue*, from the sketchiest notes jotted down ahead of time and, also like *Kind of Blue*, virtually improvised on the spot. (Although as with Miles and *Kind of Blue*, Coltrane and his group had workshopped at least two sections of *A Love Supreme* earlier, in clubs.) It is a piece of four parts of equal power and majesty, a composition as memorable and significant, from first notes to last, as any celebrated work of European classical music. And all laid down in a single recording session, in Rudy Van Gelder's Englewood studio, between 8:00 p.m. and midnight on December 9, 1964.

The work, Lewis Porter writes,

> has a carefully worked out plan. The four sections of *A Love Supreme*, "Acknowledgement," "Resolution," "Pursuance," and "Psalm," suggest a kind of pilgrim's progress, in which the pilgrim acknowledges the divine, resolves to pursue it, searches, and eventually celebrates what has been attained in song. The four parts of the suite form an archlike dramatic succession. Part 1 functions as a prelude; the tension increases in part 2 and peaks in part 3, the fastest section. A long unaccompanied bass solo introduces the last part, a relatively calm postlude.

The music itself has been described many times; yet words lead to a place of more words, a territory hemmed by the writer's abilities or inabilities and falsely illuminated by the writer's vanity. The only thing to do is listen, and listen again, from the initial splash of Elvin Jones's Chinese gong and the grand yet tranquil, muezzin-like summons of Coltrane's opening phrase in "Acknowledgement" to the dying tones of cymbals, bass, and piano at the end of "Psalm." Awe is woven throughout *A Love Supreme*, the culmination of a great musician's lifelong quest, the first part of which, for Coltrane as it was for Bird, is struggling to play what one hears in one's head, the second part being able to play it. And then (if the musician truly is great) the third part: the ability to convey to the listener the awe the player has felt in the creation.

Duke Ellington, who wrote sacred music along with the profane, expressed something of this when he said, "I'm just God's messenger boy." John Coltrane tried to say something very like it in his liner note to *A Love Supreme*, which begins:

DEAR LISTENER: ALL PRAISE BE TO GOD TO WHOM ALL PRAISE IS DUE. Let us pursue Him in the righteous path.

Yes it is true; "seek and ye shall find." Only through Him can we know the most wondrous bequeathal. . . .

He then mentions his spiritual awakening and his "period of irresolution . . . [the] phase which was contradictory to the pledge and away from the esteemed path." But now, he writes, he's thankful that

> through the unerring and merciful hand of God, I do perceive and have been duly re-informed of his OMNIPOTENCE, and of our need for, and dependence on Him. At this time I would like to tell you that NO MATTER WHAT . . . IT IS WITH GOD. HE IS GRACIOUS AND MERCIFUL. HIS WAY IS IN LOVE, THROUGH WHICH WE ALL ARE. IT IS TRULY—A LOVE SUPREME. . . .

We're invited to share his ecstatic gratitude through the music, and some of us may—but it would be a mistake to assume that *A Love Supreme* is a religious experience per se to all or even most listeners who love the piece. It's a work filled with wonders, for which "Acknowledgement" sets the stage, from that shimmering gong to Jimmy Garrison's pulse-quickening four-note theme that in effect speaks the title—the mantra, in Ashley Kahn's formulation—to Coltrane's cycling the mantra through every key, which he follows by actually speaking the title, chanting the words themselves, *a love supreme*, in unison with himself (through an overdub he did the next day) nineteen times.

It's all thrilling, even after multiple listenings, and it's thrilling because, whatever God may or may not have to do with it, it's great jazz. The urgent, ardent intro to "Resolution" isn't just an antidote to irresolution, it's a magnificent jazz tune. It's also Coltrane down to its molecules, with an instantly identifiable family resemblance to many other themes and passages of his work. And that four-note mantra in "Acknowledgement"? Take a listen to "Mau Mau," a 1953 Latin-style piece written by Art

Farmer and Quincy Jones and played by Farmer's septet, a catchy mambo
with clave percussion and, a minute and a half or so in, a four-note figure
played on baritone sax that is *exactly the same* as Coltrane's 1964 theme.
Whether Coltrane was aware of the borrowing or, as Kahn asserts, "simply drawing inspiration from the same deep, blues-filled well many others [had] visited," it's all just jazz.

And *A Love Supreme*, to use Miles's highest accolade, swings.

Yet it also, like *Kind of Blue*, possessed a serene majesty that lifted it
above other jazz albums, including Coltrane's own. Whether or not the
feelings it generated were religious, they were deep. The LP was a massive
critical success: both *DownBeat* and *Jazz* named it album of the year in
1965, and *DownBeat*'s readers voted Coltrane Jazzman of the Year and
best tenor saxophonist, and elected him to the journal's Hall of Fame,
joining the only other tenor players there, Coleman Hawkins and Lester
Young. Upon its release in January 1965—a year that would see the world
of popular music explode in a confetti conflagration of youth, and the
flight from jazz of millions of young white record buyers, not just to the
Beatles, the Rolling Stones, and Bob Dylan, but also to such newly
hatched acts as the Association, the Blues Project, Canned Heat, the
Doors, the Electric Prunes, the Grateful Dead, Jefferson Airplane, the
Lovin' Spoonful, the Mamas & the Papas, the Sir Douglas Quintet, and
the Stone Poneys, with Linda Ronstadt—in that chaotic and transitional
year, *A Love Supreme* would start selling and never really stop: by 1970
some five hundred thousand copies had been bought, more than ten times
as many as any of Coltrane's other Impulse! LPs.

But *A Love Supreme* was also John Coltrane's last completely accessible
work. "'Resolution' had been the last of Coltrane's great melodies," Ben
Ratliff writes.

> Beyond it, for the most part, lay something other than songs-for-
> the-sake-of-songs: melody lines were now a matter of intervals and
> cells, musical vitamins to keep the drone healthy. "Suite," recorded

six months after the suite that really mattered [and released post-humously in 1970, on the album *Transition*], isn't nearly as distinctive. It marks the beginning of a late Coltrane-quartet period that amounts to one interconnected song. It is a music of meditation and chant, the sound of his interior cosmos.

And so the question hangs: Is John Coltrane's interior cosmos one we are willing—or able—to share?

In the spring of 1965 Coltrane was ascending rapidly toward an empyrean all his own: his myth would grow even as his audience diminished. That spring he, Garrison, Tyner, and Jones played two fabled stands at the Half Note. Dan Morgenstern was present for one of those evenings, and though his tastes incline more toward swing and bebop than what came after, he was blown away by what he saw and heard. "The intensity that was generated was absolutely unbelievable," he recalled.

> I can still *feel* it, and it was unlike any other feeling within the music we call jazz. . . . It carried you away. If you let yourself be carried by it, it was an absolutely ecstatic feeling. And I think that kind of ecstasy was something that Coltrane was looking for in his music.

To listen to the album *Live at the Half Note: One Down, One Up*—released only in 2005, thirty-eight years after Coltrane's death—is to feel a simulacrum of the power Morgenstern felt on that ancient evening: experientially impressive, but musically divisive. To have shared the club's tiny space with those four extraordinary presences and the extraordinary sounds they made individually and together would have been breathtaking. To try to imagine the evening, to take it in merely aurally, is a different matter. The twenty-seven-minute title number contains a thirteen-minute passage in which Tyner and Garrison lay out and Coltrane and Jones play a churning duet that celebrates their profound connection. It is an awesome thing—intellectually, and if you let yourself be carried by it, viscerally. It all depends on the inclination of your viscera.

IN THE WAKE OF *A LOVE SUPREME*, COLTRANE GREW EVER MORE FASCI-
nated with free jazz—and especially with the playing of Albert Ayler, the
Cleveland saxophonist who'd taken the genre even further out than
Ornette Coleman and Cecil Taylor had, carving his own small corner of
the avant-garde by privileging sound, namely whatever sound he could
scream through his horn, over mere music. That summer Coltrane told an
interviewer that he'd had a dream seven or eight years earlier, before he'd
ever met or heard Ayler, of a whole band playing in that style. Now he had
the cultural currency and commercial power to realize his dreams. At the
end of June, Coltrane gathered ten musicians in Rudy Van Gelder's
studio—the quartet members and seven others, including Freddie Hubbard and Art Davis, as well as free-jazz exponents Archie Shepp and
Pharoah Sanders; all of them younger than he—to try to capture something approaching Ayler's conception in a large-ensemble format, mixing

in the influences of Sun Ra and Cecil Taylor. The resulting album (for Impulse!) would be called *Ascension*.

The record possessed an internal integrity—Coltrane had mapped it out carefully as a series of crescendi and decrescendi, ensemble sections and solos, though he held no rehearsals, only telling the players of his plan once they arrived in the studio. The result was two takes of two pieces of roughly twenty minutes each, all of it improvised, and sounding to the unschooled ear like barely controlled chaos. And perhaps to some schooled ears, too. The story goes that at the end of the second take of the second section, Elvin Jones "flung his snare at the studio wall, signaling his decision that for him, the date was over."

The album was a watershed for Coltrane—and, some say, for jazz itself. *Ascension*, Dave Liebman said, "was the torch that lit the free-jazz thing. I mean, it really begins with Cecil and Ornette in '59, but *Ascension* was like the patron saint saying, 'It's OK—this is valid.' I think that even had much more of an effect on everybody than *A Love Supreme*." This, George Russell said, was "when Coltrane turned his back on the money." It "signaled Coltrane's full embrace of the New Thing and its players," Eric Nisenson wrote. "He finally became a full-fledged member of the avant-garde, with no turning back."

On the other hand, as the saxophonist Frank Foster said: "That was the turning point for some musicians who had been Coltrane enthusiasts up to that time; after that they turned off."

A week after making the record, Coltrane took the quartet to the 1965 Newport Jazz Festival, where they played "One Down, One Up," followed by a leavening dose of "My Favorite Things." That was in the July 2 evening session. That afternoon, the pianist Billy Taylor, a jazz educator as well as a widely traveled ambassador for the music, had introduced the Archie Shepp Quartet this way: "One of the things that must become obvious to anyone listening to the new music is that in order to literally hear what's going on, the audience has to be very aware in terms of musical lines, and rhythmic lines. It's not easy listening; we're glad you opt to make the effort."

But as Miles Davis, who'd once walked off the bandstand at the Village Vanguard rather than perform with Shepp ("He couldn't play, and I wasn't going to stand up there with this no-playing motherfucker"), noted, fewer and fewer people were making the effort:

> Where just a few years back the music we were playing was the cutting edge, was getting real popular and finding a wide audience, all that started to stop when the critics—white critics—started supporting the free thing, pushing that over what most everybody else was doing. Jazz started to lose its broad appeal around this time.

When Shepp sat in with the Coltrane quartet at the *DownBeat* Festival in Chicago that August, there were walkouts. Young white fans, we've seen, were leaving jazz in droves. But the music was also losing a much more essential audience. As Betty Carter told Art Taylor a couple of years later: "You can go uptown and ask ten people on the street who Archie Shepp is and they won't be able to tell you. Ninety percent of his audience is white. . . . Today most of our musicians, like Ornette Coleman, avoid black people. When you go to their concerts, you don't see any black people there."

Free jazz or, as some Black musicians called it, freedom music, presented at least two fundamental problems. For one thing, it took jazz even further away from dance than bebop had, and bodily expression was a sacred Black tradition in an America that didn't recognize Black bodies as free. For another, you didn't need skill to play it, or at least to give a convincing imitation of playing it—you could just pick up a horn and blow. "The term 'free' was often a euphemism for, in my estimation, people who were total novices in some cases," Archie Shepp said. "There were certainly levels of this music, and a player like Coltrane was the consummate horn player within that African-American improvising tradition."

Yet many listeners, even those most sympathetically disposed toward Coltrane, didn't get it—or didn't want to. The composer and multi-instrumentalist Anthony Braxton remembered a dramatic moment at the Half Note: "I saw a woman come into the club and with the hook of her umbrella try to grab [Coltrane] around the arm while he was playing with the quartet. I could have killed that woman! But after the set, when she came up to scold John for playing this loud, crazy music, he was so kind to her, so understanding."

BUT HE HAD NO INTENTION OF GOING BACK. INSTEAD, HE DOUBLED DOWN on the future—almost as if, many have speculated, he knew how little time was left to him. "He knew he was going down, and God bless him that he did it before he went down," Dave Liebman said. "He told Paul Chambers, supposedly in 1965, that he didn't have much more time to live. Two years or something like that. I don't know if that's apocryphal or true. But he was not well by then. You could see that. He was a little overweight. I mean, he still played with the intensity. But Pharoah, of course, helped out a lot, second horn, take the load off of him."

Coltrane had met the Little Rock–born Farrell Sanders in 1959, in Oakland, while touring the West Coast with Miles. Sanders was still a teenager, serving the traditional apprenticeship with R&B bands but aspiring to higher musical planes. In 1961 he moved to New York, where he was homeless for a while until Sun Ra gave him work and encouraged him to change his name to Pharoah. One night in 1963, Sanders was standing outside the Half Note, dirty and hungry and having been refused admission because of his appearance. When Coltrane came outside on a break, he saw Sanders, had him let in as his guest, and insisted they stay in touch. In part through Coltrane's influence, Sanders recorded two albums as a leader in 1964.

He returned to the Bay Area, and in September 1965, went to hear the Coltrane quartet at San Francisco's Jazz Workshop, where Coltrane told him "that he was thinking about changing the group and changing the music, to get different sounds. He asked me to play with him."

By different sounds, Coltrane meant a musical realm "beyond notes." Sanders concurred with the approach: "I don't live in chord changes," he said. "They're not expanded enough to hold everything that I live and that comes out in my music."

"Coltrane was now moving quickly," Porter writes.

> He sensed that he was onto something and opened his group up right away to a whole slew of young musicians and influences. He no longer wanted to swing, and from this point on Garrison never played a walking bass with him, but broke up the beat with short phrases and strumming. Jones slashed away at full force, and Tyner's fine work receded more and more into the background.

He no longer wanted to swing. This was a fundamental, visceral problem, even for musically sophisticated listeners. David S. Ware was a young (and Black) aspiring saxophonist who in the mid 1960s virtually commuted from his home in Newark to Manhattan to hear his idol play. Ware told Ashley Kahn: "You can get almost as avant-garde as you want to be, as long as you keep that steady pulse, but Coltrane lost a lot of people when he broke that time, and went into that other world and started messing with that multidirectional time."

And still other worlds: several of Coltrane's friends told Porter that he started using LSD in 1965, and "would get so disoriented from acid during some gigs that after intermission he had to be guided back to the stage."

Both Tyner and Jones were upset with the changes in the band's sound. The problem worsened sharply during a stand at the Village Gate in late 1965, when Coltrane brought in an old Philadelphia friend, Rashied Ali, as a second drummer, and it quickly became clear that having two percussionists onstage (three, really, including Tyner) wasn't the whim of a moment on the leader's part, but a permanent plan. Jones and Ali didn't like each other, personally or musically, and a percussion battle ensued, each trying to play louder than the other. The initial (and predictable) result was cacophony; the secondary, and graver, result was the departure from the band, after five and a half years, of McCoy Tyner.

He needed to go out on his own to continue to grow as a musician, the pianist told one interviewer. But he later spoke more candidly to another writer: "I didn't see myself making any kind of contribution to that music," Tyner said. "At times I couldn't hear what anybody was doing! All I could hear was a lot of noise. I didn't have any feeling for the music, and when I don't have feelings, I don't play." Alice Coltrane, on piano and harp, would replace him.

Elvin Jones quickly followed Tyner out the door, giving an almost identical quote to *DownBeat*: "At times I couldn't hear what I was doing— matter of fact I couldn't hear what anybody was doing," he said. "All I could hear was a lot of noise."

"Though he filled the It Club in Los Angeles in 1965," Stanley Crouch wrote, "when Coltrane returned the following year with Pharoah Sanders, Alice Coltrane, Jimmy Garrison, and Rashied Ali, there were three people in the room the night I heard him."

WHITNEY BALLIETT ASSERTED THAT LATE COLTRANE—THE SAXOPHON- ist's work over the eighteen months between the end of the great quartet and his shockingly early death, a time when his music seemed to acceler- ate out of the earth's atmosphere toward interstellar space—was not the *real* Coltrane: "the peaceful, lyrical, big-toned, God-loving Coltrane, the Coltrane who was never really comfortable belaboring us with unholy shrieks and double notes and chords piled on chords, like bales stacked in a warehouse. . . . People said they heard the dark night of the Negro in Coltrane's wildest music, but what they really heard was a heroic and unique lyrical voice at the mercy of its own power."

Was Balliett projecting his own discomfort with this work onto its creator? It would appear not. Miles Davis said Coltrane told him "that even he liked some of the music he did earlier better than what he was doing now."

"Late Trane is a challenge for any listener," Dave Liebman told me. "It was difficult music. It was chaotic, it was loud, it was cacophony. For many years, you couldn't talk about late Coltrane without everybody saying, 'I don't know what happened; he lost his mind; he took too much acid. I don't know what happened.'

"It was difficult music," Liebman said. "But it was deep as hell."

"It's *supposed* to be difficult," Loren Schoenberg said. "It's all about our limitations. This is not music to tap your foot to. It's not 'Someday My Prince Will Come.' The way I interpret it is that the music of all the great African American jazz artists, and the reflection of it among non–African American jazz artists, was about changing the culture—was in some way letting America know that there were these Black geniuses, and that you have to radically rethink your attitude toward them, because this is all genius music, and it's supposed to upset your applecart in a certain kind of way. It may have jam on top; it may be on a nice roll; but nonetheless, you have to confront the fact that it's supposed to make you uncomfortable in some sense.

"And then Coltrane finally gets to the point where *all this has been done*. There's been Ornette; there's been all this; it's all happened. And maybe he knew he was sick, maybe he didn't, maybe he was experimenting with psychedelics, or maybe none of that means anything. And so consequently you're coming to hear him play—guess what? He *wants* you to be uncomfortable. In the same way Jackson Pollock or Picasso wanted you to be uncomfortable.

"John Lewis told me that John Coltrane killed jazz," Schoenberg said. "And I know what he meant. [Lewis's] whole goal in life with the Modern Jazz Quartet was to create a jazz that was accessible. It was very intellectual, it was on the highest level, but as with Armstrong and Ellington, there was some intersection with what people would listen to—wanting to be part of the pop music scene *somehow*. And I think what John meant was, Coltrane took jazz to a point where [he and his exponents] didn't care about whether people wanted to listen."

"What could have led one of the intellectual giants of jazz—one of the great bluesmen, one of the most original swingers and a master of the ballad—into an arena so emotionally narrow and so far removed from his roots and his accomplishments?" Stanley Crouch asked.

It's hard to imagine the greathearted, deeply thoughtful Coltrane consciously wanting his audience to be uncomfortable. Easier is to think of him drawing in upon himself, seeking connections with the great worlds within and without. "I know the music sounds wrong, but it's something about the sound," he once told the drummer Jack DeJohnette. "Everybody wants to hear what I've done; nobody wants to hear what I'm doing," Coltrane told a journalist. "I've had a strange career. I haven't yet quite found out how I want to play music. Most of what's happened these past few years has been questions. Someday we'll find the answers."

"I think Trane was really trying to find one with the universe," Wallace Roney told me. "I know he was trying to get that sound—that pitch, in space, that Hubbell hears now—the beginning of creation. And trying to find a vibration, what it was vibrating to. I think he was really trying to find a music that connected to more than just what we know technically as music.

"Maybe," Roney said, "his spirit outgrew his body."

And maybe John Coltrane didn't kill jazz. Maybe he just left it behind.

IN JULY 1966 COLTRANE TOURED IN JAPAN FOR THE FIRST TIME. AT A press conference in Tokyo, a Japanese journalist asked the saxophonist, who sat with Alice at his side, a question that a translator did his best to express accurately: "How you would like to be in ten or twenty years—in what kind of situation?"

"As a musician or what—as a person?" Coltrane asked.

"Let's say as a person."

"In music, or as a person—I would like to be a saint," he said. He laughed, then Alice laughed, too.

He had almost exactly one year to live.

"I talked to Coltrane right before he passed on," Sonny Rollins told me.

"How did he seem?" I asked.

"The usual way, serious," Rollins said. "But I noticed something about Coltrane's conversation at that time, and his voice. You know, they have a thing they call overtones in music, where if you play one note you also hear another. So Coltrane's voice, when he said something—in the tone of his voice I could hear the higher partials of an overtone."

I asked what this told him.

"Well, it didn't tell me anything," he said. "It was just sort of, 'Wow.'" He laughed. "But any time I talked to Coltrane, it was of an otherworldly nature. It wasn't anything that unusual."

We've seen much evidence of Coltrane's worldly side. And though he had a powerful need to keep himself to himself ("He was the type of person, he didn't care for socializing," Alice Coltrane recalled; "and I don't care for socializing, so that's sort of the way it was"), he had a domestic existence in Dix Hills, and he savored it. The presence of four young children, Alice's daughter and their three sons, would have made the household lively; the harp and grand piano in the living room would have made it tuneful. (John combed the TV listings for reruns of Marx Brothers movies: he loved to watch Harpo play.) There was a telescope in the backyard for scanning the night sky. There were shelves full of books on philosophy and spiritualism.

And then—equally hidden from the world, even from his immediate family—there was his illness. After returning from Japan, he canceled a European tour scheduled for that November; he played fewer and fewer gigs, staying closer and closer to home. He began sitting in a chair while he performed. Asked by a journalist how he liked having Pharoah Sanders in the band as a second tenor, he said, "It helps me stay alive sometimes, because physically, man, the pace I've been leading has been so hard and I've gained so much weight, that sometimes it's been a little hard physically. I feel that I like to have somebody there in case I can't get that strength. I like to have that strength in the band, somewhere."

He was a strong man, but he had abused his body in multiple ways for many years, and now something he didn't want to know about—or certainly tell anyone about, even his wife—was growing inside him. On May 7, 1967, he played what was to be his last concert, at the Famous Ballroom in Baltimore. A few days later, his stomach was hurting so badly that he went to the hospital, where he had a biopsy but declined to be operated on. He spent miserable weeks thereafter lying on the living room couch, listening to playbacks of recent recording sessions, while Alice tried to keep the kids out of the way. On July 16, when he was unable to bear the pain any longer, she drove him to Huntington Hospital, twenty minutes away. "He was such a strong man that he walked out the door himself," Alice remembered. "He was walking slow, but he made it. And then he went down so fast." He died, of cancer of the liver, at four the next morning, July 17, 1967, two months and six days shy of his forty-first birthday.

Miles's reaction to Coltrane's death was almost identical to what he'd said of Bird's passing: "In July, Coltrane died and fucked up everyone," he said. Everybody in jazz was shocked, he said. Trane hadn't been looking well; his weight gain was obvious; he'd been playing less, but—death?

Even Harold Lovett, the lawyer who represented both Davis and Coltrane, seemed to have been caught unawares. Jazz's most private genius had held his losing hand close to the vest until the very end.

And as with the death of Bird, the loss of a colossal figure central to a musical style—in Parker's case, bebop; in Coltrane's, free jazz—set a world of acolytes and epigones adrift, changing the music virtually overnight. The result after Bird's death was a joyous rebirth, the phoenix rise of a new, more soulful music. The outcome of John Coltrane's death, amid rock 'n' roll's continuing shelling of jazz—this was the summer the Doors' "Light My Fire" seemed to be playing constantly everywhere, the summer Frank Sinatra kicked his car radio through the dashboard after that goddamn song came on one more time—was more problematic.

"When Red Garland asked Coltrane if he truly believed in what he was doing—leading 'the new thing'—the saxophonist said only that if he stopped he would abandon all of those who had followed him," Crouch wrote. "Many then and now believe Coltrane's apprentices followed him into an artistic abyss."

Ornette Coleman, Cecil Taylor, Sun Ra, Albert Ayler, Pharoah Sanders, et al. may have been the progenitors of free jazz, but they were ultimately niche figures, whereas Coltrane, with the bestselling *A Love Supreme* (which wasn't free jazz, but opened the gates for Coltrane to go there), had captured the imagination not just of the jazz world, but of a wider (whiter) world beyond. He himself became an icon—and not in the modern, debased sense of the word, but in a way closer to the original religious meaning. "Toward the end of his life, Coltrane, photographed incessantly, began to look messianic," Whitney Balliett wrote. "His long, handsome, still face, usually in profile, was as serious as stone—he might have been posing for 'The Thinker'—and when he turned toward the camera he looked right into your head."

After his death, Coltrane's iconic status only grew. For Black people, Miles said, the fire and passion of Trane's late music, coherent or not, seemed to express "what H. Rap Brown and Stokely Carmichael and the

Black Panthers and Huey Newton were saying with their words, what the Last Poets and Amiri Baraka were saying in poetry." The Black liberation movement took him up as a revolutionary symbol, along with "Afro hairdos, dashikis, black power, fists raised in the air. Coltrane was their pride—their beautiful, black, revolutionary pride."

For others—for "many intellectual and revolutionary whites and Asians," as Davis said—Coltrane's image and music also struck a chord, one deeply felt if not deeply examined. For some he was a bridge from rock to jazz: in my freshman year at NYU in the late sixties, a Black dorm-mate proudly showed me his shelf full of splendidly jacketed Impulse! albums by Coltrane and others, playing some of them for me, to my near total incomprehension. But even if my understanding was next to nil, a seed was planted.

And though Coltrane was mostly joking—or maybe only partly?—when he said he aspired to sainthood, and though he bridled when an interviewer mentioned that he shared initials with Christianity's founder, two years after his death a married pair of San Francisco clergy, the Reverends Franzo W. King and Marina King, founded the Saint John Coltrane Church, with the saxophonist as its canonized patron saint. Initially the Kings hadn't been impressed with Coltrane's recorded music, but then they attended a Coltrane concert at the Jazz Workshop. "It was as though he was speaking in tongues and there was fire coming from heaven—a sound baptism," Franzo King recalled. "That began the evolutionary, transitional process of us becoming truly born-again believers in that anointed sound that leaped down from the tone of heaven out of the very mind of God, stepped from the very wall of creation and took on a gob of flesh, and we beheld his beauty as one that was called John."

And Miles, irreligious though he was, ever after kept a photograph of Coltrane on his bedroom wall.

BILL EVANS COULD CLAIM NO SUCH DISTINCTION. NOT ONLY, AT LEAST BY Miles's lights (and by the lights of some others, too), did he never again play as well as he had with Miles, but he also committed (in Miles's eyes) a peculiar sin: "It's a strange thing about a lot of white players—not all, just most—that after they make it in a black group they always go and play with all white guys no matter how good the black guys treated them," Davis said. "Bill did that, and I'm not saying he could have gotten any black guys any better than Scott and Paul, I'm just telling what I've seen happen over and over again."

This would've been news to Jack DeJohnette, who played with Evans from 1968 to 1969, a seat that brought the drummer to the attention of Miles, who then snatched him up to lead the rhythm section of his *Bitches Brew* band. But the pattern held otherwise, and it, as well as other aspects of Evans's post-Miles career—which lasted over twenty years—has been subject to extensive criticism and debate. "I think Bill could have done something different—he could've had more Black musicians in his trio," Ethan Iverson told me. "He could've reached out, after being anointed by Miles Davis, and tried a bit more than he did."

For a half year after Scott LaFaro's death, Evans sleepwalked through a fog of grief. Then he found a new bass player, a self-assured twenty-five-year-old named Chuck Israels, and set about remaking his career, starting to perform and record again. Riverside Records' Orrin Keepnews was instrumental in this process, as was a new manager introduced to Evans by Gene Lees, Helen Keane. Keane, who loved jazz, was transported by Evans's playing from the moment she first heard him; she also knew from the outset what a trial working with him would be. "Oh no . . . not this one," she said. "This is the one that could break my heart."

But Keane was very smart and very tough, and for the rest of the pianist's life she would play many roles: not just manager but fierce advocate, hand holder, and even record producer. She was essential both to building Evans's career and keeping him from falling apart entirely. "She was very strong for Bill," Lees said. "He would've been dead without her. I don't think he'd have had the career he had without her."

For there was this paradox: even as his playing, and the new trio's, solidified, Evans's "life and career [were] in hideous disarray," Lees remembered. In the summer of 1962, Lees—who was both a close friend and an

unofficial business adviser to Evans—introduced him to a rising young pianist and Bill Evans fan from Wisconsin named Warren Bernhardt. The
three had breakfast together, and Bernhardt was starstruck. "I loved him
and his gentle nature immediately," he recalled.

> After we ate we then went over to Bill's place, which was rather dirty
> and messy. It was there that I first met Ellaine and their skinny
> little pussycat named Harmony. I remember that the kitchen was
> piled to the ceiling with old newspapers and a narrow path had
> been left open to the sink and refrigerator. Quite a bizarre scene,
> but Bill had a beautiful, medium-sized Knabe grand in the living
> room, which I was afraid to touch with him there. Bill did not play
> that day, but he did invite me down to the Vanguard that very eve-
> ning, where he was performing with Paul Motian and Chuck
> Israels.

The Vanguard was packed that night, but Evans had reserved a seat for
Bernhardt—the best seat in the house: "It was magical," Bernhardt remembered.

> Right at Bill's right hand, no more than three feet from him. . . .
> A spotlight seemed to shine down on the empty seat, and at that
> moment my life changed forever. To me, being there at his side,
> in that presence, was the most beautiful moment in my life, the
> sound the greatest thing I had ever heard (except perhaps that of
> certain recordings of Rachmaninoff playing his own composi-
> tions, which had moved me deeply as a small child).
>
> We spent the breaks together, smoking cigarettes and talking
> about music. I was in heaven. Bill wrote out some changes on a
> couple of Village Vanguard folding table cards during his break.
> What a generous and loving thing for a busy man to do for a young
> fan, a kid he had only met that day! He even meticulously drew
> out the ledger lines on the blank cards.

Bernhardt was more than a young fan: though only twenty-four, he was a classically trained pianist now working in jazz, having just returned from a South American tour with the Paul Winter Sextet. His technical expertise would have made him, for Evans, the best kind of admirer: one who knew enough about music to understand what set Bill Evans apart.

Yet the stars in Bernhardt's eyes (and ears) didn't prevent him from noticing what, in Evans's home life, went beyond slobby eccentricity: "Ellaine looked like she had been in a concentration camp and Bill had tracks all over his hands, et cetera."

The et cetera covered what was too painful to elaborate on—these were two junkies in love, with each other and, perhaps just as much, with junk. And the pushers loved them: there was nothing like a steady customer. The tracks all over Evans's hands implied what wasn't seen: tracks all over his arms, legs, and feet; collapsed veins necessitating a constant search for fresh needle-access points. Keen-eyed admirers in clubs noticed that the left-handed Evans had overinjected his right hand and arm to the point of nerve damage: in early 1963 "he played one-handed throughout a week's booking at the Vanguard," Pettinger writes. "With his left hand and some virtuoso pedaling, he was able to maintain harmonic interest in support of treble lines. In morbid fascination, pianists dropped by to witness this phenomenon."

The bassist Bill Crow witnessed it on another occasion: "He would dangle the dead hand over the keyboard and drop his forefinger on the keys, using the weight of the hand to depress them. Everything else was played with the left hand, and if you looked away you couldn't tell anything was wrong."

There is a desperate sort of admirableness to this: one can't help being impressed by Evans's ingenuity and virtuosity. At the same time, his life as a human being, as a man, was sinking fast. As Miles had discovered to his sorrow, there was no keeping up with the ravening demon of heroin: the more you took, the less it did for you; the less it did for you, the more you needed. Money, sums large and small, swirled down the drain. A close friend and fellow musician recalled crossing to the other side of the street when he saw Evans, knowing the pianist would have tried to hit him up. It's the same sad story many have told about Charlie Parker and Miles: genius bends very low with a monkey on its back.

The recording tear Evans embarked on as he emerged from deep grief for LaFaro had as much to do with a need for drug money as with a reentry into life: loan sharks were threatening to break his fingers. In the summer of 1962, on the heels of laying down *Interplay*, an album with Freddie Hubbard, Jim Hall, Percy Heath, and Philly Joe Jones, Evans approached Orrin Keepnews with an idea for another quintet LP, this one to consist exclusively of his own songs—the sheet music for which he just happened to have with him. "It was obvious that he was pushing hard for all the cash he could get," Pettinger writes. "Keepnews suspected that Evans's music publisher would pay him only if his pieces were scheduled for recording." Despite feeling used, like so many who gave in to junkies' entreaties, the producer greenlighted the project. "I justified my actions this time on both humanitarian and practical grounds," Keepnews wrote later. "I found it impossible to turn down urgent financial requests from a man who was both a major creative artist and my friend."

The money wouldn't be there for long: in 1964, after the sudden death of the label's cofounder Bill Grauer, Riverside would go under. But in the meantime, Evans had signed a fat new contract with Verve, the label Norman Granz had founded in 1956. A few months after Granz sold the company to MGM in 1960, Creed Taylor left Impulse! to become Verve's executive director, sacking a number of underselling artists and putting an emphasis on recording jazz that would have the widest possible commercial impact. He had a huge success in introducing the bossa nova of Antonio Carlos Jobim to the U.S., particularly through the playing of Stan Getz. And he was determined to make a star of Bill Evans.

In early 1963, even as critics were accusing him of musical solipsism, Evans began making an album on which he accompanied himself on overdubbed tracks. It was a bravura undertaking, requiring a great deal of studio time: the project couldn't have worked without the deep pockets of Verve/MGM—and without the patient shepherding of Helen Keane and Gene Lees. Evans began suffering from heroin withdrawal during the sessions but insisted on finishing: Keane and Lees "turned the lights down low and lent their heartfelt encouragement." *Conversations with Myself* would win a Grammy in 1964.

Still, some had misgivings, not about Evans's lyricism but about his introspective nature. Whitney Balliett saw his playing as "a contest between his intense wish to practice a wholly private, inner-ear music and an equally intense wish to express his jubilation at having found such a music within himself." *The New York Times*'s influential popular-music and jazz critic John S. Wilson, who also wrote for *DownBeat*, sounded the same note: "Evans' brooding, mulling approach to his piano solos marks him as one of the rare romanticists in latter-day jazz. Playing with his trio, he seems able to shut himself off from the world around him and to move into a twilit haven where he can drift along in what seems to be a semi-comatose state as he fingers his way through long, contemplative passages."

And sometimes not all the fingers were working. One might well wonder about the similarity between such reveries and a heroin high.

MAYBE HE WAS ALSO SHUTTING HIMSELF OFF FROM THE REST OF HIS trio. With a single exception, Evans would cycle through sidemen regularly through the sixties and into the seventies, sometimes through circumstance (in the early sixties both Chuck Israels and Paul Motian now and then took time off to work in other bands), and sometimes for more pointed reasons. After making the (delightful to my ears, less so to Pettinger's) album *Trio '64* with Evans and the bassist Gary Peacock, Paul Motian departed for good, going on to develop "in more avant-garde contexts the freedom that he had experienced with the trio," according to Pettinger. But as Motian later told Ethan Iverson, he left because he was bored.

BY 1965, JOHN S. WILSON HAD HAD ENOUGH OF BILL EVANS. SELF-INVOLVED was bad enough; anodyne was a bridge too far. "The more I hear of Evans," the critic wrote in the July 15 *DownBeat*, the more I become convinced that the propagation of the Evans mystique must be one of the major con jobs of recent years. Evans' performances . . . are clean and polished, but they neither seize nor hold the attention; not mine, anyhow. There is a self-effacing quality about Evans' playing that makes the whole thing slip away from a listener so that steady listening has to be a deliberate, directed effort. This is great jazz? It's more like superior background music, music that forms a pleasant atmospheric setting but does not distract. There's nothing wrong with this sort of music, and Evans does it very well. But it scarcely seems the thing that jazz cults are based on. Still, Evans has managed to do it.

This was strong language—Wilson didn't say *cocktail music*, but he didn't have to—and there was a predictable flurry of heated reader mail on the subject, both pro Evans and con. And yet in the two and a half years since Wilson's first pan of the pianist, an awful lot of history had happened. The sixties were fast becoming the Sixties, jazz's audience was disappearing, and Bill Evans had sunk deeper and deeper into his addiction—which he was less and less able to sequester from his music. In early 1966 Chuck Israels left the trio, to "pursue his studies in arranging and composition . . . [but also] finding the pianist's drug use increasingly hard to tolerate." He was replaced soon afterward by the twenty-one-year-old Eddie Gomez, who would stay with Evans for the next eleven years.

THAT FEBRUARY, AFTER A SERIES OF STROKES, EVANS'S FATHER DIED. Shortly afterward, Evans composed a requiem for solo piano, "In Memory of His Father, Harry L. Evans, 1891–1966."

Of the man who was gentle and easygoing when sober, but raging and abusive when drunk, Bill Evans chose to remember only the good things. "The stories he shared with me about his dad were very upbeat," his late-in-life girlfriend Laurie Verchomin told me. "He didn't have any stories about his dad beating his wife, or beating [Bill and Harry]. The stories were all about how his dad was an entrepreneur who created this driving range, and they all worked in it together, as a family."

ONE ARGUMENT SAYS THAT OF THIS BOOK'S THREE SUBJECTS, BILL EVANS showed the least musical growth after *Kind of Blue*. Many, like the music writer Steve Silberman, are in agreement. "Over the decades," he wrote, "as illustrious sidemen like Eddie Gomez valiantly tried to fill the hole that LaFaro had left, Evans settled into a set of mannerisms and personal clichés that still dazzled his audiences but ultimately stultified his creative growth."

"He just stayed and played it safe, you know," Jack DeJohnette told me. "I think he was capable of much more than he did. But he fell into a kind of a pattern—a format of playing. You know, the tunes change but the approach was the same."

Dave Liebman told me a story about a college concert he and the pianist Richie Beirach played in the late seventies, opposite Evans and his final accompanists, the drummer Joe LaBarbera and bassist Marc Johnson. "Me and Richie used to play 'All Blues,' but we'd tilt it pretty modern," Liebman said. "We go backstage, and Bill's sitting there with Joe and Marc, and he goes, 'That was an interesting version, gentlemen.'

"We didn't know if he was being positive or negative. But then Richie asked him a great question, about the two opening chords of 'So What.' Those chords are voiced in a certain way—fourths—which had really rarely been used in jazz. Scriabin used them. The classical guys were way ahead of the game. And Bill is the guy who played the chords—I don't think he got those voicings from Miles. He did it himself. But he never pursued that. McCoy pursued it. McCoy's whole language was based on that voicing.

"So the question that Richie asked was, 'Why did you not pursue that,

Bill? You invented it.' And Bill said, 'It wasn't lyrical enough.' And he was right. Fourths are not lyrical like thirds. Great answer. I use it for teaching, to show that when you're playing, you can't create everything for nothing. You've got to sacrifice something."

As for free jazz, Evans's instrument itself militated against it: "Keith Jarrett said that you can't really play free on a piano," Ethan Iverson told me. "And I knew what he meant. He said it's the lever [and hammer] system—there's just no way. If you listen to Albert Ayler, that gospel cry— you can't do it on the piano. Cecil [Taylor] sounds much more like European classical music that's very disjunct. Even Paul Bley, who could play *very* out—Paul has this lyrical quality."

And yet Loren Schoenberg wondered of Evans, "Would one say that he grew less, or maybe, just in the context of what he did, did he grow exponentially in that one furrow?"

Pettinger wrote, of the pianist's February 1966 New York concert debut at Town Hall (he played solo, in trio, and with a full orchestra): "Evans had by this juncture created an entirely individual harmonic language as estimable in its thoroughness of working as those of, say, Gershwin, Messiaen, or the neoclassical Stravinsky. It was based on the tonal system of the popular song and had evolved at its own painstakingly slow pace, its creator never in a hurry to leap ahead, always content to add voicings and intensify harmony step by step, consolidating all the way."

The pianist and bandleader Jon Batiste concurs. "I would argue that of the three [Miles, Coltrane, and Evans], Bill Evans got the deepest into his conception," he told me. "Miles was always changing—which, I think, means that instead of going deeper into one thing, he explores it, implies everything that needs to be implied, for everyone else to then take it and continue it. You see everyone who left his band, especially the band with Herbie and Ron and Wayne—they took his conceptions of fusion, harmony, rhythm, improvisation, impressionism—all these were concepts that Miles would expose first. Then he moves on to the next thing.

"I would argue that Trane, in a similar way, has phases. He gets into something and explores it, and gets to the edges of it, and then once he's at the edges of it, it evolves into something else completely. Whereas Bill Evans, conceptually, has been dealing with the same root of his conception from the beginning.

"The other thing that I would say about Bill is if you listen to a record like *Conversations with Myself*, when he's overdubbing and playing, Trane didn't ever do that.* Miles didn't ever do that. To me, that's as forward thinking as what you see in current hip-hop music. Overdubbing, almost sampling yourself. To me, that's probably one of the most innovative records of the later period of all three."

What did Evans himself think? Speaking to *DownBeat*'s Len Lyons in the seventies, he complained about "this preoccupation with 'who's the most modern' instead of 'who's making the most beautiful, human music.' [The most beautiful] may very well be the most modern thing as well, but to make just avant-garde the criteria has gotten to be almost a sickness, especially in jazz."

MILES WENT HIS OWN WAY, NEITHER ESCHEWING MELODY AND RHYTHM like Coltrane nor making deep harmonic explorations like Evans. He continued to explore modes and rhythms, constantly paring away notes and resisting successions of chords; he continued living in the duality between recording, where he could experiment in repertoire and approach, and live performance, where (unlike Coltrane) he felt obliged to give audiences, at least nominally, certain footholds of familiarity where material was concerned.

Between 1965 and 1966 Davis was much distracted by his constantly fragile state of health. He had barely had time to recuperate from his second hip surgery (August of '65) when he landed in the hospital yet again (January '66), this time with a liver infection—his cocaine and alcohol habits didn't help his cause—and was laid up for the first three months of

*Unless you count his overdubbed chant on *A Love Supreme*.

the year. When the quintet went out on tour again, Miles had his management book only college dates, which demanded less of him than clubs and offered fewer temptations.

In the slim window between hospitalizations, though, he made his usual Christmastime trip to Chicago, where the quintet had a two-week stand at one of his old-favorite clubs, the Plugged Nickel. There, Columbia recorded his sets on the nights of December 22 and 23, and the power and freedom of that all-time classical hydrogen bomb and switchblade band (Miles, Shorter, Hancock, Carter, and Williams) can be heard in full, fast, sometimes chaotic flight. "At the Plugged Nickel," Wayne Shorter recalled, "we were raising so much hell that when we came off we couldn't say nothing to each other."

The Complete Live at the Plugged Nickel 1965 makes for fascinating listening: while nominally the set list is full of old chestnuts—"Walkin'," "On Green Dolphin Street," "'Round Midnight," for starters, and even "So What"—Miles's treatment of them (and the band's, the players as always following the leader's almost telepathic repertoire of cues rather any explicit instructions) was anything but nostalgic. The late 1965 Davis was not only not announcing tunes, he wasn't even ending them: each number flowed into the next with no breaks.

And the numbers themselves were transformed. "So What" becomes "Flight of the Bumblebee" fast—even faster!—its inner logic changed from mellow, moody, and meditative to coked up: jumpy, even angry. Or listen to 1961's "Walkin'," from the Black Hawk recordings, next to the Plugged Nickel version, four and a half years later: the earlier edition, though considerably faster than the mid-fifties Prestige recording, sounds rather earnest and tuneful alongside 1965's, which, once an identifying statement of the melody is (quickly) dispensed with, jumps into semi-abstract territory—not quite free jazz, not quite modal, but breathtakingly quick (Williams and Carter's pulse is relentless), with Miles's trumpet lines flying up, down, and sideways like an irritable hornet, landing here, blasting off there, following a beat all his own.

The quintet's second album, *Miles Smiles*, recorded almost two years after *E.S.P.*, was meant to be a signpost: this band, this all-new sound, had Arrived. The LP contained three new numbers by Shorter, one of them, "Footprints," destined to be a classic, and one, "Circle," by Davis. There were also two lovingly Miles-ized covers of two bebop-ish hard boppers, Jimmy Heath's 1964 "Gingerbread Boy" and Eddie Harris's 1965 "Freedom Jazz Dance."

Davis's strategy was to draw a sharp line between what the band performed in concert and what it put on record: the diminished audience for live jazz craved some kind of familiarity. "At this point," Szwed writes, "[Miles] was not willing to risk cutting himself loose from his audience. He knew how far out not to go."

This didn't always sit well with the group—a collection of brilliant young artists, each filled with musical ideas of his own, each having led a band or destined to be a leader. In his memoir Miles admitted that merely cycling through his playbook night after night was hard on his players. He confessed that it was difficult to do all the collective work necessary for preparing an album, then not play any of the record's tunes in concert. "Instead of developing the new music live which we were playing on records," he said, "we found ways to make the old music sound as new as the new music we were recording." One way was to play the old music faster and faster—but "after a while the speed really limited what we could do with them because they definitely couldn't get no faster than what they were."

And just speeding up the tempos didn't always satisfy the players' creativity. Rebellion began to set in. Shorter was sometimes drunk on the stand. Williams, who was in effect coleader, would now and then refuse to play behind a bandmate's solo if said bandmate hadn't taken the drummer's musical advice. And Herbie Hancock, filled with harmonic ideas, was baffled: Herbie said, "I don't know what to play no more," Shorter remembered.

> So Miles says, "Don't play nothin'. Only play when you feel like it." So we'd be playing a piece of music, and Herbie's sitting there with his hands in his lap . . . then all of a sudden he'd play one sound, and Miles said, "That one sound you made was a bitch." So everybody saw something happening . . . and we began playing songs without chords.

In the spring of 1967, while Ron Carter was fulfilling another obligation, the bassist Buster Williams sat in with the band on live dates. He remembered opening sets with the whimsical "Agitation," from *E.S.P.*, "the only thing that resembled a melody," Williams said.

> From there on, it was out there. I listened to Tony, and when I found that I couldn't figure out anything from Tony, I listened to Herbie. But Herbie was laying out half the time. Wayne just seemed to float on the periphery of everything, and Miles would just make his statement and go to the bar. I didn't know what I was supposed to do, man, except play the bass. . . .
>
> I learned how to keep a structure in mind and play changes so loosely that you can play for some time without people knowing

whether the structure is played or not, but then hit on certain points to indicate that you have been playing the structure all the time. When you hear these points being played, you just say, "Wow! It's like the Invisible Man. You see him here and then you don't. Then all of a sudden you see him over there and then you see him over here."

But it was the audience that was disappearing. By the latter half of the sixties, it seemed as if the Miles Davis George Avakian had envisioned—the artist who would sell millions of records on the strength of his ballads—had vanished into the past, the victim of Miles's endless creative restlessness. He continued to live in the style to which he'd become accustomed, but his records—after *Miles Smiles* came 1967's *Sorcerer* and 1968's *Nefertiti*—were now selling in the tens, rather than hundreds, of thousands. He had taken a big advance from Columbia for a promised new album with Gil Evans that kept not materializing; meanwhile, he kept making empty promises and playing for time, and management was concerned. On October 13, 1967, Teo Macero (now back in Davis's good graces after the *Quiet Nights* debacle) wrote a memo to Columbia's new president, the thirty-five-year-old Clive Davis: "The other day I discussed the possibility of doing a Miles Davis album with Miles and, as of the moment, it's only a possibility. They [Davis and Gil Evans] have been working on this possibility for three and a half years."

Clive Davis, who would soon be purging a number of old-style jazz musicians from the label's roster, handwrote a reply on the memo: "He is one of the few giants who appeal to the youth—we must keep after him."

ON HIS RELEASE FROM THE HOSPITAL IN EARLY 1966, MILES HAD TAKEN to strolling through nearby Riverside Park, sometimes with a friend—Dan Morgenstern, with whom he'd become close, lived just around the corner—and sometimes alone. On one of his strolls, he spotted Cicely Tyson, whom he'd met once or twice before: she took the traditional masculine role, asking, in effect, if he came there often. Slightly intimidated by her intense gaze, her "inner-burning fire," the man whose own dark gaze had cowed so many told her the truth: he walked every Thursday. She began showing up when he walked; they began seeing each other steadily.

By Miles's account, Tyson took the lead in their growing relationship; he resisted at first, claiming that after Frances's departure he felt empty inside. But she was "patient and persistent," and soon, by his account, he fell under her spell: "After a while she was all inside me and then she was all inside my business, too (but she won't never tell you none of hers)." Being inside his business seems to have been less about his financial dealings—he had Harold Lovett for that—than it was about taking care of an alarmingly frail forty-year-old man whose body was often prey to his worst instincts. (For one thing, she made him give up hard liquor for beer—his version of moderation after his liver troubles.) Thus began a sometimes tumultuous twenty-three-year relationship, on and off, including an eight-year marriage from 1981 to 1989. It was a bond that, Szwed says, "literally kept him alive during various illnesses."

DAVIS FREELY ADMITTED THAT HE'D LEARNED A GREAT DEAL FROM THE second great quintet's players in the three years they'd been working together—as all the players later spoke of how much they'd learned from him. He and his band of young geniuses had taken jazz to a new pinnacle. But, Wallace Roney told me, "as supersonic as the stuff they had been doing, they played a concert opposite Cannonball Adderley's band. And Miles said, 'We played our *asses* off. And people *loved* it. Then Cannonball got up there with Joe Zawinul, and electric piano, and he started playing 'Country Joe'"—Roney laughed—"I think he meant 'Mercy, Mercy, Mercy.'

"And he said the people went *off.* The people just—Cannonball drew the people *in.* I think up to that point, if they were on the same bill, Miles would've been able to take it from Cannonball. But *that* night, something about Joe Zawinul and 'Country Joe' and the audience was, 'Yeah!' Miles paid *attention* to that.

"And then they did a gig—an Andy Warhol party. And it was Joe Cocker, Janis Joplin, Rahsaan Roland Kirk—so the jazz and rock guys. Miles didn't show up that night. And while Tony and them was playing, Joe Cocker was over on the side, snorting coke and screwing girls. And Tony started telling Herbie, 'We need to get on *this* scene.'

"So then Tony start telling Miles, 'Why don't we get a guitar player in the band and start playing on the *rock* side.' Miles said, 'What? What? I don't want to hear that shit.' But Tony was his young protégé, you know, he wants to keep Tony, and Tony keeps talking about it."

And Miles kept thinking about it. He says in his memoir that whenever he played Chicago he liked going to South Side blues clubs on Monday nights to hear Muddy Waters and "the sound of the $1.50 drums and the harmonicas and the two-chord blues. . . . I knew I had to get some of what [Waters] was doing up in my music . . . because what we had been doing was just getting really abstracted."

AT A LATE DECEMBER RECORDING SESSION, HERBIE HANCOCK WAS UN-pleasantly surprised to find an electric, rather than an acoustic, piano waiting for him. "But Miles insisted," Szwed writes, "and when Herbie sat down at the [instrument], his reservations began to vanish as he found he could now be heard even over Tony Williams' drums."

The jazz guitarist Bucky Pizzarelli appeared at an early-January session; then, four days later, the up-and-coming George Benson, having been sweet-talked by Miles into sitting in, took his place. Benson was flattered to have been asked but flummoxed by Miles's methods: the trumpeter "came . . . played three or four notes, packed up his horn, and left." Same thing the next day, and the next, and the next. Benson told Miles he hated taking the money if they weren't recording; Miles assured him they would. They began. Benson wanted to solo; Miles wanted him to just double the bass line. Meanwhile, Williams—"graduate of the Berklee College of Music and a genius," Benson put it astringently—kept telling the guitarist what chords to play. Who was in charge? What were they all playing?

"So then Miles starts to get guitars on his record," Wallace Roney said, "but Tony was, like, 'No, we're not talking about [Pizzarelli or Benson]— we're talking about Jimi Hendrix.' So then Miles marries Betty, and Betty's talking about Jimi Hendrix, and now Miles wants to do a record that his wife's gonna buy. And he also wants to keep a band that Tony'll stay in—see, Tony's threatening to leave now to start *his* band. So that's how it evolved."

Betty was Betty Mabry, just twenty-three when Miles met her, and she was a fizzing, sparkling blend of style and substance: tall and long-legged and stunning, with a big, proud Afro, she was a scenester all over Manhattan, a friend to Sly Stone and Jimi Hendrix, a singer-songwriter (she'd written "Uptown" for the Chambers Brothers' bestselling LP *The Time Has Come*), a fashion designer who'd modeled for *Ebony, Seventeen, Jet*, and *Glamour*. Miles fell hard, and that was the end, for now, of his ambivalent romance with Cicely Tyson.

He was over forty now, and felt it. And Tyson was almost two years older, and here was this gorgeous, fiery young creature, and a chance at rebirth, and he grabbed it. She took him downtown for a wardrobe makeover; he began wearing collarless shirts and bell-bottom jeans. He went back to Gleason's Gym, stopped smoking. On his arm, she introduced him to her pals Jimi (whose music enchanted and baffled Davis) and Sly (whose uniquely exuberant cross of rock and R&B Miles adored). Rock 'n' roll was filling arenas; Miles's quintet was playing to half-empty clubs. It was time for a change. In January and May he recorded a new LP, *Miles in the Sky* (both the nakedly Beatles-referent title and the psychedelic cover were urged on him by Columbia), with Carter—reluctantly—on electric bass, Hancock on electric piano on one track, Davis's "Stuff," and George Benson on "Paraphernalia."

The concluding tune, "Country Son," was a gallimaufry of styles and tempi, much of it dominated by Williams's clear-the-decks drumming.

Was *Miles in the Sky* jazz? Rock? Something in between, or some strange hybrid of the two? Labels didn't matter to Miles: this was the music he wanted to hear at that moment. But labels did matter to music writers, and so the music they were soon calling fusion had officially begun.

"I WAS TELLING HERBIE THE OTHER DAY," MILES SAID AROUND THIS TIME, "we're not going to play the blues anymore. Let the white folks have the blues. They got 'em, so they can keep 'em. Play something else."

THAT SPRING, WHILE THE QUINTET WAS TOURING ON THE WEST COAST, Leonard Feather popped by Miles's Hollywood hotel suite for a quick interview. He was horror-struck by what he saw there: "I found strewn around the room records or tape cartridges by James Brown, Dionne Warwick, Tony Bennett, the Byrds, Aretha Franklin, and Fifth Dimension. Not a single jazz instrumental."

Dim and rigid as always, Feather simply failed to understand what was staring him in the face. Why should Miles listen to anyone else play jazz? He *was* jazz.

IN JUNE OF 1968, ON THE RECOMMENDATION OF EDDIE GOMEZ, JACK DE-Johnette joined Bill Evans, the new trio appearing first in a stand at Greenwich Village's Top of the Gate, then traveling to Switzerland for the second annual Montreux Jazz Festival. DeJohnette, who'd been playing (along with the pianist Keith Jarrett and bassist Cecil McBee) in what was being touted as the hippest young band around, a progressive quartet led by the tenor saxophonist and flutist Charles Lloyd, brought a new kind of energy to Evans, a youthful dynamism immediately apparent in the group's opening number at Montreux, "One for Helen." The pretty tune, a tribute to Keane, unspooled at an almost frantic pace: spurred along by the DeJohnette's ratatat sticks and insistent ride cymbal and Gomez's galloping bass line, Evans played at the kind of clip he'd rarely exhibited since George Russell's "Concerto for Billy the Kid," a dozen years earlier.

This was a new Evans, and he told anyone who asked that his new drummer was inspiring him. "As a matter of fact," Evans said at the time, "he's getting me off my musical ass."

Asked a half century later what Evans might have meant by this, De-Johnette laughed a little. "All I know," he said, "is that he used to lean over when he played, and then when I was playing with him he sat up. He sat straight up."

Might cocaine have had anything to do with his new posture? The drummer hesitated for a second, proceeding with care. "Sometimes he would rush tempos," DeJohnette said. "But other than that he was okay."

Pettinger thought differently. "The lower the head fell," he wrote, "the better Evans played."

THAT SAME JUNE, WHILE THE COUNTRY WAS BURNING AMID VIETNAM War protests and the Martin Luther King and Bobby Kennedy assassinations, Miles began making the serenely beautiful album that would become *Filles de Kilimanjaro*. Relations within the band were anything but serene. When Herbie Hancock missed the second recording session, in September—he'd gotten sick on his honeymoon in Brazil—Miles fired him. On Tony Williams's recommendation, Davis hired Chick Corea, whom Williams had gigged with in Boston. Around the same time, Ron Carter told Miles he didn't want to play electric bass anymore; Davis promptly replaced him with the young Englishman Dave Holland. And Williams, battling with Miles over several things, especially Davis's wish to add a second drummer to the band (see: Coltrane/Elvin Jones/Rashied Ali), was edging toward the door.

Meanwhile, the warm friendship between Miles and Gil Evans had continued through time and distractions, and, somewhat similarly to the way he had enlisted Bill Evans's harmonic expertise on *Kind of Blue*, Miles sought Gil's help in building the new album. And there was another similarity to the earlier record: all credit therein (and most, if not all, of the money therefrom) would go to Miles Davis.

Gil was intimately involved in shaping and creating *Filles de Kilimanjaro*. He arranged bass lines, voiced horns, and cocomposed (without credit on the album or subsequent reissues) "Petits machins (Little Stuff)," a brightly nervous up-tempo piece in 11/4 time. Gil shared Miles's love of Jimi Hendrix, and helped Davis adapt Hendrix's "The Wind Cries Mary" into the soft, pensive, and beautiful "Mademoiselle Mabry," a tribute to Miles's new young love.

Davis and Mabry married on September 30, 1968, in Chicago, with his brother and sister as witnesses. Though the marriage would only last a year, it invigorated him and helped set him and his music on a new course.

"Tony [Williams] was in the band for six months while I was there," Chick Corea told me. "Then Jack [DeJohnette] came in and everything changed. Jack was wild and loose, and Miles was trying more tunes with kind of a backbeat. And not only were the music and grooves changing, but a lot of stuff was changing. Before I knew it, we were all wearing dashikis and headbands."

At the very moment *Filles de Kilimanjaro* was released in early 1969—with, per Davis's stipulation, a striking double image of the beauteous Betty Mabry, by the fashion photographer Hiro, on the cover—Miles was railing publicly at Columbia "for not having more black promotion men and women." *The Washington Post* took up the outcry, quoting an anonymous Black source as saying, "The trouble with a company like Columbia is that when they get a good black artist they don't promote him. And they spend very little money with the black media. . . ."

But the special effort the Columbia promotion department put into alerting rock publications to the album ("*Filles* should interest rock buyers and ads should be placed in the underground newspapers," wrote the president of the Jazz Division in a memo to his staff) paid off handsomely. The *Rolling Stone* review was ecstatic: "No amount of track-by-track description here can begin to convey the beauty and intensity," it read. "There are five songs, but really they fit together as five expressions of the same basic piece, one sustained work." The sustained mood was enhanced by the flowing transitions from one track to the next, and the fact that all five tunes were in the same key (F). And a straight line can almost certainly be drawn between the *Rolling Stone* piece and the incense-and-reefer-perfumed dorm room in which this white boy first heard *Filles de Kilimanjaro.*

TEO MACERO WAS A FORMIDABLE MUSICAL FIGURE IN HIS OWN RIGHT: a Juilliard-trained conductor and composer of atonal and third-stream music, a jazz saxophonist, a cofounder with Charles Mingus of the Jazz Composers Workshop, and, after joining Columbia Records in 1957, the producer (and, often, arranger) of hundreds of albums of popular, classical, and jazz music by artists as diverse as Johnny Mathis, Leonard Bernstein, and Thelonious Monk. He was also genial and un-self-important, with an easy sense of humor that bespoke his upstate New York, Italian American roots.

Jazz was Macero's specialty and first love: he produced Brubeck's 1959 megahit *Time Out*; he signed Mingus, Monk, and the guitarist Charlie Byrd to Columbia; and he'd stepped in to complete Irving Townsend's producing work on *Kind of Blue* after Townsend was transferred to the West Coast. This was the beginning of his close, sometimes turbulent professional relationship with Miles Davis.

With the introduction of magnetic tape to the record industry after World War II, producers began to deploy tape splicing as a method of improving recordings. In short order, avant-garde composers adopted the method for their own purposes, using splicing, looping, and sampling to create original compositions. It wasn't long before Macero, an avant-gardist at heart, started making tape-splicing a key part of his record-producing toolbox, and Miles quickly became an eager participant. "Teo . . . started to splice tape together on *Porgy and Bess* and then on *Sketches of Spain*," Davis remembered, "and he did it on [*Someday My Prince Will Come*], too. We post-recorded solos on those albums, with

Trane and me doing some extra horn work. It was an interesting process that was done frequently after that."

More and more frequently, and more and more interestingly, too.

THE SESSIONS FOR THE ALBUM THAT WOULD BE CALLED *BITCHES BREW* began on August 19, 1969, the day after the end of the four-day music festival that was originally billed as an Aquarian Exposition in White Lake, New York, but came to be known as Woodstock. Four hundred thousand young people had slogged through sporadic rain and mud and inadequate sanitary facilities and drug freak-outs to hear thirty-two acts, from Joan Baez to Jefferson Airplane, Santana to the Grateful Dead, Sly and the Family Stone to Jimi Hendrix. "That many people at a concert makes everybody go crazy, and especially people who make records," Miles said. "The only thing on their minds is, How can we sell records to that many people all the time? If we haven't been doing that, then how can we do it?"

But this was also on Miles's mind. He'd continued to ask for and receive significant advances on royalties, he was in considerable debt to Columbia, and the sales of his new LPs, even when they charted, were stuck in the mid-five figures—not enough to recoup what he owed, and a fraction of the Woodstockian numbers the label's rock artists were racking up. To this end he had been browbeating Clive Davis—and, apparently, scaring him a little. "He has a raspy, low voice," the record executive recalled:

> —a fiery whisper that conveys heat over the telephone while you are straining to find out how much money he wants. He is spellbinding, and he can talk. . . . Then one day Miles called me to complain about his record sales. He was tired of low sales, and angry about it. Blood, Sweat and Tears and Chicago had borrowed enormously from him—and sold millions. These young *white* artists—he was in a rather militant frame of mind—were cashing in while he was struggling from advance to advance. If

you stop calling me a *jazz* man, he said at one point, and just sell
me alongside these other people, I'll sell more.

It was remarkable: over fifty years in America, the very word "jazz" had
gone from sex, scandal, and sensation to the low-price bins at record
stores.

It was time for an even bigger change.

Miles had booked Columbia Studio B, on East Fifty-second Street
(the final session for *Filles de Kilimanjaro* was the last time he would ever
record at Thirtieth Street), for three days, August 19 to the 21st, from
10:00 a.m. to 1:00 p.m. Davis, Shorter, Corea, Holland, and DeJohnette
all showed up promptly the first morning, but this time there were even
more musicians: Miles had hired a bass clarinetist, a second electric pianist (Joe Zawinul), an electric bassist, and three additional percussionists.

He and the band had been working out three new numbers while on
the road that summer: at Newport in July (that year's Jazz Festival also included Led Zeppelin, Sly and the Family Stone, and Jethro Tull, among
other rock bands, a decision George Wein would later regret), they'd
played two of them, "Miles Runs the Voodoo Down" and "Sanctuary."
This was not the dreamy music of his previous LP, *In a Silent Way*: the new
songs were harsh, spiky, urgent—redolent of the darkly charged atmosphere before a summer thunderstorm.

He had these tunes for the new sessions (the third was "Spanish Key"),
but there were no detailed charts: as before, Miles had sketched out some
chords and rhythms beforehand, but what he wanted from his musicians
was spontaneity. Improvisation, at the highest level. And he wanted everything they came up with: for the first time, he had Macero run the recording equipment throughout each session. Miles conducted from the
studio floor, walking around to each player and gesturing for louder or
softer, now and then whispering an enigmatic word or two. Grooves
started and stopped, then started again. The sessions, Chick Corea remembered, "were kind of wispy, they just passed right by. The recordings

themselves, from my remembrance, felt more like rehearsals. . . . There's not much romance or drama to it for me."

This is not how Miles remembered it. "That was a great recording session, man," he said, "and we didn't have any problems as I can remember. It was just like one of them old-time jam sessions we used to have up at Minton's back in the old bebop days. Everybody was excited when we all left there each day."

Did Davis know ahead of time how the album would sound? Unsurprisingly, he claimed that he did. Not writing detailed arrangements ahead of time was "not because I didn't know what I wanted; I knew that what I wanted would come out of a process and not some prearranged shit." And whether he felt certain of the process or not—and even by his own account there was a great deal of uncertainty in Miles's molten core—he knew how important it was to *seem* certain. Contrary to custom, Betty was in the studio for the entire date (Max Roach was present, too): Davis the leader would have wanted to demonstrate leadership for his young wife.

And Miles the great artist wanted complete ownership of *Bitches Brew*. "Some people have written that doing *Bitches Brew* was Clive Davis's or Teo Macero's idea," he said, striking a familiar note. "That's a lie, because they didn't have nothing to do with none of it. Again, it was white people trying to give some credit to other white people where it wasn't deserved because the record became a breakthrough concept, very innovative."

Doing the album may not have been Clive Davis's or Teo Macero's idea, but as a great editor, Macero had a great deal to do with making *Bitches Brew* what it finally became. Working from almost nine hours of tape, he, the recording engineer Ray Moore, and Miles mixed and spliced for more than a month, in a process that might have impressed Karlheinz Stockhausen. The contrast between this LP and *Kind of Blue*, which contained exactly one tape splice, could not have been starker. "With all that music, what we know as *Bitches Brew* could have been assembled twenty different ways," the producer Bob Belden said on the occasion of the

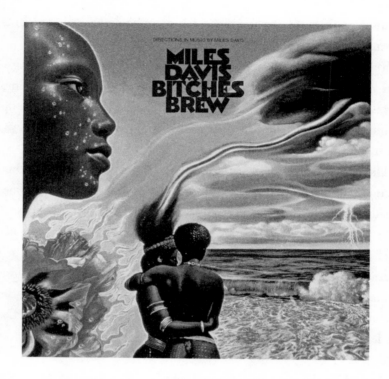

album's reissue almost thirty years later. "And Teo found logical, and musically interesting, ways to present it."

Months before the album's release in March 1970, Macero sent advance tapes of it to Ralph J. Gleason, arguably Miles's biggest fan in the music media. Gleason—who would write the gushing, e. e. cummings-style liner notes for *Bitches Brew*—mock-criticized: "No wonder jazz is dead, guys like you are killing it." Teo answered: "I may have killed jazz, but I have established a new kind of music. What have you done lately?"

FROM ITS DARING-AT-THE-TIME TITLE (IT'S QUAINT AND RATHER SWEET in these days of routinely scabrous hip-hop to think that there was serious consternation at Columbia about the phrase *Bitches Brew*, but worried memos flew around Columbia before the title was approved) to the trippy, ominous cover art by the Israeli painter Mati Klarwein, which seemed to speak of both racial pride and racial strife, to the dark, echoey urgency, the "brilliant and infectious jungle-like chaotic energy" of the music itself, the album commanded instant—and predictably mixed—attention around the country. "A double-record release of mostly pretentious and dull music," wrote a San Antonio reviewer. "Ralph J. Gleason's stream-of-consciousness jacket notes hail this as a new concept that will change the world. We'll see."

But a long syndicated piece by the Associated Press writer Mary Campbell cast Miles as the savior of a music that had become moribund. "After swing came bebop," she wrote,

> and after bebop came cool or progressive jazz, which became more and more intellectual and introverted, pursuing an ever-narrowing path that fewer and fewer listeners were interested in following. Jazz was said to be dead and cool jazz was said to have forced it beyond its endurance and killed it. . . .
>
> But a lot of jazz people, in and outside the business, have been waiting for jazz to progress from progressive, to prove that cool did not cool the whole thing. And we may just be standing at that moment. Hopefully, thankfully, we are.
>
> Columbia has just released a two-LP record set by Miles Davis called "Bitches Brew" that is terribly exciting.
>
> It's a new direction, an ongoing from the cool that sounds like a widening of the path. Those who liked the cool should love it and from the open, welcoming sound of it, a whole lot of new listeners should join in.

A whole lot of listeners did join in. *Bitches Brew*, wrote Columbia Records historian Gary Marmorstein, "charted higher and longer than any other Davis album—or, for that matter, any other jazz record of the period. The Mati Klarwein–[Columbia art director] John Berg cover, its voodoo themes rendered in bright arresting colors, seemed to be displayed in every record store you walked into."

Was *Bitches Brew* jazz? "The whole album leaves you wildly enthusiastic that jazz is alive and back on the track," Mary Campbell wrote. But the grumpy purist Stanley Crouch begged to differ. "Beginning with the 1969 *In a Silent Way*," he wrote,

> Davis's sound was mostly lost among electronic instruments, inside a long maudlin piece of droning wallpaper music. A year later, with *Bitches Brew*, Davis was firmly on the path of the sellout. It sold more than any other Davis album, and fully launched jazz-rock with its multiple keyboards, electronic guitars, static beats, and clutter.

When Miles played parts of the album over the phone for his brother, Vernon Davis said, "I don't care for it." When Miles asked Vernon why, his brother told him that a woman he worked with at the IRS had always bought every record Miles made, but, she said, "Now he done lost us."

DAVIS WAS KEENLY AWARE OF COLUMBIA MANAGEMENT'S UNHAPPINESS about continually advancing him money that he wasn't earning back. "What they didn't understand," Miles said,

> was that I wasn't prepared to be a memory yet, wasn't prepared to be listed only on Columbia's so-called classical list. I had seen the way to the future with my music, and I was going for it like I had always done. Not for Columbia and their record sales, and not for trying to get to some young white record buyers. I was going for it for myself, for what I wanted and needed in my own music. *I* wanted to change course, *had* to change course for me to continue to believe in and love what I was playing.

And, it goes almost without saying, to continue to make the kind of money he was used to making. But when Clive Davis suggested he could expand his audience by starting to play big rock venues like the Fillmore East in New York and the Electric Factory in Philadelphia, Miles erupted. "He wasn't going to play for 'those fucking long-haired white kids,'" he told Columbia's president. "He would be 'ripped off'; [rock promoter] Bill Graham wouldn't pay him enough *money*. . . . He wanted 'off the fucking label!'"

He would quickly adjust his thinking.

In March 1970 Miles and the quintet, with the addition of the Brazilian percussionist Airto Moreira, opened for Neil Young and Crazy Horse, and the Steve Miller Band, at the Fillmore East. A month later Davis and the same band opened for the Grateful Dead at San Francisco's Fillmore West. At first, by his account, the long-haired white kids in the audience were walking around and talking while the sextet played, but then they started to listen. "The *Bitches Brew* shit . . . really blew them out," Miles recalled.

"The gigs I did for Bill [Graham] during this time were good for expanding my audience," he said. "We were playing to all kinds of different people. The crowds that were going to see Laura Nyro and the Grateful Dead were all mixed up with some of the people who were coming to hear me. So it was good for everybody."

Meanwhile, thanks in good part to Miles's widening audience, and to the delight of Columbia brass, *Bitches Brew* kept flying off the shelves. The album would go on to sell over a million copies, second only, among jazz recordings, to *Kind of Blue*.

SOON AFTER CHARLES LLOYD'S BAND BROKE UP, KEITH JARRETT JOINED Miles. He played alongside Chick Corea until Corea and Dave Holland left at the end of 1970 (to form their own short-lived quartet, Circle), then stayed on through 1971. Jarrett revered Miles but hated the music the group was playing. Nor did he have much respect for the other musicians. "The funk and the non-knowledge of the past was beginning to take a toll on the band," he said.

Miles and I were like a duo with a group who had no idea of what they were doing. He did get back to the old tunes once in a Boston club and it was terrible. I was the only one who knew them. The bass player was playing notes like he didn't know how to play the bass. The rest of the band were aliens. [Miles] was in bad shape.

———

THE BEATLES BROKE UP IN 1970. JIMI HENDRIX DIED, AT AGE TWENTY-seven, in September of that year (Miles flew to Seattle to attend the funeral, a big gesture for a man who hadn't gone to see his own mother off); Janis Joplin passed the next month, at the same age. Jim Morrison, also twenty-seven, went out the door the following July. While rock absorbed these body blows, the thing called fusion flourished: Tony Williams Lifetime began in 1969; Joe Zawinul and Wayne Shorter formed Weather Report in 1970; during the next year, John McLaughlin created the Mahavishnu Orchestra and Herbie Hancock started Mwandishi; after Circle, Chick Corea went solo for a while before beginning Return to Forever in 1972. These bands had pulse and excitement and even, in many cases, memorable tunes: they kept alive the idea of jazz (or something like it) as entertainment.

All Miles's children, and all selling more records than Miles.

IN 1971 A STUDENT INTERVIEWER ON THE COLUMBIA UNIVERSITY RADIO station WKCR-FM asked Charles Mingus what he thought of Miles's new music.

Mingus: Who?

Interviewer: Miles Davis.

Mingus: Never heard of him. I knew a guy by that name who used to play with Bird, but I thought he was dead.

———

IN EARLY 1970, BILL EVANS, ON HIS WAY TO PERFORM IN THE SOVIET Union, was busted at John F. Kennedy International Airport when heroin was found in his suitcase. He was jailed but not charged, thanks, according to Laurie Verchomin, to a political connection of Ellaine's. As a result (and as a condition of his release), Evans and Ellaine stopped using heroin and entered an experimental methadone program at Rockefeller University, turning over a new leaf as the new decade began.

Methadone, a synthetic opioid usually administered orally, relieves heroin cravings and reduces or eliminates withdrawal symptoms. It itself is addictive, but, under carefully controlled maintenance therapy, provides a hygienic (societally as well as medically) substitute for all the ills associated with heroin, including the many hazards of intravenous injection. On the program, Pettinger writes,

> [Evans's] lifestyle improved beyond recognition . . . friends and fans observed a changed personality, almost a metamorphosis. The frequently sullen, withdrawn, and unapproachable figure of old manifested a new frankness in acknowledging the people around him. Likewise on the bandstand, that apparent indifference to audience presence was replaced by a smile and a nod, albeit reserved, toward the listeners' welcome.

But, Verchomin told me, methadone treatment "kind of killed [Bill and Ellaine's] relationship, 'cause it just wasn't the same. And Bill wanted to have a family, and she was infertile because they had been junkies for eleven years."

Junkies in love: the tragic romance of heroin—the scoring, the shooting up, the incomparable high, and the anxious urgency of scoring again; the dark inside humor of it all—was the center of their life together, and now the center had fallen away.

Eddie Gomez, Eliot Zigmund, Bill Evans. Seventies.

FUSION HELD NO TEMPTATIONS FOR BILL EVANS. UNLIKE MILES, HE HAD no need for Lamborghinis or leopard-skin coats. Thanks to his reputation and Helen Keane, he had steady if not highly remunerative work in jazz clubs—and a regular concert schedule in Europe, where jazz, and Evans, were revered. He was used to living on the cheap, and out of a suitcase.

The seventies did have their effect on Evans: the junkie-professor look disappeared along with his heroin habit (as did his severely deteriorated teeth: while the pianist was touring in London, an English dentist and jazz fan provided him with a full set of dentures, gratis). He put on weight and grew a resplendent mane, then a mustache, then a full beard. The shirt collars also grew, as did an unfortunate proclivity for patterned polyester.

Musical growth was another matter. Due in no small part to the advent of the electronic bass pickup, Eddie Gomez had become, by some accounts, the most venturesome member of the trio. This was the creative standstill for the pianist that many critics have pointed out, along with the rise of the domineering bass solo that some observers have deplored.

Evans didn't seem to mind. Overseas adulation continued to buoy him: packed theaters in Great Britain, Scandinavia, and Europe fell into an awed hush—so unlike the atmosphere in American clubs—when he sat down at the piano. On the trio's first tour in Japan in early 1973, "We . . . arrived to television cameras, banners, flowers, and everything but a marching band," Helen Keane recalled. "Everyone seemed to know who Bill was—from bellboys to waiters to giggling girls with autograph books—and as always, he handled each situation with genuine charm. I think one of the most endearing qualities of Bill's personality was the almost childlike pleasure he got from the star treatment he received wherever he went."

Soon after returning to the States, Evans played a gig at a new club, Concerts by the Sea, in Redondo Beach, California, the latest venture of Howard Rumsey, the founder of Hermosa Beach's Lighthouse. There he met a young cocktail waitress named Nenette Zazzara, and they were both struck by a bolt of sexual electricity. Zazzara was honey haired and full bodied, with wide-set eyes that seemed to contain more than a hint of danger. She was lush, sensual, provocative: everything Ellaine wasn't—including a potential mother to Evans's child. (Zazzara was the single mother of a young daughter, Maxine.) She wasn't much of a jazz fan, but she loved his intelligence and dry sense of humor, and she especially loved him in bed. After a short but intense romance, he proposed and she said yes.

On returning to New York, he confessed all to Ellaine. For twelve years they had shared everything, including needles (and pain), subsisting on saltines and milk with Hershey's chocolate syrup (him) and Häagen-Dazs coffee ice cream (her). They'd lain next to each other in freezing apartments where the electricity had been turned off, an extension cord run out to the hall powering the TV, had spent Bill's earnings on heroin and candles and food for the twin Siamese cats she joked she had given birth to, Harmony and Melody. In some ways she had become more of a doting mother to him than a lover. At first she seemed accepting of Evans's moving on, but when he returned to California, Ellaine withdrew all the money from their bank account, flew to Las Vegas and gambled it away, then came back to New York and threw herself in front of a subway train. Helen Keane had to identify the tiny body.

Evans and Nenette were married that August, in a festive ceremony at the Plaza Hotel.

MILES WAS IN THE STUDIO OFTEN DURING THE REST OF 1972, AND PLAYED several concerts with a semi-electric nonet that included sitar and tabla. The music continued in the vein of *Bitches Brew*—electric, echoey, urgent, or doomy. On songs such as "Ife," "Chieftain," and "Rated X," Miles continued to work in brief phrases rather than solos. Often he played organ rather than trumpet. He'd been using an electronic pickup in his horn for a while, and now and then he employed a wah-wah pedal, an innovation he may have picked up from Randy Brecker. A September show at Lincoln Center was attended by a twelve-year-old, jazz-precocious Wallace Roney. "It was one of the greatest concerts I ever seen," Roney told me.

> It was Miles's new sextet—[drummer] Al Foster had just joined the band; [soprano saxophonist] Carlos Garnett; [keyboard player] Cedric Lawson; [electric bassist] Michael Henderson; Mtume [James Mtume Forman, percussionist and son of Jimmy Heath]. They were playing stuff from [the recently released LP] *On the Corner*. And I was up to date with it, by the way. It was the first time I heard Miles play with the wah-wah pedal; but he still had a piano player in his band. So he still had ties to the band with Chick, or Keith—still had that sound.

Three weeks later, Davis's physical woes multiplied when, jet-lagged after returning from a concert in Palo Alto, he fell asleep at the wheel of his Lamborghini on the West Side Highway and ran into a grassy median, breaking both legs in the wreck. He was hospitalized for several weeks and homebound for the rest of the year.

But in early 1973 he began touring actively again, at first with the nonet, and after May with a new working septet: Dave Liebman on tenor and soprano sax, and flute; Pete Cosey (who could play like Hendrix) and Reggie Lucas on electric guitars; Michael Henderson on electric bass; Al Foster on drums; and Mtume on conga and other percussion. All the musicians but Miles were in their twenties, and all except for Liebman were Black. "I was the only white guy around except for the roadie," he told me.

> This was Black Panther time, 1973. We're in the belly of the beast. The Yamaha equipment was painted red, green, and black, the colors of the Black Panther flag, and there's Dave up there, a little Jew. I mean, you could feel the tension. Some of the guys in the band definitely resented that I was there. It wasn't even personal. One day, Miles said—this is out of nowhere, when I was hanging out—he said, "They don't like you." I said, "Who are they?" He named a couple of them in the band, especially one guy. "I told them you ain't got no color. Is that okay?" I said, "Thanks, Miles."

The group traveled extensively—to Japan, Switzerland, France, Italy, Sweden, Denmark, Germany, Yugoslavia, the UK—but there was frequent tardiness, and there were occasional cancellations, due to Davis's fragile health.

"During my time with Miles, he was addicted to painkillers," Liebman said. "And I partook with Miles. Everything he did, I did. Percodan. We'd start out with a hundred and end up with none. He took ten a day sometimes. I don't know how he went to the bathroom.

"I kept him company because he couldn't sleep, he couldn't be alone. I had a lot of time with him, a lot of face time. I can't say I understood what he was saying half the time, because it wasn't only the growl that we all know; it was [the drugs]."

"On Sunday, February 10, the legendary Miles Davis turned out one of the worst performances of his career at the Masonic Temple in Detroit," one 1974 review began.

It started out badly, as Miles was an hour and a half late. . . . When
Miles finally showed up, things went for the worse. His band was
sensational, no, indescribably delicious, but Miles appeared sick
and possibly drunk and played out of key, and without energy. He
kept spitting on the floor, grossing the audience out. Amid catcalls
and boos (his pants were even falling down), Miles finally walked
off stage, only to return after heated arguments offstage and continue with a lackluster showing. It's sad, too, as the other people
in his entourage were remarkable in their show, and also seemed
irritated with Miles's unusual weirdness. . . .

Alas, there was nothing especially unusual about it. He was suffering
from walking pneumonia—this accounted for the spitting—along with
everything else.

Nevertheless, during his two-and-a-half-year tenure with Miles, Liebman came to an acute understanding of what had made Davis a genius as
both a leader and a player over the last three decades. "One thing about
Miles that I saw—he was super-confident," Liebman said.

He never doubted what he played. He never looked around for an
answer. He didn't pose questions. He made statements. And I've
never seen such surety in a person. Maybe Albert Einstein [had
it]—I don't know. But I never saw such absolute, "What I just
played is all there is—there *is* nothing else."

MILES HAD BEEN THREATENING TO RETIRE SINCE THE LATE 1950S—IT
was a great way to make writers sit up and take notice—and in 1971, when
his health problems were multiplying and he'd temporarily stopped touring, "there were reports that [he] was going to retire by midsummer,"
Szwed writes. He didn't, of course, but in the spring of 1974, when Davis
wound up in the hospital while on tour in Brazil—he'd indulged in vodka,

marijuana (which he normally stayed away from), "a lot of coke," and Percodan—he started to give serious consideration to hanging it up.

He had a kind of miraculous recovery—which is mostly to say that he didn't die—and over the summer and into the fall, though considerably weakened, he took an octet on a U.S. tour with Herbie Hancock's ultra-hot jazz/funk/rock sextet Headhunters: *opening* for Hancock, whose *Head Hunters* LP was outselling *On the Corner* ten to one. "Deep down that pissed me off," Miles said. But not very deep down: when Hancock went to Davis's dressing room to say hi, Miles "told him that he wasn't in the band and that the dressing room was off limits to anybody who wasn't in the band." That's the memoir version. What Miles actually told Herbie, according to Wallace Roney, was "Get the fuck out of here."

THE LIFE OF A TOURING JAZZ MUSICIAN IS NOT CONDUCIVE TO DOMESTIC relationships, as many players have acknowledged ruefully. In late 1974 Jack DeJohnette's replacement, Marty Morell, married a Canadian woman and decided to settle down in Toronto, ending his days with Bill Evans and leaving a hole in the trio.

When a drummer friend of Morell's, Eliot Zigmund, heard that the pianist was holding auditions at the Village Vanguard, he arranged with Helen Keane to try out and, to his astonishment, got the spot. After playing for a couple of weeks at the Vanguard, the trio set out for a tour of Europe and Scandinavia.

"I was thirty years old," Zigmund said. "So I looked at Bill almost like a god. I was so in awe of people from that generation, and especially him, just for the revolutionary nature of what he had done." The young drummer found Evans pleasant but somewhat distant. "I think had I been in a more confident place in my own life I could have developed a stronger friendship with him," he said. "But he was very mysterious, too. When we were on the road for weeks at a time he would just disappear. He just stayed in his hotel room. He didn't come out, he didn't socialize—at the end of the last set you would turn your head and he'd be gone. It was like, *Where's Bill?* I realize now how burnt out he must have been at that age, with all the touring he had done."

Evans, Nenette, and Nenette's young daughter, Maxine, had been living in an apartment in Riverdale, a quiet neighborhood just north of Manhattan. But in early 1975 Nenette found she was pregnant, and Evans bought a house in Closter, a leafy suburb in Bergen County, New Jersey. The house was commodious, with a big backyard next to woods—and Evans had to tour almost constantly to afford the mortgage payments.

Still, Eliot Zigmund told me, it was a relatively good time in the pianist's life. "He was really trying to control his health," Zigmund told me. "Bill was on methadone maintenance. He had a new wife, and then a new baby"—his long-awaited first child, Evan Evans, was born in September 1975—"and he was very positive about life, he was really trying to stay clean. There was no intravenous drug use at all when I was in the band." Evans's cocaine use, too, appeared to have stopped entirely. He wasn't rushing tempos anymore.

Evans was relatively clean and healthy, but he was afflicted with a strange kind of nostalgia. "Bill was more romantic about his history as a drug addict than he was about his history as a musician," Zigmund told me. "On planes occasionally we'd sit together, and he would reminisce sometimes about all the weird shit he did copping—there was a certain mystery and romance, almost like a *noir* feeling about his drug use."

The drummer laughed. "He had a *badge*, actually, a cop's badge, that he could flash if he ever got caught copping, or ever got into hot water in Harlem. He'd also go to the weirdest places to cop drugs—you could go to the Village and call somebody to meet you on the street, you know. I heard that when he went back [to using] in the seventies, he would go back up to Harlem to cop, when at that point you could get drugs anywhere. I just think it brought back the romance of the beginning of his tenure as a jazz musician."

But in the moment he also tasted real happiness. Evans and Tony Bennett had long been mutual admirers—they periodically ran into each other in airports—and in mid-1975 the idea of their making an album to-gether quickly became a reality. Over two days in June, in Fantasy's Berke-ley, California, studios, they recorded *The Tony Bennett/Bill Evans Album*, and it was a thing of quiet magnificence—only the two musicians, the re-cording engineer, and Helen Keane were in the studio—and a perfect blending of two great and intimate arts.

The birth of his son, Evans told the writer Len Lyons, had given him a sense of completeness. "My personal life has become so happy in the last couple of years, getting a whole family thing going, buying a home, be-coming a father. All of this contributes to my motivation, which is a mys-terious element in anybody's life. . . .

"I'm just feeling more alive now, alive in a broader way than just being a musician or an individual on the music scene. When you have children, it seems you're more tied to the future and to everything that's going on in the world."

MILES KEPT UP A GRUELING TOURING SCHEDULE FOR THE REST OF 1974 and into the beginning of 1975: Cleveland, San Francisco, Los Angeles; three weeks in Japan in January and February. In March, having patched things up with Herbie Hancock, Davis swallowed his pride and took his septet out once again as the keyboardist's opening act, starting in Wash-ington, D.C., and proceeding into the Midwest. In St. Louis in late March, at a party after a concert at the Kiel Opera House, Irene Oliver, the mother of Miles's children, showed up and created a scene. Their two sons, Gregory and Miles IV, were lost in life, she exclaimed—failures, and it was all Miles's fault. According to Davis, the partygoers kept expecting him to retaliate—maybe even slap her around—but he just stood there weeping, knowing everything she said was true. Soon afterward, Miles collapsed with a bleeding ulcer and was hospitalized yet again.

And soon was out playing again, though playing what is a fair ques-tion. Davis rationalized it as "a deep African thing, a deep African-American groove, with a lot of emphasis on drums and rhythm, and not on individual solos." He'd been studying Stockhausen, he said, taking in the idea of "performance as a process." Whatever that meant.

One thing it meant for certain was that for Miles, the idea of jazz (that word he didn't use) as entertainment, a concept about which he'd always been ambivalent at best, had now well and truly passed. "I didn't want to ever play again from eight bars to eight bars," he said. "I had to do what I was doing if I was going to keep thinking of myself as a *creative* artist."

Dizzy, with his capacious spirit, defended him: "The creators are supposed to step forward," he wrote. "That's why I can appreciate Miles. I don't care whether you like his music or not, he has stepped forward. It's up to your personal taste, but the music is there for you to taste whether you like it or not. He did have the courage to step up there."

But not always the wisdom to step back. On July 1, 1975, Davis played a concert at Avery Fisher Hall: against a tired musical tapestry of swishing, funking, and wah-wah-ing, he came in now and then on his horn, briefly, with a barely recognizable imitation of Miles Davis. The only thing that could be said was that, whatever his musical inadequacies, this tiny skeletal presence in beads and giant sunglasses, the world-historical figure, was at least actually present. It was *Miles Davis*. That was it, though. He had been reduced to a spectacle.

Yet maybe it's not that simple—with Miles, things were never simple. The following month Columbia released a double album, *Agharta* (the title came from the name of a mythical subterranean city), recorded at Davis's February concert in Osaka. Gary Giddins, then the *Village Voice*'s jazz critic, "*decimated* the record. Because Miles plays so badly on it." But Giddins later had second thoughts: "[Saxophonist] Sonny Fortune — maybe the best playing he ever recorded, and Pete Cosey is amazing on guitar. It's true, Miles plays terribly. But he's *choreographing*." Giddins wrote an apology for his review. Two more live albums in the same vein, *Pangaea* and *Dark Magus*, would be released in 1976 and 1977, and along with *Agharta*, have had fans ever since. Even if he couldn't feature himself, Miles could still use his young musicians to produce a spontaneous work unlike any that had been heard before. He could still make it new, whether you liked it or not.

But after appearing at the Schaefer Music Festival in Central Park in September 1975, he decided to hang it up in earnest. "I felt artistically drained, tired," he said. "I didn't have anything else to say musically." It was the first real rest he'd taken in over thirty years, since he had started playing professionally. "I thought that after I was a little better physically I would probably start to feel better spiritually also. I was sick and tired of going in and out of hospitals and hobbling around, on and off stage. I was beginning to see pity in people's eyes when they looked at me, and I hadn't seen that since I was a junkie. I didn't want that. I put down the thing I loved most in life—my music—until I could pull it all back together again."

He thought he might be gone for six months. It would be almost six years.

WARREN BERNHARDT VISITED BILL EVANS AND HIS YOUNG FAMILY IN Closter and found a scene of cozy domesticity. The baby slept under the table while the two pianists analyzed and played Rachmaninoff's Third Concerto together. Richie Beirach also paid a call and was amazed at what he found: "He was actually openly happy, which was completely un-like him. And it threw everybody."

But it soon became horribly clear that Evans was ready to sacrifice his new happiness to his old god. Someone—some say a musician he was close to—offered him cocaine, and, hopeless addict that he was, he ac-cepted it gratefully. "And then he just dove into it," Zigmund said. "I mean, I don't know of anybody that used cocaine intravenously except Bill Evans. And he was using *massive* amounts of cocaine. With the full knowledge that his doctors had told him, If you return to intravenous drug use, you're gonna kill yourself, basically."

He was using massive amounts because—whether or not he paid the mortgage on time—all that concertizing meant steady cash flow. And Nenette knew about his relapse all too soon, and didn't want the children around it. In early 1978 she took Maxine and Evan and moved to a house on the Connecticut shoreline. Bill took his Chickering baby grand and relocated to an apartment on the ninth floor of a narrow white high-rise in Fort Lee, New Jersey, just south of the George Washington Bridge.

ACROSS THE HUDSON, MILES DESCENDED INTO HIS OWN DARKNESS. DAYS and seasons went by on West Seventy-seventh Street, and he stayed inside, connected to the world only by the television that was never turned off and friends who now and then stopped by: Gil Evans, Al Foster, Jack DeJohnette, Max Roach, Dizzy Gillespie, Herbie Hancock, Ron Carter, Tony Williams, Philly Joe Jones, Richard Pryor, Cicely Tyson. Sometimes he wouldn't let them in. After they'd been turned away a few times, many of them stopped coming.

He was, by his own estimation, "a hermit." His one-year marriage to Betty Mabry had foundered on the shoals of his disapproval and boredom: he came to see her as "a high-class groupie, who was very talented but . . . didn't believe in her own talent." The serene moment of the album whose cover she graced had vanished like smoke. But serenity was anathema to Miles anyway. While he and Mabry were still together, he had started seeing two other women simultaneously, Marguerite Eskridge and Jackie Battle. Both were young, Black, beautiful, quiet, and self-possessed; neither presented any competitive challenge. In 1971, Marguerite had borne him a son, Erin. But Miles's cocaine craziness would drive both women away. His general chaos—besides the cocaine (five hundred dollars a day's worth), he was also addicted to Percodan and Seconal, and was drinking quantities of Heineken and cognac—drove nearly everyone away.

His house, he said, "was a wreck, clothes everywhere, dirty dishes in the sink, newspapers and magazines all over the floor, beer bottles and garbage and trash everywhere. The roaches had a field day." He shuttled through cleaning women quickly. It wasn't just the filth that horrified them; it was Miles himself. Soon they stopped coming, too.

Sex kept happening, though—a lot of it. It didn't matter that he was a severely debilitated, agoraphobic forty-nine-year-old: brigades of young women passed through, often more than one at a time; every possible kink was explored. All customers were satisfied, by Miles's accounting. All of it was consensual, he claimed. Many Polaroids were taken. He made no apologies.

Over time, inevitably, the pleasures lost their edge and the isolation mounted. Having always resisted nostalgia, he now succumbed to it: he missed his fellow geniuses and the sorcery they had all woven together. And so hungry was he for human contact that, as Jack DeJohnette told me of visiting Miles during this period, "He had pictures up of musicians he had worked with all around the wall." Bird. Trane. Dizzy. Max. Keeping him company when few others would.

AFTER OVER A DECADE WITH EVANS, EDDIE GOMEZ DECIDED TO MOVE ON. He feared becoming permanently pigeonholed as Bill Evans's bassist, and, like Marty Morell before him, he had a family he wanted to see more of. Eliot Zigmund left around the same time: "You'd find yourself playing the same ten or twelve tunes over and over and over again, and on nights when you weren't feeling that inspired, sometimes it was hard," he said. In January 1978 Evans held auditions for a new bassist, and finally settled on Michael Moore, whose quiet strength and delicacy of touch impressed him. To fill in temporarily on drums, the pianist tapped his old partner in crime, the great Philly Joe Jones, who was known for many things besides quiet or delicacy.

Moore had come up revering Bill Evans, but he quickly came to regret his decision to sign on. Evans was once again rushing on up-tempo numbers, and Philly Joe was happily abetting him. "It was," Pettinger writes, "the old junkie-buddy syndrome again: before, Evans and Jones had both been on heroin; now it was cocaine and alcohol, respectively. They were like a couple of vampires in their exclusive club, swapping stories on another planet."

Moore was soon history; his replacement was a twenty-four-year-old from Dallas, Marc Johnson. Johnson, too, was awed to play with the great

Bill Evans, but his combination of musical inventiveness and openhearted respect for Evans inspired the pianist, and the trio's chemistry changed for the better. When Philly Joe had to move on, Evans took the recommendation of his friend the guitarist Joe Puma and auditioned a thirty-year-old upstate New Yorker named Joe LaBarbera. He liked what he heard, and yet another Bill Evans trio was born. This one would be the last.

LaBarbera came from a musical family and had listened to a lot of jazz piano growing up. But "hearing Bill Evans play was transformative for me," he told me. As was becoming Evans's friend. The drummer was a warm and generous man, and the pianist met him halfway.

"I grew to love him like a brother," LaBarbera said. When he first went to work with the trio, he and his wife had just had their first child, necessitating a move from Manhattan to Woodstock in upstate New York. "And so when I would work in town, Bill would let me stay on a foldout bed in his living room. So we spent a lot of time together."

"I grew to love him because we had a *lot* of common ground," LaBarbera said. "We had both listened to a lot of the same music, even though Bill was a generation ahead of me—Nat Cole and Lester Young and Earl Hines. Bird, of course. But Bill and I had also both been Boy Scouts. We used to have a laugh about that. We had both been in the service—both been in the army and in an army band. Different times, different places, but similar, shared experience.

"And then, just as a human being, he was so personable. He was so open and friendly; extremely intelligent. Just easy to be around. No airs, no pretension about who he was or what he was. He knew full well what he was capable of delivering musically and he knew he worked hard for it. But that's as far as it went, because when we got on the bandstand, we were, all three of us, working for that common goal of the music, *all* the time. It was never about, you know, 'I'm the star and you guys are backing me up.' *Never* like that."

The new trio quickly found its footing, a "tough and resilient interplay . . . an inner fiber, a healthy three-way dynamism," Pettinger writes. "The minute you sat down and played with him," LaBarbera recalled, "the minute the first note came out, he was so strong and so positive about his direction that if you were any kind of a musician at all, you intuitively knew where he wanted it to go. He would never say anything to you like, 'Do this, do that.' He gave you the room to find it on your own."

At the beginning of 1979 they went out on the road. While playing at a club in Edmonton, Alberta—a converted church, packed with awe-struck college jazz students and professors—Evans met a twenty-two-year-old waitress named Laurie Verchomin. She was petite, pretty, and big-eyed, with a dancer's slim body, and when she asked if she could bring him anything, he asked if she was available later: he had something he wanted to talk to her about.

Verchomin was struck, while she was serving, "by the intensity of the music and the spell it's able to cast on the room. The fans are so preoccupied with the music, they ignore me when I approach the table. I am trying to be as quiet as possible. If I speak at all I am given dirty looks."

"I'd really like to spend some time with you," Evans told her after the show. "We leave tomorrow for Calgary, maybe you could join me for a few hours tonight at my hotel?"

"That sounds great," she said. "Can I bring my boyfriend, too? He's a really big fan of yours."

He broke into a thin laugh. "No, that's not what I had in mind."

She was, by her own description, "soft wax," young and impressionable and dying to escape an abusive father and the dead boredom of frigid Edmonton. When they went back to her apartment, it wasn't just the two of them: a gaggle of persistent jazz fans tagged along. She made Evans tea and gave him a stash of coke she'd been holding for a dealer friend; he took out one of Helen Keane's business cards, wrote something on it, and handed it to her. On the back of the card, in his neat handwriting, was a short note ("Lori—You seem very special to me—Bill (Evans)") along with his address and phone number in Fort Lee.

ON APRIL 26, 1979, HE WROTE HER FROM A PLANE EN ROUTE FROM PHOE-nix to Tucson:

Thank you for the lovely note and a most interesting quote from Sartre. It came at a time when it was most welcome since I lost my brother last Friday—my only brother and to whom I was closer than even my parents. He was two years older and led me into sports, music, jazz and in general was a model and hero to me. He was an educator who built the 164 schools of Baton Rouge, La. into a music system ahead of its time and dedicated to ideals far above the "football marching band" that epitomizes many schools depts of music.

It was a great shock and I received your note upon my return from Baton Rouge. If we see each other I will tell you more.

He told her of his upcoming schedule: free the latter part of May, either off or working in New York City (one week at the Vanguard, starting the twenty-ninth); free for much of June, also. "So if you would like to spend a few days with me—I would love it," he wrote. "Just call and I'll arrange your tickets." He signed the letter with love.

She flew east at the end of May.

HARRY EVANS HAD SHOT HIMSELF BECAUSE HE WAS SEVERELY DEPRESSED, Peter Pettinger writes. But there was more to it than that. Harry had been schizophrenic, Bill told Laurie Verchomin. He recounted "the hours he spent listening to [his brother's] paranoid ranting about the nature of the universe. How he really wanted to believe that Harry was just ahead of his time, onto something the rest of the world didn't understand yet."

He told her all this soon after she arrived, as he sat on the bench of his Chickering in the Fort Lee apartment. Then he played her a tune he'd started to write just before Harry's death. He'd now decided to call it "We Will Meet Again."

Her first visit lasted only a week, but it was densely packed with events: between a steady round of snorting cocaine and making love, Laurie and Bill explored downtown Manhattan, had dinner with "crusty New Yorkers" Max Gordon and his wife, Lorraine, the proprietors of the Village Vanguard; and went to the racetrack, where Evans was just "some guy from New Jersey who [bet] on horses" and where his racetrack pals, "slimy, hairy-chested men from New York," leered at his young girlfriend. Evans asked Laurie if she wanted to meet Miles Davis. He offered to take her to Michael's Pub to hear Woody Allen play clarinet. It was all head-turningly strange for this very young woman from the provinces.

One day, with a childlike faith that complete candor would only deepen their new relationship, Evans showed Verchomin a pile of letters and photographs from the women he'd had sex with over the last couple of years.

> Since his separation from his wife, he emphasizes. He looks at their pictures fondly, his treasure chest of sexual/emotional experience. The expressions of these women are all variations on the theme of longing. I imagine they are all longing to be with him. Some are married. Some are single. They are all very young. I wonder how he is able to reach inside the souls of these women so easily. Is it the drugs, the sex, the music? I know what it is for me. It is his own transparency, giving me the permission I need to be myself.

The last photo Evans showed her was of Nenette. With a pang, Verchomin saw how young and sexy the pianist's wife was; she took envious notice of Nenette's lush blond mane. Evans asked Laurie if she'd like to drive up to Connecticut to meet his family. "I see the look in his eyes, this is something really important to him," Verchomin wrote. "I would do anything for this man."

In Connecticut, Nenette smoked pot with Laurie and told her that she, Laurie, was "just one in a series of women Bill has brought up to her house to meet her. Then she [talked] about his health and her concern for him." Evans had only "an eighth of a liver left, after all his bouts with hepatitis during his heroin years. And . . . his doctor has warned him that even one drink would be deadly to him in his condition."

Verchomin found this strange, since Evans didn't drink at all. She assumed Nenette was referring to his cocaine use.

LAURIE VERCHOMIN TURNED DOWN EVANS'S OFFER TO INTRODUCE HER to Miles: "I was afraid to meet Miles Davis, 'cause I had heard too many crazy stories about him," she said. "Bill was starting to strike up his friendship again with Miles, and Miles was in a really dark place. And it seemed like a scary place—he was in his full exploration of debauchery."

THAT JULY, EVANS GAVE A TELEPHONE INTERVIEW TO WKCR-FM FOR A multiday Miles Davis Festival. Miles had been completely off the scene for almost four years now, and rumors about his ill health abounded, but Evans said that he and Gil Evans had recently visited Davis at home and found him looking well and in good spirits. Bill had "somewhat prevailed upon him that the world was waiting for him," he told the interviewer.

BORED WITH DEPRAVITY AND DRUGS, "TIRED OF BEING FUCKED UP ALL the time," Miles was beginning to listen to the world's entreaties. In 1978, George Butler, Columbia Records' new head of A&R for jazz and progressive music, had started a gentle campaign, against the resistance of some at the label who didn't believe Davis would ever return to playing, to woo him back. Butler started by phoning just to talk; soon he was paying visits to 312 West Seventy-seventh. Miles didn't make it easy for him. "In the beginning," the trumpeter recalled, "I was so indifferent to what he was talking about that he must have thought I would never [come back]. But he was so goddamn persistent and so pleasant when he would come by, or call and talk on the telephone. Sometimes we would just sit around watching television and not saying nothing."

It helped, a lot, that Butler was Black, a calm, comforting presence, and distinguished: conservative in his dress and manner, with an academic background (a master's in music education). Miles began to entertain the possibility of picking up his trumpet again. He sat down at his piano and played some chords: it felt good.

It also helped that his head was clearer. During this same period, Cicely Tyson had come back into his life, first just dropping by, but soon taking charge, applying the considerable force of her personality to purging his house of louche characters and cleaning Miles himself up. She brought him healthy food, introduced him to vegetables; told him he had to quit smoking or she wouldn't kiss him. She said that he must stop taking drugs and cut down on drinking. He mostly listened—though by his own testimony he both quit cocaine and continued to take it. ("It wasn't the coke that fucked me up—it was the whiskey," he told me. "The only thing wrong with coke is that they'll bust you for it.")

In early 1980 he called George Butler and said he wanted to record again.

IN HER MEMOIR OF HER TIME WITH BILL EVANS, LAURIE VERCHOMIN DEscribes her initial arrival at Kennedy airport, "wearing what I thought a man my father's age would find attractive—something from the 1940s. A long pleated skirt, platform shoes and a prim white blouse with a tweed jacket." On their way to his apartment, they stop at an all-night supermarket "to pick up a few supplies (hot dogs, Pepsi and cigarettes for him—soda water for me)." And, she writes, while they're standing in the checkout line, "I can't help but wonder if people think I am his daughter. This gives me a little kick. Like we are getting away with something."

"I think he attracted a lot of women like me," Verchomin told me. She shifted, as she frequently did when talking about Evans, into the present tense. "All the women he's been with that I know of have that thing that they need to be healed, and that he is seen as the healer of that trauma. And it has a lot to do with their dads."

Evans had his own daddy issues. "He told me that he never felt like a man," Verchomin said. "He said, 'I am still a *boy*.' It explained a lot to me.

Why he could be so soft, and so receptive, and so unformed by the world. You know, unhardened. He was extremely in touch with his feminine side. So he not only got to be my child—I could cut his food up, and give him a bath, and totally care for him—he also got to be the dad! He was the guy who was leading the show, and telling everyone what to do, and protecting me."

The idea of this ravaged, almost fifty-year-old man being babied, even bathed, by the fresh-faced twenty-two-year-old is strange and unsettling. In her memoir Verchomin describes her first sight of Evans's thin legs, cratered and scarred by two decades of drug injections, "something like the surface of the moon. . . . I've never seen scarring like this." He returns her look without shame or regret and explains "that they are old scars and don't hurt anymore."

For the first half of their sixteen-month relationship they lived separately, Verchomin periodically flying back from western Canada to join Evans while he toured, both in America and overseas. It was the life he knew best and loved best. "His whole life was very much like hotel life all the time," Verchomin told me. "That was just a really efficient style of living for him. He liked to get room service; he kept his life very simple so there wouldn't be a lot of"—she laughed ruefully—"nesting going on, or anything like that. He was a traveler. He was a transient person passing through this world, circling the globe over and over again with his giant suitcases."

She was struck by the sharp difference between the way jazz was treated in Europe and how it was received in the U.S.: "Jazz in Europe was really high-esteem," she said. "It's so high-end over there—it's opera houses, and we stayed in beautiful hotels, and Bill made *lots* of money. And then in America, you'd come back, and, well—look at the Vanguard. I know it's like a church, but it only holds like ninety-five people."

Most of the money Evans made went straight into the pockets of cocaine dealers. And bill collectors and the IRS were after him, so more had to be made. At the end of 1979, the trio went on a grueling European tour: twenty-one cities in twenty-four days. In Paris, his two sold-out sets at the 750-seat Espace Cardin were recorded by Radio France; in 1983, Warner Brothers' Elektra-Musician label issued the recordings as *The Paris Concerts, Editions One and Two.* Pettinger calls the concerts "performances that have long been acclaimed as among the finest from the Bill Evans trio," citing "an excitement in the air, a feeling that anything could be made to happen at any time." But the pianist Kenny Werner sensed a manic quality to the excitement: "You can hear this intensity that wasn't there earlier, but that also has to do with switching from heroin to cocaine," he told me. "He had lost his most precious possession, which was his touch. It now had an aggressiveness to it."

From the start of their relationship, even as they did drugs together, Evans and Verchomin had nourished a mutual fantasy of her as the angel who would rescue him from addiction: "Like, 'I have this problem; I brought you here to help me with it,'" she said. "Of course I wanted Bill to quit." But for Evans, quitting was never really an option.

"He was totally inflexible on this point," Joe LaBarbera told me. "I mean, so many people that loved the guy tried to talk to him from the beginning—Scott LaFaro talked to him, Helen Keane talked until she was blue in the face. I tried to talk to him *time* and time again—we actually had screaming matches. I mean, he simply did *not* want to change his habits.

"One day—we were driving in a car—he said, 'Look, I know that you're well-intentioned, but don't try to help me out.' He said, 'This is a personal decision that I've made. I don't need anybody's help.'"

In the spring of 1980, Evans told Verchomin, "You have to come and stay with me now."

When she arrived, "he was in a very paranoid state," Verchomin said. "He thought that the FBI was following him; he thought there were listening devices in all the hotels we went to." In his Fort Lee bedroom, she said, he had nailed a blanket over the window.

And yet, she said, "he made it easy for me to accept that. He somehow made it funny for me." When she offered to look for the listening devices, she said, "He's like, 'No, because they know you're gonna look for them, so they hide them really well.'" She laughed. "No matter what I would say to him, his psyche had already established this alternative universe, and so I just had to respect that. It's like, Oh, well, he's living in *that* universe."

And the rescue fantasy had also changed. "I think he knew that he was really close to dying," she told me. "And he wanted someone to sit with him while he was doing it." All her roles—angel, mother, daughter—had transformed. "We were very aware that those were just costumes and illusions, and that there was something much larger happening than that. It had to do with being present in every moment. Because when you're aware of death, you have a gift of presence. It's just an incredible, intense state of awareness—always knowing that it could just end, in any moment."

"While my exterior is in decline," Evans told LaBarbera, "I have a completely pure core. My spirit is pure."

Living on methadone, cocaine, and unfiltered Camels, he kept playing. In June, at the Vanguard; in July, at Ronnie Scott's Jazz Club in London; at the end of August, at the Hollywood Bowl. On the afternoon of this show, Verchomin writes, Evans was in their hotel room, "finally relaxing after another questionable dose of methadone. High blood pressure is creating headaches and tension, and a persistent fever has him deep under the covers warding off a chill from the air conditioning." He somehow peeled himself out of bed; at the venue, he immediately lay down in the green room and told Marc Johnson and Joe LaBarbera that he wasn't sure he could play, but would try. "When the time comes for him to hit," she writes, "he gets up and shuffles out on stage to play one of the most powerful shows I've ever witnessed. Sitting in the stands . . . , I am awed by the enormity of Bill's playing, his ability to fill the expanse of the amphitheater with sheer energy."

In the second week of September he returned to New York for a stand at Fat Tuesday's, a club in a former German beer hall at Third Avenue and Seventeenth Street. He opened on Tuesday the ninth and played on the night of the tenth. "But by the second night," LaBarbera recalled, "we were literally carrying him in from the car to the piano." Yet again, once he sat down to play, "somehow he completely suspended any physical limitations and just played his *ass* off. I mean, it was unbelievable."

Driving down the FDR as Evans and Verchomin headed to the club on the evening of the eleventh, he nodded out at the wheel and nearly crashed into an overpass abutment. Her screaming roused him, and disaster was narrowly averted. He pulled off the highway, badly shaken, and she called a cab. At Fat Tuesday's Evans told Johnson and LaBarbera that he was unable to play. A substitute pianist was found, and Bill and Laurie returned to Fort Lee.

LaBarbera, who was bunking on a foldout bed in the front room of the apartment, said that when he got back from the gig on Sunday night, he and Verchomin finally prevailed on Evans to check in to a hospital the next day. "We were actually pretty excited," the drummer recalled. "We thought, 'Oh my God, this is fantastic.'"

On Monday morning, September 15, Evans had to be helped through the lobby and into the back seat of his car. With LaBarbera at the wheel and Verchomin next to him, they drove across the bridge and into Manhattan. As they sat in crosstown traffic, Evans spotted a beautiful woman and said, "This really must be the end, because I really don't feel a thing for that woman." The three of them laughed.

Verchomin took the opportunity to address a serious subject—the pianist's incessant financial woes—in a lighthearted way. "Hey, Bill," she said, "what do you think about having a memorial concert to raise money for you?"

"You mean a tribute, my dear, as I am still alive," he said, dryly.

The three of them laughed again, and Evans began to cough up blood. In a moment a steady stream was flowing from his mouth; hilarity turned to horror. Evans gave LaBarbera directions to Mount Sinai Hospital. "Lay on the horn, Joe," he said. "Tell them it's an emergency."

Verchomin turned in her seat, keeping a desperate watch on Evans. "He gives me the fear in his eyes," she writes. "I want to tell him that I need more, that we aren't done yet. He tells me, 'I think I'm going to drown.' I'm not sure a person can lose that much blood."

They pulled up to the hospital. LaBarbera: "I remember picking him up—he weighed almost nothing—and carrying him into the emergency room." Evans's blood was everywhere, leaving a trail through the waiting room. He was laid on a gurney, and doctors and nurses took over. Back in the waiting room, sitting with his jacket on her lap, Verchomin watched a janitor mop up his blood. "A nurse appears and in a soothing voice describes Bill's condition as something similar to a nosebleed that just needs cauterizing." A woman sitting next to Verchomin told her, in great detail, about a similar experience her husband had gone through. She spoke of him in the present tense. A young doctor came out and took Verchomin into a small office. "We couldn't save him," he said.

"BILL EVANS," GENE LEES SAID, "COMMITTED THE LONGEST, SLOWEST suicide in musical history."

EVANS'S DEATH, MILES'S MEMOIR SAID,

> made me real sad, because he had turned into a junkie, and I think he died from complications of that. The year before Bill died, Charlie Mingus had died, so a lot of my friends were going. Sometimes it seemed like just a few of us were left from the old days. But I was trying not to think about the old days, because in order to stay young I believe a person has to forget the past.

He began to record again.

It helped that George Butler had sent him a tasty bribe—a Yamaha grand piano—and that his sister Dorothy's son Vincent Wilburn, Jr., had turned out to be a decent jazz drummer. In May 1980, Miles returned to Columbia Studio B, this time with Wilburn and three of his nephew's Chicago friends on electric bass, synthesizers, and celeste, as well as the singer Angela Bofill and a new young saxophonist referred to Davis by Dave Liebman—named, ironically enough, Bill Evans.

The song they recorded, "The Man with the Horn," became the title tune of Miles's first comeback album. It was a silky, loping, mellow thing with the sound of a Blaxploitation movie theme, and *Shaft*-like lyrics to match:

> Smooth, suave, debonair—describes a man so rare,
>
> Like fine wine, he gets mellower with age. He's the man with
> the horn.

The man himself played in the background, Harmon-muted, wah-wahed, and heavily echoed: it was identifiably Miles, that plangency was there, but it was also wan and somewhat dispirited. After Wilburn and his friends returned to Chicago, Miles formed a new band: Evans on soprano and tenor sax, flute, and electric piano; Mike Stern on guitar; Marcus Miller on electric bass; Al Foster back on drums; and a percussionist named Sammy Figueroa. It was this group that recorded most of the rest of the album, and Miles seemed more comfortable with them: he was more front and center on the record's better tracks—"Back Seat Betty" (a backhanded tribute to Mabry); "Ursula"—but this also meant he was more exposed.

Critics carped ("a bunt single"; "It misses by several Miles"), but as usual, Davis paid them no mind. His prolonged self-exile from music had, if anything, only burnished his iconhood. The portion of the music-listening public that still cared about jazz thought about him, worried about him, yearned after him. Newspaper pieces called him "the Greta Garbo of the jazz trumpet," wondered about "the reasons for his five-year seclusion in his Manhattan brownstone . . . , the state of his health."

To give his public what it ardently desired (and to put some money in the bank), he took the new group out on the road, with an initial four-night gig at the end of June, at a Boston club, a four-hundred-seat former disco called Kix. All four nights sold out fast. Miles's comeback was an epochal occasion—journalists flew in from as far away as Japan— to which he gave the theatrics it deserved: he pulled up at the club in his yellow Ferrari, with Cicely Tyson seated at his side; he wore a black jumpsuit, big sunglasses, and, most theatrical of all, the facial hair he'd been unable to grow back in the Dexter Gordon days, a beard and a mustache. The whiskers, sitting oddly on his small, still boyish face, somehow looked pasted on.

We want Miles, the crowd chanted.

The *Boston Globe*'s review was ecstatic:

> Last night Miles Davis gave solid evidence that he was back to stay, that the chops are still as impressive as ever and the famed mystique has not dimmed an iota. . . . Davis alternated brooding, elongated lines with brief, swinging interludes. Evans, on soprano, was superb and the group interplay seemed contagious, taking its lead from Davis who, despite five years of inactivity, was playing with seasoned assuredness as he continually inserted pauses like a nervous suitor.

But was the review for the music or the mystique? His mystique had always been one of his great creations; more and more, it was all he had left.

Davis and Tyson were married, on Thanksgiving Day 1981, at Bill Cosby's country house in Massachusetts. Andrew Young, then the mayor of Atlanta, performed the ceremony; Dizzy Gillespie, Max Roach, and Dick Gregory were in attendance, along with many others. It should have been a gala occasion, except that the groom was seriously ill: "I had that gray look of almost-death in my face," Miles recalled. "Cicely saw it. I told her I felt like I could die at any minute. During the summer I had shot some dope in my leg and it had fucked it up."

He wasn't doing his own health any favors. Though he had cut back on cocaine, he was still swilling Heinekens and smoking several packs of Camels a day. There was blood in his urine; his liver was severely compromised. One of his doctors asked him, point-blank, if he wanted to live. Miles said that he did. "Well, Miles," the doctor said, "if you want to live, you've got to cut all this stuff out, including smoking." Miles went on doing what he was doing.

Why had he married Tyson? He said in his memoir that he'd lost any sexual feeling for her. She craved romance; he had none to give. She was a year and a half older; he needed the attentions of young, pretty women to ease the pain of aging. She mother-henned him, which he both needed and hated. Five days after the wedding he was unfaithful. When Tyson went to Africa at the start of 1982 to make a film, he ran riot—until he woke up one day to find his right hand had gone dead. At first he believed he was suffering from a semi-mythological malady called Honeymoon Syndrome: "You're making love to your woman," he told me, "and y'all just make love so much, it numbs your arm." But it turned out that he'd suffered a minor stroke. Tyson returned from Africa to take care of him. She kept him alive; he repaid her with his friendship and attention—and by cheating on her constantly and, occasionally, hitting her.

ON FEBRUARY 17, 1982, MONK DIED, AT SIXTY-FOUR YEARS OLD. JAZZ MAY have left dance behind, but Thelonious kept dancing till the end of his career.

WITH PHYSICAL THERAPY, MILES REGAINED ENOUGH USE OF THE HAND to play trumpet again. Against medical wisdom, he went back out on the road. "I knew that I looked like death waiting to eat a soda cracker," he said. "I was so thin and had lost most of my hair. . . . I was so weak a lot of the time that I had to play while sitting down." What he omits saying is that he was sometimes playing from a wheelchair. It hardly mattered;

he was greeted rapturously wherever he went—Japan, Sweden, Denmark, Germany, London, Rome, Paris—whether he played well or not (or played at all: as before, he often he put down his horn and tapped out notes on the electric organ). And whether he played well or not, he still led a tight band, still had a singular genius for conducting with the minutest glances and gestures.

Was it jazz? If Miles was involved, it must be—at least so the thinking went.

"Why did he come back? Because he needed the money!" said Dave Liebman, who still sat in with Davis now and then in New York. "That's why he came back. He needed the damn money. He was existing on checks from Columbia. He would get the check, he would give it to us, we had to go cash it at the Chinese restaurant at Eighty-first and Broadway. He'd say, 'Take the check to them; they know who I am.' Somebody like me would take the check to this Asia de Cuba joint—it was like six hundred dollars, something like that. I'd go back and give him six hundred dollars. He'd go immediately and get coke with it."

But Liebman's respect and affection for Davis never wavered. "I felt that Miles in the eighties—as far as I was concerned, he gave another generation a chance to see him, because [otherwise] they would never have known about him," he said. "They would have known him as an historical figure, like I know Charlie Parker. But here they could go and see him play—and they did. I was glad that at least people could see him play again, even if the music was watered down."

After a couple more tours—four cities in Japan in May 1983, Warsaw and Berlin in October—he returned to New York at the beginning of November to be feted at Radio City with a mammoth celebration organized by Columbia Records and Cicely, "Miles Ahead: A Tribute to an American Music Legend." Cosby emceed. The program featured Quincy Jones leading a big band; the trio of Herbie Hancock, Ron Carter, and Tony Williams; and an all-star Miles Davis alumni group consisting of Jimmy Heath, Philly Joe Jones, Wayne Shorter, and a dozen others. The evening was rich with remembrance, but Davis wasn't having any.

"Efforts were made to have Miles play in one of his older styles," Szwed writes, "but he ignored them, and instead did a half-hour set with his current band"—two electric guitarists, two drummers, a clarinetist, a synthesizer player, and Davis playing another synthesizer with his right hand and trumpet with his left. It was a bravura touch, and a body blow to nostalgia.

In a long night of highlights, one of the highest was the big finish of the program's first half, a seven-trumpet fanfare for Miles as a prelude to a midnight presentation that included, among other accolades, an honorary doctor of music degree from Fisk University. The trumpeters were an all-star group themselves, their ages running the gamut from the fifties (Art Farmer and Maynard Ferguson) to the thirties (Jimmy Owens, Lew Soloff, Randy Brecker, Jon Faddis) to the youngest by far, a handsome, broad-faced twenty-three-year-old from Washington, D.C., who, while

still in his teens, had twice won *DownBeat*'s Award for Best Young Jazz Musician of the Year. His name was Wallace Roney.

EIGHT YEARS ON. TIME HAD DONE MILES NO FAVORS: GIL EVANS, ARGUably his only close friend since Freddie Webster, had died, of peritonitis, in 1988. Davis's own maladies had only advanced as he approached, then passed, the age of sixty-five. He had a permanent limp, his plastic hip never having gotten quite right; his diabetes was out of control; his vision was fading; he had respiratory difficulties; he was skeletally thin and still losing weight. In spite of it all, he kept moving, the thing he knew best. In July 1991 he traveled to the Montreux, Switzerland, Jazz Festival for a gig Quincy Jones had finally succeeded in talking him into after fifteen years of trying: a retrospective of the Gil Evans–arranged big band recordings *Birth of the Cool*, *Porgy and Bess*, and *Sketches of Spain*.

Had the nostalgia-proof Miles Davis succumbed to nostalgia? Wallace Roney, who at Miles's invitation had joined the band at Montreux, asserted that he had not. If someone had told him a year earlier that Davis had agreed to play his old material again, "I would've said, 'You're just bullshitting. That's what you'd *like*.' But I knew that Miles was *so* into it now. And he wasn't into it as looking *back*. He was looking at, 'Let's develop it. Let's play this music. Hasn't been played enough now.'"

Roney had spent the past eight years literally and figuratively sitting at Miles's feet, playing for him, listening to him play, taking in his musical ideas. "I wanted to learn what he had to say," he told me. "So I listened, you know."

But all the to-do surrounding this simple musical friendship—the cobbled up Roney-Marsalis rivalry; the Miles-Marsalis battles, culminating in the 1986 Vancouver incident—all this was old news in July 1991: Marsalis was a superstar, Roney was having a middling-successful career in a niche art. Miles was in steep decline.

Then something magical happened. In all the many hours he had spent with Davis, Roney had never actually played trumpet *with* him: "I might've played in [his] house, or he might've played and I played back something," he told me. Even in rehearsals on the afternoon of the eighth, Roney hadn't dared to play along with him: "When he came—I stepped back."

But in performance that night, Roney said, "Man! Now he gets to hear his *son*. Play his stuff." He laughed. "All the lessons, all that stuff that I learned! Oh God! So I'm up there playing 'Boplicity,' and all this stuff— I don't know, man. It was like a dream. At first I was thinking, Oh, shit, what is he thinking? Then he came over to me and whispered in my ear: *'Phrase this with quarter-note triplets.'*

"Man, I'm playing, he's whispering in my ear, then he takes out his horn. And he starts to play *with* me. I heard that sound a million times. But next to my sound—oh, *man*. Oh, God! I mean, that was *Miles Davis*.

"And now I'm more and more comfortable. And I'm *playing*. And we're playing something—I think 'Sketches of Spain.' And all of a sudden, Miles *stops*. He stops playing. And he looks like he's angry. And he walks off the stage. And Quincy walks off the stage.

"Then Quincy comes back—he says, 'Well—show must go on.' We all thought that Miles said, 'Fuck, I don't want to do this.' And I was wondering if I overstepped my bounds—you know, that I *played* too much. So—Miles is *gone*. And we keep playing 'Sketches of Spain.' Now that he's not on my shoulder, I'm *really* going for it, you know? Now I gotta take his slack. So I'm playing like I'd play if I had to lead this band. I'm going for it, and after we finish, Miles comes back. He just wanted to take a rest, that's all it was; I don't know why he didn't *say* that."

But Miles was just doing what Miles had always done: walking off the stage achieved the dual purpose of yielding the spotlight to one of his players and keeping the audience thinking about him, Miles (*Where'd he go?*). And as always, few if any had truly understood.

When Davis returned, Roney remembered, he put his arm around his protégé's shoulder and said (Roney shifted into Miles-voice): "'You sure sound good playin' that shit up there.'

"And I said, 'No, man, I'm just playing your stuff.' And Miles said,

'No, Wally—no. Stop that. No more of that humble stuff. You sound *good* playing that stuff up there.'

"But I can't not be humble," Roney told me. "I said, 'Chief, I'm just playing what I learned from you.'

"He looked at me," Roney said. "He said, 'Okay. I'll buy that. 'Cause I ain't doin' shit but playin' Dizzy's shit with Freddie Webster's tone.'"

AT THE END OF AUGUST, MILES AND HIS BAND PLAYED THE HOLLYWOOD Bowl. Wayne Shorter, who was also performing at the concert, visited Davis in his dressing room: "He had lost so much weight from the time I saw him in July," he remembered. "But still he had a sort of illumination around his skin, his face and everything: there was slight illumination emanating from within him—from within to without, and I could see there was something different."

Over the Labor Day weekend, Miles started vomiting blood. His final lover, the artist Jo Gelbard, drove him to St. John's Hospital in Santa Monica, where he was admitted with what was once more thought to be pneumonia. Days later, he suffered a stroke that paralyzed the left side of his body. Agitated, struggling to keep from falling asleep, he kept saying, "I don't want to die."

He was still fully engaged in life: still painting; working on a hip-hop album, as well as a collaboration with Prince. He wanted to record *Tosca*, to star in a Broadway show based on his life. Ever restless, straining against the petty bonds of time and illness.

"He was pulling the wires and tubes out of himself," Gelbard recalled, "and the situation was getting difficult to handle, even though he was down to eighty pounds." A male nurse managed to get him back into bed; Gelbard lay down next to him. All at once, she felt him go limp: he had fallen into a coma.

He never regained consciousness. Three weeks later, on September 28, 1991, he died, a very old (and very young) sixty-five.

———

I HEARD THE NEWS AS I DROVE UP THE WEST SIDE HIGHWAY FROM AN-
other interview: it felt unreal somehow. My mind went back two and a
half years, to the moment I was to leave at the end of our talk. As I shoul-
dered my backpack and shook his hard, spidery hand, thanking him and
saying goodbye, he looked at me with dark, glittering eyes. "You comin'
back?" he asked.

Acknowledgments

In the fall of 2017 I was a biographer without a subject, at sea without a sail or a rudder. The second and final volume of my life of Frank Sinatra had been published two years earlier, and my feelings about what I might write next were somewhat akin to those expressed by Sinatra's first wife, Nancy, when asked why she never married again: "After Frank Sinatra, who?" It seemed formidably difficult to come up with a biography subject—or any nonfiction subject—as big, as impactful. So I was flailing, and pushing: never a good place for a writer to be. That autumn I wrote a proposal for a group biography, somewhat akin to Lytton Strachey's *Eminent Victorians*, of four men who died in 1955: Albert Einstein, Charlie Parker, Wallace Stevens, and James Dean. There was a surface cleverness to the idea—all four were vivid characters, and they were vividly different. Yet Strachey's subjects defined a particular, and perhaps simpler, age. What linked my four subjects except for the coincidence of the year of their deaths? *Eminent Eisenhowerians* just didn't have the same ring.

The editors who read my proposal found it ingenious but not compelling. But one of them, Scott Moyers of Penguin Press, asked if I wanted to get together to discuss ideas—other ideas. And so on a very cold December afternoon, Scott and I met for the first time, for coffee at a tapas restaurant on lower Sixth Avenue, and after a few getting-acquainted pleasantries, he mentioned a book idea *he* had: Miles Davis, John Coltrane, and Bill Evans, the three geniuses of the historic jazz album *Kind of Blue*.

My reaction was instantaneous. "Let's do it," I said.

The notion excited me for a couple of reasons. One was that, like many people, jazz aficionados and general listeners alike, I knew and loved *Kind of Blue*, the bestselling jazz album of all time. The 1959 record was in a timeless category all its own: deep, mysterious, transcendent. Another reason was that I had once interviewed Miles, in 1989, for a *Vanity Fair* piece pegged to the publication of his memoir, and, contrary to his fearsome reputation, he had been sweet and expansive: I liked him very much.

And I immediately had an idea for expanding on Scott's idea. I knew that the jazz writer Ashley Kahn had published an excellent and highly readable, if somewhat specialized, book about the making of *Kind of Blue*. But what if, instead of just writing about the album, I were to tell the stories of these three great artists both as men and musicians, before, during, and after the recording of the record that brought them together? There was a lot there: musically, historically, psychologically. Racially. There was the big story of the devolution of jazz—the only purely American art form— in the second half of the twentieth century, from a music that brought the country together, made it dance, to an art music, a niche music, one that fewer and fewer people found understandable or compelling. *Kind of Blue* seemed to sit almost precisely at the hinge between jazz's 1950s glories and its slide into esotericism. I said all this to Scott.

"Let's do it," he said.

And so we did, and here you have it, and my unceasing gratitude goes to Scott Moyers, an editor of brilliance, originality, and bigheartedness.

To Miles Davis I also owe an immense debt, not just for his kindness to a raw and uneducated young reporter but for setting me on a path toward loving and beginning to understand this great music.

I was fortunate to begin the project with the Miles interview in my pocket, and as my work proceeded, my luck held: I was able to interview many musicians of the highest caliber, beginning with the great Sonny Rollins, who astounded me with his candor, generosity, and thoughtfulness about matters musical and beyond.

Wallace Roney, Miles's only protégé and a kind of genius himself, was extraordinarily generous with his time and incisive in his thinking about the musical era my three subjects lived in, as well as the creative evolution of each man.

Every musician I spoke with had astounding things to say, and every one of them educated me. I'm especially grateful to Monty Alexander, Jon Batiste, Randy Brecker, Chick Corea, Jack DeJohnette, Jon Faddis, Billy Hart, Eddie Henderson, Ethan Iverson, Sheila Jordan, Lee Konitz, Joe LaBarbera, Dave Liebman, Christian McBride, Kenny Werner, Denny Zeitlin, and Eliot Zigmund.

I'm also indebted to the musical polymaths who gave so freely of their time: Gary Giddins, Dan Morgenstern, Ted Panken, and Loren Schoenberg.

Monica Getz, Maxine Gordon, and Laurie Verchomin provided invaluable detail and insight about the times, and the Life.

Jessica Butler went beyond the call of duty to help me find the beautiful photographs that illustrate the book.

I'm also grateful to Andy Arleo, Jessica Brecker, Stephanie Crease, Mark Gould, Emily Hunt, Aaron Kaplan, Avery Kaplan, Jacob Kaplan, Peter Losin, and Leif Bo Petersen.

My deep thanks to the team at Penguin Press: Mia Council, Tom Dussel, Hal Fessenden, Sarah Hutson, Daniel Lagin, Heather Lewis, Darren Haggar, Danielle Plafsky, Mollie Reid, Greg Villepique, Chelsea Cohen, Claire Vaccaro, Eric Wechter, Aly D'Amato, and Ann Godoff.

A very special thank-you to Ken Langone, a true friend.

Once again I'm profoundly grateful to my longtime agent, the great Joy

Harris, for accompanying and encouraging me on another voyage together, and emboldening me for the road ahead.

Each of my three sons, Jacob, Aaron, and Avery, has a different relationship to music, but all are equally passionate about it, and all continue to inspire and teach me.

And to my wife, Karen Cumbus, my vast gratitude for living with me, for giving me hope when my hopes were low—and for putting up with all the times I raised a shushing hand as I tried to identify, for the umpteenth time, which saxophonist we were hearing on the radio.

Notes

Prelude

11 **visits to yoga clubs:** Twenty-two years later, Talese would write of jaded suburban couples seeking even more unusual amusements in his bestseller *Thy Neighbor's Wife*.

11 **"He makes each performance":** John S. Wilson, "Thelonious Monk Plays Own Works," *New York Times*, Mar. 2, 1959.

12 **Buried in the back pages:** Ibid.

Chapter 1: The blue trumpet

17 **We settled down:** James Kaplan, "Miles Davis Blows His Horn," *Vanity Fair*, Aug. 1989.

19 **It didn't help matters:** Francis Davis, "You're Under Arrest," *Rolling Stone*, July 4, 1985.

19 **The first time the two:** Gourse, *Wynton Marsalis: Skain's Domain*, p. 89.

20 **"See, you laughing":** Author's interview with Miles Davis.

21 **In Wynton's 2015 retelling:** Wynton Marsalis blog, wyntonmarsalis.org/blog/entry/my-1986-encounter-with-miles-davis-in-vancouver.

21 **"Wynton Marsalis surprised everyone":** United Press International (UPI) report of July 2, 1986.

22 **furious. "Get the fuck off":** Davis and Troupe, *Miles*, p. 374.

22 **"Wynton can't play":** Ibid.

22 **The story, Marsalis said:** Wynton Marsalis blog, wyntonmarsalis.org/blog/entry/my-1986-encounter-with-miles-davis-in-vancouver.

23 **"Now Wynton talks about":** Author's interview with Wallace Roney.

25 **Still, some who knew Miles:** When I look back at my interviews with Miles, I find that he used the word only four times over the course of three-plus hours.

25 **Some have also contended:** And some have gone much further: "The book," Stanley Crouch wrote, "is overwhelmingly an outburst of inarticulateness, of profanity, of error, of self-inflation, and of parasitic paraphrasing of material from Jack Chambers' *Milestones*" (Crouch, *Considering Genius*, pp. 252–53).

26 **Brown didn't swing:** As a not entirely tangential point, let it be noted that in the index of Miles's voluminous memoir, a virtual catalog of twentieth-century jazz musicians, the names of Lee Morgan and Freddie Hubbard are nowhere to be found.

Chapter 2: Dentist's son

31 **"seemed to be middle class":** Davis and Troupe, *Miles*, p. 14.

32 **"Dr. Miles D. Davis":** "Entertainments, Society and Meetings, Upper Alton," *Alton Evening Telegraph*, Mar. 7, 1925, p. 3.

33 **"I got whatever artistic talent":** Davis and Troupe, *Miles*, p. 14.

34 **"he was a bad little dude":** Early, *Miles Davis and American Culture*, p. viii.

35 **At Lincoln High he met:** Irene (1924–2007) was known by three surnames during her life: at birth, Cawthon; then by her stepfather's name, Birth; and last, probably through a marriage after she left Miles, Oliver. See wikitree.com/wiki/Cawthon-223.

37 **"People would start to dance":** Gillespie and Fraser, *To Be, or Not . . . to Bop*, p. 190.

37 **"No other band like this":** Ibid., p. 188.

38 **"I remember one place we worked":** Ibid., p. 190.

39 **"The way that band was playing":** Davis and Troupe, *Miles*, p. 7.

39 **"Come on, we need a trumpet":** Ibid., p. 8.

40 **"you couldn't even hear him":** Gillespie and Fraser, *To Be, or Not . . . to Bop*, p. 191. Miles recalled (Davis and Troupe, *Miles*, p. 154) that as the youngest member of the band, he was required by Eckstine to sit on a wooden Coke box instead of a chair during gigs—and to pick up the leader's suits at the cleaner, fetch him cigarettes, and make sure Eckstine's shoes were shined.

40 **"that I had to leave":** Davis and Troupe, *Miles*, p. 9.

Chapter 3: It must be heard with the brain and felt with the soul

43 **"a smokescreen, a stopover":** Davis and Troupe, *Miles*, p. 52.

44 **"fed up with travel":** DeVeaux, *The Birth of Bebop*, p. 350.

44 **"hipper-looking clubs":** Davis and Troupe, *Miles*, p. 55.

45 **"long, low-ceilinged":** DeVeaux, *The Birth of Bebop*, p. 284.

45 **"The tables were three inches":** Shaw, *52nd Street*, p. 280.

45 **"Up front trumpet":** Russell, *Bird Lives!*, p. 171.

45 **"Listeners were rocked":** Ibid., p. 172.

46 **"Sometimes you can listen":** Gillespie and Fraser, *To Be, or Not . . . to Bop*, p. 203.

46 **"Jazz in the Swing Era":** Giddins, *Visions of Jazz: The First Century*, p. 89.

47 **"I remember listening with awe":** Davis and Troupe, *Miles*, p. 55.

48 **Wincing at the appellation:** Ibid.

48 **"My best advice":** Ibid., p. 56.

49 **"playing my ass off":** Ibid., p. 60.

49 **"Plus, they were so":** Ibid., p. 59.

49 **"I used to win *awards*":** Author's interview with Davis.

50 **"I wanted to see what was going on":** Davis and Troupe, *Miles*, pp. 60–61.

51 **"I said, 'Listen, Dad'":** Ibid., pp. 73–74.

51 **"You know, my father":** Author's interview with Miles Davis.

52 **"He was very gifted":** Early, *Miles Davis and American Culture*, p. 83.

52 **"That shit be going so fast":** Gillespie and Fraser, *To Be, or Not . . . to Bop*, p. 226.

53 **"I used to try to play":** Davis and Troupe, *Miles*, p. 62.

53 **His death two years later:** It would also be rumored that Webster had injected bad heroin—possibly laced with battery acid or strychnine—that someone, possibly a vengeful dealer cheated out of money, had intended for Sonny Stitt.

53 **"a great and genius musician":** Davis and Troupe, *Miles*, p. 65.

53 **"Bird was *out*"**: Author's interview with Miles Davis.

54 **"talk to street people"**: Giddins, *Celebrating Bird*, p. 95.

54 **"You took advantage"**: Gillespie and Fraser, *To Be, or Not . . . to Bop*, p. 177.

55 **"This is my home"**: Gioia, *The History of Jazz*, p. 231.

55 **thinking it was cocaine**: Spunt, *Heroin and Music in New York City*, p. 53.

55 **"but I hated that clowning"**: Davis and Troupe, *Miles*, p. 163.

56 **"Then they all quit at once"**: Stearns, *The Story of Jazz*, p. 159.

56 **"'Shut up, Junior'"**: Hayde, *Stan Levey, Jazz Heavyweight*, p. 68.

56 **"Everyone in the room heard"**: Giddins, *Celebrating Bird*, pp. 95–96.

57 **"had been struggling to find"**: DeVeaux, *The Birth of Bebop*, p. 417.

57 **"I'm almost sure by now"**: *Dizzy Gillespie/Charlie Parker: Town Hall, New York City, June 22, 1945*, Uptown Jazz CD, June 2005.

59 **"Things didn't work out"**: Gillespie and Fraser, *To Be, or Not . . . to Bop*, p. 223.

59 **In late July he returned**: Besides Bird and Byas, the group consisted of Al Haig on piano, Curley Russell on bass, and either Stan Levey or Max Roach on drums.

59 **"Dizzy's quitting the group"**: Davis and Troupe, *Miles*, p. 68.

59 **"'Here's my trumpet player'"**: Ibid.

59 **In early October, Parker began**: Ibid. Miles and Troupe write, incorrectly, that the stand was at the Three Deuces. See Peter Losin's authoritative Parker chronology: http://www.plosin.com/milesAhead/Bird/Charlie%20Parker%20Chronology%201945.html.

60 **"Bird and [Arnold] Schoenberg"**: Author's interview with Dave Liebman.

60 **"I just couldn't play it high"**: Davis and Troupe, *Miles*, pp. 68–69.

60 **"That's how bad"**: Gillespie and Fraser, *To Be, or Not . . . to Bop*, pp. 215–16.

60 **"I think it's the same reason"**: Author's interview with Loren Schoenberg.

61 **even more privileged**: Gordon was bona fide Los Angeles Black royalty. His father, one of the first African American physicians in L.A., treated Duke Ellington and Lionel Hampton; his mother was the daughter of a Medal of Honor recipient in the Spanish-American War.

61 **"'you playing in Bird's band?'"**: Davis and Troupe, *Miles*, pp. 110–11.

62 **"'Why don't you get'"**: Ibid., p. 111.

62 **"The cabaret licenses"**: "4 Night Clubs Penalized," *New York Times*, Nov. 5, 1945, p. 21.

62 **"hustlers and fast-living pimps"**: Davis and Troupe, *Miles*, p. 72.

63 **Dizzy Gillespie told**: Gillespie and Fraser, *To Be, or Not . . . to Bop*, p. 211.

63 **"After the hearings ended"**: "4 Night Clubs Penalized."

64 **"with little apparent"**: Broven, *Record Makers and Breakers*, pp. 57–59.

64 **"a rather profane cheapskate"**: Scott Yanow, "Artist Biography: Herman Lubinsky," *AllMusic*, allmusic.com/artist/herman-lubinsky-mn0000678736/biography.

64 **"who mastered the art of networking"**: Ritz, *Faith in Time*, p. 71.

64 **later to become Sadik Hakim**: Black jazz musicians started to embrace Islam and adopt Muslim names as early as the late 1940s.

64 **"The material consisted"**: Dave Gelly, "The Immortal Charlie Parker," *Jazz Journal*, Feb. 5, 2020. Fascinatingly, on the outtake of "Ko-Ko," the musicians actually start to play Ray Noble's "Cherokee," the number "Ko-Ko" is based on—only to have Reig run out of the control room yelling "Hold it! Hold it!" and whistling and clapping his hands to nip in the bud this dangerous breach, which would've been money out of Herman Lubinsky's pocket and into Noble's. See https://www.npr.org/2000/08/27/1081208/-i-ko-ko-i.

65 **"I didn't make no bones"**: Davis and Troupe, *Miles*, p. 75.

65 **nor to lose face**: "It was like one guy with two heads was playing together," the bassist Ray Brown said. "It's hard to go back and find any two horns that played together any better at any time. And such fantastic soloists. And they were playing a different thing" (Gillespie and Fraser, *To Be, or Not . . . to Bop*, p. 250).

66 **"after Bird got high"**: Davis and Troupe, *Miles*, p. 76.

67 **"altercations and a reshuffling"**: Russell, *Bird Lives!*, p. 211.

67–68 "Bird was never organized": Davis and Troupe, *Miles*, p. 89.
68–69 "He wasn't no musician": Ibid., pp. 89–90.
    69 "He rolled up his sleeves": Russell, *Bird Lives!*, p. 211.
    69 "After each of": Ibid., p. 212.

Chapter 4: Serious

75 "the unforgettable night": Bob Bernotas, "Moving Ever Forward: Benny Golson," jazzbob .com/articles.php?id=8.

75 and "Salt Peanuts": The true authorship of this 1942 number is uncertain. Charlie Parker has also been credited with its composition, and its signature octave-jump riff appeared in Count Basie and Glenn Miller recordings in 1941.

75 "right between the eyes": John Coltrane with Don DeMicheal, *DownBeat*, Sept. 29, 1960.

76 "We got to the club": Bob Bernotas, "Moving Ever Forward: Benny Golson," jazzbob.com /articles.php?id=8.

76 "if it started with Coltrane": Porter, *John Coltrane*, p. 60.

77 "This session was inspired": Ibid., p. 43.

77 "Dizzy had cashed in": Russell, *Bird Lives!*, p. 243.

78 "copying like mad": Porter, *John Coltrane*, p. 44.

78 "a very reserved individual": Ibid., p. 39.

78 like Parker himself: For the story of how the recording was found, see Porter, *John Coltrane*, p. 308. It can be heard (Bernie's Bootlegs: "Young John Coltrane Live w/Navy Band '46 & Johnny Hodges '54," YouTube audio, 42:29, Sept. 17, 2017) at youtube.com /watch?v=3Qn7123lcTM.

79 "the connection that would": Porter, *John Coltrane*, p. 50.

79 Upon his discharge: Ibid., p. 40.

80 "My family liked church music": DeVito, *Coltrane on Coltrane*, p. 62.

81 "practiced *all* the time": Ibid., p. 33.

81 "a very rhythmic fellow": Tom Steadman, "Coltrane: The Quiet Boy Who Grew Up in High Point and Became a Jazz Legend," Greensboro.com, Sept. 21, 1991, greensboro .com/coltrane-the-quiet-boy-who-grew-up-in-high-point-and-became-a-jazz-legend /article_b7bcc0dc-0d9b-5d95-9561-0d2ce971bb75.html.

81 "It was mostly": DeVito, *Coltrane on Coltrane*, p. 62. Coltrane is using an anachronism to refer to rhythm and blues—the term "rock and roll," as applied to popular music, didn't enter common usage until the early 1950s, several years after he graduated high school.

82 "horn wasn't squeaking": Porter, *John Coltrane*, p. 31.

82 "He just loved": Ibid., p. 33.

82 "I threw myself": DeVito, *Coltrane on Coltrane*, p. 130.

83 acts such as Ralph Dunbar's: Advertisement, *Philadelphia Inquirer*, May 20, 1917, p. 19.

83 "many social clubs": Porter, *John Coltrane*, p. 35.

83 "so many jam sessions": Ibid., p. 36.

84 "would sit at my vanity": Ibid., p. 33.

84 "a kind of cocktail music": DeVito, *Coltrane on Coltrane*, p. 130.

84 "A good place to learn": Ibid., p. 62.

85 he jammed with Bird: Losin, *Miles Ahead*, jam session of Feb. 19, 1947, plosin.com /milesAhead/Bird/Charlie%20Parker%20Chronology%201947.html.

85 "a great reader": Porter, *John Coltrane*, p. 79.

85 "We were in tune": Smithsonian Institution Jazz Oral History Program: Lewis Porter interviews with Jimmy Heath, Mar. 3 and 4, 1995.

85 a botched conk job: See *The Autobiography of Malcolm X* for a full description of the torments early– and mid-twentieth-century Black men, including Malcolm in his youth, went through to conk—straighten—their hair.

86 **"If you're going to play"**: "Eddie Vinson Puts Emphasis on Youth," *Detroit Tribune*, Screen/Radio/Stage section, Jan. 15, 1949, p. 15.

86 **"sounded like Dexter Gordon"**: Porter, *John Coltrane*, p. 74.

86 **"also a popular performer"**: Ibid., p. 73.

87 **"'Yeah, little ol' Coltrane'"**: "Jazzman of the Year: John Coltrane," *DownBeat's Music 1962—The 7th Annual Yearbook*, 1962, pp. 66–69.

87 **"I've picked up something"**: Ibid., p. 66.

87 **"Parker had me strung"**: Ibid., p. 63.

Chapter 5: Move

90 **even Duke Ellington**: Crease, *Gil Evans*, p. 138.

90 **"The legendary Billy Eckstine"**: Travis, *An Autobiography of Black Jazz*, p. 318.

90 **made a record with the honking**: Davis and Troupe, *Miles*, pp. 98–99.

90 **"They can get it out"**: Chan Richardson letter of Feb. 7, 1947 in Russell, *Bird Lives!*, p. 238.

90 **Duke Jordan soon signed**: Losin, *Miles Ahead*, Three Deuces stand of Aug. 7–Sept. 24, 1947, plosin.com/milesAhead/Bird/Charlie%20Parker%20Chronology%201947.html.

90 **"but the inducement of being"**: Russell, *Bird Lives!*, p. 243.

91 **"he'd just smile"**: Davis and Troupe, *Miles*, pp. 101–02.

91 **"Because then we couldn't"**: Ibid., p. 102.

92 **The spontaneous freedom**: History can be unkind to its chroniclers: soon after Benedetti taped "All the Things You Are," Sammy Kaye kicked him out of the club for failing to buy any food or drink.

92 **"The first session was made"**: The reliably exhaustive jazz researcher Leif Bo Petersen says the session was on Oct. 28, 1947. See Losin, *Miles Ahead*, plosin.com/milesAhead/Bird/Charlie%20Parker%20Chronology%201947.html.

92 **"'mad, blowing mood'"**: Russell, *Bird Lives!*, p. 249.

93 **and finally, two ballads**: Ibid., p. 250.

93 **"Playing with Bird and being seen"**: Davis and Troupe, *Miles*, p. 105.

94 **"Miles's musical gift"**: Author's interview with Jon Batiste.

95 **"Take me as you would"**: Priestley, *Chasin' the Bird*, p. 73; Giddins, *Celebrating Bird*, p. 135; Reisner, *Bird*, p. 229.

96 **"within stumbling distance"**: Crease, *Gil Evans*, p. 130.

96 **"He'd come in with"**: Davis and Troupe, *Miles*, p. 120.

97 **"Like bull sessions"**: Crease, *Gil Evans*, p. 131.

97 **"we started utilizing"**: Ibid., pp. 131–32.

97 **on the quintet's first**: Actually it was a modified version of the quintet, with Bud Powell on the piano instead of Duke Jordan. Powell was by far the better player—great to Jordan's good—but he and Bird seldom worked together because, according to Miles (Davis and Troupe, pp. 75, 114), they simply didn't like each other. "Donna Lee" was named after Curley Russell's daughter.

97 **"really flipped me"**: Marc Crawford, "Miles and Gil: Portrait of a Friendship," *DownBeat*, Feb. 16, 1961.

98 **"We heard sound"**: Davis and Troupe, *Miles*, p. 104.

98 **"bothered me less"**: Ibid., p. 104.

98 **tied Dizzy for first**: Ibid., p. 108.

98 **"I didn't come to New York"**: Ibid., p. 120.

99 **"allowing more flexibility"**: Crease, *Gil Evans*, p. 156.

99 **"a rehearsal band"**: Ibid., p. 157.

99 **"I hired the rehearsal halls"**: Davis and Troupe, *Miles*, p. 116. Troupe seems to be, to put it kindly, paraphrasing Gerry Mulligan's famous remark: "Miles called the rehearsals, hired the halls, called the players and generally cracked the whip" (Cook, *It's About That Time*, p. 16).

99 *"not* widely respected": Crease, *Gil Evans*, p. 156.
99 "Listen to him with Dizzy": Author's interview with Wallace Roney. "Fat Girl" was Miles's nickname for Navarro; Navarro called Miles "Millie."
100 "Max was perfect": Crease, *Gil Evans*, p. 157.
100 Kaye begged him: Ibid., pp. 114–15.
101 a Miles Davis–led quintet: Losin, *Miles Ahead*, recording session of Sept. 25, 1948, plosin .com/milesAhead/Sessions.aspx?s=480925.
101 "I had the club": Davis and Troupe, *Miles*, p. 117.
102 "their first tune, a thing": Losin, *Miles Ahead*, Royal Roost concert of Sept. 4, 1948, plosin .com/milesahead/Sessions.aspx?s=480904.
103 "The music at times": Joey Soane, "Music Makers . . . ," *Lyndhurst* (N.J.) *Leader*, Sept. 23, 1948, p. 10.
103 "I didn't know what they": Chambers, *Milestones*, p. 106.
103 it's hard to guess: Losin, *Miles Ahead*, Royal Roost concert of Sept. 18, 1948, plosin.com /MilesAhead/Sessions.aspx?s=480918b.
103 "higher than a motherfucker off": Davis and Troupe, *Miles*, p. 123.
104 "the Davis trumpet highlighting": "In the Groove," *Amarillo* (Tex.) *Sunday News-Globe*, Mar. 13, 1949, p. 13.
104 "There is a strange": Ed Caswell, "'Say, Man, What's This Bebop Got That Dixieland Ain't Got?,'" *Stanford Daily*, July 22, 1949, p. 8.
105 "Vooph! It's great": Howard Lee, Record Parade column, *Cleveland Call and Post*, Mar. 19, 1949, p. 9-B.
105 "along with Sidney Bechet": Davis and Troupe, *Miles*, p. 126.
106 "had the crowds dancing": Russell, *Bird Lives!*, pp. 270–71.
106 "represented both liberation": Morgenstern, *Living with Jazz*, p. 214.
106 "When I finally": Davis and Troupe, *Miles*, p. 126.
106 "I like your playing": Russell, *Bird Lives!*, p. 271.
107 "cared a lot for Irene": Davis and Troupe, *Miles*, p. 126.
107 "sinking faster than": Ibid., p. 127.

Chapter 6: Walking the bar

109 "technically . . . the best": Gillespie and Fraser, *To Be, or Not . . . to Bop*, p. 355.
109 "A dance band": Ibid., p. 356.
110 "They'd just stand": Ibid., pp. 356–57.
110 "It's either me": Ibid., p. 357.
110 "When you put it in your nose": Porter, *John Coltrane*, p. 62.
111 "That way they all": Ibid., p. 85.
111 Heath found him: Heath believed he saved Coltrane's life. As he recalled in his memoir: "Coltrane took off first. He cooked up his stuff, drew it up, and shot it into his arm. He immediately fell out on the floor. The guy who had sold it to us was still hanging in the restaurant, so we asked him to come up and bring some milk so that we could try to revive Coltrane. The milk was supposed to be an antidote, we thought. We were slapping him, throwing water in his face, trying to get him to come to. When the guy brought the milk, we poured that down his throat and eventually Coltrane got up. He said that the last thing he remembered when he fainted was my saying, 'Come on, man. Come on, man. Give me the works.' If we hadn't revived him, he certainly would have OD'd, and the Coltrane that people know now would never have existed. This was before *My Favorite Things* or *A Love Supreme*. His monstrous and legendary career came later. Of course, we revived him because he was our friend, not because he was going to make history" (Heath and McLaren, *I Walked with Giants*, pp. 69–70).
111 who had just fired: Dizzy's words, according to Jimmy Heath: "You junky motherfuckers. You're fired" (Heath and McLaren, *I Walked with Giants*, p. 70).

112 "I heard Charlie Parker": Steve Voce, "Obituary: Red Rodney," *The Independent*, May 30, 1994, independent.co.uk/news/people/obituary-red-rodney-1439684.html.

112 "When you're very young": Lees, *Cats of Any Color*, p. 103.

112 "Heroin was our badge. It was": Jonnes, *Hep-Cats, Narcs, and Pipe Dreams*, p. 119.

112 "sweated like a horse": Hawes, *Raise Up Off Me*, p. 14.

112 After he'd sat there: Ibid., p. 15.

113 "made a believer": Ibid.

113 "I started using": July 26, 1966, interview of Dexter Gordon by Mike Hennessey in *Melody Maker*, a British music magazine.

114 "it was our fight": Author's interview with Sonny Rollins.

114 "To live once": Russell, *Bird Lives!*, pp. 260–61.

115 but then asked Fremer: Björn Fremer, "The John Coltrane Story, as Told to Björn Fremer," *Jazz News*, May 10, 1961.

115 "It's such an uncertain": Ibid., p. 77.

115 playing an extended stand: The ornate and magnificent club, at Broadway and Fifty-second Street, opened on December 15, 1949, so named to garner publicity from Charlie Parker's reputation—though ironically, because of Parker's incessant financial demands, the eponym rarely played there.

115 It is magnificent: Bernie's Bootlegs, "Dizzy Gillespie & John Coltrane, Live at Birdland 1951—Unknown Radio Broadcast," 32:13, Sept. 18, 2017, youtube.com/watch?v=A63IsX -5HM8&t=595s.

116 "I was somewhat disgusted": DeVito, *Coltrane on Coltrane*, p. 131.

116 "'Gee, I wish'": Porter, *John Coltrane*, p. 86.

116 on Wyalusing Avenue: Jimmy Heath believed (Porter, *John Coltrane*, p. 60) that he'd first introduced Coltrane to Miles at Philadelphia's Downbeat Club in December 1947, when Miles was in town with the Charlie Parker Quintet. For his part, Miles remembered first meeting Coltrane in the summer of 1950, when Coltrane was playing with Gillespie "at a club up in Harlem" (Davis and Troupe, *Miles*, p. 133). Lewis Porter writes (*John Coltrane*, p. 86) that Coltrane played a dance job at the Audubon Ballroom with Miles, Sonny Rollins, Bud Powell, and Art Blakey, but places the gig in March 1951.

117 "He has fabulous": John Coltrane with Don DeMicheal, *DownBeat*, Sept. 29, 1960.

117 "had not reached the point": Fremer, "The John Coltrane Story, as Told to Björn Fremer."

117 "walked right out": Porter, *John Coltrane*, p. 92.

117 "in Las Vegas lounges": Ibid.

117 jump-blues tunes: Ibid. Jackson's best-remembered number may be 1952's "Big Ten Inch Record."

118 Dorothy Fields and: Coltrane Research, "John Coltrane with Johnny Hodges 1954," YouTube audio, 30:00, publication date unknown, youtube.com/watch?v=OCTXcUGKcw8&t=245s.

118 "It was my education": DeVito, *Coltrane on Coltrane*, p. 42.

118 "That was a lot": Porter, *John Coltrane*, p. 62. Eighty dollars in 1950 was the equivalent of over nine hundred dollars today.

118 an old school friend: Ibid., p. 91.

Chapter 7: Junkie time

121 "who were copying": Davis and Troupe, *Miles*, p. 129.

121 "Those were listless": Morgenstern, *Living with Jazz*, p. 214.

122 "'Yeah, he gets high'": Szwed, *So What*, p. 88.

122 "a four-year horror": Davis and Troupe, *Miles*, p. 132.

123 "Then suddenly everyone": Szwed, *So What*, p. 86.

123 hiding Miles's shoes: Ibid., p. 87.

123 closer to sources: *The Negro Travelers' Green Book*, Spring 1956, issuu.com/dafiyab.benibo /docs/negro_traveler_s_green_book.

124 "nice, quiet, honest": Davis and Troupe, *Miles*, p. 136.

124 "I'd do anything": Ibid., p. 136.

124 "as well as from those": Szwed, *So What*, p. 90.

125 He had, he said: Davis and Troupe, *Miles*, p. 136.

125 date his birth to: wikitree.com/wiki/Davis-7198; legacy.com/obituaries/name/muhammad
-abdullah-obituary?pid=176218353.

125 why Miles named: Miles IV (1949–2015), who as an adult resembled Miles not at all,
would change his name to Muhammad Abdullah: wikitree.com/wiki/Davis-7198.

125 "it was just over": Davis and Troupe, *Miles*, p. 138.

126 that would culminate: Owen Callin, "Record Reviews," *Bakersfield Californian*, Sept. 8,
1950, p. 23.

126 "Cut that shit out": Davis and Troupe, *Miles*, p. 139.

126 "arrested for being black": Reich, *The World of Jim Crow America*, p. 34; Taylor, *Notes and
Tones*, p. 240.

127 "He didn't like the fact": Szwed, *So What*, p. 94.

127 notoriously racist L.A. police: "All the policemen are Southerners, and all of them mess
with you," Philly Joe Jones told Arthur Taylor. "A policeman is a public servant and supposed to be protecting citizens. In California it's just the opposite. That's the SS troops
out there, man. They're storm troopers" (Taylor, *Notes and Tones*, p. 43).

127 spent his first time: Gordon, *Sophisticated Giant*, p. 102.

127 "been arrested for carrying": Nick La Tour, "On the Scene in Harlem Town," *Jackson Advocate*, Nov. 18, 1950, p. 4.

128 "a lot of respect for": Pat Harris, "Nothing but Bop? 'Stupid,' Says Miles," *DownBeat*, Jan.
27, 1950.

128 a scathing editorial: Vail, *Miles' Diary*, p. 35.

128 "It was pure": Vail, *Miles' Diary*, p. 36.

129 "really opened my eyes": Michael Jarrett, Penn State York, unpublished fall 1995 interview with Bob Weinstock, audio file at https://dcr.lib.unc.edu/record/4e4804f4-3b90-4ba0
-8f8e-dd90f121413c.

130 Miles said he'd rather: Miles Davis Official Artists Channel, "Miles Davis—Meeting
Producer Bob Weinstock (from The Miles Davis Story)," YouTube audio, 2:53, Aug. 18,
2017, youtube.com/watch?v=tVdYzPXlGgM.

130 "'ask him to call me'": Vail, *Miles' Diary*, p. 37.

130 "put a little money": Davis and Troupe, *Miles*, p. 140.

130 "willing to take a chance": Ibid., p.143.

131 "a very different Miles": Goldberg, *Jazz Masters of the 50s*, p. 70.

131 head arrangement–cum–improvisation: *Head arrangement*: played from memory, learned
by ear.

132 "Jazz to me is": Gillespie and Fraser, *To Be, or Not . . . to Bop*, p. 360.

132 "They copped that part": Ibid.

132 "fucked-up, raw": Davis and Troupe, *Miles*, pp. 142–43.

133 "Davis is rather unfamiliar": Jack Tracy, review of "Morpheus" and "Blue Room" (Prestige 734), *DownBeat*, Apr. 6, 1951.

133 "If only I could": Davis and Troupe, *Miles*, p. 143.

134 "we all need the joy": Cab Calloway, "Is Dope Killing Our Musicians?," *Ebony*, Feb.
1951.

135 "all I care about": Nisenson, *Open Sky*, p. 39.

135 "Heroin just became": David Hutchings, "Jazz Great Dexter Gordon Blows an Elegant
New Note as an Actor," *People*, Nov. 24, 1986, p. 113.

135 "sticking a needle": Ibid.

135 "I remember really being": Nisenson, *Open Sky*, p. 39.

135 "Money can cover up": Gourse, *Art Blakey*, p. 38.

135 "But I felt so": Davis and Troupe, *Miles*, p. 96.

136 **"Sometimes it was so hot"**: Heath and McLaren, *I Walked with Giants*, p. 71.
136 **"it's a great way"**: Author's interview with Randy Brecker.
136 **"forgot the bassman"**: DeVito, *Coltrane on Coltrane*, p. 25.
137 **It was a Sunday afternoon**: Vail, *Miles' Diary*, p. 40.
137 **"Release of items like"**: Jack Tracy, review of "Down" and "Whispering" (Prestige 742), *DownBeat*, Sept. 7, 1951.
138 **Davis's first album as**: Weinstock cannily opted not to lead with the tunes Miles played so poorly on his first Prestige session in January: the tracks made their way onto subsequent Prestige LPs.
139 **"rude, unswinging drumming"**: Jack Tracy, review of "Dig (I & II)" (Prestige 777), *DownBeat*, Dec. 3, 1952. "Dig" would later be called "Donna," and credited to Jackie McLean.
139 **"*Blue Period* is the title"**: *DownBeat*, Apr. 3, 1953.
139 **before the trademark rasp**: The pre-rasp Davis voice can be heard at length on a St. Louis radio interview Miles did in July or August 1953: Miles Davis Jazz Central, "Miles Davis 1953 Interview with DJ Harry Frost on KXLW, East St. Louis," YouTube audio, 12:26, Aug. 31, 2020. youtube.com/watch?v=5CvG3jEGr9w.
140 **"pimping women for money"**: Davis and Troupe, *Miles*, p. 148.
140 **"like a little boy again"**: Ibid., p. 149.
141 **"whose parents owned"**: Ibid., p. 150.
141 **too sick and mistrustful**: Jazz musicians treated there over the years included Dexter Gordon, Jackie McLean, Chet Baker, Sam Rivers, Wilbur Ware, Sonny Stitt, Red Rodney, Elvin Jones, Lee Morgan, Tadd Dameron, and Sonny Rollins. "Over the years, so many musicians were in Lexington that the facility had big bands and also several small combos," writes Barry Spunt in his *Heroin and Music in New York City* (p. 64). "They called their treatment the cure, and it took four and a half months," Rollins recalled. "They treated drug addiction like an illness, not a crime, and you felt more like a patient than a convict. It was very compassionate treatment. They used dolophine, which was an early form of methadone" (Nisenson, *Open Sky*, p. 68). Dameron, imprisoned at the facility for three years, was transformed by the experience: "Tadd rekindled his enthusiasm for composing after the recent, lost years of heroin-induced lethargy," his biographer writes. "He used the various [Lexington] bands to try out his own new compositions and also those of others, many of whom had never composed or arranged before. He encouraged everyone to write" (MacDonald, *Tadd*, p. 61).
141 **went their separate ways**: Maybe, too, Miles was just too much of a solitary cat to want to consign himself to a population of fellow musician addicts: Red Rodney, a Lexington inmate at the time, told, poignantly, of being thrilled that Miles was checking in, and rushing to greet him, only to find that Davis had left (Vail, *Miles' Diary*, p. 42).
141 **"Miles in the past year"**: Leonard Feather, "Poll-Topper Miles Has Been at a Standstill Since Back in 1950," *Melody Maker*, Feb. 23, 1952.
142 **"even thinking of myself"**: Davis and Troupe, *Miles*, p. 156.

Chapter 8: Take off

145 **"renewed. He had no working"**: Losin, *Miles Ahead*, recording session of May 9, 1952, plosin.com/milesAhead/Sessions.aspx?s=520509.
145 **"(25 lbs heavier)"**: Vail, *Miles' Diary*, p. 44.
146 **all the musicians were Black**: Besides Miles: J. J. Johnson, Jackie McLean, Milt Jackson, Percy Heath, and Kenny Clarke. Halfway through the tour McLean left and was replaced briefly by tenor player Zoot Sims, who then left and was replaced by Jimmy Heath.
146 **there was the uncomfortable**: The tour also played several Black clubs.
147 **"And his grosses"**: Vail, *Miles' Diary*, p. 44.
147 **"and, he thought"**: Davis and Troupe, *Miles*, p. 159.

147 **"The solid sender was"**: Dorothy Kilgallen, The Voice of Broadway, syndicated column, Aug. 15, 1952.

147 **"skipping and sliding"**: Davis and Troupe, *Miles*, p. 160.

148 **calls the sessions "desultory"**: Losin, *Miles Ahead*, recording session of April 20, 1953, plosin.com/milesAhead/Sessions.aspx?s=530420.

148 **Bird drank a full fifth**: Losin, *Miles Ahead*, recording session of Jan. 30, 1953, plosin.com /milesahead/Sessions.aspx?s=530130.

148 **"we played some"**: Davis and Troupe, *Miles*, p. 161.

149 **"higher than a motherfucker when"**: Ibid.

149 **"but it's still Miles"**: John Tebben, Jazz Mill column, *Independent Press-Telegram Southland Magazine* (Long Beach, CA), Nov. 1, 1953.

149 **new hundred-dollar bills**: Davis and Troupe, *Miles*, p. 164.

150 **Rumsey was white**: If, that is, they deigned to come. There were those who called Rumsey's primarily white bands the Lightweight All-Stars; some said that the only times the Lighthouse gigs were any good was when Black greats like Wardell Gray and Roach joined them. The recording of West Coast jazz, much of it on Dick Bock's Pacific Jazz label, produced further dissension. "The jazz out of the East was heavy and black and out of the West light and white, that's the way it sounded," the tenor player Teddy Edwards told an interviewer in 1994. "We had plenty of hard hitters [on the Coast] but we didn't get recorded—Sonny Criss, Hampton Hawes, Wardell, all of us, but we were ignored for mostly a racial thing. It was very racially motivated." Bob Rusch, "Teddy Edwards Interview Taken & Transcribed by Bob Rusch," *Cadence*, Apr. 1994.

151 **now and then breaking**: Davis and Troupe, *Miles*, pp. 165–66.

151 **"copied a lot"**: Davis and Troupe, *Miles*, p. 167.

152 **"rich white guy"**: Ibid.

153 **"Then it was over"**: Don DeMicheal, "Miles Davis: The *Rolling Stone* Interview," *Rolling Stone*, Dec. 13, 1969.

153 **"The rest of it"**: Davis and Troupe, *Miles*, pp. 169–70.

154 **"He knew that I had"**: Ibid., p. 170.

155 **"went on the bandstand and"**: Bjorn and Gallert, *Before Motown*, pp. 134–35.

155 **"his man Freddie Frue"**: Szwed, *So What*, p. 109.

155 **"because of guys like him"**: Davis and Troupe, *Miles*, p. 172.

155 **"I saw this"**: Szwed, *So What*, pp. 109–10.

156 **"pulled me through some"**: Davis and Troupe, Miles, p. 174.

156 **"strong, both musically"**: Ibid., p. 175.

156 **"when he bothered"**: Ibid.

157 **listening and demonstrating**: Miles, nothing if not competitive, would have been sharply aware that Silver had recently been playing and recording with Art Blakey, in a quintet that included Clifford Brown.

157 **the American Sublime**: Bloom, *Thomas Pynchon*, p. 1.

157 **optometrist turned recording engineer**: It was actually the home of Van Gelder's parents. The living room there not only had great acoustic characteristics for recording, but also a beautiful Steinway grand.

158 **"at a high speed"**: Szwed, *So What*, p. 111.

159 **"melody broke loose"**: Ibid.

159 **an upbeat Eddie Vinson**: Whose opening notes are thisclose to the opening notes of Rodgers and Hart's 1935 standard "The Most Beautiful Girl in the World."

159 **"in striking contrast"**: Losin, *Miles Ahead*, recording session of Mar. 15, 1954, plosin.com /milesahead/Sessions.aspx?s=540315.

160 **a lot like Bird**: So much so that Charles Mingus, listening to the record a few months later in a *DownBeat* blindfold test, would mistake Schildkraut for Parker. Miles rewarded the young altoist by leaving him out of his memoir altogether.

160 **Miles's "Solar"**: Miles clearly appropriated this tune from "Sonny," written by the guitar-

ist Chuck Wayne in the mid-forties and dedicated to the short-lived trumpeter Sonny Berman, but never registered for copyright. Miles's title is a punning catch-me-if-you-can tease. He had something of a reputation for lifting tunes from others—a habit that would, five years hence, come into play on *Kind of Blue.*

160 **"Davis has another chorus"**: Losin, *Miles Ahead,* recording session of Apr. 3, 1954, plosin .com/milesahead/Sessions.aspx?s=540403.

160 **doing good business**: Vail, *Miles' Diary,* p. 58.

161 **"going over the valves"**: Szwed, *So What,* p. 113.

162 **"an uptempo blues"**: Ibid.

162 **"showed him the stopwatch"**: Ibid., p. 114.

162 **"turned my whole life"**: Davis and Troupe, *Miles,* p. 177.

163 **"'Walkin'" was something new**: Miles's *treatment* of "Walkin'" was something new. The tune itself had begun as "Gravy," a 1950 recording by Gene Ammons, who credited the song to the tenor saxophonist, composer, and arranger Jimmy Mundy. At various times, Davis would also title the number "Weirdo" and "Sid's Ahead."

163 **"sound rather frail"**: Vail, *Miles' Diary,* p. 59.

163 **"a gig-skipping"**: J. D. Considine, "When Miles and Trane Made History," Special to *The Globe and Mail,* May 27, 2006, theglobeandmail.com/arts/when-miles-and-trane-made -history/article18164154.

163 **faulted his "articulation"**: See, for example, the Feb. 11, 1953, *DownBeat* review of *Young Man with a Horn* (Blue Note 5013).

164 **Listen to *Miles Davis with Sonny Rollins***: Now part of a compilation, *Miles Davis: The Complete Prestige 10-Inch LP Collection.*

164 **"'This is who I am'"**: Greg Cwik and David Marchese, "Understanding Miles Davis, in 9 Parts," *Vulture,* Sept. 25, 2015, vulture.com/2015/09/miles-davis-lives-9-parts.html.

165 **"Depression was one"**: Crouch, *Considering Genius,* pp. 46–47.

165 **"rendered invisible by"**: Tyson, *Just as I Am,* p. 168.

166 **"But most of all"**: Davis and Troupe, *Miles,* p. 180.

Chapter 9: Left-handed pianist

170 **"truly cannot fathom"**: Golson and Merod, *Whisper Not,* p. 110.

170 **"I was overwhelmed"**: Ibid., p. 111.

171 **"Sometimes we have to"**: Ibid.

171 **"with split fingernails"**: Brian Hennessey, "Bill Evans: A Person I Knew," *Jazz Journal International,* Mar. 1985, pp. 8–11.

171 **"couldn't play 'My Country'"**: Louis Cavrell, dir., *The Universal Mind of Bill Evans,* a 1966 film of Evans talking about music with his older brother, Harry.

172 **"opened a whole new world"**: Don DeMicheal, untitled essay in *Bill Evans Plays,* a 1969 booklet of Evans transcriptions. Downloadable at https://www.scribd.com/doc/284267153 /Bill-Evans-Plays.

172 **"got a lot of experience"**: Ibid.

173 **"had been quite unconscious"**: Pettinger, *Bill Evans,* p. 16.

173 **"I began to think"**: Don Nelsen, "Bill Evans: Intellect, Emotion, and Communication," *DownBeat,* Dec. 8, 1960, pp. 16–19.

173 **"had to build my music"**: Hennessey, "Bill Evans: A Person I Knew."

174 **"finally it revealed itself"**: Cavrell, dir., *The Universal Mind of Bill Evans.*

174 **"His relationship with his mother"**: Author's interview with Laurie Verchomin.

174 **"by all accounts he was"**: Pettinger, *Bill Evans,* p. 5.

175 **"the same old story"**: Ibid.

175 **"keep bread on the table"**: Reminiscence of Pat Evans at https://harryevanstrio.com/The _Two_Brothers.pdf, pp. 3–4.

175 **"saturated with music"**: Ibid., p. 3.

175 "Birthdays were more": Ibid., p. 4.
175 "One thinking for the other": Ibid., p. 2.
175 "bespectacled, introspective": Ibid.
176 "roomed together in a house": Ibid., p. 5.
176 "immersed himself in the music": Ibid., p. 2.

Chapter 10: Now's the time

179 "would just sit and listen": Kelley, *Thelonious Monk*, p. 106.
180 "'It took me a long time'": Miles Davis taped interview with Quincy Troupe, June 16, 1988, Quincy Troupe Collection, Schomburg Center for Research in Black Culture.
180 "[He's] the one who": Ibid.
180 "pay strict attention": Kelley, *Thelonious Monk*, p. 107.
180 "but if you're bullshitting": Miles Davis taped interview with Troupe.
181 "'This is my mother's house'": Kelley, *Thelonious Monk*, pp. 165–66.
181 "After he lit up": Ibid., p. 166.
182 "he was already a bit": Ibid., p. 183.
182 "You got to have": Davis and Troupe, *Miles*, p. 187.
182 "'purest moments of beauty'": Losin, *Miles Ahead*, recording session of Dec. 24, 1954, plosin .com/milesahead/Sessions.aspx?s=541224.
183 "I don't have to sit": Gourse, *Straight, No Chaser*, p. 96.
183 Ira Gitler remembered: Kelley, *Thelonious Monk*, p. 183.
183 "Hey, Rudy, put": ktdchon22, "The Man I Love (take 1)—Miles Davis," YouTube audio, 8:31, Aug. 28, 2017, youtube.com/watch?v=f13hyaCuU9U.
183 "Miles'd got killed": Kelley, *Thelonious Monk*, p. 182.
184 "picked my little ass up": Davis and Troupe, *Miles*, p. 187.
184 "Roy Eldridge had his piano": Kelley, *Thelonious Monk*, p. 182.
184 "produced something extraordinary": Vail, *Miles' Diary*, p. 64.
185 "Get me out": Szwed, *So What*, p. 116.
186 "These are sick": Santoro, *Myself When I Am Real*, p. 112.
186 "remark a morgue attendant made": Russell, *Bird Lives!*, p. 359.
187 "Mr. Parker was ranked": "Charlie Parker, Jazz Master, Dies," *New York Times*, Mar. 15, 1955.
187 "fucked everyone up": Davis and Troupe, *Miles*, p. 188.
188 exuberant and assured: Nat Hentoff would give *The Musings of Miles*—Davis's first twelve-inch LP—five stars in a *DownBeat* review (*DownBeat*, Nov. 2, 1955).
189 "'a bebop Bobby Hackett'": Szwed, p. 118. Hackett (1915–76) was a swing-era trumpeter and cornetist whose flowing lyricism was much admired by Miles.
190 "That was my first": Wein, *Myself Among Others*, p. 457.
190 "Miles had a way": Ibid., p. 458. According to several sources, Whittemore didn't become Miles's agent until after Newport.
190 Davis still didn't have: He had a quintet he wanted to work with—Rollins, Garland, Chambers, and Philly Joe—but couldn't afford to tour with them. Four days before Miles went to Newport, the five played the recently opened Café Bohemia in Greenwich Village, but this was a one-off, a special appearance, not a stand.
191 "*Miles Davis*, trumpet!": Milestones: A Miles Davis Archive, "All Star Jam Session featuring Miles Davis—July 17, 1955 Newport Jazz Festival, Newport," YouTube audio, 24:36, July 16, 2016, youtube.com/watch?v=1UxxXnfgmmU&t=167s.
191 "playing the same music": Davis and Troupe, *Miles*, p. 121.
192 "high priest of bop": "All Star Jam Session featuring Miles Davis—July 17, 1955."
193 "people were running": Davis and Troupe, *Miles*, p. 191.
193 "Sign him—now!": Stuart Nicholson, "Miles Davis—Highs and Lows at Newport,"

Jazzwise, April 21, 2016, jazzwise.com/profile/article/miles-davis-highs-and-lows-at-newport.

194 **"then it was four years"**: Szwed, *So What*, p. 117.

194 **"It was a sad"**: John McDonough, "Fifty Years Later, George Avakian Remembers Miles Davis," *Wall Street Journal*, July 7, 2005, wsj.com/articles/SB112068802064678822.

194 **"Miles Davis is perhaps"**: Liner notes, *Miles Ahead*.

195 **"a very high quality"**: McDonough, "Fifty Years Later, George Avakian Remembers Miles Davis."

195 **"people who know nothing"**: Ibid.

195 **"ask anyone's permission"**: Ibid.

195 **"a wild idea"**: Szwed, *So What*, p. 118.

195 a two-thousand-dollar advance: Worth about twenty-one thousand dollars today.

195 **"a lot of money for jazz"**: Ratliff, *Coltrane*, p. 20.

196 where the house band: Dorothy Kilgallen, Voice of Broadway syndicated column of May 12, 1955: "The new existentialist place in Greenwich Village, Café Bohemia, boasts a downtown version of [Birdland's dwarf doorman] Pee Wee Marquette, cool sounds, and a clientele right out of Central Casting. Prop types: beards, lasses with pale pink lipstick, and a token sprinkling of Ivy Leaguers. Once in a while a group of tourists from out-of-town wander in, and do they register surprise!"

197 shouted with the sheer joy: Sheridan, *Dis Here*, pp. xvi–xviii.

197 in her syndicated column: Dorothy Kilgallen, Voice of Broadway syndicated column, Sept. 26, 1955.

197 **"gorgeous swooping tone"**: Sheridan, *Dis Here*, p. 3.

198 **"just kind of fluffed"**: Davis and Troupe, *Miles*, p. 193.

198 complete his teaching contract: Sheridan, *Dis Here*, p. 9.

198 **"had been pushing"**: Szwed, *So What*, p. 120.

198 **"Philly Joe brought up"**: Davis and Troupe, *Miles*, pp. 194–95.

Chapter 11: Why he picked me, I don't know

201 **"never heard anything so great"**: Priestley, *John Coltrane*, p. 29.

202 **"We were too musical"**: Porter, *John Coltrane*, p. 95.

202 **"had a lot of arrangements"**: Ibid.

202 **"a little of Philly Joe"**: Davis and Troupe, *Miles*, p. 200.

203 **"in a situation like that"**: DeVito, *Coltrane on Coltrane*, p. 131.

204 **"my silence and evil looks"**: Davis and Troupe, *Miles*, p. 195.

204 **"practically had to beg"**: Ibid.

204 **"we hit it off"**: Ibid., p. 196.

205 the LP, *'Round About Midnight*: The three-word handle had become common usage, though Monk preferred his original *about*-less title.

205 **"enable you to blow"**: Losin, *Miles Ahead*, recording session of Oct. 26, 1955, plosin.com/milesAhead/Sessions.aspx?s=551026.

205 **"the thing I needed"**: John McDonough, "Fifty Years Later, George Avakian Remembers Miles Davis," *Wall Street Journal*, July 7, 2005, wsj.com/articles/SB112068802064678822.

206 **"fired from Dizzy's band"**: Author's interview with Loren Schoenberg.

206 **"not fumbling exactly, but"**: Bill Evans interview by Bill Goldberg and Eddie Karp, WKCR, New York, July 4, 1979, jazz.fm/rare-interview-with-bill-evans-recounts-the-story-of-miles-davis-and-kind-of-blue.

206 **"He was just a spiritual"**: Author's interview with Sonny Rollins.

206 **"was naturally frustrating"**: Kitty Grime, "John Coltrane Talks to *Jazz News*," *Jazz News*, Dec. 27, 1961.

207 **"that [Coltrane] was working"**: Szwed, *So What*, p. 122.

207 **"it was the trumpeter"**: Morgenstern, *Living with Jazz*, p. 217.

207 **"used to send chills"**: Davis and Troupe, *Miles*, p. 196.

208 Coltrane clearly won: Porter, *John Coltrane*, p. 99.

208 **"debuted their pianoless"**: Kahn, *Kind of Blue*, p. 57.

208 **"destroyed West Coast jazz"**: Porter, *John Coltrane*, p. 99.

209 certain amount of studio chatter: At the end of "Woody 'n' You," on *Relaxin'*, Miles asks Weinstock, "Okay?" and Weinstock jokes that they'll have to do another. Miles responds, fake-sharply: "*Why?*"—then Coltrane asks, "Could I have the beer opener?" It's like a frat-house gig!

210 **"Coltrane," Miles quickly**: Miles Davis Official Artist Channel, "Sweet Sue, Just You (false start with discussion by Leonard Bernstein & Miles Davis)": YouTube audio, 1:56, Dec. 26, 2016, youtube.com/watch?v=RDGb_H3nxvQ.

210 **"gave him all the room, man"**: Bill King, "Rare interview with Bill Evans recounts the story of Miles Davis and Kind of Blue," jazz.fm, May 24, 2019, jazz.fm/rare-interview -with-bill-evans-recounts-the-story-of-miles-davis-and-kind-of-blue/.

210 *"Hey, we're looking"*: Louis Cavrell, dir., *The Universal Mind of Bill Evans*, a 1966 film of Evans talking about music with his older brother, Harry.

211 **"rode down to Rockaway"**: Pettinger, *Bill Evans*, p. 25.

211 **"I hope it doesn't"**: Don Nelsen, "Bill Evans: Intellect, Emotion, and Communication," *DownBeat*, Dec. 8, 1960, pp. 16–19.

212 **"only the European classical"**: Pettinger, *Bill Evans*, p. 55.

212 **"'I knew then and there'"**: Ibid., pp. 31–32.

214 **"You have to be deeply"**: Liner notes for Russell's Decca album *Jazz in the Space Age*, 1960.

215 **"vigor and vitality"**: Ibid.

215 two albums of standards: Kelley, *Thelonious Monk*, pp. 185, 190.

217 his Monk-ish "Five": Though the piece is literally named for its clusters of five-beat bars, its title has to have been an admiring if cheeky reference to Miles's (and Eddie Vinson's) 1954 hard-bop classic "Four."

217 **"comparable to a piano vignette"**: Pettinger, *Bill Evans*, p. 37.

217 **"Miles's head was"**: Bill Evans interview with Brian Hennessey, *Along Came Bill*, BBC Radio 2, 1990.

218 **"almost immediately got"**: Nisenson, *Ascension*, p. 30.

218 **"Unbeknown to the band"**: Szwed, *So What*, p. 125.

219 **"He just wasn't too"**: Porter, *John Coltrane*, p. 104.

219 **"clothes sometimes filthy"**: Szwed, *So What*, p. 125.

219 more arguments with Davis: Vail, *Miles' Diary*, p. 84.

219 **"Coltrane is the best"**: Ibid., p. 86.

220 **"sometimes nodding out"**: Davis and Troupe, *Miles*, p. 209.

220 didn't even like the word: Szwed, *So What*, p. 139; Vail, *Miles' Diary*, p. 95.

220 **"kept right on shooting"**: Davis and Troupe, *Miles*, p. 209.

221 **"creased up and dirty"**: Porter, *John Coltrane*, p. 104.

221 **"could get [Davis] into *Newsweek*"**: Szwed, *So What*, pp. 127–28.

221 **"picking his nose"**: Davis and Troupe, *Miles*, p. 212.

221 there is good reason: Ibid., p. 207. Miles's memoir dates the attack to October 1956, when Davis *first* fired Coltrane. Lewis Porter, on the other hand, says that Monk couldn't have offered Coltrane work then because he, Monk, was still without a cabaret card. He then adds a caveat about the memoir: "Unfortunately, [*Miles*] must be used with caution; in compiling it Troupe combined his interviews of Davis with material from other publications—uncredited—so it is hard to tell whether Davis actually told this to Troupe or whether Troupe took it from Thomas." Meaning J. C. Thomas, who wrote the biography *Chasin' the Trane: The Music and Mystique of John Coltrane* (Porter, *John Coltrane*, p. 317).

Chapter 12: I began to accept the position in which I had been placed

223 "A fellow homeboy": Kelley, *Thelonious Monk*, p. 209.

224 "a longstanding friendship": Ibid., p. 212.

224 "begun rehearsing informally": Porter, *John Coltrane*, p. 105.

224 she reminisced, laughingly: Rothschild, *The Baroness*, p. 187. Monk titled a blues, "Ba-Lue Bolivar Ba-Lues-Are," after the hotel.

225 "one night at the Algonquin": Kelley, *Thelonious Monk*, p. 218.

225 "one genius too far": Rothschild, *The Baroness*, p. 187.

226 "we'd just get one tune": DeVito, *Coltrane on Coltrane*, pp. 17–18.

226 "like a big brother": Bret Primack, "The Real McCoy," *Jazz Times*, Jan.–Feb. 1996.

227 "has been granted": Liner notes, *A Love Supreme*, 1964.

227 "a duty we owe": Ira Gitler, "'Trane on the Track," *DownBeat*, Oct. 16, 1958.

227 "I felt so fortunate": Liner notes, *Dakar* (1981 compilation album, Prestige 24104).

227 recorded his first LP: Along with the trumpeter Johnnie Splawn, baritone saxophonist Sahib Shihab, Paul Chambers, Tootie Heath, and one pianist for each side of the album, Red Garland and Mal Waldron.

228 "Riverside's most important": Nat Hentoff, *Brilliant Corners* review, *DownBeat*, June 13, 1957.

229 "He walked out with": Kelley, *Thelonious Monk*, p. 225.

229 "Thelonious vacillated between": Ibid., p. 222.

231 "*the* local place": Ibid., p. 227.

231 "a blackjack and a napkin": Ibid.

231 "not intimidated but": Baraka, *The Autobiography of LeRoi Jones/Amiri Baraka*, p. 133.

232 Eight weeks turned: Five months and twenty-two days, to be exact. The quartet's final night at the Five Spot was Dec. 26, 1957.

232 "I just heard something": Porter, *John Coltrane*, p. 110.

232 predicted Coltrane's impact: Ibid.

233 "that was a *stimulant*": DeVito, *Coltrane on Coltrane*, pp. 17–18.

233 "Opening night he was struggling": LeRoi Jones, "The Acceptance of Monk," *Down-Beat*, Feb. 27, 1964.

233 "served as models": Porter, *John Coltrane*, p. 110.

233 "exploring our different": Ibid., p. 132. Wilson replaced Dunlop early on when Dunlop had union problems. The expatriate saxophonist Steve Potts, who used to finagle his way into the Five Spot as a teenager, recalled (in conversation with my friend Andy Arleo, a musician and teacher in Nantes, France) a night in the early sixties when Monk's bandmates were waiting for the pianist, who as usual was late. Hearing a ruckus outside, Potts went to check out what was happening—and saw Monk, dancing in the street while a crowd threw coins his way. When Potts told Monk the band was waiting for him, Monk said he was making more money dancing than playing, and decided to go home (Andy Arleo, email).

234 "he got something": DeVito, *Coltrane on Coltrane*, p. 21.

234 "A lot of fun": Ibid., p. 19.

234 "playing out on the *fringes*": Author's interview with Wallace Roney.

235 "'found myself down there'": Ibid.

236 "Miles was in a buoyant mood, strolling": John Tynan, "Caught in the Act: Miles Davis Quintet," *DownBeat*, May 2, 1957.

236 "I found myself missing": Davis and Troupe, *Miles*, p. 216.

237 "He was very effective": Crease, *Gil Evans*, p. 191. According to the author, Miles went to Clark Terry for advice on the instrument.

237 "Gil Evans was the arranger": Liner notes, *Miles Ahead*.

237 "then he'd be gone": Davis and Troupe, *Miles*, p. 184.

238 "couldn't use more than": Crease, *Gil Evans*, p. 192.

239 "Why not a black": Giddins, *Visions of Jazz*, p. 347.

239 he'd worn it out: Davis and Troupe, *Miles*, p. 215.

239 if he was ever depressed: Ibid., p. 122.

240 "Thank goodness I made": Vail, *Miles' Diary*, p. 106.

242 "Shorter came out of Coltrane": Author's interview with Wallace Roney.

242 "He's a real musical thinker": John Coltrane with Don DeMichael, *DownBeat*, Sept. 29, 1960.

243 "direct and free-flowing lines": Ibid.

244 "Hinton's gutty bass": Paul Little, Needle in the Groove column, *Arlington Heights Herald*, June 27, 1957, p. 35.

245 "'I ain't never heard'": Davis and Troupe, *Miles*, p. 223.

246 propulsive new composition: There was some initial confusion about the song's title. While he was playing with Charlie Parker in 1947, Miles had recorded a completely different tune with the same name, written for him by John Lewis. On initial pressings of the 1958 Columbia album *Milestones*, the song was simply listed as "Miles," but its title soon changed to match the name of the LP.

246 "when the other scale [comes]": Szwed, *So What*, pp. 158–59.

249 "But I could see where": Author's interview with Wallace Roney.

249 "Red got mad at me": Davis and Troupe, *Miles*, p. 224.

250 "'Bring him over'": Pettinger, *Bill Evans*, p. 52.

250 "asked me to stay": Ibid.

250 "the position in which": Vail, *Miles' Diary*, p. 117; Mike Hennessey, "Evans the Jazz," *Melody Maker*, Feb. 27, 1965.

Chapter 13: Fucking up the blues

253 "if you're hearing him": Milestones: A Miles Davis Archive, "Miles Davis—May 17, 1958 Café Bohemia, New York City," YouTube audio, 20:07, May 16, 2016, youtube.com/watch?v=pag1SFz341g&t=728s.

254 "because their cost risks": George Avakian, "Jazz Record Sales Reach All-Time Peak," *Syracuse Post-Standard*, Nov. 17, 1957.

254 "seem to be rather aimless": Don Gold, review of *Relaxin' with the Miles Davis Quintet*, *DownBeat*, May 15, 1958.

255 "Everyone was tired": Davis and Troupe, *Miles*, p. 229.

255 "one of those crucial moments": Pettinger, *Bill Evans*, p. 54.

255 The band recorded: Plus, to let off some steam at the end of the session—Chambers and Cobb having grown impatient with holding back—a swinging twelve-minute version of Cole Porter's "Love for Sale" that wouldn't appear on a recording until 1975.

256 some say Cannonball: Pettinger, *Bill Evans*, p. 56.

256 to lay claim: And to make an artistic statement: see Ira Gitler, "Julian 'Cannonball' Adderley, Part I," *Jazz*, Summer 1959.

256 "Touch is your": Author's interview with Jon Batiste.

257 "such is the depth": Pettinger, *Bill Evans*, p. 55.

257 "having the feelings": Lyons, *The Great Jazz Pianists*, pp. 224–25.

258 "if it's expressed": Gitler, "Julian 'Cannonball' Adderley, Part I."

258 "'nothing was wrong, and'": Szwed, *So What*, pp. 162–63.

258 "these recordings had": Ibid., p. 162.

259 "Don't snore on": Losin, *Miles Ahead*, recording session of May 26, 1958, plosin.com/milesAhead/Sessions.aspx?s=580526.

260 "And I was so": Author's interview with Chick Corea.

260 "As long as they can": Davis and Troupe, *Miles*, p. 231.

261 "We don't want no": Author's interview with Wallace Roney.

261 "looked at him and smiled": Davis and Troupe, *Miles*, p. 226.

262 "sparkling water cascading": Ibid.

262 "showing him some voicings": Kahn, *Kind of Blue*, p. 207.
262 "Miles *loved* Bill": Author's interview with Wallace Roney.
262 "drug-grounded fellowship": Pettinger, *Bill Evans*, p. 61.
263 "And boy, did he become": Author's interview with Eliot Zigmund.
263 junkie-buddies, in: Pettinger, *Bill Evans*, p. 62.
263 "That will never be": Smithsonian Jazz Oral History Program interview of Jimmy Cobb, July 26–27, 2010, americanhistory.si.edu/sites/default/files/file-uploader/Jimmy-Cobb -Transcription-2020.pdf.
263 "not to ever mention": Davis and Troupe, *Miles*, p. 228.
264 "had to blur the world": Pettinger, *Bill Evans*, p. 62.
264 "Coltrane never quite approved": Ibid. Strikingly, though Evans was very much on the record with his admiration for Coltrane, one is hard-pressed to find any mention at all of Evans among all of Coltrane's many interviews.
264 fourth album as a leader: For reasons best known to those who can no longer enlighten us, the song "Soultrane"—a lovely ballad written by Tadd Dameron for his 1957 album *Mating Call* (on which Coltrane played)—was not on this LP.
264 "He had that type of": Porter, *John Coltrane*, pp. 252–53.
265 "Trane's 'sheets of sound'": *Soultrane* liner notes.
265 an interest in the harp: Porter, *John Coltrane*, p. 138.
266 "groups like fives and sevens": John Coltrane with Don DeMicheal, *DownBeat*, Sept. 29, 1960.
266 "more confusing to listeners": Don Gold, review of the Davis sextet's performance at the 1958 Newport Jazz Festival, *DownBeat*, Aug. 7, 1958.
266 he recorded abundantly: Recording, ideally as a leader, was also an economic necessity for all of Miles's musicians: an early experiment with paying them retainers hadn't worked out, and though Davis lived richly from his Columbia money—in 1958 he traded his gull-wing Mercedes for a red Ferrari—his sidemen only got paid per gig (Pettinger, p. 57).
267 a new Lincoln Continental: Porter, *John Coltrane*, p. 140.
267 "catalyzed new depths": Pettinger, *Bill Evans*, p. 63.
267 "When you play a note": Gitler, "Julian 'Cannonball' Adderley, Part I."
268 "He reordered Gershwin's": Crease, *Gil Evans*, p. 199.
269 "It did me a lot": Don Nelsen, "Bill Evans," *DownBeat*, Dec. 8, 1960.
270 "trying to get hold": Ellison and Murray, *Trading Twelves*, p. 193.
270 "This guy caint": Ibid., p. 202.

Chapter 14: Outside of time

273 "has split into": *New Yorker*, Goings On About Town, Jan. 3, 1959.
274 It was Balliett, after all: Whitney Balliett, Jazz Records column in *New Yorker*, May 17, 1958.
274 "three bandleaders in the group": Davis and Troupe, *Miles*, p. 233.
274 "Cannonball and Trane loved him": Davis and Troupe, ibid.
275 "thought maybe I'd wake up": Quoted in Orrin Keepnews, liner note to *Peace Piece and Other Pieces*, Milestone M-47024, 1975.
275 "was too busy": Pettinger, *Bill Evans*, p. 67.
276 *Portrait of Cannonball* colleagues: Keeping up with the Joneses: Sam Jones and Philly Joe Jones weren't kin, and neither was related to Count Basie's majestic drummer Jo Jones—nor to Elvin Jones, who would become the drummer in Coltrane's great quartet—and who was the youngest brother in the eminent musical family that produced the pianist Hank Jones and the trumpeter, composer, and bandleader Thad Jones. Likewise, the multifarious Quincy Delight Jones was on his own genealogical page.
276 and "Some Other Time": This tune didn't appear on the LP, but was included as a bonus track on the album's 1987 CD reissue.

277 "play the finger piano": Davis and Troupe, *Miles*, p. 225.
277 "I got a concept": Ibid., p. 226.
278 went back to the show: Szwed, *So What*, p. 173.
278 "that was the only way": Davis and Troupe, *Miles*, p. 233.
278 "The music was too thick": Ibid, p. 230.
278 "they often spent hours": Szwed, *So What*, p. 161.
279 "crucial to the character": Pettinger, *Bill Evans*, p. 81.
279 "I planned that album": Davis and Troupe, *Miles*, p. 233.
279 If you have to call: Szwed, *So What*, p. 173.
279 "but Miles called": Pettinger, *Bill Evans*, p. 82.
280 "went home and wrote": Ibid.
280 "First-take feelings": Kahn, *Kind of Blue*, p. 105.
280 "'You play *this*'": Bill Goldberg and Eddie Karp radio interview of Bill Evans, WKCR-FM, New York, July 4, 1979. Transcribed by Allan Chase, 2019: allanchase.files.wordpress .com/2019/05/bill-evans-interview-wkcr-7.4.79c.pdf.
280 "forms were so simple": Kahn, *Kind of Blue*, p. 99.
280 "interplay between those dancers": Davis and Troupe, *Miles*, p. 234.
281 "go in at 10 o'clock": Kahn, *Kind of Blue*, p. 145.
281 "instruments on various stools": Ibid., pp. 94, 96.
281 "'Hold it before you go'": Ibid., p. 95.
282 "CO 62290, no title": Losin, *Miles Ahead*, recording session of Mar. 2, 1959. plosin.com /milesAhead/Sessions.aspx?s=590302. In addition to the overall project number, Columbia assigned three consecutive catalog numbers to the as yet untitled tunes to be recorded that afternoon.
282 the straight-ahead blues: The song's title came from the nickname Miles had given to an actual person, Fred Tolbert, an eccentric bartender and hanger-on from Philadelphia (Kahn, *Kind of Blue*, p. 104).
282 "not at his best": Pettinger, *Bill Evans*, p. 37.
283 The old church echoed: Losin, "Miles Ahead": recording session of Mar. 2, 1959.
283 "one note contains": Goldberg and Karp radio interview.
283 "like he was possessed": Davis and Troupe, *Miles*, pp. 222–23.
283 "sounded like a continual": Kahn, *Kind of Blue*, p. 107.
284 R&B hit by Junior Parker: Ibid., p. 110.
284 "the other noises": Losin, *Miles Ahead*, recording session of Mar. 2, 1959, plosin.com /milesAhead/Sessions.aspx?s=590302.
285 "Bobby Timmons's comparable": Pettinger, *Bill Evans*, p. 82.
286 "find something captured": *Kind of Blue* liner notes.
286 "opened up a whole vista": Kahn, *Kind of Blue*, p. 117.
287 "leaving for New York": Szwed, *So What*, p. 175.
287 "'wrote a little song'": arte.tv, "Dennis Hopper—Interview Retrospective 2008/part 1": YouTube audio, 8:09, Dec. 20, 2008, youtube.com/watch?v=3VM-vYafxtM.
289 "gave him a sketch": Davis and Troupe, *Miles*, p. 234.
289 "sketched out the melody": Goldberg and Karp radio interview.
289 "playing those six bars": Ibid.
289 "a small matter to me": Brian Hennessey, "Bill Evans: A Person I Knew," *Jazz Journal International*, Mar. 1985, pp. 8–11.
289 "I don't want to make": Marian McPartland, *Piano Jazz*, recorded Nov. 6, 1978, broadcast May 27, 1979, npr.org/2010/10/08/92185496/bill-evans-on-piano-jazz.
290 "Miles Davis the jazz phenomenon": Kahn, *Kind of Blue*, p. 130.
290 from the musical: Evans and Tony Bennett would record "Some Other Time" for their 1975 LP *The Tony Bennett/Bill Evans Album*.
291 "a little dissonant": Kahn, *Kind of Blue*, p. 142.
291 "serve as a little vamp": Ibid.

291 "waltz-like bounce": Ibid.
292 "It sounds reflective": Author's interview with Loren Schoenberg.

Chapter 15: Annus mirabilis

295 "I've been so free here": DeVito, *Coltrane on Coltrane*, p. 57.
296 "the fury of the search": Liner notes, *Giant Steps*.
296 "So it'd be, you know": DeVito, *Coltrane on Coltrane*, p. 56.
296 "At times we had": Bob Snead, "Jazz Corner" column, *Cleveland Call and Post*, Jan. 24, 1959.
297 "we all merely followed": Golson, *Whisper Not*, pp. 34–35.
298 "I tried to figure out": John Tynan, "Ornette: The First Beginning," *DownBeat*, July 7, 1960.
299 "you could play sharp": Litweiler, *Ornette Coleman*, p. 25.
300 "immediately finish the song": Ibid., p. 45.
301 "Norris couldn't forget": Ethan Iverson, "Ornette 2: This Is Our Mystic," ethaniverson.com/rhythm-and-blues/this-is-our-mystic.
301 "They're almost like twins": Litweiler, *Ornette Coleman*, p. 66.
301 "These are *not* musicians": Ethan Iverson, "Ornette 2: This Is Our Mystic."
301 Clarke told Loren Schoenberg: Author's interview with Loren Schoenberg.
303 "quartet still sounded friendly": Szwed, *So What*, p. 169.
303 "Your fucking *band* don't": Ibid., p. 419.
304 "He burst on the scene": Gunther Schuller, "Two Reports on the School of Jazz," *Jazz Review*, Nov. 1960.
304 "the surging bitterness": Milton R. Bass, The Lively Arts column, *The Berkshire Eagle*, Sept. 10, 1959.
304 "trying to play a kind": Ibid.
304 "'Damn it, tune up!'": Litweiler, *Ornette Coleman*, p. 70.
304 "never knew from which": Bass, The Lively Arts.
305 "I was waiting": Kahn, *Kind of Blue*, p. 157.
305 "staying within the confines": review (unbylined) of *Kind of Blue*, *Billboard*, Aug. 31, 1959.
305 "taking no chances": B.C., review of *Kind of Blue*, *Metronome*, Oct. 1959.
305 "technical perfection has sold": Jack Coffman, Just Jazz column, *Hutchinson* (Kansas) *News*, Nov. 1, 1959.
305 "It was beautiful but": Kahn, *Kind of Blue*, p. 160.
305 "Buy it and play it": C. H. Garrigues, "Recapturing the Magic of Miles," *San Francisco Examiner*, Oct. 11, 1959.
306 "*Porgy & Bess* was": Kahn, *Kind of Blue*, p. 194.
306 "I've decided not to show": Dorothy Kilgallen, Voice of Broadway syndicated column of June 9, 1959.
307 "distinction without a difference": Author's interview with Sonny Rollins.
308 "Best sides are": review (unbylined) of *The Shape of Jazz to Come*, *Billboard*, Nov. 9, 1959.
309 "largest collection of VIP's": George Hoefer, "Caught in the Act," *DownBeat*, Jan. 7, 1960.
309 "the internal emigrants": Francis Newton in *New Statesman*, quoted by Nat Hentoff in *Jazz Review*, Nov. 1960.
310 "He says, 'That's Leonard'": Will Friedwald, "At the 92nd Street Y, Jazz for All," *New York Sun*, July 24, 2008.
310 pronounced Ornette a genius: Lee Santa, "Celebrating 100 Years of Jazz in America," *The Reader*, Sept. 2, 2015, sandpointreader.com/celebrating-100-years-of-jazz-in-america.
310 "gets to you emotionally": Charles Mingus, "Mingus on Ornette Coleman," *DownBeat*, May 26, 1960.
310 "I think he's jiving": Nat Hentoff, "Ornette Coleman: Biggest Noise in Jazz," *Esquire*, Mar. 1961.

310 Yet Lionel Hampton: Gillespie and Fraser, *To Be, or Not . . . to Bop*, p. 105; Michael J. West, "Ornette Coleman's Music Polarized Jazz, then Became Part of Its DNA," *Washington Post*, June 11, 2015.

310 He would eventually: Gillespie and Fraser, *To Be, or Not . . . to Bop*, pp. 486–87.

310 "Come on down here": Litweiler, *Ornette Coleman*, p. 83.

311 "sounded more the same": Author's interview with Sonny Rollins.

311 "'Well, you know, that'": DeVito, *Coltrane on Coltrane*, p. 102.

312 "man is all screwed up": Goldberg, *Jazz Masters of the 50s*, p. 231.

312 "jumped up one night": Davis and Troupe, *Miles*, pp. 249–50.

312 "White people are especially": Ibid., pp. 250–51.

313 Even Bob Brookmeyer: Litweiler, *Ornette Coleman*, p. 82.

313 "just sat in and played": Davis and Troupe, *Miles*, p. 250.

313 "don't know what's wrong": Ibid.

313 "And it wasn't true": Kart, *Jazz in Search of Itself*, p. 179.

313 "a full-fledged modern art": Francis Davis, "Ornette's Permanent Revolution," *The Atlantic*, Sept. 1985.

313 "On Why Jazz Isn't Cool": Nicholas Payton, "On Why Jazz Isn't Cool Anymore," on Nicholas Payton's personal website, November 27, 2011, nicholaspayton.wordpress.com /2011/11/27/on-why-jazz-isnt-cool-anymore/.

314 "Jazz died in 1959": *Free Jazz* was the name of a 1960 Ornette Coleman album. The phrase soon came to stand for the kind of music—unrooted in popularly understood concepts of rhythm, harmony, and melody—that Coleman, Cecil Taylor, Albert Ayler, and many others were playing.

Chapter 16: After

318 "Appearing with him will be": "Jazztet of Miles Davis in Concert," unbylined article, *San Mateo Times*, Feb. 20, 1960.

318 "a great little piano player": Davis and Troupe, *Miles*, p. 232.

318 "He never came back": Ibid., p. 240.

319 "we have corrupted it": *Cannonball Adderley Quintet in San Francisco*, CD remastered in 2007.

319 now had to go back: Davis and Troupe, *Miles*, p. 240.

320 "I just felt I needed": Ibid., p. 241.

320 "This record is": Bill Mathieu, review of *Sketches of Spain*, *DownBeat*, Sept. 29, 1960.

320 "catapulted Davis into": Robert Christgau, "Jazz Annual," *The Village Voice*, May 21, 1970.

320 even revealing that Jimmy Heath: Davis and Troupe, *Miles*, p. 237. Heath joined Miles briefly in 1959, but then had to quit: having recently been released early from prison (heroin possession), he found that the conditions of his parole restricted him to a fifty- or sixty-mile distance from Philadelphia. (Jimmy Heath, *I Walked with Giants*, p. 98.)

321 "'John, make your own group'": Porter, *John Coltrane*, p. 171.

321 "The energy he brought": Ibid., p. 173.

322 "not wholly essential": Kitty Grime, "John Coltrane Talks to *Jazz News*," *Jazz News*, December 27, 1961.

322 "I never met anybody": Porter, *John Coltrane*, p. 176.

322 Tyner brought a new: Postif, *Les Grandes Interviews de Jazz Hot*, pp. 133–34.

323 "fourth chords seem to add": Porter, *John Coltrane*, p. 177.

323 "took him to a barbecue": Thomas, *Chasin' the Trane*, p. 130.

323 "quite unknown and": DeVito, *Coltrane on Coltrane*, p. 128.

323 "I guess you could say he has": Quoted in Nat Hentoff's liner notes for *John Coltrane "Live" at the Village Vanguard*, 1962.

323 "He's just a": Porter, *John Coltrane*, p. 180.

324 latterly out of favor: Except by the groundbreaking avant-garde reed player Steve Lacy.

324 "almost like a human voice": Davis and Troupe, *Miles*, p. 224.

324 **"a universal concept unifying":** Scott Anderson, "John Coltrane, Avant Garde Jazz & the Evolution of 'My Favorite Things,'" honors thesis, Gustavus Adolphus College, St. Peter, Minnesota, Spring 1996, coltrane.room34.com/thesis.

325 **"we've stretched . . . through":** DeVito, *Coltrane on Coltrane*, p. 133.

326 **"The saxophonist's departure":** Carr, *Miles Davis: The Definitive Biography*, p. 164.

327 **"He has remained close":** Leonard Feather, "Miles Davis," *Melody Maker*, Sept. 17, 1960.

327 **"We were very comfortable":** Davis and Troupe, *Miles*, p. 255.

327 **tended to spend money:** Ibid.

327 **"I want you out":** Szwed, *So What*, p. 147.

328 **"Stravinsky, Arturo Michelangeli":** Davis and Troupe, *Miles*, p. 256.

328 **"perhaps the only period":** Carr, *Miles Davis: The Definitive Biography*, p. 170.

328 **"Playing with Hank":** Davis and Troupe, *Miles*, p. 252.

328 **"ferocious, lonely and romantic":** Norman Mailer, "Superman Comes to the Supermarket," *Esquire*, Nov. 1960.

329 **"freshness and a strength":** Pettinger, *Bill Evans*, p. 94.

329 **"I sneaked down":** DeVito, *Coltrane on Coltrane*, p. 233.

329 **"some kind of freak":** Davis and Troupe, *Miles*, p. 252.

329 **"And I've been playing":** Russ Wilson, "Miles Davis to Retire?," *DownBeat*, July 6, 1961.

330 **"'I'll divorce myself'":** Gilbert Millstein, "On Stage: Miles Davis," *Horizon*, May 1961.

331 **"such a beautiful musician":** Davis and Troupe, *Miles*, p. 256.

331 **"we now have the license":** Pettinger, *Bill Evans*, p. 91.

331 **"like a bucking":** Liner notes by Conrad Silvert, *Spring Leaves* (Milestone compilation, 1976).

332 **"developed as we performed":** Brian Hennessey, "Bill Evans: A Person I Knew," *Jazz Journal International*, Mar. 1985, pp. 8–11.

332 **"filling space between sets":** Gordon, *Live at the Village Vanguard*, pp. 84–85.

332 **"perfect empathy and telepathy":** C. Michael Bailey, *All About Jazz* website, Nov. 1, 2005, allaboutjazz.com/bill-evans-trio-sunday-at-the-village-vanguard-and-waltz-for-debby -by-c-michael-bailey.

333 **"how do you start again":** Hennessey, "Bill Evans: A Person I Knew."

333 **"She was small, dark":** Bruce Spiegel, dir., *Bill Evans: Time Remembered*.

334 **"bent on pursuing an anarchistic":** John Tynan, Take 5 column, *DownBeat*, Nov. 23, 1961.

334 **"Everybody has quite a bit":** Don DeMicheal, "John Coltrane and Eric Dolphy Answer the Jazz Critics," *DownBeat*, Apr. 12, 1962.

335 **"The live experience of hearing":** Author's interview with Denny Zeitlin.

335 **"torrential and anguished outpouring":** Pete Welding, untitled review, *DownBeat*, April 26, 1962.

335 **"yawps, squawks, and countless":** Ira Gitler, review of *Coltrane "Live" at the Village Vanguard*, *DownBeat*, April 26, 1962.

335 **"turning them in every conceivable":** Martin Williams, review of *Africa/Brass*, *DownBeat*, Jan. 18, 1962.

336 **"He'll just end up imitating":** Gene Lees, liner notes for the LP *John Coltrane Quartet: Ballads*, Jan. 1963.

336 **"seemed to be something":** Frank Kofsky, "John Coltrane: An Interview," *Jazz and Pop*, Sept. 1967.

337 **"some bossa nova shit":** Davis and Troupe, *Miles*, p. 259.

338 **"became difficult to talk to":** Szwed, *So What*, p. 235.

338 **"were very good musicians, but":** Davis and Troupe, *Miles*, p. 262.

339 **"You're making the record":** Ibid., p. 263.

339 **"He was something else, man":** Ibid., p. 264.

339 **"so his head was open":** ALL MAN CORP, "TALKING MILES DAVIS.mpg," YouTube video, 7:43, Mar. 13, 2010, youtube.com/watch?v=QRl3weG4HIs.

340 **charging the owner with:** Losin, *Miles Ahead*, concert recording of Sept. 20, 1963, plosin .com/milesAhead/Sessions.aspx?s=630920. When the band returned to the Workshop

the following April, an ad for the gig, sounding like something from 1863 rather than 1963, noted that "for the next two weeks the saloon's liquor license will be lifted to let an eighteen year old Negro play the drums."

340 **"probably the best drummer"**: Robert Christgau, Consumer Guide, *Village Voice*, Apr. 23, 1970.

340 **"expressing the drums"**: *Miles Ahead: The Music of Miles Davis*, 1986 documentary.

340 **"And he was that"**: Ibid.

341 **"some tricky little figures"**: Szwed, *So What*, pp. 240–41.

341 **"I pay you to practice"**: Tingen, *Miles Beyond*, p. 35.

341 **"like being out of key"**: Davis and Troupe, *Miles*, p. 268.

341 **"champagne, women, cars"**: Szwed, *So What*, pp. 240–41.

342 **"bottom was falling out of jazz"**: Balliett, *American Musicians II*, p. 443.

342 **"found work as sidemen"**: Mary Campbell, "Miles Brews Up New Life for Jazz," Associated Press, May 20, 1970.

343 **"There was a fixed structure"**: Szwed, *So What*, p. 251.

343 **"seemed to transport the audience"**: Liner notes, *Miles Davis Quintet, 1965–1968*.

343–44 **"hydrogen bomb and switchblade band,"** in: Szwed, *So What*, p. 252.

344 **"learned a lot from her"**: Davis and Troupe, *Miles*, pp. 26, 267.

344 **"[The] music in general is"**: Kenny Dorham, review of *E.S.P.*, *DownBeat*, Dec. 30, 1965.

345 **the abstract and**: Szwed, *So What*, p. 252.

346 **"'You're not going'"**: Ibid., p. 249.

346 **a picture of Frances**: *Someday My Prince Will Come* was the first.

347 **"You can add that"**: Howison, *God's Mind in That Music*, p. 108.

347 **"Naima appears to have"**: Porter, *John Coltrane*, p. 270.

348 **"I felt I was receiving"**: Thomas, *Chasin' the Trane*, p. 173.

348 **"I've brought you a present"**: Ibid., p. 138.

348 **He brushed her off**: Ibid., p. 157.

349 **"That was a funny time"**: DeVito, *Coltrane on Coltrane*, p. 303.

349 **"Said he had a headache"**: Thomas, *Chasin' the Trane*, pp. 162–63.

350 **"So I called her"**: Porter, *John Coltrane*, p. 272.

350 **"stayed in a hotel sometimes"**: Thomas, *Chasin' the Trane*, p. 166.

350 **"help him fulfill"**: Ibid., p. 172.

350 **"Monk, Mingus, Freddie Webster"**: Davis and Troupe, *Miles*, p. 411.

351 **"go humbly to it"**: DeVito, *Coltrane on Coltrane*, p. 314.

351 **"way of giving thanks"**: Ibid., p. 245.

351 **"a complicated mood"**: Ratliff, *Coltrane*, p. 86.

352 **"stylistic resting point"**: Kahn, *A Love Supreme*, p. 79.

353 **"A long unaccompanied"**: Porter, *John Coltrane*, p. 232.

354 **"IT IS TRULY"**: Liner notes, *A Love Supreme*, 1964.

354 **in unison with himself**: Of this excursion in modulation, Porter says Coltrane is "telling us that God is everywhere—in every register, in every key" (*John Coltrane*, p. 242). This is poetic, and persuasive, but there's another, not necessarily contradictory interpretation: that the passage "portends the final, experimental extreme of Çoltrane's career" (Kahn, *A Love Supreme*, p. 103). Or as Dave Liebman puts it, "It's really looking towards what he's about to go into, which is very, very free and non-key-centered improvisation" (Ibid.).

355 **"same deep, blues-filled well"**: Kahn, *A Love Supreme*, p. 99.

356 **"a music of meditation"**: Ratliff, *Coltrane*, p. 92.

356 **"that kind of ecstasy"**: Porter, *John Coltrane*, p. 217.

357 **That summer Coltrane told**: DeVito, *Coltrane on Coltrane*, pp. 247–48.

358 **"flung his snare"**: Kahn, *The House That Trane Built*, p. 137.

358 **"more of an effect"**: Kahn, *A Love Supreme*, pp. 181–82.

358 **"member of the avant-garde"**: Nisenson, *Ascension*, p. 173.

358 **"That was the turning point"**: Kahn, *A Love Supreme*, p. 182.

358 "It's not easy listening": Billy Taylor—Topic, "Spoken Introduction to Archie Shepp's Set by Billy Taylor (Live, 1965 Newport)," YouTube audio, 2:02, July 26, 2018, youtube.com /watch?v=n8N6TRUpJhM.
359 "Jazz started to lose": Davis and Troupe, *Miles*, pp. 268, 271.
359 "you don't see any": Taylor, *Notes and Tones*, p. 278.
359 "the consummate horn player": Kahn, *A Love Supreme*, p. 184.
360 "'he was so kind'": Porter, *John Coltrane*, p. 252.
360 "take the load off": Author's interview with Dave Liebman.
360 "asked me to play": Elizabeth van der Mei, "Pharoah Sanders," *Coda*, June–July 1967, p. 4.
361 "not expanded enough": Ibid., p. 5.
361 "Tyner's fine work receded": Porter, *John Coltrane*, pp. 264–65.
361 "started messing with": Kahn, *A Love Supreme*, p. 183.
361 "had to be guided": Porter, *John Coltrane*, p. 265.
362 "when I don't have feelings": Ibid., pp. 266, 42.
362 "matter of fact I couldn't hear": Ibid., p. 266.
362 "three people in the room": Crouch, *Considering Genius*, p. 213.
362 "at the mercy of": Balliett, *Collected Works*, pp. 828–29.
362 "liked some of the music": Davis and Troupe, *Miles*, p. 286.
363 "But it was deep": Author's interview with Dave Liebman.
363 "took jazz to a point": Author's interview with Loren Schoenberg.
363 "removed from his roots": Crouch, *Considering Genius*, p. 214.
364 "it's something about the sound": Author's interview with Jack DeJohnette.
364 "Someday we'll find": Graham Lock, "Trane Talk," *Wire*, Apr. 1991.
365 "his spirit outgrew": Author's interview with Wallace Roney.
365 He laughed, then Alice: DeVito, *Coltrane on Coltrane*, p. 270.
365 "It wasn't anything": Author's interview with Sonny Rollins.
365 "don't care for socializing": Ratliff, *Coltrane*, p. 90.
366 "that strength in the band": Frank Kofsky, "John Coltrane: An Interview," *Jazz and Pop*, Sept. 1967.
366 "And then he went down": Garland, *The Sound of Soul*, p. 227.
366 "In July, Coltrane died": Davis and Troupe, *Miles*, p. 285.
367 "Many then and now": Crouch, *Considering Genius*, p. 213.
367 "His long, handsome, still face": Balliett, *Collected Works*, p. 828.
368 "Coltrane was their pride": Davis and Troupe, *Miles*, p. 286.
368 "and we beheld": M. H. Miller, "The Canonization of Saint John Coltrane," *T: The New York Times Style Magazine*, Dec. 3, 2021.
369 "what I've seen happen": Davis and Troupe, *Miles*, p. 232.
369 "He could've reached out": Author's interview with Ethan Iverson.
369 "This is the one": Lees, *Meet Me at Jim and Andy's*, p. 154.
369 "I don't think he'd have": Bruce Spiegel, dir., *Bill Evans: Time Remembered*.
369 "in hideous disarray": Lees, *Meet Me at Jim and Andy's*, p. 152.
370 "Bill did not play": Pettinger, *Bill Evans*, p. 133.
370 "drew out the ledger lines": Ibid., pp. 133–34.
371 "Bill had tracks": Ibid., p. 150.
371 "pianists dropped by": Ibid., p. 145.
371 "Everything else was played": Quoted in booklet accompanying the CD compilation *Bill Evans—The Secret Sessions (Recorded at the Village Vanguard 1966–1975)*, Milestone, 1996.
371 A close friend and fellow: Bruce Spiegel, dir., *Bill Evans: Time Remembered*.
372 "Keepnews suspected that": Pettinger, *Bill Evans*, p. 137.
372 "both a major creative artist": Orrin Keepnews, liner notes to *The Solo Sessions, Vol. 1*, Milestone, 1989.
373 "turned the lights down": Pettinger, *Bill Evans*, p. 144.
373 "to express his jubilation": Balliett, *Such Sweet Thunder*, p. 80.

373 **"a semi-comatose state"**: John S. Wilson, *Moonbeams* review, *DownBeat*, Jan. 31, 1963.
373 **less so to Pettinger's**: "[T]he album was prepared hurriedly [it was recorded in a single day] and did not truly represent what the artists had achieved elsewhere" (Pettinger, *Bill Evans*, p. 153). Maybe, but Evans also had the taste and courage to give a solid effort to Irving Berlin's frankly sentimental "Always," a tune not easily translatable to jazz, and the taste, courage, and sense of humor to lay down a charming version of "Little Lulu," Buddy Kaye, Fred Wise, and Sidney Lippman's theme song from the 1940s animated shorts based on Marjorie Henderson Buell's ("Marge") great comic-strip character.
373 **"in more avant-garde contexts"**: Pettinger, *Bill Evans*, p. 153.
373 **Motian later told Ethan Iverson**: Author's interview with Ethan Iverson.
374 **"Still, Evans has managed"**: John S. Wilson, *Trio '65* review, *DownBeat*, July 15, 1965.
374 **"finding the pianist's drug use"**: Pettinger, *Bill Evans*, p. 173.
375 **"they all worked in it"**: Author's interview with Laurie Verchomin.
375 **"mannerisms and personal clichés"**: Steve Silberman, "Broken Time: 'Nardis' and the Curious History of a Jazz Obsession, *The Believer*, Aug. 1, 2018.
375 **"the tunes change but"**: Author's interview with Jack DeJohnette.
376 **"You've got to sacrifice"**: Author's interview with Dave Liebman.
376 **"Paul has this lyrical"**: Author's interview with Ethan Iverson.
376 **"did he grow exponentially"**: Author's interview with Loren Schoenberg.
376 **"intensify harmony step by step"**: Pettinger, *Bill Evans*, p. 173.
377 **"To me, that's probably"**: Author's interview with Jon Batiste.
377 **"almost a sickness"**: Len Lyons tape recording, Institute of Jazz Studies, Rutgers University, Newark, N.J.
378 **"raising so much hell"**: Szwed, *So What*, p. 256.
379 **destined to be a classic**: Shorter had already recorded the song for his album *Adam's Apple*, but the record wouldn't be released until October 1967, a year after *Miles Smiles* hit stores. Both versions became jazz immortals.
379 **"He knew how far"**: Szwed, *So What*, p. 256.
380 **"couldn't get no faster"**: Davis and Troupe, *Miles*, pp. 278–79.
380 **"everybody saw something happening"**: Scherman and Rowland, *The Jazz Musician*, p. 13.
381 **"'Then all of a sudden you see'"**: Berliner, *Thinking in Jazz*, p. 340.
381 **"one of the few giants"**: Teo Macero Collection, Music Division, New York Public Library for the Performing Arts.
382 **"all inside my business"**: Davis and Troupe, *Miles*, p. 284.
382 **"literally kept him alive"**: Szwed, *So What*, p. 258.
383 **"Tony was his young protégé"**: Author's interview with Wallace Roney.
383 **"what we had been doing"**: Davis and Troupe, *Miles*, p. 288.
383 **At a late December**: Actually, per Losin, *Miles Ahead*, recording session of Dec. 28, 1967, plosin.com/milesAhead/Sessions.aspx?s=671228, two pianos, a Wurlitzer and an RMI Electra.
383 **"his reservations began"**: Szwed, *So What*, p. 266.
384 **Benson put it astringently**: Ibid., p. 267.
384 **"So that's how it evolved"**: Author's interview with Wallace Roney.
385 **"Play something else"**: Chambers, *Milestones*, p. 135.
385 **"Not a single jazz"**: Leonard Feather, "Miles Davis Blindfold Test," *DownBeat*, June 13, 1968.
386 **"he's getting me off"**: McPartland, *All in Good Time*, p. 107.
386 **"The lower the head fell"**: Pettinger, *Bill Evans*, p. 166.
387 **nervous up-tempo piece**: "Gil developed it orchestrally and structurally when he formed a new band a couple of years later," Stephanie Stein Crease writes. "Retitled 'Eleven,' it became a standard in Gil's book, and Davis was listed as co-composer when the piece was included on subsequent Evans albums" (Crease, *Gil Evans*, p. 199).
387 **"we were all wearing"**: Author's interview with Chick Corea.
387 **fashion photographer Hiro**: Also at Miles's insistence, the notation "DIRECTIONS IN

MUSIC BY MILES DAVIS" appeared above his name. "It means I tell everybody what to do," he told *Rolling Stone* (Dec. 27, 1969). "It's my date, y'understand? I get tired of seeing 'produced by this person or that person.' When I'm on a date, I'm usually supervising everything." This was perhaps a direct pushback at Teo Macero, who was becoming ever more involved in producing Davis's LPs, and who—to Miles's annoyance—had been given a prominent "produced by" credit on the cover of the irksome *Quiet Nights*.

387 "black promotion men": Marmorstein, *The Label*, p. 419.

387 "spend very little money": Hollie I. West, "Black Tune," *Washington Post*, Mar. 13, 1969.

387 "five expressions of": Unbylined review of *Filles de Kilimanjaro*, *Rolling Stone*, Apr. 19, 1969.

389 "an interesting process": Davis and Troupe, *Miles*, p. 252.

389 "If we haven't been": Ibid., p. 297.

389 significant advances on royalties: On June 18, Teo Macero forwarded to Columbia's president a note from Miles: "[Tell Clive Davis] I need $20,000. My albums are doing well. I am a star. I am going to do three more albums for him this year and I need money" (Teo Macero Collection, Music Division, New York Public Library for the Performing Arts).

389–90 "If you stop calling me": Davis with Willwerth, *Clive*, p. 260.

391 "There's not much romance": Pete Gershon, "Class of '69," *Signal to Noise* (Nov.–Dec. 1998), p. 22.

391 "Everybody was excited": Davis and Troupe, *Miles*, p. 300.

391 "a breakthrough concept": Ibid.

392 "And Teo found": Tom Moore, "Bitches Back," *Guitar World*, Dec. 1998.

392 "What have you done": Teo Macero Collection, Music Division, New York Public Library for the Performing Arts.

392 worried memos flew: From Teo Macero to Irving Townsend, now a Columbia VP: "Miles wants to call the new album *Bitches Brew*. Please advise." Ibid.

393 "jungle-like chaotic energy": Sharee Fruck on Steve Hoffman Music Forums, Feb. 5, 2020, forums.stevehoffman.tv/threads/miles-in-a-silent-way-re-imagined-as-bitches-brew .933244/page-5.

393 "stream-of-consciousness jacket notes": Jeff Duffield, Records column, *San Antonio Express and News*, May 17, 1970.

393 "Those who liked the cool": Mary Campbell, "Miles Brews Up New Life for Jazz."

393 "displayed in every record store": Marmorstein, *The Label*, p. 421.

394 "back on the track": Mary Campbell, "Miles Brews Up New Life for Jazz."

394 "fully launched jazz-rock": Crouch, *Considering Genius*, p. 251.

394 "Now he done": Szwed, *So What*, p. 303.

394 "*had* to change course": Davis and Troupe, *Miles*, p. 298.

395 "He wanted 'off'": Davis and Willwerth, *Clive*, p. 261.

395 "So it was good": Davis and Troupe, *Miles*, p. 301.

396 "[Miles] was in bad": *The Man with a Horn*, radio series produced for the Canadian Broadcasting Company (CBC) by Ross Porter, 1994.

396 "knew a guy by that": Sharif Abdus-Salaam interview of Charles Mingus, WKCR-FM, New York, July 6, 1971. Szwed, *So What*, p. 313.

397 "replaced by a smile": Pettinger, *Bill Evans*, p. 198.

397 "she was infertile": Author's interview with Laurie Verchomin.

399 "star treatment he received": Helen Keane, booklet accompanying *The Complete Fantasy Recordings*, 1989.

400 employed a wah-wah pedal: Author's interview with Randy Brecker.

400 "still had ties to": Author's interview with Wallace Roney.

401 "I said, 'Thanks'": Author's interview with Dave Liebman.

401 "wasn't only the growl": Ibid.

402 "also seemed irritated": Losin, *Miles Ahead*, concert recording of Jan. 27, 1974, plosin .com/milesAhead/Sessions.aspx?s=740127.

402 "What I just played'": Author's interview with Dave Liebman.

402 **"retire by midsummer"**: Szwed, *So What*, p. 320.
403 **"off limits to anybody"**: Davis and Troupe, *Miles*, pp. 330–31.
403 **What Miles actually:** Author's interview with Wallace Roney.
404 **"with all the touring"**: Author's interview with Eliot Zigmund.
404 **"brought back the romance"**: Ibid.
405 **"everything that's going on"**: Lyons, *The Great Jazz Pianists*, p. 220.
406 **been studying Stockhausen:** Davis and Troupe, *Miles*, p. 329.
406 **"keep thinking of myself"**: Ibid.
406 **"He did have the courage"**: Gillespie and Fraser, *To Be, or Not . . . to Bop*, p. 487.
406 **Giddins wrote an apology:** Author's interview with Gary Giddins.
407 **"the thing I loved most"**: Davis and Troupe, *Miles*, p. 332.
407 **"And it threw"**: Interview by Win Hinkle in the 1989–1994 bimonthly newsletter *Letter from Evans*, vol. 5, no. 3.
407 **"you're gonna kill yourself"**: Author's interview with Eliot Zigmund.
408 **by his own estimation:** Davis and Troupe, *Miles*, p. 335.
408 **"a high-class groupie"**: Ibid., p. 305.
408 **"The roaches had"**: Ibid., p. 335.
409 **"He had pictures up"**: Author's interview with Jack DeJohnette.
409 **"sometimes it was hard"**: Author's interview with Eliot Zigmund.
409 **"like a couple of vampires"**: Pettinger, *Bill Evans*, p. 254.
410 ***Never* like that**: Author's interview with Joe LaBarbera.
411 **"gave you the room"**: Pettinger, *Bill Evans*, p. 262.
411 **"No, that's not"**: Verchomin, *The Big Love*, p. 31.
412 **He signed the letter:** Ibid., pp. 28–36.
412 **"rest of the world didn't understand"**: Ibid., p. 42.
414 **assumed Nenette was referring:** Ibid., pp. 43–54 passim.
414 **"seemed like a scary place"**: Author's interview with Laurie Verchomin.
414 **"somewhat prevailed upon him"**: Pettinger, *Bill Evans*, p. 263.
414 **"sit around watching television"**: Davis and Troupe, *Miles*, p. 339.
415 **"only thing wrong with coke"**: Author's interview with Miles Davis.
415 **"Like we are getting away"**: Verchomin, *The Big Love*, p. 39.
416 **"guy who was leading"**: Author's interview with Laurie Verchomin.
416 **"they are old scars"**: Verchomin, *The Big Love*, pp. 40–41.
416 **"like a church"**: Author's interview with Laurie Verchomin.
417 **"an excitement in the air"**: Pettinger, *Bill Evans*, p. 267.
417 **"now had an aggressiveness"**: Author's interview with Kenny Werner.
417 **"Of course I wanted"**: Author's interview with Laurie Verchomin.
417 **"'I don't need anybody's'"**: Author's interview with Joe LaBarbera.
418 **"could just end"**: Author's interview with Laurie Verchomin.
418 **"My spirit is"**: Author's interview with Joe LaBarbera.
418 **"awed by the enormity"**: Verchomin, *The Big Love*, p. 120.
419 **"thought, 'Oh my God'"**: Author's interview with Joe LaBarbera.
419 **"not sure a person"**: Verchomin, *The Big Love*, p. 131.
420 **"remember picking him up"**: Author's interview with Joe LaBarbera.
420 **"couldn't save him"**: Verchomin, *The Big Love*, pp. 131–32.
420 **"longest, slowest suicide"**: Lees, *Friends Along the Way*, p. 284.
420 **"in order to stay young"**: Davis and Troupe, *Miles*, p. 345.
421 **"misses by several Miles"**: H. A. H., Reflections in Vinyl column, *Blytheville* (Arkansas) *Courier News*, Sept. 11, 1981.
421 **"the Greta Garbo"**: Ibid.
421 **"his five-year seclusion"**: James V. Murray, Knight-Ridder News Service, July 26, 1981.
422 **"continually inserted pauses"**: Ernie Santosuosso, "Miles Is Back, No Mistake," *Boston Globe*, June 27, 1981.

422 "had shot some dope": Davis and Troupe, *Miles*, p. 348.
423 "cut all this stuff out": Ibid.
423 "y'all just make love": Author's interview with Miles Davis.
423 "I was so weak": Davis and Troupe, *Miles*, p. 350.
423 sometimes playing from: Szwed, *So What*, p. 360.
424 "even if the music": Author's interview with Dave Liebman.
425 a bravura touch: Szwed, *So What*, p. 364; "Musicians Pay Tribute to Jazzman Miles Davis,"
    Associated Press, Nov. 8, 1983.
426 "Hasn't been played enough": Author's interview with Wallace Roney.
428 "playin' Dizzy's shit": Ibid.
428 "slight illumination emanating": Szwed, *So What*, p. 399.
428 he had fallen into a coma: Ibid.

Bibliography

Baker, Chet. *As Though I Had Wings: The Lost Memoir.* New York: St. Martin's Press, 1997.

Baldwin, James. *The Fire Next Time.* New York: The Dial Press, 1963.

Balliett, Whitney. *American Musicians II: Seventy-One Portraits in Jazz.* Jackson: University Press of Mississippi, 2006.

———. *Collected Works: A Journal of Jazz, 1954-2001.* New York: St. Martin's Press, 2002.

———. *Such Sweet Thunder: 49 Pieces on Jazz.* Indianapolis: Bobbs-Merrill Company, 1966.

Baraka, Amiri. *The Autobiography of LeRoi Jones/Amiri Baraka.* New York: Freundlich Books, 1984.

Berliner, Paul F. *Thinking in Jazz: The Infinite Art of Improvisation.* Chicago: University of Chicago Press, 2009.

Bernotas, Bob. *Reed All About It: Interviews and Master Classes with Jazz's Leading Reed Players.* Candler, N.C.: Boptism Music Publishing, 2002.

Bjorn, Lars, and Jim Gallert. *Before Motown: A History of Jazz in Detroit 1920–1960.* Ann Arbor: University of Michigan Press, 2001.

Bloom, Harold. *Thomas Pynchon: Bloom's Modern Critical Views.* New York: Chelsea House, 2003.

Broven, John. *Record Makers and Breakers: Voices of the Independent Rock 'n' Roll Pioneers.* Champaign: University of Illinois Press, 2011.

Carr, Ian. *Miles Davis: The Definitive Biography.* Boston: Da Capo Press, 2006.

Chambers, Jack. *Milestones: The Music and Times of Miles Davis to 1960.* Sag Harbor, N.Y.: Beech Tree Books, 1983.

Cook, Richard. *It's About That Time: Miles Davis On and Off Record.* New York: Oxford University Press, 2007.

Crease, Stephanie Stein. *Gil Evans: Out of the Cool.* Chicago: Chicago Review Press, 2003.

Crouch, Stanley. *Considering Genius: Writings on Jazz.* New York: Basic Books, 2009.

———. *Kansas City Lightning: The Rise and Times of Charlie Parker.* New York: HarperCollins, 2013.

Davis, Clive, and James Willwerth. *Clive: Inside the Record Business.* New York: William Morrow, 1975.

Davis, Miles, and Quincy Troupe. *Miles: The Autobiography*. New York: Simon & Schuster, 1990.

DeVeaux, Scott. *The Birth of Bebop: A Social and Musical History*. Oakland: University of California Press, 1997.

DeVito, Chris. *Coltrane on Coltrane*. Chicago: Chicago Review Press, 2012.

Early, Gerald Lyn. *Miles Davis and American Culture*. St. Louis: Missouri Historical Society Press, 2001.

Ellison, Ralph. *Shadow and Act*. New York: Vintage Books, 1995.

Ellison, Ralph, and Albert Murray. *Trading Twelves*. Washington, D.C.: National Geographic Books, 2001.

Gabbard, Krin, editor. *Representing Jazz*. Durham, N.C.: Duke University Press, 1995.

Garland, Phyl. *The Sound of Soul: The Story of Black Music*. Bloomington: Indiana University Press, 1969.

Gavin, James. *Deep in a Dream: The Long Night of Chet Baker*. Chicago: Chicago Review Press, 2011.

Giddins, Gary. *Celebrating Bird: The Triumph of Charlie Parker*. Minneapolis: University of Minnesota Press, 2013.

———. *Visions of Jazz: The First Century*. New York: Oxford University Press, 2000.

Gillespie, Dizzy, and Al Fraser. *To Be, or Not . . . to Bop*. Minneapolis: University of Minnesota Press, 2009.

Gioia, Ted. *The History of Jazz*. New York: Oxford University Press, 1997.

Goldberg, Joe. *Jazz Masters of the 50s*. Boston: Da Capo Press, 1983.

Golson, Benny, and Jim B. Merod. *Whisper Not: The Autobiography of Benny Golson*. Philadelphia: Temple University Press, 2016.

Gordon, Max. *Live at the Village Vanguard*. Boston: Da Capo Press, 1982.

Gordon, Maxine. *Sophisticated Giant: The Life and Legacy of Dexter Gordon*. Oakland: University of California Press, 2020.

Gourse, Leslie. *Art Blakey: Jazz Messenger*. New York: Schirmer Trade Books, 2002.

———. *Straight, No Chaser: The Life and Genius of Thelonious Monk*. New York: Schirmer Trade Books, 1997.

———. *Wynton Marsalis: Skain's Domain*. New York: Schirmer Trade Books, 1999.

Griffin, Farah Jasmine, and Salim Washington. *Clawing at the Limits of Cool: Miles Davis, John Coltrane, and the Greatest Jazz Collaboration Ever*. New York: Thomas Dunne Books, 2013.

Hawes, Hampton, and Don Asher. *Raise Up Off Me: A Portrait of Hampton Hawes*. Boston: Da Capo Press, 2001.

Hayde, Frank R. *Stan Levey: Jazz Heavyweight*. Solana Beach, Calif.: Santa Monica Press, 2016.

Heath, Jimmy, and Joseph McLaren. *I Walked with Giants: The Autobiography of Jimmy Heath*. Philadelphia: Temple University Press, 2010.

Hentoff, Nat. *Jazz Is*. New York: Random House, 1976.

Howison, Jamie. *God's Mind in That Music: Theological Explorations Through the Music of John Coltrane*. Eugene, Or.: Wipf and Stock Publishers, 2012.

Jones, LeRoi (Amiri Baraka). *Black Music*. Brooklyn: Akashic Books, 2010.

Jonnes, Jill. *Hep-Cats, Narcs, and Pipe Dreams: A History of America's Romance with Illegal Drugs*. Baltimore: Johns Hopkins University Press, 1999.

Kahn, Ashley. *A Love Supreme: The Story of John Coltrane's Signature Album*. New York: Penguin, 2003.

———. *Kind of Blue: The Making of the Miles Davis Masterpiece*. Boston: Da Capo Press, 2000.

———. *The House That Trane Built: The Story of Impulse Records*. New York: W. W. Norton & Company, 2007.

Kart, Larry. *Jazz in Search of Itself*. New Haven: Yale University Press, 2008.

Kelley, Robin D. G. *Thelonious Monk: The Life and Times of an American Original*. New York: Free Press, 2009.

Lees, Gene. *Cats of Any Color: Jazz Black and White*. New York: Oxford University Press, 1994.

———. *Friends Along the Way: A Journey Through Jazz*. New Haven: Yale University Press, 2003.

———. *Meet Me at Jim & Andy's*. New York: Oxford University Press, 1988.

Liebman, Dave, and Lewis Porter. *What It Is: The Life of a Jazz Artist*. Lanham, Md.: Scarecrow Press, 2012.

Litweiler, John. *Ornette Coleman: A Harmolodic Life*. New York: William Morrow, 1992.

Losin, Peter. *Miles Ahead* website, www.plosin.com/milesahead/.

Lyons, Leonard. *The Great Jazz Pianists*. Boston: Da Capo Press, 1989.

MacDonald, Ian. *Tadd: The Life and Legacy of Tadley Ewing Dameron*. London: Jahbero Press, 1998.

Marmorstein, Gary. *The Label: The Story of Columbia Records*. New York: Thunder's Mouth Press, 2007.

McPartland, Marian. *All in Good Time*. New York: Oxford University Press, 1987.

Mingus, Charles. *Beneath the Underdog: His World as Composed by Charles Mingus*. New York: Alfred A. Knopf, 1971.

Morgenstern, Dan. *Living with Jazz*. New York: Pantheon, 2009.

Nisenson, Eric. *Open Sky: Sonny Rollins and His World of Improvisation*. New York: St. Martin's Press, 2000.

———. *The Making of Kind of Blue: Miles Davis and His Masterpiece*. New York: St. Martin's Press, 2001.

———. *Ascension: John Coltrane and His Quest*. Boston: Da Capo Press, 1995.

Pearson, Nathan W. *Goin' to Kansas City*. Champaign: University of Illinois Press, 1987.

Pepper, Art, and Laurie Pepper. *Straight Life: The Story of Art Pepper*. New York: Schirmer, 1979.

Pettinger, Peter. *Bill Evans: How My Heart Sings*. New Haven: Yale University Press, 1998.

Porter, Lewis. *John Coltrane*. Ann Arbor: University of Michigan Press, 1999.

Postif, François. *Les Grandes Interviews de Jazz Hot*. Paris: Editions de l'Instant, 1989.

Priestley, Brian. *Chasin' the Bird: The Life and Legacy of Charlie Parker*. New York: Oxford University Press, 2007.

———. *John Coltrane*. New York: Apollo Publishing International, 1987.

Ratliff, Ben. *Coltrane: The Story of a Sound*. New York: Macmillan, 2007.

Reich, Steven A., editor. *The World of Jim Crow America: A Daily Life Encyclopedia* [two volumes]. Santa Barbara: ABC-CLIO, 2019.

Reisner, Robert. *Bird: The Legend of Charlie Parker*. Boston: Da Capo Press, 1977.

Ritz, David. *Faith in Time: The Life of Jimmy Scott*. Boston: Da Capo Press, 2009.

Rothschild, Hannah. *The Baroness: The Search for Nica, the Rebellious Rothschild*. New York: Vintage Books, 2013.

Russell, Ross. *Bird Lives!* Boston: Da Capo Press, 1996.

Santoro, Gene. *Myself When I Am Real: The Life and Music of Charles Mingus*. New York: Oxford University Press, 2001.

Scherman, Tony, and Mark Rowland. *The Jazz Musician: 15 Years of Interviews. The Best of Musician Magazine*. New York: St. Martin's Press, 1994.

Schoenberg, Loren. *The NPR Curious Listener's Guide to Jazz*. New York: Penguin, 2002.

Shaw, Arnold. *52nd Street: The Street of Jazz*. Boston: Da Capo Press, 1977.

Sheridan, Chris. *Dis Here: A Bio-Discography of Julian "Cannonball" Adderley*. Westport, Conn.: Greenwood Publishing Group, 2000.

Spunt, Barry. *Heroin and Music in New York City*. New York: Springer, 2014.

Stearns, Marshall W. *The Story of Jazz*. New York: Oxford University Press, 1970.

Szwed, John. *So What: The Life of Miles Davis*. New York: Simon & Schuster, 2004.

Taylor, Arthur. *Notes and Tones: Musician-to-Musician Interviews*. Boston: Da Capo Press, 2009.

Thomas, J. C. *Chasin' the Trane*. Boston: Da Capo Press, 1976.

Tingen, Paul. *Miles Beyond: Electric Explorations of Miles Davis, 1967–1991*. New York: Billboard Books, 2001.

Travis, Dempsey Jerome. *An Autobiography of Black Jazz*. Chicago: Urban Research Institute, 1983.

Troupe, Quincy. *Miles and Me*. Oakland: University of California Press, 2000.

Tyson, Cicely. *Just as I Am*. New York: HarperCollins, 2021.

Vail, Ken. *Miles' Diary: The Life of Miles Davis 1947–1961*. London: Sanctuary Publishing, 1996.

Verchomin, Laurie. *The Big Love: Life & Death with Bill Evans*. Scotts Valley, Calif.: CreateSpace, 2011.

Wein, George, and Nate Chinen. *Myself Among Others: A Life in Music*. Boston: Da Capo Press, 2009.

Werner, Kenny. *Effortless Mastery*. Van Nuys, Calif.: Alfred Music, 1996.

Wilmer, Val. *As Serious as Your Life: Black Music and the Free Jazz Revolution, 1957–1977*. London: Profile Books, 2018.

X, Malcolm, and Alex Haley. *The Autobiography of Malcolm X*. New York: Grove Press, 1965.

Captions and Credits

Image Captions and Credits

p. xii, top right: Miles Davis in the studio recording *Kind of Blue* (1959), New York, 1959. Photo: Don Hunstein.
(© SONY MUSIC ENTERTAINMENT.)

p. xii, center left: John Coltrane and Miles Davis (background) in the studio recording *Kind of Blue* (1959), New York, 1959. Photo: Don Hunstein.
(© SONY MUSIC ENTERTAINMENT.)

p. xii, bottom right: Miles Davis, Bill Evans, and Paul Chambers (background) in the studio recording *Kind of Blue* (1959), New York, 1959. Photo: Don Hunstein.
(© SONY MUSIC ENTERTAINMENT.)

p. 14: Miles Davis, New York, 1986. Photo: William Coupon.
(© WILLIAM COUPON/TRUNK ARCHIVE.)

p. 20: Wynton Marsalis and Miles Davis at the Vancouver International Jazz Festival, 1986. Photo: Chris Cameron.
(© CHRIS CAMERON 1986.)

p. 30: Miles Davis at about age nine or ten, ca. 1935–36.

p. 35: Miles Davis (back row, far right) playing with Eddie Randle's Blue Devils at the Rhumboogie Club, East St. Louis, 1944.
(ALBUM/ALAMY.)

p. 42: Publicity photo of Miles Davis, 1948.

p. 54: Tommy Potter, Charlie Parker, Dizzy Gillespie, and John Coltrane performing at Birdland, New York, 1951.
(BRIDGEMAN IMAGES.)

p. 66: Charlie Parker (foreground), Miles Davis (right), Tommy Potter, and Max Roach performing at Three Deuces, New York, ca. 1947. Photo: William P. Gottlieb.
(WILLIAM P. GOTTLIEB/IRA AND LEONORE S. GERSHWIN FUND COLLECTION, MUSIC DIVISION, LIBRARY OF CONGRESS.)

pp. 72, 74: John Coltrane watching Charlie Parker on the saxophone performing with the Jimmy Heath Orchestra at Elate Club Ballroom, Philadelphia, December 7, 1947.

p. 76: United States Navy portrait of John Coltrane, ca. 1945.

p. 88: Miles Davis, ca. 1960. Photo: G. Marshall Wilson.
(JOHNSON PUBLISHING COMPANY ARCHIVE/COURTESY J. PAUL GETTY TRUST AND SMITHSONIAN NATIONAL MUSEUM OF AFRICAN AMERICAN HISTORY AND CULTURE.)

p. 94: Gil Evans conducting, date unknown.
(ALBUM/ALAMY.)

p. 108: John Coltrane in his backyard, Queens, New York, 1963. Photo: Jim Marshall.
(© JIM MARSHALL PHOTOGRAPHY LLC.)

p. 120: Cover of Miles Davis's *Miles Davis Group* (Barclay Disques, 1956).

p. 144: Miles Davis during a Miles Davis Quartet session at Van Gelder Studio, New Jersey, March 6, 1954. Photo: Francis Wolff.
(© BLUE NOTE RECORDS/UMG RECORDINGS INC.)

p. 161, clockwise, from top left:
Irving Penn, *The Palm of Miles Davis*, New York, 1986. (© THE IRVING PENN FOUNDATION.)
Irving Penn, *The Hand of Miles Davis*, New York, 1986. (© THE IRVING PENN FOUNDATION.)
Irving Penn, *The Hand of Miles Davis (B)*, New York, 1986. (© THE IRVING PENN FOUNDATION.)
Irving Penn, *The Hand of Miles Davis (C)*, New York, 1986. (© THE IRVING PENN FOUNDATION.)

p. 168: Bill Evans yearbook photo for the Kappa Delta Pi National Education Society at Southeastern Louisiana University, 1949.
(COURTESY SOUTHEASTERN LOUISIANA UNIVERSITY.)

p. 178: Charles Mingus, Thelonious Monk, Miles Davis, Gigi Gryce, and Max Roach at Tony's, New York, March 7, 1954. Photo: Jimmy Morton.
(PHOTO BY JIMMY MORTON FROM THE ARCHIVE OF FRED BRATHWAITE.)

p. 200: John Coltrane and Miles Davis (background) in the studio recording *Kind of Blue* (1959), New York, 1959. Photo: Don Hunstein.
(© SONY MUSIC ENTERTAINMENT.)

p. 222: John Coltrane, Shadow Wilson, Thelonious Monk, and Ahmed Abdul-Malik performing at the Five Spot Café, New York, 1957. Photo: Don Schlitten.
(COURTESY DON SCHLITTEN.)

p. 228: Thelonious Monk outside the Five Spot Café, New York, 1963. Photo: Ben Martin.
(GETTY IMAGES.)

p. 247: Miles Davis, Red Garland, Philly Joe Jones, and Paul Chambers in the studio recording *Milestones* (1958), New York, February 4, 1958.
(MICHAEL OCHS ARCHIVES/GETTY IMAGES.)

p. 248: Miles Davis and Red Garland in the studio recording *Milestones* (1958), New York, February 4, 1958. Photo: Dennis Stock.
(© DENNIS STOCK/MAGNUM PHOTOS.)

p. 252: The Miles Davis Sextet performing at the Newport Jazz Festival, Rhode Island, July 3, 1958. From left: Bill Evans, Jimmy Cobb, Paul Chambers, Cannonball Adderley, John Coltrane, Miles Davis. Photo: Vernon L. Smith.
(VERNON SMITH COLLECTION, COURTESY VERNON SMITH II/SONY MUSIC ARCHIVES.)

p. 259: Miles Davis and Bill Evans in the studio recording *Kind of Blue* (1959), New York, 1959. Photo: Don Hunstein.
(© SONY MUSIC ENTERTAINMENT.)

p. 272: Bill Evans, Miles Davis, Cannonball Adderley, and John Coltrane in the studio recording *Kind of Blue* (1959), New York, 1959. Photo: Don Hunstein.
(© SONY MUSIC ENTERTAINMENT.)

p. 294: Ornette Coleman, Hollywood, 1959. Photo: William Claxton.
(COURTESY DEMONT PHOTO MANAGEMENT, LLC.)

p. 299: Page detail from the *Long Beach Independent*, May 5, 1951.

p. 316: John Coltrane, New York, April 1962. Photo: Chuck Stewart.
(© CHUCK STEWART PHOTOGRAPHY, LLC.)

p. 330: Bill Evans performing for a TV special in Copenhagen, 1964. Photo: Jan Persson.
(© JAN PERSSON/CTSIMAGES.)

p. 341: Miles Davis performing with Tony Williams in Copenhagen, October 4, 1964. Photo: Jan Persson.
(© JAN PERSSON/CTSIMAGES.)

p. 346: Cover of Miles Davis's *E.S.P.* (Columbia Records, 1965).

p. 357, clockwise, from top left: John Coltrane, McCoy Tyner, Elvin Jones, and Jimmy Garrison of the John Coltrane Classic Quartet, Oslo, October 23, 1963. Photos: Randi Hultin.
(THE NATIONAL LIBRARY OF NORWAY.)

p. 364: Mark Doox, *St. John Coltrane The Divine Sound Baptist*, 1992, acrylic and gold leaf on wood board, 38 x 34 1/2".
(© MARK DOOX.)

p. 378: Miles Davis performing with Herbie Hancock, Tony Williams, Ron Carter, and Wayne Shorter at the Berliner Jazztage, Berlin, September 25, 1964. Photo: Jan Persson.
(© JAN PERSSON/CTSIMAGES.)

p. 392: Cover of Miles Davis's *Bitches Brew* (Columbia Records, 1970).

p. 398: Bill Evans (right) poses with Eddie Gomez and Eliot Zigmund (The Bill Evans Trio), ca. 1975.
(MICHAEL OCHS ARCHIVES/GETTY IMAGES.)

p. 425: Wallace Roney and Miles Davis performing at the Montreux Jazz Festival, Switzerland, July 8, 1991. Photo: Herman Leonard.
(© HERMAN LEONARD PHOTOGRAPHY LLC.)

Text Credits

This page constitutes an extension of the copyright page.

Excerpts from *Miles: The Autobiography* by Miles Davis with Quincy Troupe, copyright © 1989 by Miles Davis. Reprinted with the permission of Simon & Schuster, Inc. All rights reserved.

Excerpts from "The John Coltrane Story, as told to Björn Fremer" by Björn Fremer, *Jazz News* (May 10, 1961). Used by permission from the National Jazz Archive.

Excerpts from *To Be, or Not . . . to Bop* by Dizzy Gillespie and Al Fraser, copyright © 1979 by John Birks Gillespie and Wilmot Alfred Fraser. Used by permission from University of Minnesota Press.

Excerpt from *Whisper Not: The Autobiography of Benny Golson* by Benny Golson and Jim B. Merod, copyright © 2016 by IBBOB, Inc. Used by permission of Temple University Press.

Excerpts from "John Coltrane Talks to *Jazz News*" by Kitty Grime, *Jazz News* (December 27, 1961). Used by permission from the National Jazz Archive.

Excerpts from *Bill Evans: How My Heart Sings* by Peter Pettinger, copyright © 1998 by Yale University. Reprinted with the permission of Yale University Press. All rights reserved.

Excerpts from *John Coltrane: His Life and Music* by Lewis Porter, copyright © 1998 by the University of Michigan. Used by permission from the University of Michigan Press.

Excerpts from *Bird Lives! The High Life and Hard Times of Charlie (Yardbird) Parker* by Ross Russell, copyright © 1973 by Ross Russell. Reproduced by permission of the University of Texas and Harold Ober Associates Incorporated.

Excerpts from *So What: The Life of Miles Davis* by John Szwed, copyright © 2002 by John Szwed. Reprinted with the permission of Simon & Schuster, Inc. All rights reserved.

Excerpts from *Thelonious Monk: The Life and Times of an American Original* by Robin D. G. Kelley, copyright © 2009 by Robin D. G. Kelley. Reprinted with the permission of The Free Press, a division of Simon & Schuster, Inc. All rights reserved.

Index